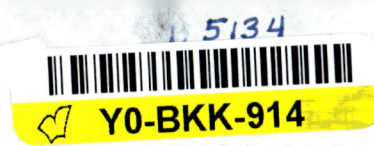

Studies in Indian Tradition Series No. 6

New Essays in the Philosophy of
SARVEPALLI RADHAKRISHNAN

Edited by
S.S. RAMA RAO PAPPU

KANSAS SCHOOL OF RELIGION
UNIVERSITY OF KANSAS
1300 OREAD AVENUE
LAWRENCE, KANSAS 66044

Sri Satguru Publications
A Division of
Indian Books Centre
Shakti Nagar, Delhi, INDIA

Sri Satguru Publications
Indological & Oriental Publishers
A Division of
Indian Books Centre
40/5, Shakti Nagar,
Delhi-110007 INDIA

© All rights reserved.

First Edition : Delhi, 1995

ISBN 81-7030-461-X

Printed at:
Mehra Offset Press, Delhi-2.

PRINTED IN INDIA

New Essays in the Philosophy of
SARVEPALLI RADHAKRISHNAN

To
Bimal K. Matilal
Troy Oragan
Paul Arthur Schilpp

Foreword

This collection of 'new essays' on Radhakrishnan's personality and thinking is the most comprehensive to come out after the volume on his philosophy edited by P.A. Schilpp. This contains 38 essays dealing almost exhaustively with different aspects of his thought.

Till today Radhakrishnan is the only Indian philosopher who has expounded in English a particular type of idealism in a most charming and elegant manner. In its own way his idealism is an original development, under the influence of western philosophy, of what he takes to be the Upanishadic view. He contends that the highest value and the truly real are inseparable. The Absolute is real, consciousness and freedom. Sometimes he substitutes "delight" or "spirit" for "freedom". The real (he wrote) includes ideas and if these are interpreted as ideals or values, an idealist view of the universe results. Such a view, according to him, finds the universe to be meaningful and life to be purposeful.

For years before he came to occupy high offices Radhakrishnan devoted himself to develop what he called a self-understanding of religion and a fitting of religious convictions with facts known from empirical experience and science. He took this endeavour to be an exposition of and exhortation to spirituality. He believed that the fundamental spiritual conviction is "the consubstantiality of the spirit in man and God". He also phrased it thus: that which is in the very centre of man's being is akin to the Supreme. He also spoke of the unity of the universe and its being essentially Spirit. He expressed these ideas beautifully and attractively. The papers in this book have evaluated his work in various ways.

Quite from an early age Radhakrishnan began concerning himself with civilizational, national, social, ethical and political issues. He read, thought and expressed views on them. As Vice-President and President of India he spoke often on democracy, secularism and other subjects. These later speeches of his are as important as what he wrote and spoke earlier; perhaps in these spontaneous outpourings there is more originality than in his writing and earlier speeches.

It is to Radhakrishnan's *Indian Philosophy* and his translations and commentaries of the *Upanishads* and *Gita* that ;the interested Indian elite (e.g. Jawaharlal Nehru, Jayaprakash Narayan) turned in the intra-war period. From 1952 to 1967 when Radhakrishnan was in high offices of State, not only his writings attained greater vogue, but the media daily communicated to the Indian people what he was saying on things which mattered to them. During this period he travelled extensively all over the world receiving numerous honours and making impact on very important persons as well as on ordinary people. Academic Indian philosophy was more or less symbolised by him; by and large people considered that only what he wrote and said was Indian Philosophy. There were of course philosophers in universities, some in Indian and more in other countries, who did not think so. But India has not yet produced a University Professor of Philosophy who has exerted greater influence than him on its people.

Professor S.S. Rama Rao Pappu has been making an invaluable contribution to the promotion and propagation of Indian philosophy through his conferences at Miami University. The conference on Radhakrishnan organised by him, judging by the number and quality of its paticipants, is one of the most successful among them. This volume will bear permanent witness to this. I hope it will be read widely.

17 September 1994   **K. Satchidananda Murty**
Chairman,
Indian Philosophical Congress

Preface

The essays included in this volume are revisions of papers originally presented in the Radhakrishnan Centennial Conference I Had organized at Miami University in April, 1988. Due to circumstances beyond my control, the publication of these "new essays" was delayed, but the delay did not fortunately make them "old." Only three papers in this volume were published in philosophy journals elsewhere. They are now reprinted in this volume. Unfortunately, however, three contributors to this volume, B. K. Matilal, Troy Organ and Paul Arthur Schilpp did not live to see this volume in print. This volume is dedicated to the memory of these three scholars.

There are, it seems to me, four anthologies consisting of essays on Radhakrishnan, the earliest and the most erudite being Paul Schilpp's Library of Living Philosophers' volume on *The Philosophy of Sarvepalli Radhakrishnan* published in 1952. The essays included in this volume are not merely a repetition of the old themes. They contain new perspectives on Radhakrishnan. It is the sign of a great philosopher that he is read and re-read, criticized and defended continuously. This continuous evaluation is a sign of vitality of a great philosopher, not an exercise in superfluity. That these essays are appearing almost fifty years after the publication of Paul Schilpp's volume in the Library of Living Philosophers is an indication that Radhakrishnan's volume philosophy is alive and thriving. Indian philosophers have lived in the shadow of

Radhakrishnan during his life-time. Though recent trends in Indian philosophy seems to be a struggle to walk away from Radhakrishnan's shadow, he has entered the Indian philosophic consciousness so deeply that it will take some time to be weaned away from Radhakrishnan's influences. A review of the contents of the present volume will reveal that most of the contributors to the volume live in the West and are taking an "external" point of view on Radhakrishnan both in time and distance. This volume is also comprehensive in covering all important aspects of Radhakrishnan's thought. Last but not least, these essays are also written as a tribute to a great philosopher on the centennial of his birth anniversary.

My work as Editor of this volume was made easier and enjoyable because of the help given by many friends, especially K. Satchidananda Murty for writing the Foreword to this volume, Purusottama Bilimoria, General Editor of the series, Naresh Gupta of the Indian Books Centre who has patiently waited for the manuscript to reach his hands and who has expeditiously printed it when it has reached him. My thanks are also due to Miami University for providing me a modest grant to organize the Radhakrishnan Conference and finally to my wife, Suryakantham, who knew the Radhakrishnan family since childhood and has provided me some missing biographical insights about Radhakrishnan.

Oxford, Ohio
June 15, 1995

S. S. Rama Rao Pappu

Contents

Foreword   vii

Preface   ix

PART I
RADHAKRISHNAN : THE PERSON, HIS WRITINGS AND HIS LEGACY

1. Sarvepalli Radhakrishnan : The Philosophical Bridge between Orient and Occident/ *Paul Arthur Schilpp*   3
2. Radhakrishnan's LutheranConnection/ *Visvaldis V. Klive*   15
3. Perennial Issues in Radhakrishnan Scholarship/ *Robert N. Minor*   29
4. Remarks on Three Radhakrishnan Introductions/ *Alex Wayman*   43
5. Radhakrishnan and the Problems of Modernity in Indian Thought/ *B.K. Matilal*   55
6. Kavis or Ṛsis : The Legacy of Radhakrishnan and the Discipline of Hindu Studies/ *Christopher Chapple*   65
7. Radhakrishnan's Contributions to Western Thought/ *Troy Organ*   75
8. Radhakrishnan's Contributions to Philosophy/ *Krishna Mallick*   89

PART II
RADHAKRISHNAN AND RELIGIOUS PLURALISM

9. Radhakrishnan's Conception of the Veda/ *George Chemparathy*   103

10. Radhakrishnan's Approach to Yoga/
    S. Gopalan 129
11. Radhakrishnan and the Development of a Global
    Paradigm of Meaning/*David M. Brookman* 143
12. Radhakrishnan and the Doctrine
    of Karma/*Narayan Champawaat* 163
13. On Having More than One Home/*Harry Buck* 173
14. Radhakrishnan's Approach to Religious Diversity/
    J.G. Arapura 187
15. Radhakrishnan as the Exponent of Advaita
    Vedanta on the question of Encounter
    of Religions/*Anindita N. Balslev* 211
16. Radhakrishnan : The Prophet of the Religion of
    'the Spirit/*Ishwar C. Harris* 225
17. Radhakrishnan's Eternal Religion (*Sanātana Dharma*)
    and the Religions/*Donald Tuck* 245
18. Sarvepalli Radhakrishnan's Use of Christian Scripture/
    Boyd Wilson 265
19. Radhakrishnan and Tolerance in Hinduism/
    S.S. Rama Rao Pappu 299
20. Radhakrishnan's Philosophy of Religion/
    John M. Koller 309

PART III
RADHAKRISHNAN'S METAPHYSICAL QUEST

21. 'Saving the Appearances' in Plato's Academy/
    Puruṣottama Bilimoria 327
22. Radhakrishnan's Pantheism :
    Internal Relations to God's Mode of Being/
    Richard Stadelman 345
23. Radhakrishnan's Understanding of the Human Body/
    Carl Olson 367
24. The Perceptual, the Conceptual and the Spiritual :
    Radhakrishnan's Metaphysical Quest/*K. Sundaram* 383
25. The Nature and Significance
    of Intuition/*Hope K. Fitz* 393
26. The Individual and the Avatāra in the Thought
    of Radhakrishnan/*Judy Saltzman* 405

27. The Third Sense of Idealism /*Arindam Chakravarty*   423
28. The Advaita of Sankara and Radhakrishnan/
   Sakunthala Gangadharam   443
29. The Idealist Tradition : Radhakrishnan and Berkeley/
   B. David Burke   461
30. The Mystery of Creation in the Thought of
   Radhakrishnan and Sri Aurobindo/   485
   Robert M. Kleinman
31. The Problem of Evil in Radhakrishnan and Aurobindo/
   Kevin Sullivan   497
32. Radhakrishnan and Whitehead : Their Philosophic
   Methods From West-East Perspective/*Anil Sarkar*   507

PART - IV
RADHAKRISHNAN, SOCIETY AND ART

33. Radhakrishnan on Man, God and
   the State/*Anand Mohan*   525
34. Radhakrishnan and Humanism/*Yeager Hudson*   547
35. Perspectives on Social Philosophy :
   Radhakrishnan's View/*T.S. Devadoss*   561
36. Radhakrishnan's Philosophy of
   World Involvement/*Kaisa Puhakka*   577
37. Radhakrishnan's Philosophy of Art/*Fred G. Sturm*   591
38. Radhakrishnan, Religion and World Peace/
   Jerald Richards   603

PART I

RADHAKRISHNAN : THE PERSON, HIS WRITINGS AND HIS LEGACY

1
Sarvepalli Radhakrishnan : The Philosophical Bridge Between Orient and Occident

PAUL ARTHUR SCHILPP
Southern Illinois University

Though Radhakrishnan was famous as a philosopher, he was also a distinguished diplomat in his own right. First (1946-1949), he was appointed as India's representative in UNESCO. During the last year of that appointment he became Chairman of the Executive Council; then (1949-1952), Jawaharlal Nehru appointed him India's Ambassador to U.S.S.R. in Moscow. In that capacity, Radhakrishnan performed so well that, on his return to India in 1952, he was elected Vice-President of India. He held that position for ten years (1952-1962). Then, finally, in 1962 he was elected to the highest position in the Indian Government, namely President of the Republic of India (1962-1967), thereby he became the first *Philosopher-King* since Marcus Aurelius (121-180 A.D.).

In those twenty one years (1946-1967), he proved himself the true *statesman* in the best Socratic sense of that term, rather than the merely successful politician. His philosophy obviously served him well in all those years. Plato had argued that "philosophers should be kings!" Here, in the middle of the twentieth century was one who carried that injunction out literally, and did so in the nation with the second largest population on earth.

But it is not my function to celebrate Radhakrishnan's achievements and greatness as a "King." Rather, I would like to point out that, even in the field of his first (and, we dare say, major profession of his life, that is to say in *philosophy*) in my judgment he also occupies a unique role, namely that of a bridge between Oriental and Occidental philosophy.

Yes, of course, there have been other philosophers who contributed significantly to that "bridge." But, at least insofar as I am acquainted with the recent history of philosophy, I know of no name, either in the East or in the West who has been more successfull - in aiming at mutual understanding - than Sarvepalli Radhakrishnan.

Let me try to present you with evidence for this claim.

As many of you are aware, I had the privilege of spending six months in India during 1951, when I lectured at fifteen Indian universities, conferred with Radhakrishnan, attended the 25th anniversary of the Indian Philosophical Congress in Calcutta, and ultimately completed the *Library of Living Philosophers* volume on the *The Philosophy of Sarvepalli Radhakrishnan* in the seclusion of a houseboat near Srinagar, Kashmir, during the final six weeks.

Radhakrishnan was not only the first *Oriental* philosopher in my *Library of Living Philosophers*, just twelve years after I founded the series; he was also the first Absolute Idealist. (In the years since then, *The Philosophy of Brand Blanshard*, published in 1980, became the next one - over 30 years later.)

Apparently Radhakrishnan wrote only two autobiographies. The first one, published in India in 1937, when

Radhakrishnan was 49 years old, was entitled *My Search for Truth* (only 50 pages). (By 1937, Radhakrishnan had already, for a year, been appointed as Professor of Eastern Religions and Ethics at Oxford University, England.) *My Search for Truth, not* its achievement! That was an appropriate title for an autobiography by a philosopher who, in all of his mature years, proved that he was a "*seeker*" and that truth, for him, was not absolute but a relative term. How true! "The Religion of the Spirit and the World's Need : Fragments of a Confession" was the title of a second autobiography published in my *The Philosophy of Sarvepalli Radhakrishnan*, "The World's Need" to be met by "The Religion of the Spirit" again : how descriptive of Radhakrishnan's entire life. "Fragments of a Confession" he sub-titles this second autobiography. "Fragments" they may be, but they are also "Fragments of a Commitment" as much as of a "Confession!"

Radhakrishnan took both his Bachelor's as well as his Master's degrees at Madras *Christian* College, even though he was - and always claimed to be - a Hindu philosopher. But, at Madras Christian College, it was inevitable that most of his teachers would be "Christians." As much they had a profound and life-long influence on him and especially, of course, on his thinking.

Yes, Radhakrishnan *did* resent the too often derogatory way which many "Christian" missionaries took toward Hinduism. Under their teaching he came not only to read, but also to appreciate the *New Testament* which already had a profound effect upon the great Mahatma Gandhi. But they introduced him also to the great varieties of Western Philosophy.

In fact Radhakrishnan admits that, even as late as 1937, most courses in philosophy taught in almost all Indian universities were courses in Western - rather than in Indian philosophy. Radhakrishnan himself gives continuous proof of this fact not only in his own philosophy but also in both of his autobiographies.

His opening sentence of his second chapter of *My Search for Truth*[1] begins with reference to Hegel (not exactly an Indian philosopher). On the second page of his third chapter in the same book he writes : "True knowledge is to know one's own ignorance, an insight which reiterates Socrates' own famed saying."

On the side of Hinduism we find him saying (on the same page 7): "I know that the people of India are the victims of paralyzing superstitions." And, on page 8 he says : "This attitude of respect for all creeds, this elementary good manners in matters of spirit, is bred into the marrow of one's bones from the Hindu tradition . . . . Religious tolerance marked the Hindu culture from its very beginning." On the following page Radhakrishnan quotes Clement of Alexandria (again not a Hindu philosopher!) as saying that "there was always a natural manifestation of the one Almighty God amongst all right-thinking men." The same page also has references to both Jesus and St. Augustine, two other Western thinkers. Consider this telling sentence : "The challenge of Christian critics compelled me to make a study of Hinduism and find out what is living and what is dead in it."[2]

Radhakrishnan quotes "the preacher" as saying : "God has put eternity into the heart of man." And, we find this distinctly *New Testament* idea : "To have a vision of God requires a pure heart. To know the truth, not learning but the heart of a child is needed." Radhakrishnan refers to the fact that he has been contributing to such Western "learned" (i.e. philosophical) magazines as the *International Journal of Ethics*, the *Monist*, etc.[3]

Radhakrishnan also writes : "I published a series of articles in *Mind* on Bergson's philosophy . . . I examined the philosophical views of Leibniz, James Ward, William James, Rudolf Eucken, Hastings Rashdall, Bertrand Russell, Lord Balfour, etc."[4] And when, in 1920 Macmillan published his well known book, *The Reign of Religion in Contemporary Philosophy*, Radhakrishnan notes that the book "had a warm reception."[5] Radhakrishnan refers to such additional Occidental philosophers, like J.H. Muirhead, J.S. MacKenzie, J.E.C. McTaggart, Hinman of Nebraska, as well as the famous British idealist Bernard Bosanquet.[6]

In fact, Professor J.H. Muirhead, in 1921, invited Radhakrishnan to write a systematic and readable account of Indian philosophy for his *Library of Philosophers*, a set which was published in two volumes. No less than the editors of the *Encyclopaedia Britannica* invited Radhakrishnan to write the article on "Indian Philosophy" for the fourteenth edition of this great encyclopaedia. This essay was on Indian Philosophy, but all the way through Radhakrishnan showed his thorough acquaintance with, and understanding of Occidental Philosophy. Western philosophers as well as ordinary Occidental readers of the International Journal, the *Hibbert Journal*, had an opportunity to read Radhakrishnan's incisive articles in that magazine.

Radhakrishnan was invited in September 1926, on the occasion of the International Congress of Philosophy at Harvard University, and in June previously at the Congress of the Universities of the British Empire in Oxford and Cambridge. This, his first visit to both England and America were, according to his own statement, high points in his early career.

At the Philosophical Congress at Harvard, Radhakrishnan deplored "the lack of a spiritual note in modern civilization," an idea which he developed in further detail in his small book entitled, *Kalki : or the Future of Civilization*.

Radhakrishnan's knowledge of the rest of the world was by no means limited to his major field of philosophy. For example, he did not shy away from critically discussing psychological behaviourism. Nor did he shrink from discussing the Russian experiment of Communism. About it he says : "it is at least an honest attempt to secure for all an equal share in the things which constitute the physical basis of life."[7] On the consequences of both Communism and Fascism, he notes, they lead only to "the *unfortunate result* of mutual conflict and suppression of individual liberty." He deplores "the tendencies to seek salvation in herds."[8] For them "society has become a prison."

This discussion leads him to write : "let us by all means establish a just economic order, but let us also note that the economic is *not* the whole man." He deplores Aldous Huxley's *Brave New World* and adds : "The present crisis of civilization is the direct result of the loosening hold of ethical and spiritual ideas."[9] "The perilous rivalries of national states are accompanied by a furious competition in armaments." And that was written by him 50 years before the world's greatest armaments merchant was living in the White House. And on the same page he says, "nothing is inevitable in human affairs except peace. It is the world's desperate need."[10]

We find the future President of India, way back in 1937 - twenty-five years before he became President - writing as follows : "There is something fundamentally defective in the present organization of society. It is not sufficiently democratic. The basis of democracy is the recognition of the dignity of human beings. It affirms that no individual is good enough to be trusted with absolute power over another and no nation is good enough to rule another."[11] And he continues : "But the present organization of society, national and international, works on the principle that the strong do what they can and the weak suffer what they must.

Dictatorships are political devises born of despair."[12] And now listen to this at once simple and yet daring statement. "Things are never settled until they are settled right."[13]

"Man is not a detached spectator of a progress eminent in human history," says Radhakrishnan, "but an active agent remoulding the world nearer to his ideas. Every age is much what we choose to make it!"[14] "Only a humanity that strives after ethical and spiritual ideas can use the great triumphs of scientific knowledge for the true ends of civilization . . . to form man is the object of philosophy." And "religion is what we do with ourselves when we are alone . . . silent communion is an essential part of all worship . . . worship does not consist in fasts and prayers, but in the offering of a pure and contrite heart ... interest, meaning, purpose, value are qualities given to events by the individual mind."[15]

What other philosopher, whether from the East or from the West, has ever annually commuted for fourteen years from Oxford University to several Indian universities, as Radhakrishnan did? Obviously no scholar could do that unless he were thoroughly at home in both Eastern and Western philosophy. And, all of his writings - whether in book, or essay-form, give constant proof of this. And he was, of course, master of the King's English. In this regard, from my own point of view, Radhakrishnan was second only, among philosophers, to Bertrand Russell.

As a philosopher, Radhakrishnan freely admitted that he was personally not interested in the popular movements in philosophy of our day, namely logic and epistemology. His approach to philosophy was primarily from the viewpoint of religion.[16] He was doubtlessly aware of Einstein's comment of the epistemological and logical movements in philosophy as the "malady of contemporary empiricistic philosophizing."[17] (Einstein once joked with me about the "twittering of little birds on the same subjects.")

Radhakrishnan stood for what he called the "splendour of the Spirit," and proclaimed that the Spirit creates the world and controls its history by a process of perpetual incarnation. . ." or "Spirit working in matter so that matter may serve the Spirit." The world, he said, was not "a matter of machine," but rather "an act of worship, and of life." "The Supreme" he saw as an infinite with "Infinite possibilities." He called freedom the "primordial source and condition of existence, preceding all determinism."[18]

In his later autobiography, "Fragments of a Confession" in the *Library of Living Philosophers,* he writes : "This is teaching not only of the Upaniṣads and Buddhism but also of the Greek mysteries and Platonism, of the Gospels and the schools of Gnosticism. This is the wisdom to which Plotinus refers, when he says : "This doctrine is not new; it was prefessed from the most ancient times though without being developed explicitly; we wish only to be interpreters of the ancient sages, and to show by the evidence of Plato himself that they had the same opinions as ourselves."[19] This is the religion which Augustine mentions in his well-known statement : "That which is called the Christian religion existed among the Ancients, and never did not exist, from the beginning of the human race until Christ came in the flesh, at which time the true religion, which already existed, began to be called Christianity."[20]

Although as I mentioned earlier, Radhakrishnan was not only a life-long Hindu, he was certainly not orthodox, and in fact he was widely read in Christian literature, including the Bible. This was in part due to his early and later education and in part due to his natural broad range intellectual approach to matters of theology. Indeed he spoke of the day that all men and religions might be joined as brothers "in a Universal Church" and that George Bernard Shaw's comment be realized : "O God, that madest this beautiful earth, when will it be ready to receive thy saints."[21]

The first twelve years of Radhakrishnan's life were in Christian Missionary institutions - the Lutheran missionary school in Tirupati, in South India, from the impressionial age of eight from 1896 to 1900; Voorhees Preparatory Academy at Vellore from 1900 to 1904 and Madras Christian College from 1904 to 1908.[22] Yet Radhakrishnan was never at any time converted to Christianity as a result of this educational influences, but remained true to Hinduism. But he was very "disturbed" and "shaken regarding the traditional props on which I leaned." Indeed he said that as a result of so many Christian-oriented teachers, he became a seeker after truth for himself - standing in the "primordial situation in which all philosophy is born."

Radhakrishnan began his professional career as a teacher of philosophy at Madras Christian College in April 1909 almost 80 years ago. During the next years he undertook an intense study of the Hindu Classics such as the *Bhagavad Gītā*, and critical guides of others works such as the *Brahma Sūtra*, and also studies of Buddhism and Jainism. He talked with trusted friends and intellectuals, including Gandhi and Tagore. He read the works of Plato, Kant and Bergson, among other Western thinkers. Like the true scholar he was, he spent a lot of time thinking and searching, and did not arrive quickly nor haphazardly at his philosophy of religion.

During the long years that Radhakrishnan lived in England, he became very fond of the British, "especially their love of justice, their hatred of doctrinairism, their sympathy for the underdog" made a profound impression on him. Although he was a very travelled man, and spent time in France, America, and Russia, as well, it was the English who held first place in his heart as a foreigner. Thus perhaps because of Radhakrishnan's appreciation of British ways and culture, as well as his deep dedication to his own India, he also served as a bridge during the years India fought for its independence and freedom from English benevolent despotism. May be it was less hard for him than most Indians to heed Gandhi's cry to reject British foreign rule but love the British people - and to rally in a mode of non-violence. He was a living bridge between East and West during those years, and he stood for the most idealistic injunctions of the prophets of East and West, preaching peace and love, yes, even understanding of one's enemies, while marching in an opposite direction. And he was able to influence countless of his native countrymen as well as personages in the West. Indeed, he praised "All Souls College" at Oxford University as his second home.

Radhakrishnan has observed that the central concern of our time is not so much the wars and dictatorships which "disfigured" it, but rather the "impact of different cultures on one another, their interaction, and the emergence of a new civilization based on the truths of Spirit and the Unity of mankind."[23] He has also observed that some scientists claimed that life originated on our planet twelve million years ago. But, he noted that man had come into existence only half a million years ago. Man, he called, "in his infancy," and with "a long period ahead" on this planet.[24]

Despite "innate obstinacy of human nature," Radhakrishnan said in his book *Recovery of Faith*, in 1955 : "Man is not body and mind, he is also a spirit, and all progress is due to individual effort."[25] Above all he concluded, "we live in an age of tensions, danger, and opportunity. We are aware of our insufficiencies and we can remove them if we have the vision to see the goal and the courage to work."[26]

To carry on in earnest effort for East-West rapprochement in both culture and politics, we must take to heart - and to action - the ideas of Sarvepalli Radhakrishnan as one of the great seers of the twentieth century. He lit a candle in our times and pointed the way to peace and understanding.

Physically the great Philosopher - King, Sarvepalli Radhakrishnan, is dead. But, mentally, morally and spiritually, long - beyond this Centennial his birth - live his peerless example, his matchless inspiration, and his worldwide, globe-encircling influence!

References

1. S. Radhakrishnan, *My Search for Truth* in *Religion in Transition,* edited by Virgilius Ferm (New York : MacMillan & Co., 1937).
2. *Ibid.*, p. 10.
3. *Ibid.*, pp. 12-13.
4. *Ibid.*, p. 15.
5. *Ibid.*
6. *Ibid.*, p. 16.
7. *Ibid.*, p. 20.
8. *Ibid.*
9. *Ibid.*, p. 21.
10. *Ibid.*, p. 22
11. *Ibid.*, p. 23.
12. *Ibid.*
13. *Ibid.*, p. 26.
14. *Ibid.*, p. 26.
15. *Ibid.*, pp. 36-38
16. S. Radhakrishnan, "Fragments of a Confession," in *The Philosophy of Sarvepalli Radhakrishnan,* edited by Paul Arthur Schilpp (New York : Tudor Publishing Company, 1952), p. 6.
17. *Ibid.*, p. 17.
18. *Ibid.*, p. 40.
19. *Ibid.*, p. 80.

20. *Ibid.*
21. *Ibid.,* p. 81.
22. *Ibid.,* p. 7.
23. *Ibid.*
24. *Ibid.,* p. 82.
25. S. Radhakrishnan, *Recovery of Faith* (World Perspectives Series, Vol. 4., New York : Harper, 1955), p. 63.
26. *Ibid.,* p. 205.

2
Radhakrishnan's Lutheran Connection

VISVALDIS V. KLIVE
Wittenberg University

1.

Perhaps a more appropriate title for this paper would be "Radhakrishnan and the Tirupati Experience," for it was none other than in the unique place - the famous temple town and Hindu pilgrimage centre of Tirupati - that he encountered the Lutherans for the first time. Radhakrishnan in his *Fragments of a Confession* writes :

> "I spent the first eight years of my life (1888-1896) in a small town in South India, Tirutani, which is even today a great centre of religious pilgrimage. My parents were religious in the traditional sense of the term. I studied in Christian Missionary institutions for twelve years, Lutheran Mission High School, Tirupati (1896-1900), Voorhees College, Vellore (1900-1904), and the Madras Christian College (1904-1908). Thus I grew up in an atmosphere where the unseen was a living reality. My approach to the problems of

philosophy from the angle of religion as distinct from that of a science or of history was determined by an early training. I was not able to confine philosophy to logic and epistemology."[1]

What we call the "Tirupati experience" speaks to this "early training." Many commentators and writers on Radhakrishnan - probably under the impact of his *My Search for Truth* (particularly Chapter III) — have stressed, in connection with this "early training," two things : (1) the crucial importance of the later Madras experience that led to the writing of *Ethics of Vedanta* in 1908, and (2) Radhakrishnan's "annoyance" with Christian missionaries (for example, his taking issue with the "criticisms levelled by Christian Missionaries on Hindu beliefs and practises,"[2] which "roused his pride" and also presented a serious challenge, which "impelled/him/to make a study of Hinduism and find out what is living and what is dead in it."[3] Jochim Wach in "Radhakrishnan and the Comparative Study of Religion."[4] traces what he regards as Radhakrishnan's "bitterness" towards Christianity back to these early experiences - a position which Radhakrishnan later felt obliged to deny.[5] Most literature has generally placed primary emphasis on the word "missionary" rather than "Christian" or "Lutheran," when talking about Radhakrishnan's early religious development and first contacts with Christianity. This has been provided support to the idea, which to my mind is a rather restrictive position, that Radhakrishnan's philosophy should be seen as some sort of Hindu "apologetic" against zealous Christian proselytizers.

In this paper I will not, however, argue the last point, but, rather, concentrate on something else and suggest that there may be another dimension to Radhakrishnan's "early training" or "early experience" : his being at Tirupati (rather than just at Vellore or Madras) during his early formative years did his being in a Lutheran institution (rather than some other Christian institution). There could be special significance to this coincidence. Thus, in this "Tirupati experience," there may be more than meets the eye, or even more than Radhakrishnan himself cares to admit or totally understands. Of course, he was quite young at that time - a child turning into a teenager, but that does not preclude that these early experiences could have illuminated his later thought, particularly his notion of "faith," as evidenced in his well-known claim : ". . . from the time I knew myself, I have had firm faith in the reality of an unseen world behind the flux of phenomena . . . and even when I was faced by grave difficulties, this faith has remained unshaken."[6] Maybe in the light of the early experiences, the significant element in this claim is not so much the obvious statement of a metaphysical idealism ("the reality of an unseen world behind the flux of phenomena"), as it is sometimes understood by readers of Radhakrishnan, but rather the attitude of complete belief or commitment, which was greatly emphasized in the later *Recovery of Faith*.[7]

It is not our intention to somehow make Radhakrishnan into a good Lutheran. Far from it, for there is a deep tradition of "faith" in the Indian thinking itself (note, for example, the entire tradition of *prapati* or self-surrender). But I would like to suggest that Radhakrishnan's being both in a Lutheran setting and in the Śrī Venkateśvara cult centre at the same time and under the same circumstances had a profound experiential effect that involved much more than just becoming "familiar not only with the teachings of the New Testament, but with the criticism levelled by Christian missionaries on Hindu beliefs and practises," as Radhakrishnan tells us.[8] These early four years at Tirupati may have had considerably deeper and more lasting effects.

2.

Two seemingly unrelated developments or observations prompt such considerations : (1) Radhakrishnan's frequent recourse to the terminology of faith, particularly in his later works (for example, in *My Search for Truth*, he writes, "if faith and hope in the spiritual direction of the universe are not there, he/any person/is not a religious man,"[9] and his increasing admiration for such thinkers as Kierkegaard, Jaspers and other existentialists, who emphasize this element of faith; (2) our better understanding of the growth of the Śrī Venkateśvara cult in Tirupati that Radhakrishnan found as a young person. It is true that this last element has not been discussed by Radhakrishnan, but this may be due to the fact that most of his autobiographical statements were written for a Western audience, who were not particularly familiar with the various Vaishnavite religious cults of South India. Also, Radhakrishnan's family might not have been interested in this question.

In general, people do not look upon Radhakrishnan as a young person, with a young boy's sensibilities, who came from Tirutani to Tirupati in 1896. The reason for this seems to be that many writers on Radhakrishnan have not literally made such a trip and probably presume that either Tirupati is or was very much the same kind of temple town as Tirutani, or they consider that the only important point about Radhakrishnan's coming to Tirupati was his entrance into a completely new religious environment (that is, the Christian community) that ultimately challenged all of his previous religious ideas. This seems to be an oversimplification.

Quite obviously the year 1896 represented a significant break in Radhakrishnan's life. This was the first time that the young boy was away from home. This was the first time he encountered a different religious and social life. From the

Hindu point of view, Tirupati did not at all resemble his very familiar Tirutani, for its focus was a completely different Vaishnavite tradition. Śri Venkateśvara, who was worshipped at Tirupati (actually in Tirumala, on top of the sacred hills), was *The Lord* (God) who "burns away" or "burns out" (extinguishes) the sins of mankind, and He should be approached with a contrite heart and a complete commitment and trust in His grace. The gracious actions of Śri Venkateśvara came through faith. One of the basic rituals at Tirumala called for complete prostration and rolling around on one's back in the sacred chamber, as a sign of personal penance and submission. In addition, the tradition called for the shaving of one's hair (men, women, children) as a sign of complete surrender and anticipation of the Lord's divine grace. (Nothing of this sort happened at Tirutani.) All of the stories of the Śri Venkateśvara cult focused on the deeds of the Lord, who was magnanimous to those particular devotees who placed complete trust in Him. The sins were "extinguished" by grace through trust in the Lord. When hearing such language, one is struck by the basic similarities between these attitudes of the Vaishnavites at Tirupati and Martin Luther's thinking about religion and the struggle to find a "merciful God." (As Luther once confided to Staupitz : "Um einen bahrmherzigen Gott zu kriegen" - "how to find a merciful God.") The Lutheran answer was that the sins are "extinguished" only by the grace of God through faith and commitment (*Sola fides, sola gratia*). This was the spirit dwelling in Tirupati, and this was the spirit of the Lutheran mission in Tirupati with its High School that young Radhakrishnan attended.

In philosophical terms, the Śri Venkateśvara tradition was more or less related to the Viśista-Advaita tradition - a view still popularly shared by many Tirupati inhabitants. Śri Venkateśvara was taken to be a personal expression of Brahman — a God who really cared for individual devotees.

The idea of a personal *Iśwara* was always there. God acted always in specific providential ways. He had settled in the serpentine-like sacred mountains of Tirumala, in order to help with individual salvation. This was a highly popular tradition.

In Lutheran terms, the East Mission Compound (as the place of Radhakrishnan's school is known today) was the place where repentance, faith and forgiveness through the grace of God was constantly preached and taught. It was basically the 19th century Lutheranism from Germany, basically pietistic rather than doctrinaire in character, that found its way to Tirupati and was communicated to the Indians. The location was not accidental.

Historically this was the Hermannsburg Lutheran Mission, which had opened its Mission High School in 1880. It carried its very Germanic designation - "Hermannsburg Mission High School" - up to World War I. For the Hermannsburg Mission this was one of their principal places of operation in India. Reverend Wickert was the Principal at the time. The teaching staff consisted basically of German missionary teachers, such as Pastor Johann Mancke, Herr Poppe, Pastor Peterson and others, all who held appointments during the last part of the 19th century. The only exception seems to have been teacher Natesa Iyer. Although the language of instruction was basically English, most of the teachers communicated in German. Imagine the problems of the students who came from Tamil or Telugu backgrounds! It was essentially a "German school" in its pedagogical outlook, approach and "spirit."

In the East Mission Compound area, in addition to the Mission High School there was also a Lutheran congregation, which at that time was the only Christian organization in Tirupati. Similarly to a number of other German Lutheran missions, it was serviced entirely by foreign missionaries, rather than local Indian pastors or evangelists. The worship life (hymns, liturgy) reflected the German Lutheranism of that period, and it is still very much evident today in the South Andhra Lutheran Church (as distinct from other Lutheran Church bodies in India). All of the students from the Mission High School had to participate in the worship activities of the Lutheran congregation. An important activity was to learn how to sing the hymns, which were all translations from German hymnals. We are dwelling upon these historical details, for they reveal what sort of Christianity or, for that matter, what sort of first non-Hindu religion Radhakrishnan actually encountered. (There was a very small Islamic presence in Tirutani, not to mention other religious groups.)

In religious terms, one should recognize that the German missionaries who taught Radhakrishnan at the East Mission Compound (from where, incidentally, one also had a good view of the sacred hills and road to Tirumala, where the main temple of Lord Śrī Venkateśvara was located) were for the most part trained in the 19th century German theology characterized by emphasis on personal religious experience. (This may be one of the reasons why Radhakrishnan later never doubted their religious sincerity and devotion, although he did complain about their religious exclusivism). Radhakrishnan was essentially taught by people who were more or less trained in terms of the religious thinking of Daniel Friedrich Schleiermacher, whose theology was becoming increasingly prevalent in Germany. The period of Luthern "scholasticism" and rationalism was over. The new thinking was that religion should be approached in terms of experience - the experience of the "dependence upon the Infinite" (using Schleiermacher terminology). This experience was the experience of faith. Schleiermacher had developed this relationship between experience and faith in his monumental work, *Christian Faith,* which had become the official theology text for many German universities. Radhakrishnan does not speak much about

Schleiermacher, but relates more or less to his later followers, such as Rudolph Otto and others.

The basic point we are trying to make is that one could learn at Tirupati certain things that one was not able to do at Tirutani. Tirupati truly was a new religious and intellectual venture. Maybe this was only coincidental, but a number of insights and experiences converged here. In spite of external differences and official professions (or even intentions) of faith, one could sense a basic similarity between what was going on at the Lutheran High School (and the Church, which was at the centre of the Mission Compound) and at the pilgrimage centre atop Tirumala, to which people ascended on foot, on their knees or were carried up in palanquins. There was, if we my suggest, a certain distinctive "core" to the Tirupati Experience - the experience of God, who can be approached with a contrite heart in faith.

It is probably here that Radhakrishnan as a young person learned many things that affected his thinking later. For example, Tirupati gave evidence that despite external differences there are certain similarities between religions, such as between the theistic Vaishnavism of Tirumala and the Lutheranism of the East Mission Compound. The rituals themselves may have suggested this. Consider, for example, Radhakrishnan's continuing later concern about the relation of *Brahman* to *Īśvara*, which he regarded as one of the most difficult problems in the philosophy of religion. After all, Śrī Venkateśvara reflected a very special sort of *Īśvara* - the merciful and forgiving Lord, who cares. In *My Search for Truth* there is a unique passage where Radhakrishnan compares the absolute faithfulness of a Hindu wife to the faithfulness of the Eternal, "who loves us with the same love, awaiting us patient and unwearied when we return, weary with false pleasures, to him."[10] Such a statement could only grow out of an experience of a personal *Iśvara*, who is truly merciful. Consider Radhakrishnan's own attitudes towards Christianity and other religions, both in the positive and negative sense. There is always a tension, attractiveness and criticism going together as Radhakrishnan writes about Christianity. Again and again he resorts to expressing his thoughts with Christian terminology, even as he talks about *Brahman*. (See, for example, the Introduction to *The Principal Upanishads*.[11] Why is it that, when he writes about the personality of God, he has to compare his views with those of Aquinas or Karl Barth? Is this simply because he presumably was writing for Western audiences, or is this a reflection of some deeper personal experience gained in Tirumala, and which was not so different from what took place in the Lutheran Missionary Compound? Maybe both factors are involved.

3.

In later years there appeared Radhakrishnan's *Recovery of Faith*, as a response to the growing sense of insecurity or of an impending atomic conflict in the world. Radhakrishnan wrote : "No centre holds the world together. Religion has been the discipline hitherto used for fostering wisdom and virtue. But the drift from religious belief has gone much too far, and the margin of safety has become dangerously small.[12] Within this context comes his call for "a recovery of faith" or "spiritual reawakening." Radhakrishnan uses both of these phrases interchangeably.

Although *Recovery of Faith* has been sometimes dismissed as a popular call for a religious revival and a work where already previously developed and expressed ideas have been reiterated, the presentation or, for that matter, the restatement of these ideas is interesting. The selection of terminology may provide new insights into Radhakrishnan's thinking, particularly as far as his understanding of the conditions of faith is concerned. In the central chapter entitled "The Need for Belief," Radhakrishnan discusses the tension between doubt and belief:

> "The age of faith is always with us; only the object of our faith changes. We depart from one creed only to embrace another. The new cults are built on something which is more fundamental than the desire for truth. It is the desire for faith. However much we may avoid the recognition of that necessity, we need some certainty, some view that makes sense of life."[13]

This notion of the "desire for faith," as contrasted by Radhakrishnan to the "desire for truth," is interesting for it suggests a certain "deeper" grounding of one's religious convictions in the nature of human existence. Radhakrishnan writes thus:

> "Man is never nearer God than in the extremity of his anguish. Then, and *not till then* [our emphasis - VVK], do we hear an echo of that bitterness of all human cries - 'They have taken away the Lord . . . and we know not where they have laid Him.' Where shall we go, to what God shall we make our offering? Who has the words of eternal life? This imploring cry does not proceed from the lips of the righteous orthodox . . . . It is the unhappy creatures, who have passed through the depths of doubt, who have nowhere left to turn, it is they who are engaged in what Karl Jaspers calls 'the impassioned struggle with God for God.'"[14]

One is inevitably reminded of Luther's and Kierkegaard's inner struggles - the context of despair for faith. Faith, as Radhakrishnan puts it, is at the "rock bottom of despair," and the search for it "may be difficult." For Radhakrishnan all persons, even the greatest, know of this "nihilistic despair." It is a stage one cannot hope to evade; it is something that one has to go through and transcend.

At this juncture then a new faith - Radhakrishnan explicitly calls it a rational faith - should be offered to struggling and aspiring humanity. It consists of a "new vision of God in whose name we can launch a crusade against the strange cults which are now competing over the souls of man."[15]

Does this not sound a little bit like missionary talk? What Radhakrishnan has in mind is what he calls the "substitutes for religion," such as "paganism," "humanism," "nationalism" and others. This new faith is not a matter of "arbitrary dogmas or hesitating negations," but of experience. It is the true *sanātana dharma,* the eternal religion. It is a rational faith, not in the sense that it somehow rests on reasons or arguments, but rather that it asserts the fundamental truths of all major religions and allows particular religions to transform themselves to approximate the religion of spirit.

Within this context faith can be thought of as "the experience of reality," or simply a "personal experience," It does not stand apart from what people commonly describe as "religious experience." It is a change of consciousness, an inner development, a radical transformation of the human being. As such it involved the whole being of the believer, not just a few faculties. Radhakrishnan identifies this experience explicitly with Kierkegaard's apprehension of truth as "subjectivity" and a "matter of inwardness."[16] It is a personal appropriation in the Kierkegaardian sense. All of this has resonance in the Lutheran tradition, which emphasizes the idea of faith as committing one's whole being to God : "You shall love the Lord, thy God, with all your mind, heart and soul."

To be sure, Radhakrishnan goes on and identifies this "experience of reality" with the "participation of the knowing subject in the spiritual reality"[17] or the "immediate awareness of Being itself" or the "direct experience" and makes other statements which constitute his well-known interpretation of religion. Yet this transition from the Kierkegaardian (or, for that matter, Lutheran) terminology to essentially an Indian mode is interesting and may tell something about Radhakrishnan's own religious development over the years.

One is tempted at this point to raise certain critical questions. Is Radhakrishnan really justified or correct in linking Kierkegaard's apprehension of truth as subjectivity or spiritual inwardness with one's participation in spiritual reality or the immediate awareness of Being itself? Is the "existential truth," whatever it may be, the same as the "immediate awareness of reality"? Maybe not, but this is a topic to be considered for itself. The major question, however, is how to account for this linkage in terms of Radhakrishnan's own growth as a religious thinker. The fact is that Radhakrishnan somehow saw this linkage and, as time went on, became increasingly concerned with the existentialist thinkers, who thought in terms of faith and existential appropriations. In seeking for answers to these questions, the early Tirupati experience may become illuminating. Maybe at that time the "Recovery of Faith" had started, and the insights from two quite diverse religious traditions contributed to that "recovery." It could be that it was not only in Madras, but already in Tirupati, with its singular religious climate, that the search for the common elements between religions had started, elements which were rooted in the "faith in the reality of an unseen world." Maybe the element of faith, coupled with the concept of a merciful God, as propounded at Tirumala or at the East Mission Compound, provided the first steps and bridges.

Perhaps in old age Radhakrishnan came back to what he had experienced in youth. After all, Tirupati was his first experience away from home.

References

1. Paul A. Schilpp. *The Philosophy of Sarvepalli Radhakrishnan* (New York : Tudor Publishing Co., 1952), p. 6.
2. "My Search for Truth," in R. McDermott, ed., *Basic Writings of S. Radhakrishnan* (Bombay : Jaico Publishing House, 1972), p. 37.
3. *Ibid.*, p. 40.
4. *The Philosophy of Sarvepalli Radhakrishnan*, 443ff.
5. *Ibid.*, p. 807.
6. *Basic Writings of S. Radhakrishnan*, p. 35.
7. S. Radhakrishnan, *Recovery of Faith* (Delhi : Oriental Paperbacks, 1967).
8. *Basic Writings of S. Radhakrishnan*, p. 37.
9. *Ibid.*, p. 41.
10. *Ibid.*, p. 37.
11. S. Radhakrishnan, *The Principal Upaniṣads* (London : George Allen & Unwin, 1953).
12. *Recovery of Faith*, p. 9.
13. *Ibid.*, p. 71.
14. *Ibid.*, p. 72.
15. *Ibid.*
16. *Ibid.*, p. 99.
17. *Ibid.*

3
Perennial Issues in Radhakrishnan Scholarship

ROBERT N. MINOR
The University of Kansas

From the time Radhakrishnan began writing, he received both praise and criticism for his work. This was to be expected, for he never thought of himself as a descriptive historian of religion or philosophy but as a constructive thinker and apologist for a tradition which he believed was threatened by the criticisms of outsiders and by the scholasticism and emphasis upon non-essentials of those within. Radhakrishnan kept this the focus of his work and, thus, fended off biographical issues as unimportant.[1] He seldom responded to critics of his own work directly, except to a negative review of his *Indian Philosophy* by E.J. Thomas, to allegations of plagiarism made in *The Modern Review* of Calcutta, and, as was expected of him, to the essays in the volume of the Library of Living Philosophers Series dedicated to this thought. These last he called only "a few considerations which may help to elucidate my position."[2]

Radhakrishnan's writings were, however, a response to criticism, but this was criticism of his tradition in general, of "Hinduism." Trained as an ethicist under an ethicist, Radhakrishnan's responses centered around issues of ethics.

Even his final constructive position, variously called monistic idealism, Hinduism, and then the religion of the spirit,[3] was recommended as the future religion of the world because he believed it was experientially based, tolerant of religious variety, and ethically effective.

Though scholars have also differed over the accuracy of his understanding of the tradition of Indian thought, it is in these three areas that scholars have most often analyzed Radhakrishnan's thought : his experientially based integralism, his place as a "bridge-builder" between East and West, and his construction of an idealist ethics. To his credit his thought has been a continual part of academic discussion, but, as in most such cases I would guess, the evaluation has been appreciative but mixed, for in these three key areas scholars continue to disagree about the satisfactoriness of Radhakrishnan's system. Yet Radhakrishnan himself held these three issues as most crucial.

His Experientially Based Integralism

Experience for Radhakrishnan, as noted by Phillips[4] is "conceived of in broader terms than those which are acknowledged by the naturalist." Like the scientist, whose work is based upon experiment, so philosophers and religious thinkers should base their conclusions upon experience, particularly that which is intuitive. Intuition, defined as self-authenticating and free from the possibility of doubt, he says, is a super-conscious level of knowledge in which the individual realizes his or her union with the Absolute. Phillips, as others have, notes that this corresponds to an age-old teaching identified as *philosophia perennis*. "Radhakrishnan's highest merit lies in his great ability to present this ancient doctrine in its essential purity, freed from the obscuring and partisan details which have so often attached themselves to it."[5] Phillips and Browning both consider Radhakrishnan's use of the term "intuition" as inconsistent, though normally clear in each context.[6]

Yet, even more, Radhakrishnan is identified as a bold reinterpreter of the Advaita Vedanta of the eighth century Indian thinker Śaṁkara. Raju accuses critics of Radhakrishnan's reading of Śaṁkara of being "worshippers of tradition." "It would not be surprising, therefore, if Radhakrishnan should appear to some as reading too much of Western thought into Indian and too much of Indian thought into Western. But when a given concept is first reinterpreted and seen in a new light, it is likely to disclose a new meaning unseen by us before."[7] R.P. Singh summarized Radhakrishnan's reading of Śaṁkara as more rational and as introducing a natural theology, revising Śaṁkara's conception of scripture, developing the idea of a fellowship of faiths, defining the main problem as "saving the world" rather than "saving Brahman," emphasizing a divergent aspect of *māyā*, and maintaining the liberated individual to save the world.[8] Raju sees all of this as having a great influence upon contemporary Indian thought, the greatest influence, however, centering upon the place of intuition : "The great contribution which Radhakrishnan has made to Indian epistemology and which has influenced many Indian writers is the idea that intuition is not opposed to intellect but is its completion."[9]

Others have not been as happy with this reconstruction. Bharati asserts that, in spite of Radhakrishnan's hopes, this is "theology" not "philosophy" because, like "all the schools of Vedānta," it puts its emphasis on ontology and metaphysics.[10] Raghavachar considers it quite daring to ascribe to Śaṁkara such teachings as *sarva-mukti*,[11] and Rambachan considers Radhakrishnan's description of the place of *śruti* in his and Śaṁkara's thought a clear misunderstanding.[12]

Many of the early analyses, though valuable, such as those in the Library of Living Philosophers volume, were limited because the authors often had not read Radhakrishnan's works widely. They were based upon one or two of his main writings. However, three major critical studies based upon a more complete reading of his writings appeared within seven years of each other. The first was Bürkle's *Dialog mit dem Osten*, the second, Arapura's important *Radhakrishnan and Integral Experience*, and the third, a more critical study by Urumpackal called *Organized Religion According to Dr. S. Radhakrishnan*.

Arapura looks at Radhakrishnan's method and application of integral experience. He argues that though Radhakrishnan began with an absolute idealism, he progressively developed a philosophy of integral experience. At a number of points Radhakrishnan departed from Advaitin thought, for example by declaring that "manifest personality or empirical self is not an illusion."[13] But this, Arapura points out, is more reconcilable with personalism than the advaitin insistence on the unitary with regard to self.[14]

Urumpackal's analysis is similarly thorough, including an analysis of the secondary literature. Radhakrishnan's definition of Hinduism is a reinterpreted and idealized one, but, Urumpackal argues. Radhakrishnan fails to give a reasonable explanation of the relationship between the Absolute and God. Instead he labels the problem *māyā*, "an admission of the insolubility of the problem."[15] In this Urumpackal echoes M.N. Roy's previous criticism : "From the Aupaniṣadic Ṛṣis down to Śaṁkarācārya, no orthodox Hindu speculative thinker has been able to prove how the diversities of nature could arise from a common cause. The sheer impossibility of this task ultimately drove Indian speculation to the moumental absurdity of the *Māyāvāda.*"[16]

Bürkle views Radhakrishnan as a defender of Hinduism more than a constructive thinker. He is particularly critical of Radhakrishnan's resort to Śaṁkara and the Hindu scriptures at the same time that Radhakrishnan is critical of Western thinkers for being under "the reign of religion."[17] Bürkle suggests that there is little "integral" about Radhakrishnan's vision, for the ultimate result of *sarva-mukti* is not the salvation of the individual but its ceasing to be.[18]

Among the studies of Radhakrishnan devoted centrally to his understanding of *māyā*, the variety of meanings it takes on in Radhakrishnan's thought have been noted. Braue and Tuck have produced the most detailed studies of *māyā* in Radhakrishnan, clarifying Radhakrishnan's meaning as denying the illusoriness of the world. Braue, in fact, observes six meanings of the term "other than 'illusion'."[19] However, in his dissertation and a later article, Tuck argued that : "Radhakrishnan is taking subsidiary statements in Śaṁkara, elevating them beyond their intent, and in fact, undermining an otherwise well executed system."[20] These studies too support Urumpackal's conclusion that by saying the relationship of the one and the many is *māyā*, Radhakrishnan has renounced his claim to giving a rational explanation of the relationship between the universe and the absolute.[21]

On the issue of Radhakrishnan's experiential integralism, scholarship remains unsettled about its solution to the problems of philosophy. The debate continues about its integral nature, about its ability to move beyond the claim of faith that integral experience is behind the all, and, thus, about its ability to explain the relationship between the personal and impersonal and the many and the one in satisfactory terms.

His System as Bridge-Builder

On the one hand, scholars have praised Radhakrishnan as a bridge-builder between the East and the West, an apostle of tolerance for the variety of religious positions. Raju, among others, believes that Radhakrishnan "has succeeded in showing that the spirit of man is the same everywhere in spite of differences of outlook. The differences are only non-essentials."[22] Inge is representative of those who put the matter in terms of East and West : "No one has done more than Radhakrishnan to interpret East and West to each other.[23] But the most exhaustive study is that of Harris, who concludes that Radhakrishnan has given humanity a philosophy of universalism which not only implies "the unity of religions, but all human knowledge and experience," while it affirms the oneness of intentionality between all religions, and the unity of humankind.[24]

But this is not the unanimous position of scholarship. For example, in 1970 McDermott concluded that "Radhakrishnan's synthesis falls short of the range and precision required of a system which would synthesize the variety of philosophical systems as we are now coming to know them."[25] He, apparently prematurely, on the basis of the broader scope and richer variety of data which has become available, pronounced the end of the philosophical search for "a universal philosophical synthesis."[26]

Other scholars have also observed problems of method in Radhakrishnan's attempt which go far beyond the availability of data. Radhakrishnan posits an integral experience at the heart of all religions which provides their unity, an experience which he believes is above the interpretations of history. Yet, Kaylor pointed out that his definition of this experience is not outside of history, for ". . . Radhakrishnan locates the primary source of authentic religion in the geographical East, and the primary source of danger to modern life in the geographical West."[27] Moreover, it has also been argued that Radhakrishnan's understanding of the essential uniting experience, is more than just an "Eastern" understanding but a form of Hindu understanding. Again, McDermott is clear : "What Radhakrishnan considers to be the essence of religion would seem to be scarcely distinguishable from the view of reality and disciplines that characterize the Idealist and Hindu views."[28]

To go even further, it is not merely a Hindu, but, more precisely, a form of advaitin understanding. As such, it functions to allow him to accept the understanding of Śaṁkara, only one of the Indian historical positions available to people, as correct, while it limits his ability to accept even other elements of his own tradition as they accept themselves. His position as to the essential unity of religions in this manner, which has been called "an inclusivistic absolutism,"[29] actually insulates him from taking other options seriously. They are accepted as they fit into his own interpretation. For Radhakrishnan, then : "Tolerance is an affirmation of one's own viewpoint when held by others and a placing of all other viewpoints within one's own by rejecting all absolute claims of other positions . . . . This definition of tolerance will not satisfy outsiders or those who do not find tolerance of one's own position virtuous."[30]

The frustration of those outside of Radhakrishnan's understanding, who have attempted to communicate their problem with this approach and failed, reflects the very inability of Radhakrishnan's approach to see the other positions as other. This is because the position Radhakrishnan takes assumes that it knows more about the other positions and religious experiences than the others do. At times this is merely seen as a misreading of the other positions. On Buddhist traditions, for example, Murti concludes that Radhakrishnan's treatment is not balanced : "Radhakrishnan does not, it appears to me, sufficiently emphasize their [Buddhist and Hindu] differences; in fact, he even tends to minimise them. This is evident especially in his treatment of the relation between the *Upaniṣads* and Buddha and to a certain extent also between the absolutisms of Mādhyamika, Yogācāra and Advaita Vedānta."[31]

At other times his approach is understood as hostile. Wach sees "a notable trace of bitterness in a great number of references to Christianity in Radhakrishnan's writings."[32] Radhakrishnan could hardly relate to such criticisms. To Wach he responded : "If he finds it so, there must be a basis for his statement and I am sincerely sorry for it."[33] Likewise, Kung argued that, far from accepting other positions, when Radhakrishnan affirms that "the *only* thing that has any ultimate validity is that inner experience of the Absolute ... he is taking up a *dogmatic* standpoint."[34] More recently, Almond has placed the issue in terms of three problems : the problem of approximation (How does one determine which religion most truly reflects the core of religion?), the problem of the priority of religious experience (It is a normative judgment to place a high priority on religious experience particularly if other religions do not, as Radhakrishnan himself admits), and the problem of unity of the actual experiences.[35]

Among scholars at present, then, the status of Radhakrishnan's "bridge-building" receives mixed reviews. Some laud him as an advocate of the key to religious unity while others question the appeal of his solution outside of those who have already accepted his basic premises. In fact, if it is unable to take the positions of the others as serious positions, but relativizes their absolute beliefs, his position appears to be unable to speak to their actual positions but only to a caricature[36] or to a neo-advaitin reading of them.

His Advocacy of Idealistic Hindu Ethics

From the writing of his M.A. thesis, *The Ethics of the Vedānta and its Metaphysical Presuppositions*, to his last works, Radhakrishnan was fighting criticisms of an ethical position which he identified with "Hinduism," that position particularly related to Advaita Vedānta.[37] Critics contended that there was no basis for ethics in "Hinduism" or "Indian thought," by which they most often meant the tradition of Advaita Vedānta. The world is, in this view point, *māyā*, which has been understood to affirm that the world is not ultimately real. Radhakrishnan, Tuck and Braue have shown most extensively, does not understand the concept of *māyā* in this manner.

Radhakrishnan asserts that *māyā* designates that the world, unlike the Absolute, is not independently real. The world, as a place to do ethics and morality, is dependent upon the Absolute for the reality that it has. But what is that dependency? It is *māyā*, which designates also that the relationship between the One and the many is inexplicable. Moore commends this solution. "The great significance of the doctrine of *māyā* - of special relevance for ethics - is essentially the reminder that the empirical world is not the ultimate; for, to hold that it is would be the essence of ignorance, and ignorance is the cause of bondage, suffering, and false living."[38] He concludes then that, "Radhakrishnan has built a solid foundation for the ethical and religious life which he and Hinduism advocate so strongly and so effectively."[39]

Arapura, on the other hand, has questioned the practical applicability of Radhakrishnan's approach : either it is an ethics of perfection, "a species of dogmatics," or a conversion of ethics into the acting out of unique intuitions.[40] However, other scholars have found a more basic theoretical flaw at the heart of his apologetics. Just as scholars have noted that Radhakrishnan's designation of the metaphysical problem as *māyā*, as inexplicable, is not a rational, systematic explanation of the relationship of the One and the many, so some analysts of his ethical apologetics have criticized this usage to answer critics. It amounts to a statement of faith rather than a demonstration of a basis for ethics in the tradition.

Hunnex and Goodwin have placed the issue in terms of Radhakrishnan's answer to his fellow mystic Albert Schweitzer. Hunnex traces the issues of ethics and mysticism between the two, concluding that the essential difference is "the support which each brings to bear on behalf of ethics." For Schweitzer : "The problem of ethical mysticism is identity with particular beings as wills-to-live rather than identity with universal Being."[41] As Phillips had previously written, the problem is not that Radhakrishnan finds life unsatisfactory, but that he fails to find it "finally satisfactory."[42]

Goodwin in the most sustained manner argues that Radhakrishnan's answer to Schweitzer's criticism is inadequate. Radhakrishnan fails to show what the relationship is between Brahman and the world and, thus, how there are values in the world, i.e. how the values of Brahman are transferred to the world. And the term *māyā* will not do, for it merely indicates that the system cannot explain this, it is mysterious.

> Schweitzer's contentions are not fully met. They are not met for the reason that, as Radhakrishnan himself points out, the *concept* of the infinite, of spirit, of Brahman, is held to be without empirical content. The *concept* of Brahman is the experience of the mystic philosophically interpreted. And we can rightly raise the question, what is the relationship of Brahman, so conceived, to the world as we understand the latter. And to *this* question there is, as Radhakrishnan admits, no answer.[43]

Without an answer to this question, Goodwin points out, one cannot offer an account of the nature and continuity of the value which links ethics and Brahman, "Radhakrishnan endeavours mightily to fill the axiological gulf between 'the infinite and the finite;' but to no avail." Though Radhakrishnan asserts a relationship, he cannot explain or describe it and, thus, is unable even to show why the system should be called "world and life-affirming." The only resort is to a faith which might be called as blind as those Radhakrishnan criticizes.

On this third issue, then, scholars continue to debate the adequacy of Radhakrishnan's system. Is it more than a faith stance? This, then, joins the other two issues as matters of continuing debate among scholars who analyze Radhakrishnan's position. Radhakrishnan himself defined these three issues as the keys to a religion of the future and his own "religion of the spirit," but scholars continue to question whether he has established these as any more than affirmations of faith. Are they philosophically justifiable? If so, are they more so than other religious positions? Ignatius takes the skeptical view : "What makes his view less coherent and therefore less acceptable is the fact that he wants to defend *philosophically* (that is, by pure reason) what most of our Hindu ancestors defended *theologically* (that is, on the authority of the supposed revealed word of God).[4] As such, Radhakrishnan's reconstruction of "Hinduism" solves few of the problems Radhakrishnan himself set out to solve and his system is as non-philosophically based as the critics say. In any case, that Radhakrishnan's system is so much the object of debate, shows how it continues to dominate comparative thought and modern discussions of the definition of "Hinduism" as one of the world's religious traditions.

References

1. For example, see his letter to the editor in Paul Arthur Schilpp, ed., *The Philosophy of Sarvepalli Radhakrishnan* (New York : Tudor, 1952), 3.
2. "Reply to Critics," in Schilpp, 789.

3. Robert N. Minor, "Sarvepalli Radhakrishnan and 'Hinduism' Defined and Defended," in *Religion in Modern India*, 2nd. rev. ed., ed. by Robert D. Baird (New Delhi : Manohar, 1989), 421-54.
4. Bernard Phillips, "Radhakrishnan's Critique of Naturalism," in Schilpp, 132.
5. *Ibid.*, 148.
6. Robert W. Browning, "Reason and Types of Intuition in Radhakrishnan's Philosophy," in Schilpp, 177-8. See also S.J. Samartha, *Introduction to Radhakrishnan : The Man and His Thought* (New Delhi : Y.M.C.A., 1964), 29-31.
7. P.T. Raju, "Radhakrishnan's Influence on Indian Thought, in Schilpp, 528.
8. Ram Pratap Singh, "Radhakrishnan's Substantial Reconstruction of the Vedānta of Śaṁkara," *Philosophy East and West*, XVI, 1-2 (January-April 1966), 31-2. See also his "Śaṁkara and Radhakrishnan," in *Dr. S. Radhakrishnan Souvenir Volume*, ed. by J.P. Atreya (Moradabad: Darshana International, 1964), 440-452.
9. Raju, Radhakrishnan's Influence . . .," 534.
10. Swami Agehananda Bharati, "Radhakrishnan and the Other Vedānta," in Schilpp, 464.
11. S.S. Raghavachar, "Radhakrishnan, A Philosopher with a Difference," *Indian Philosophical Annual*, I (1977-78), 7.
12. Anantanand Rambachan, "Śaṁkara's Rationale for *śruti* as the Definitive Source of *Brahmajñana* : A Refutation of Some Contemporary Views," *Philosophy East and West*, XXXVI, No. 1 (January 1986), 25-40.
13. J.G. Arapura, *Radhakrishnan and Integral Experience : The Philosophy and World Vision of Sarvepalli Radhakrishnan* (New York : Asia Publishing House, 1966), 154.
14. *Ibid.*, 162.
15. Thomas Paul Urumpackal, *Organized Religion According to Dr. S. Radhakrishnan* (Roma : Universita Gregoriana Edtrice, 1972), 224.
16. M.N. Roy, "Radhakrishnan in the Perspective of Indian Philosophy," in Schilpp, 555.

17. Horst Bürkle, *Dialog mit dem Osten: Radhakrishnans neuhinduistische Botshcaft im Lichte chrislicher Weltanschauung* (Stuttgart : Evanglisdhes Verlagawerk, 1965), 85.
18. *Ibid.*, 91.
19. Donald Braue, "*Māyā*" *in Radhakrishnan's Thought : Six Meanings Other Than Illusion* (Columbia : South Asia Books, 1985). For an earlier study, see Samartha, 45-49.
20. Donald Richard Tuck, The Doctrine of Maya : Radhakrishnan," *Darshana International*, XV, No. 4 (October 1976), 56. See also his "Māyā : Interpretive Principle for an Understanding of the Religious Thought of Śaṁkara and Radhakrishnan." Unpublished Ph.D. dissertation, University of Iowa, 1970.
21. Cf. P.T. Raju, "The Idealism of Professor Sir S. Radhakrishnan," *Calcutta Review* (3rd Series), LXXVI (August 1940), 182-3.
22. *Ibid.*, 169.
23. W.R. Inge, "Radhakrishnan and the Religion of the Spirit," in Schilpp, 332.
24. Ishwar C. Harris, *Radhakrishnan : The Profile of a Universalist* (Columbia : South Asia Books, 1982), 287.
25. Robert A. McDermott, "Radhakrishnan's Contribution to Comparative Philosophy," *International Philosophical Quarterly*, X, No.3 (September, 1970), 435.
26. *Ibid.*, 440.
27. R. David Kaylor, "Radhakrishnan as Proponent and Critic of Religion," *Indian Philosophical Annual*, XII (1977-78), 59.
28. Robert A. McDermott, "Introduction," In *Radhakrishnan : Selected Writings on Philosophy, Religion, and Culture* (New York : E.P. Dutton, 1970), 25.
29. William Halbfass, "India and the Comparative Method," *Philosophy East and West*, XXX, No. 1 (January 1985), 12-13.
30. Robert N. Minor, "Sarvepalli Radhakrishnan on the Nature of 'Hindu' Tolerance," *Journal of the American Academy of Religion*, L. No. 2, 287.

31. T.R.V. Murti, "Radhakrishnan and Buddhism," in Schilpp, 569.
32. Joachim Wach, "Radhakrishnan and the Comparative Study of Religion," in Schilpp, 448.
33. S. Radhakrishnan, "Reply to Critics," in Schilpp, 807.
34. Hans Kung, "The World's Religions in God's Plan of Salvation," in *Christian Revelation and World Religions*, ed. by J. Neuner (London : Burns and Oates, 1967), 48-9.
35. Philip C. Almond, *Mystical Experience and Religious Doctrine : An Investigation of the Study of Mysticism in World Religions* (Berlin : Mouton Publishers, 1982), 13.
36. See Urumpackal, 213ff; Hendrik Kraemer, *Religion and the Christian Faith* (London : Lutter worth Press, 1956), 134; and Stephen Neill, *Christian Faith and Other Faiths* (London : Oxford University Press, 1962), 83-6.
37. For a study of the development of Radhakrishnan's thought and apologetics, see Robert N. Minor, *Radhakrishnan : A Religious Biography* (Albany : State University of New York Press, 1987).
38. Charles A. Moore, "Metaphysics and Ethics in Radhakrishnan's Philosophy," in Schilpp, 305.
39. *Ibid.*, 310.
40. J.G. Arapura, 132.
41. Milton D. Hunnex, "Mysticism and Ethics : Radhakrishnan and Schweitzer," *Philosophy East and West*, VIII, No. 3-4 (October, 1958-January 1959), 136.
42. Bernard Phillips, 144.
43. William F. Goodwin, "Mysticism and Ethics : An Examination of Radhakrishnan's Reply to Schweitzer's Critique of Indian Thought," *Ethics*, LXXVII, No. 1 (October 1952), 34.
44. Gnanapragasam Ignatius, "Sarvepalli Radhakrishnan and Jnana," *The Modern Schoolman*, XXXVI, No. 4 (May 1959), 277.

4
Remarks On Three Radhakrishnan Introductions

ALEX WAYMAN
Columbia University

Here I shall go into Radhakrishnan's introductions to three works, *The Bhagavad Gītā*[1] (1948), *The Dhammapada*[2] (1950), and *The Principal Upaniṣads*[3] (1953). It appears useful to mention some contemporary introductions, namely, three by the Swiss psychologist Carl Jung, to Suzuki, *An Introduction to Zen Buddhism*[4] (1949); his psychological commentary to Wilhelm's translation from the Chinese of *The Secret of the Golden Flower*[5] (1955), and one for Evans-Wentz, *The Tibetan Book of the Dead*[6] (1957). On the Suzuki work, Jung mentioned, "The original Buddhist writings themselves contain views and ideas which are more or less unassimilable by the average Western understanding." For the Secret of the Golden Flower, Jung admitted that he was "deeply impressed by the strangeness of the Chinese text." And for the Tibetan Book of the Dead, Jung (p. xliii) finds the Eastern theory of *karma* beyond our scientific knowledge or our 'reason.' Jung stressed that these Asiatic works are intellectual riddles for the Westerner. But this does not prevent him from his kind of comments, and he does contact these systems but only in the area of his own prevalent interest, that of 'consciousness' while also pushing his theory of the 'unconscious.' One may conclude that Jung was only partially successful in these introductions and commentaries, since he was mainly exposing his own system; and the introductions are valuable in this sense, since Jung is an important writer of this century. Also worth mentioning is the introduction by Ananda K. Coomaraswamy and I.B. Horner, to the canonical selections published with the title *Gotama the Buddha* (1948, the same year as Radhakrishnan's version of the *Bhagavad Gītā*). This introduction claims that the usual explanations of Buddhism as adhering to a theory of 'non-self' (*anātman*) has misconstrued what Buddhism is talking about, that in fact it did not deny a self, in particular a 'great self.' Therefore, Jung and Coomaraswamy agree that the Westerners simply do not get into the spirit of these Asian religions or philosophies; Westerners are baffled by the terms, continually miss the point. Even so, both Jung and Coomaraswamy put themselves forward as the rare interpreters who, also by a kind of mystery, are able to get inside these systems and to reveal what they amount to.

One may also notice that Coomaraswamy shares with Radhakrishnan the feature of an Indian background, so they would presumably be 'insiders' from this fact - though of course not from this fact alone. And by the same argument Carl Jung was not an 'insider' to these Asian topics, and again not by his birthplace alone. Nowadays, it is believed by various Westerners that they can spend a period of time in India under the tutelage of gurus and become thereby 'insiders' for communication purposes; but, after all, this is their illusion, because if that is what it takes to be an 'insider,' all residents of India would be insiders by virtue of living there, or of having gurus there. Turning to Radhakrishnan, we find a person who is apparently bilingual, writing fine English with ease while writing on - topics which Carl Jung deemed recondite and hard to penetrate intellectually. We shall observe that Radhakrishnan is not the 'insider' in the classical sense of the fervent

Remarks On Three Radhakrishnan Introductions 45

sectarian, for he writes with a broad-mindedness and kindliness to all his topics of discourse which belies the intense sectarian connotation, even combativeness of the original Indian classics.

Thus, all three of the texts which Radhakrishnan has introduced belong to that great revolt against the older theory of the Brahmanical sacrifice that transformation consists in the external ritual cooking. The Upaniṣads inaugurated the revolt by insisting that true transformation is internal, and that the sacrifice takes place in the head. The Buddhist text *Dhammapada* writes about the internal transformation without even the terms of the old sacrificial cult. The *Bhagavad Gītā* is conciliatory, praising the various ways of getting to the Hindu goal, be it of *mokṣa*.

Radhakrishnan in his introductions has a distinct advantage over Carl Jung since in the case of Radhakrishnan the introductions are to texts which he has himself translated, granted of course that the translations are not pioneer and that he has been helped by previous translation labour on these same texts. Accordingly, he contacts these texts on the level of the original sentence (the *vākya*). Perhaps that is why he does not make the kind of remarks we find in Jung, namely, that the text is strange and has many untranslateable terms. For, whatever language we speak or write, it is not strange to us - it is the foreigner who finds it strange. The sense of strangeness sometimes helps for understanding a text if one has a mind for the strange things, and perhaps this is Carl Jung's way. It does not seem to be Radhakrishnan's way.

Radhakrishnan, while not admitting difficulties for himself as the one to understand, apparently does not expect the reader to readily grasp these matters, so cites the Christian gospels, Plotinus, the Middle East mystical writers like Rumi, Confucius and the Christian theologian Thomas

Aquinus; besides a fund of Indic materials, Vedic, Vedāntic, Nyāya, Sāmkhya, and so on. These citations are in a context of directing attention to a comparable idea or ideas. Thus, Radhakrishnan is not among those who discount East-West parallels as arbitrary and lacking in cogency. He accepts East-West parallels to be as feasible as comparisons within or among the doctrinal or religious systems of India itself. On the other hand, such citations have a certain amount of drawback, as suggesting that this is the way to understand the Indic systems. There is no suggestion with such citations that they were necessary for Radhakrishnan's own understanding of the three books for which he wrote introductions. Indeed, it is not right for anyone to insist that a topic needs a different topic in order to be understood, since what is necessary in any case is the understanding itself; and if understanding is lacking for a given topic, why does it appear by dint of another topic?

One theme that runs through all three of Radhakrishnan's introductions is his treatment of ethics. Indeed, this must have been his chief interest in the Buddhist *Dhammapada*. There are ethical problems left over by all three of the texts on which he comments. In his Upaniṣad introduction, Radhakrishnan addresses himself to the thorny problem left by Śaṁkara's arguing for 'knowledge' (*jñāna*) as producing the salvation which works cannot. Radhakrishnan says of work that it "purifies the heart and produces the illumination which is the immediate condition of salvation." His solution is to credit the ethical life with taking one to a stage just prior to salvation (*mokṣa*), and then allowing 'knowledge' - be it supernatural knowledge - as taking the person the final distance. In a way, this solution seems consistent with the *Chāndogya-Upaniṣad*, IV, 15, 5 & 6, reference to a non-human (*amānava*) guide who leads the deceased to Brahman, since 'non-human' leaves out 'human acts' (*puruṣakāra*).

Then there is the problem of evil, and he says, "Evil is the result of our alienation from the Real." And he also says, "Man is of the divine race, but he has in him the element of non-being, which exposes him to evil." This kind of talk labels man's fallen nature as 'non-being,' so his divine nature, what is called also his 'freedom,' is 'true being.' As man sinks he is more and more fettered by *karma*. Radhakrishnan explains : "The freedom of the individual increases to the extent to which he identifies himself with the Absolute in him, the *antar-yāmin*." And he continues in this Upaniṣad introduction to interpret that the Upaniṣads enjoin a spirit of detachment (*vairāgya*), namely, from the objects of the world - and this, of course, is a prevalent teaching of the *Bhagavad Gītā*. But in his *Bhagavad Gītā* introduction he presents what appears to be an alternate solution, saying, "Evil is caused by the bondage to the *guṇas*." And further, "When we recognize the self as distinct from prakṛti with its guṇas we are released." This is of course the Sāṁkhya school terminology. It follows that the 'self' is here a name for Puruṣa (the pure consciousness), which should get disengaged from matter, the phenomenalization of the *prakṛti* with its three *guṇas*, or distinct powers. Hence, we should practise *yoga*, according to the precept or *sūtra*, gain cessation of the modifications of the mind (the *citta*), in Radhakrishnan's words (p. 57) "fold up the phenomenal series." But this solution for getting released does not seem to be consistent with the former solution. My reason for saying this, is the necessity to identify oneself with a reality within; but in the Sāṁkhya system this internal reality can be *prakṛti* with its three *guṇas*, just as real as is *puruṣa*; and when the yogin identifies with seems the reality within, granted it is not the Sāṁkhya *manas*, then is it the Ahaṁkāra? And if not that, it is the *buddhi*, also called Mahat? It is a big problem for the Sāṁkhya as to what is in bondage, the *puruṣa* or the subtle body (*sūkṣma-śarīra*) produced by the *prakṛti* evolutes. And so, when one identifies with the *antar-yāmin*, the inner controller, to revert to Radhakrishnan's expression, it is indeed a question of what this is.

Again in his Upaniṣad introduction, Radhakrishnan clarifies the 'fallen nature' (cf. p. 98) as the objective world, "in which the subject is alienated from the object of knowledge. It is the world of disruption, disunion, alienation. In the 'fallen' condition, man's mind is never free from the compulsion exercised by objective realities." And his introduction to the *Dhammapada* would credit the same attitude to Buddhism (p. 45) : "This view is corroborated by the Buddhist formula : 'This is not mine; I am not this; this is not myself'." Adding, "These negations aim at expressing the absolute difference of self from non-self or object." The point is that by virtue of this separation of subject and object, the object exerts a fascination for the subject, and so the term 'fallen' applies both to the object and to the subject. By the Buddhist insistence that these objects are "not mine," there is severance of relation between subject and object, whereupon the object can no longer affect the subject; and this ends the 'disunion' and 'alienation,' to use Radhakrishnan's terms.

I sense that the *Dhammapada* introduction was Radhakrishnan's hardest. Only his ever-present benevolence, a kindly attitude toward all the Indic systems, and to other religions of the world as well, carries him through this introduction. He tries to derive Buddhism from the Upaniṣads, saying (p. 29), "The Upaniṣads, from which the Buddha's teaching is derived, hold that the world we know, whether outward or inward, does not possess intrinsic reality. Intrinsic reality belongs to the knower, the Ātman, the self of all selves." But the best he could do with the Buddhist teaching of 'non-self' is to say (p. 44) : "The doctrine of non-self (*anatta*) asserts that the ego is a process of becoming." Then he cites Buddhist scripture showing the Buddha advises the search for the self, intending of course that this is a superior self, not the one that people accept as self. In so writing, he agrees with the position I previously alluded to as that of Coomaraswamy and Horner in their own introduction to a book of Buddhist selections. While agreeing with these authors that the Buddhist teaching of non-self is not the denial of the Upaniṣadic self that can be equated with the great Brahman of the universe, it seems to me that these authors, in trying to make Buddhist teachings agree with the preceding Upaniṣads, have missed the main point of why Buddhist literature itself does not make such an identification. The reason can be seen in Buddhist scripture after scripture, indeed ubiquitous; and yet largely misunderstood. Even when Radhakrishnan speaks of the "doctrine of non-self" we see the problem of terminology, as when he calls it a 'doctrine.' Indeed, read this Buddhist literature with an unprejudiced mind, and one must conclude that 'non-self' has nothing to do with a real self, just as the Yogācāra insistence on non-existence of external objects has nothing to do with the reality of objects. What all these kinds of statements intend is, first of all, that the human state is the only one of the various destinies, gods, men, hungry ghosts, animals, and hell-beings, that has the possibility of changing one's perception of the world. Each of these destinies has its own way of perceiving; and also among humans it is clear that men and women have among themselves as a class different ways of perceiving the opposite sex. And we think our perceptions are free to make, but it is taught that they are in bondage. The prescription for loosening this bondage starts with using the intellect to make denials of the reality of the object and of the subject. It is a claim that this is the way to gradually loosen this bondage so that there can be a real change in the nature from the ordinary person to a saint and then to a master of nature's forces. Now, one might argue that this is not the way to do it - that there is better way, or surer way, to change from the ordinary person to the saint and to the master in such sense. But one thing is certain : this was Gautama Buddha's way, his prescription. And it is certain that Buddhism is not understood by the attempts to derive it from the Upaniṣads, well intentioned as these may be. And yet it is also true, and this agrees with Radhakrishnan's intuition, that the great revolt of the Upaniṣads prepares the way for such a programme as that of Gautama Buddha, for it is the Upaniṣadic insistence on the subjectivity of true transformation that prepares the way for what would follow. I presume that any system that stresses the illusion of the world, as does the Advaita-Vedānta and before it the Mādhyamika school of Buddhism, has behind it a similar implication of loosening and then destroying the bondage in the human condition; but almost invariably surveys of Indian philosophy take such positions as doctrinal and try to fit them into some philosophical framework and pigeonhole.

On a more technical note, there is Radhakrishnan's remarks about symbols. In the Upaniṣad introduction he says (p. 138) : "Symbols belong to an order of reality different from that of the Reality which they symbolize. They are used to make the truth intelligible, to make the unhearable audible." He goes on to mention some of these symbols, like fire and light, as used for contemplation and in fact are employed by other religions besides the Indic ones. Since the Supreme is not ordinarily contacted directly, mankind has provisional intimations by way of symbols. Radhakrishnan points out that these symbols have meanings. Such symbols are partial glimpses of reality. In the Upaniṣads these are the special passages called *upāsana*, or worship, or called *vidyā* as a type of spiritual knowledge. Perhaps the most famous one of such passages of symbolic nature is the Gāyatrī. Radhakrishnan states (p. 139), "We may use any symbols and methods which help to bring about a change of consciousness, a new birth." He means that symbols are of different value, and the preferable ones are those that bring about the desired change of consciousness, the 'new birth.' And these very remarks perhaps reveal why the Buddhists do not trace their path procedure to the Upaniṣads. Such use of symbols is the positive way, while Buddhism prefers the negative approach, speaking of 'non-self' and the various kinds of voidness (śūnyatā). However, it must be conceded that Buddhism has its positive passages of symbols; and as the centuries passed on, various Buddhists preferred the positive statement, and so there is the famous 'parable of the burning house' of the Lotus Scripture (*Saddharma-puṇḍarīka*) which is in the form of the positive symbol, as are many other fine passages of Buddhist literature. When tantrism, whether Hindu or Buddhist, became popular, the use of symbols became the life of such literature and the associated practises; and all this kind of literature is much indebted to the early as well as the later Upaniṣads.

Of course, one cannot treat Radhakrishnan's introduction to the *Bhagavad Gītā* without considering the portrayal of Arjuna. For Radhakrishnan, Arjuna "typifies the representative human soul seeking to reach perfection and peace." Yet his mind is clouded, his position is impossible to resolve, and he is assailed by doubt and despair. And it is at such a time, when human acts (*puruṣakāra*) are of no avail, that he becomes receptive to divine counsel. It is a curious feature of this famous text that the dialogue between Kṛṣṇa (representing the divine counsel) and Arjuna (the receptive human) should take place on the battlefield between the two hostile arrayed armies. Why should all the hostilities remain in suspension while this dialogue is going on? Or is it, strange to say, that the dialogue, which takes some chapters to write out and some time to read, took place in a moment, so to say?

Radhakrishnan goes on to consider how this goal of perfection is to be attained. "To escape from bondage we must get rid of ignorance, which is the parent of ignorant desires and so of ignorant actions. Vidyā or wisdom is the means of liberation from the chain of *avidyā-kāma-karma.*" He points out that wisdom and ignorance are opposed as are light and darkness, to wit, only one of these can be in a given place, so if light prevails there is no darkness; and if darkness triumphs, gone is light. Wisdom is differentiated from scientific knowledge, and also from the intellectual pathway. In his Upaniṣad introduction he refers to the Upaniṣad distinction between the lower knowledge (*a-parā vidyā*), i.e. knowledge of the Vedas and the sciences; and the higher wisdom (*parā vidyā*) that gives knowledge of the Imperishable. Now, while the scientific knowledge is deemed to be lower, it is not discounted as valueless. It helps us in an intellectual way to appreciate the path, indeed to learn about Arjuna and his dilemma, and the associated doctrines. Indeed, it is this lower knowledge that is used to read the three Radhakrishnan introductions, but they are rewarding nevertheless. The rational order is called *smṛti*, wherein the experiences of the sages have been reduced to a form that can be applied to govern individual conduct as well as social contracts. The higher wisdom is the experience (*anubhava*) of Reality. It is recorded in the *śruti* as the direct revelation. The higher wisdom, according to Radhakrishnan, requires Arjuna to lose the passions directed to external objects, and to enter the inward silence with initial contact with the 'Eternal' from which it was sundered, so to experience in his words the 'Indwelling God.' This means, I suppose, that Arjuna has made within a pure place for this Indwelling God, the inner temple to which the deity can be invited.

There is an easier path for Arjuna if he takes the 'Way of Devotion' (*bhakti-mārga*). This is trust and love to a Personal God, and avoids the ascetic discipline or the strenuous control of thinking processes. This way requires service to the deity with daily remembrance. Arjuna should avoid the 'holier than thou' attitude.

Or Arjuna could follow the 'Way of Action' (*karma-mārga*), but then he would have to fight, if that is the Dharma of his birth. Indeed, we could not really avoid action - which in grammar is the virtuality of the verb. We should not be attached to the ends. As Radhakrishnan mentions, "We have to act in the world as it is, while doing our best to improve it." Hence, if Arjuna follows this way, he should try to be an exemplar, an inspiration for others.

If Arjuna succeeds in attaining the transcendent condition, then for him the Eternal is always present. Radhakrishnan reels off the titles - he can be called the *yogin*, the *siddhapuruṣa*, the *jītātman*, the *yuktacetas*, and in the Sāṁkhya terminology, he is *prakṛtilīna*, merged in *prakṛti*. But did Arjuna succeed? Let us assume that if not that Arjuna, then some other.

The topic of Dharma comes up especially in Radhakrishnan's introduction to the *Dhammapada*. It is a fine intuition of Radhakrishnan's to treat the matter of *dharma* here in various ways. This could lead to much discussion. Let me mention now, as I have elsewhere, that Mrs. M. Geiger and Prof. W. Geiger long ago in their 1921 monograph published at Munich, compared the Pāli term *dhamma* with the Upaniṣad *brahman* and found an equivalence of usage. I am confident that this equivalence will stand up in further research. It is part of my agreement with Radhakrishnan that Buddhism did take important teachings from the Upaniṣads, although changing the technical terms. But what the Buddha did not take from that wonderful literature is his theory of the path, the Buddhist way of gaining perfection.

I hope by the foregoing to have provided a fair idea of Radhakrishnan's three introductions. Naturally, much more could be said, although a rule would intervene called the law of diminishing returns. I should not leave the topic without again remarking on Radhakrishnan's remarkable broadmindedness, his love for and appreciation of all the religious currents of his beloved India.

References

1. S. Radhakrishnan, *The Bhagavad Gītā* (New York : Harper, 1948).
2. S. Radhakrishnan, *Dhammapada* (New York : Oxford University, Press, 1966).
3. S. Radhakrishnan, *Principal Upaniṣads* (London : Allen & Unwin, 1953).
4. D.T. Suzuki, *An Introduction to Zen Buddhism* (London : Rider, 1949).
5. Richard Wilhelm (tr) : *Secret of the Golden Flower* (New York : Harcourt, Brace & Co., 1938).
6. W.Y. Evans-Wentz, *Tibetan Book of the Dead* (New York : Oxford University Press, 1957).

5

Radhakrishnan and the Problems of Modernity in Indian Philosophy

BIMAL KRISHNA MATILAL
Oxford University

Bertrand Russell in 1923, in a review of Radhakrishnan's first volume of *Indian Philosophy* (Allen & Unwin), commented:

> His work is admirably done, though, perhaps, for English readers, it would have been well to give more account of the political history which accompanied the successive schools of philosophy. One of the main documents of Buddhism is the 'Questions of King Milinda,' this was the Greek King Menander, of the end of the second century B.C. The Western reader wishes to know what influence Greek philosophy had on Buddhism, the more so as Buddhist art suffered a powerful Hellenic influence; but on this subject the book contains no information.

This appeared in *The Nation and the Athenaeum* on 15 September, 1923. About 65 years later, the question that Russell asked still remains unanswered. In this regard, at least, we have not done anything better than what Radhakrishnan did at that time.

The question had two distinct parts. Both parts, I venture to add most respectfully to Russell whom I regard as one of the greatest philosophers of modern times, had originated unconsciously from a Western bias. Recently when I have lectured at various philosophy departments of Western universities, I have frequently faced almost the similar question, almost in identical language. It seems that with majority of professional Western philosophers today, the Western understanding of Indian philosophy has not progressed much further.

The first part of the question relates to the political history of India and perhaps it is a valid question that springs from a genuine spirit of inquiry. But the fact is that the so-called different 'schools' of Indian philosophy did not originate under different political regime, as far as we can tell. Or if they did, their history or pre-history is entirely lost to us. And it would certainly be of interest if we could, by miracle, recover that history. But the question is why is that question important? I believe it assumes importance in the background of the implicit premise that those who are doing Indian philosophy today are at best historians of philosophy and at worst historians of ideas of cultural anthropologists. There is, of course, some truth in the idea that political and, of course, social realities exerted influences upon the philosophical doctrines that developed in a particular age. And this could be an interesting line of research uncovering in any hidden peculiarities of such philosophical ideas. Russell's mistake, repeated by many today, was not to see that the basic philosophical systems developed within a very short span of time, if not all together, and that there was a continuous on-going philosophical dialogue among the upholders of different schools or positions for over a millennia, in fact for 14 hundred years or more, meanwhile political history in India was as varied and different as it could be. In such a situation, it is impossible to find any direct link between the political upheavals (such as the Muslim conquests, wars between small states, and despots coming to power) and the philosophical concerns of the age. This is a drawback and perhaps had something to do with the nature of philosophy in India in general, which was concerned with epistemology, logic and metaphysics, but not so much with moral or social philosophy. (Moral and social concerns, however, were not completely absent. Such concerns are often reflected in the literature, in different versions of the epics and in the narrative literature. But this is another issue.)

The second part of the question is a non-starter. I have often faced it while talking about logic and epistemology : 'what influence Greek philosophy had on Indian philosophy?' The plain truth is that we do not know, and perhaps, there was not any influence either ways. Had there been any, we could have found out by now. May be, some day, some Indologist will discover a Sanskrit text written in the beginning of the Christian era, which would be translation of Plato's *Republic* or Aristotle's *Metaphysics* or *Prior Analytics*. Then we would know. But until then let us assume that there wasn't any influence. Yes, the Hellinic influence on the Buddhist art is discernable. But in philosophy, Buddhism was an Indian product. Its origin has been well-documented.

In fact there might have been some influence, very indirect as it was, in the other way around. Some have mentioned (although it has not been well-authenticated or proven beyond reasonable doubt) that Pyrrho (of Sextus Empiricus) was influenced by the Indian sceptics, or even the Neo-Plationists had absorbed some influence from the Mahāyāna Buddhist or Upaniṣads. But that is marginally possible. Russell's question was already loaded for he was moved by the Hellenic influence on the Buddhist art. However when I face today this question of possible Hellenic influence on Indian philosophy or Indian philosophers, after I have presented a paper or given a lecture on the contribution of an Indian philosopher of say ninth or tenth century A.D. to the ongoing debate on epistemology in India, I feel somewhat at a loss about how to answer or react.

The problem of modernity in Indian philosophy today cuts deeper here. A large section of those who are working today on Indian philosophy should be regarded not mere historians of ideas, but philosophers in their own right who are deriving insights and inspirations from their close study of the classical Indian tradition. Many of those who are doing Greek or scholastic philosophy today are also regarded as philosophers in their own right. The same should hold for the Indian philosophers. And I believe such questions as those about Greek influence tend to deflect the philosophical issues and hence the main points made in a paper or a book are thereby glossed over. (Russell did the same while reviewing Radhakrishnan's book, as noted above.)

There is another point to be made here. Historical issues are of course important within a tradition. And I for one would not dream of undermining them at all. But philosophical problems are in the habit of recurring at different times in different contexts, and it is interesting to see why they recur and how far they take on the contextual colouring and to what extent they transcend contexts. Study of Indian philosophy is also important in the light of these observations.

A brief comment on the problem of interpretations. Indologists for a long time have been taking others to task for distorting, misrepresenting and reading anachronistically new ideas in the old texts by taking them out of context. And surely there is a danger of misinterpretation if we do not keep within our view the age of the textual material. But the old Indological idea about discovering scientifically through archaeological excavations, as it were, the *virgin meanings* of the texts, in their pristine purity, has by now been exploded. And some modern hermeneutic philosophers have gone so far as to say that there is no original meaning of the texts anyway for the meaning is what you make of it today, or even that the meaning percolates through the mind of the reader, modern or ancient. While I do not endorse this extreme view completely for I do not understand it fully, I believe this would have sobering influence upon the Indological criticism of some modern interpreters' representations. Any outstanding philosophical text would be rich with ambiguities so that it would admit of several, sometimes contesting interpretations. Indian philosophical texts should be edited, re-edited, translated, interpreted and re-interpreted several times over by a number of scholars over a few generations, then and then only I believe we would be talking with confidence about such outstanding philosophers as Nāgārjuna, Dharmakīrti, Uddyotakara, Udayana, Śaṁkara, Kumārila, Vācaspati Miśra and Gaṅgeśa. Nowadays when we write a book on Indian philosophy we still talk in terms of different schools, as Radhakrishnan did, Vedānta, Nyāya, Buddha, and Mīmāṁsā. A lot of spade work has still to be done. In the near future, if the research programmes are satisfactory, one can pay attention more fully to the individual philosophers I have listed a moment ago. This would be a welcome outcome of the kind of research started by Radhakrishnan along with many others a couple of generations back. I now move on to *Sarvepalli Radhakrishnan.*

He was probably the only person in recent history, who, from being well-known as a professional philosopher, came to be the head of a state, President of India; and I might add, without being unnecessarily reticent about my own country, that India is probably the only place where this could happen. A man does not have to devote his entire life in politics and public work in order to be the head of the state.

Plato's idea of a philosopher-king could be a distinct possibility in the case of India.

Radhakrishnan was primarily a philosopher concerned with such broader issues as whether the task of philosophy should be only *interpreting* life or changing it as well; what role, if any, religion should play in contemporary philosophy, and what is the meaning of life, spirit and freedom. By his own admission, he was mostly influenced by Śaṁkara, Rāmānuja and Madhva of classical India, as well as by Plato, Plotinus and Kant in the West. In spite of his abiding interest in classical India, he was more a creative thinker than a classical scholar. He used the comparative method, being well-aware of its limitations as well as the difficulties involved in any adequate historical interpretation of Indian thought. But he realized, as most of us often do when we become well-acquainted with the classical philosophical texts of India, that this could not be simply an antiquarian's pursuit. He wrote :

> Ancient Indians do not belong to a different species from ourselves. An actual study of their views shows that they ask questions and find answers analogous in their diversity to some of the more important currents in modern thought.[1]

Radhakrishnan participated in the rather persistent debate about whether the Buddha was inclined towards the metaphysics of the Upaniṣadic soul, although the Buddha openly repudiated the notion of the empirical soul. Here he disagreed with his pupil, T.R.V. Murti, and gave a positive answer. With regard to the *bodhi* of Buddhism, he raised the question, which often seems pertinent : what can it be, if it is not the universal self? A tentative answer may be that it is exactly what the universal self is NOT.

With regard to the broader questions of philosophy and religion, Radhakrishnan held several distinct views. He believed that the human consciousness has three levels, that of perceptions, that of reason, and that of intuitive insight. The first helps us to collect observed data, the second to exercise rational reflection, and the third to add meaning, value and character to the observed reality. He defines the third as *ānanda*, a spiritual insight, and (using Sri Aurobindo's term) as 'integral consciousness.' He believes that scientific knowledge, where the first two levels are dominant, is 'inadequate, partial and fragmentary, but not false.' Our intuitive insight, he claims, is what gives fullness to man as a man, leads to his spiritual joy which is akin to aesthetic satisfaction, and brings about the fulfilment of his inner being.

The last point brings us to two other components of Radhakrishnan's thought : his idealistic view of life and his idea of a universal religion, i.e. a universal spiritual life for everybody. Regarding the first, he contributed to a world-view which he called 'idealism,' but refused to identify it with the usual meaning of 'idealism,' a sort of panpsychism or a pan-fictional approach to the world. The use of this term was perhaps unfortunate and confusing, as his critics pointed out. But his meaning was not entirely unclear. His 'idealism' has to do with the third level of human consciousness, what he described as the integral insight. It is what tries to make our life on this world neither 'an irrational blind striving,' nor 'an irremediably miserable blunder,' It is what is supposed to add meaning, value and worth to our life. Without it, it is believed, our civilization would be bankrupt. 'It finds life significant and purposeful.'[2] We may rightly disagree about what worth, if any, should we assign to our life, but we cannot deny the presence of a worth-assigning component in human awareness. Radhakrishnan, I believe, referred to this component by his use of the term 'idealism.' Further, he believed that this part of human awareness, when properly cultivated, will take us away from the pursuit of materialistic pleasure towards the quest for the infinite joy of the Absolute. In this respect, he was an optimist.

When one reads this part of Radhakrishnan's philosophy, one tends to have a *deja vu* experience if one has read Rabindranath Tagore's *The Religion of Man* or some of his Bengali essays on such topics. That Radhakrishnan was deeply influenced by Tagore's thought, i.e., Tagore's poetic vision of the cosmos, is proven by the fact that he was partly instrumental in the process that led the University of Oxford to confer its Ph.D. *honoris causa* to Poet Tagore at a special convocation at Santiniketan on 7 August, 1940. The university was represented on this occasion by Sir Maurice Gwyer, Dr. Sarvepalli Radhakrishnan and Mr. Justice Henderson of the Calcutta High Court. This was exactly a year before Tagore died. He died on 7 August 1941, and at his death, Radhakrishnan said : 'He [Tagore] was the greatest figure of the modern Indian Renaissance.' Tagore's universalism was not just an echo of the universalism that was prevalent in Europe at that time (in Goethe and others). It was less romantic and based more on pragmatic consideration. I believe Radhakrishnan's universalism was partly influenced by his reading of Tagore.

Radhakrishnan's idea of a universal religion has been criticised by many. Religions encouraged, if anything, respective dogmas and intensifying prejudices about other's religious beliefs. A true believer in one particular religion invariably and necessarily claims monopoly over truth and ultimate value. In the face of this state of affairs, how can one even hope to see common ties and underlying unity in different conflicting religious traditions? Radhakrishnan thought that this can be countered, for we can find a basis, the discovery of 'the World of Spirit' as he called it, which will enable us to ignore the concrete formulations of the Divine in different traditions and work towards a unity. For, according to Radhakrishnan, the Divine is 'formless and nameless and yet capable of manifesting all forms and names.'[3]

Whether this optimism or 'idealism' is justified or not, it certainly has a perennial charm for the humans in all ages. Radhakrishnan was, however, well-aware that his use of the term 'philosophy' would not agree with that of others, specially those belonging to the Anglo-American Analytic Tradition. He was also far from being an Indianist, who would claim that India, and India alone, can save the world from disaster. For his search was for a universal religion (he called it philosophy too) which would be found in all lands and cultures, in the meeting point of the Upaniṣadic seers and, Plato, Plotinus and Philo, Jesus and Paul. He believed that such a meeting point exists, and as it resides in the spirit which alone can save us from the meaninglessness of the present situation.

References

1. Paul A. Schilpp, *The Philosophy of Sarvepalli Radhakrishnan* (New York : Tudor Publishing Co., 1952), p. 13.
2. S. Radhakrishnan, *An Idealist View of Life* (London : George Allen & Unwin, 1931), p. 15.
3. Paul A. Schilpp, *The Philosophy of Sarvepalli Radhakrishnan*, p. 796.

6
Kavīs or Ṛṣis :
The Legacy of Radhakrishnan and the Discipline of Hindu Studies

CHRISTOPHER CHAPPLE
Loyola Marymont University, USA

Radhakrishnan : The Way of Accommodationism

The year 1988 marks the centennial celebration of the birth of Sarvepalli Radhakrishnan, the philosopher and President of India. In his 1939 work entitled *Eastern Religions and Western Thought,* Radhakrishnan reveals himself to be brilliantly and intimately familiar with two traditions : Christianity and Vedāntic Hinduism. His facility in dealing simultaneously with both fields remains unparalleled. In the first part of this century, it was easy to regard his interpretations of the Christian message as clearly Hinduized. Yet, at the same time, it must be noted that his presentation of Hinduism is similarly somewhat Christianized. Although he is careful (and correct) to point out the grotesque deficiencies in Schweitzer's reading of Asian religious traditions, Radhakrishnan tends to present a highly intellectualized, even sanitized view of the Hindu world, a world which is certainly recognizable if not appealing to the mystically inclined Christian. This accommodationism is certainly understandable; as a child Radhakrishnan underwent twelve years of training in Christian institutions, while at the same time receiving family based training in the Brahmanical tradition. This dual perspective child rearing tradition has been the norm for English language educated Indians of the last 150 years, since the passing of Lord Macaulay's "Minutes of 1835." As practical and necessary as this "bringing together of two worlds" was in the colonial era, it does seem to have left a lasting and perhaps negative influence on those of us who engage in the study of Indian thought.

With the advent of text and redaction criticism of Biblical literature, the scripture scholar in the 19th century became saddled with the double hermeneutical task of determining the integrity of a text in light of social and historical concerns as well as its meaning. In *Eastern Religions and Western Thought,* Radhakrishnan is primarily concerned with meaning and successfully arrives at a mystical interpretation appropriate to both traditions. However, in his more widely used *Source Book in Indian Philosophy,* coedited with Charles A. Moore, he clearly falls sway to a redaction criticism in the Orientalist approach that fails to adequately convey the full meaning of the literary tradition. For instance, in his introduction to the section entitled "The Vedic Period," Radhakrishnan refers to "the different strata of thought which indicate marked development from 'polytheistic' religion to monistic philosophy" (*Source Book,* p. 4). This statement, which bespeaks a creeping commitment to evolutionism, lacks sensitivity to the vitality of the continuing Vedic ritual tradition. By separating religion from philosophy and "polytheism" from monism, an ethic of outsider posture is assumed. The judgment that "the most important section of Vedic hymns, from the point of view of philosophical content, is . . . 'Monotheistic and Monistic Tendencies,' where the transition from early polytheism to the more philosophical monism of later hymns is depicted"

(*Source Book*, pp. 4-5), shortchanges the fluidity, versatility, and excitement of the kathenotheistic/henotheistic tradition. By reading the *Ṛg Veda*, with its multiplicity of gods and powers, one becomes equipped to comprehend multiple deity temples in a philosophical manner. Herein lies a key to understanding plurality. At its worst, the categorization of aspects of a tradition as polytheistic or monotheistic borders on an attempt to mitigate the radical otherness of the Hindu tradition, with its cyclic conception of time and its near shamanistic invocation of power.

By way of contrast, two scholars from the latter half of this century have celebrated the challenge presented by the Vedas. Using philosophical methodology, Antonio T. DeNicolas engages the reader in a nonmonistic, nonmonotheistic interpretation, using the pluralistic way of the Vedas to reveal the Vedas. Similarly, using a religious methodology, Raimundo Panikkar celebrates the raw immediacy and diversity of the Vedas without rationalizing the motivations of its authors. These approaches, however, are the exception and not the rule.

Kavis : The Way of the Imagination

With the rise of the social sciences (over and against the humanities) since the Second World War, and since the "discovery" of Asia by itinerant American scholars, a new trend in Indian studies has emerged. No longer do the respected schools with Indological concentrations in this country tolerate purely Sanskritic studies. Emphasis has shifted to "new" material, folk-based, for which field study may be conducted. Kabir, Sur Dass, Tukaram, and others have come into their own as truly representing the Hindu tradition, and rightly so. Oxford University Press has taken to publishing such works as *The Deeds of God in Rdhhipur* by Anne Feldhaus and *The Lord as Guru: Hindu Sants in North Indian Tradition* by Daniel Gold. One of my favorite books of the past couple of years in this vein is *Gods of Flesh, Gods of Stone*, edited by Joanne Waghorne. These works tell of another Hinduism, not unrelated to Radhakrishnan's elevated form, but a Hinduism rooted in flesh, in ritual, in what some nineteenth century scholars would label superstition. Gripping concerns foreign to polite scholarship are discussed here openly: possession, healing, exigencies of caste. At the same time, scholars such as Wendy O'Flaherty have turned from the traditional philosophical/ religious texts to the rich story tradition in recent works such as *Dreams, Illusion, and Other Realities* and *Tales of Sex and Violence : Folklore, Sacrifice, and Danger in the Jaiminiya Brahmana*. O'Flaherty recognizes, in her own words, that concern for such texts "could be regarded as idiosyncratic at best, perverse at worst, and certainly contrary" (*Tales,* p. 3). And yet there is something to be learned, something authentic in the marginality of these traditions, perhaps something more compelling than that which is found in more staid scholarship of fifty years ago. With this emerging literature, we get a sense of the Dionysian elements of the Hindu tradition, an aspect long overshadowed and disdained by the Aristotelian and Apollonian demands for sobriety and order that have long dominated Europeanist sensibilities.

Ṛṣis : The Way of Rationality

While a concern for the exotic has come to dominate many of those involved with the field of religion, for those involved with philosophy a more sober emphasis has emerged. Radhakrishnan, as a philosopher, may be characterized as a humanist. His writings address all aspects of the human as situated in the world. He simultaneously is a metaphysician, a cosmologist, epistemologist, and ethicist. However, with the rise of Anglo-American analytical tradition, it has become no longer fashionable to speak thus about the whole person without the jargon of truth claims.

Just as Radhakrishnan introduced his anthologies with evolutionary terminology appropriate to his time, so now studies in Indian philosophy come packaged with such chapter headings as "The Issue of Pragmatic Intersubjectivity, Should Non-mystics Believe Objective Mystic Claims, and The Issue of Mystic Exemption from Requirements of Coherence," as found in Stephen H. Phillips recent book *Aurobindo's Philosophy of Brahman*. Using a tightly argued, rigorous approach, Phillips in fact does legitimate the mystical experience and Aurobindo's work in light of the analytic tradition. But does Aurobindo require - or deserve - such legitimation? Perhaps more appropriately, the work of B.K. Matilal, Douglas Daye, Karl Potter and others has an affinity between traditional Indian and European forms of logic. Yet in both cases one is left wondering if such enterprises of cross cultural comparison in any way illuminate the indigenous Indian tradition. The fundamental suppositions of *mokṣa* and *māyā, jīvan mukta, puruṣa, prakṛti*, so central to the Indian discussion, become relegated to the background when one focuses on theories of knowledge, inference, and perception and whether a given author passes the coherence test.

In B.K. Matilal's recent work *Perception : An Essay on Classical Indian Theories of Knowledge*, as well as his earlier volume coedited with J.L. Shaw entitled *Analytical Philosophy in Comparative Perspective*, one gets the sense that in some way the theories of Russell, Brentano, Quine, Strawson and others have determined what aspects of Indian thought are best suited to participate in the contemporary philosophical arena. But the converse also can be found. John Taber's *Transformative Philosophy : A Study of Śaṁkara, Fichte, and Heidegger* attempts to "read" Fichte, Heidegger, and Rorty in light of Indian antecedents, thus attempting to legitimate edifying and transformative philosophies. For Taber, Śaṁkara determines the agenda.

Both religionists and philosophers owe a debt to

Radhakrishnan. Like Vivekananda before him, he helped revive Indian religious traditions by infusing them with a Western-style certainty of definition, in opposition to and in response to Christian criticisms of Hindu pessimism and ethical deficiency. He introduced Indian thought to the wider arena of philosophical discourse. This reformed Hinduism survives in the work of various Vedānta societies, the Theosophical movement, and in some basic textbooks on Hinduism. However, with the subsequent advance of scholarship, Neo-Vedānta has been criticized as hybrid, synthetic, nonrigorous. Even the work of Radhakrishnan himself, which claims to be beyond doctrinal formulations, has been questioned due to the fact that, as Minor note, "he (Radhakrishnan) never entertained the possibility that his own definition ... was itself a doctrine" (Minor, p. 134). His Neo-Vedāndic hermeneutics of oneness has become suspect.

Research of the past several decades has exposed more and more differences between Asian ways of thought and worship. Radhakrishnan's evolutionary scheme of theism leading to monism no longer suffices as representing the "Hindu" tradition. But neither has Radhakrishnan's overarching scheme been replaced. Just as pluralism is evident in the many gods of the Indian pantheon, so also has the task of interpretation become increasingly plural. Radhakrishnan, following the lead of his missionary Professor A.G. Hogg, used as his departure point the philosophers current in his own time (James Ward, N.K. Smith, A.E. Taylor, William James, etc. as noted by Robert Minor). Similarly, modern day interpreters gaze through the windows provided by their own training. The influence of Freud is evident in the work of Jeffrey Masson-Mausaiff and Wendy O'Flaherty; Ortego y Gasset in Antonio DeNicolas; Quine in Matilal; and so forth. As Husserl and others have noted, increased knowledge is mediated by what we already know.

And yet, is it possible to truly enter into a culture so that it may be understood on its own terms? Radhakrishnan's synthetic views allowed a colonialized country to proudly assert the supremacy of Vedāntic monism; Radhakrishnan advanced a new cultural perspective, in an appropriate heuristic fashion. Today new challenges confront us. One of the most exciting developments in cross cultural studies is the attempt by B.K. Matilal to draw radically divergent traditions into dialogue with one another in a manner that is thoroughly Jaina. In *Perception*, Nyāya realism is juxtaposed with Buddhist phenomenalism in a way that these world views are seen as complementary. By looking at one system that asserts the reality of things and another that denies abiding reality, it is assumed that the two combined will offer not an absolutist view but a "fairly coherent and comprehensive picture" (*Perception*, p. 425). The method here typifies Hindu and Jaina qualified tolerance by recognizing the impossibility of any statement of reality as being all-inclusive and yet acknowledging, as did the Jainas, that all positions hold some truth (*anekanta-vāda*). This indeed is the dilemma that faces modern persons living in a pluralistic world . . . and scholars operating in today's interdisciplinary multiplicity.

Radhakrishnan's life work brought forth a bridge between the Christian and Hindu world views, a bridge vital to India's transition from colony to sovereign state. His writings prescind from a unified, idealistic, essentially spiritualized vision of the world. However, he moves his many tapestries in a day when it was possible to speak of synthesis and sameness. Today, as evidenced in such works as MacIntyre's *After Virtue*, we live in a fragmented world; synthesis is increasingly difficult to achieve and perhaps not even desirable. We live today in an era of pluralism, not of homogeneity. As scholars of the Indian tradition, we find ourselves using myriad approaches, from the earthiest of field study to the most elevated of philosophical debates. To build on the example of Radhakrishnan, our research must be cognizant of the perspectives of various disciplines, as well as various traditions. Like in Vedic times, we find ourselves divided into poets or *kavīs* who tell grand stories of exotic peoples and *ṛṣis* or seers who sternly alert us to what is appropriate and correct. Just as the later Purāṇic tradition brought these two traditions together, and just as Radhakrishnan brought East and West together with elegant ease, so too must we resist the utterly non-Hindu requirement of limiting the scope of our inquiry to either a Dionysian poetic frenzy or a dry, Apollonian analytic approach. With both perspectives, and a cognizance of the power that our hermeneutical tools hold, we can hope to approach a totality of understanding without sacrificing the plurality that is so central to the expansive Hindu horizon.

Bibliography

DeNicolas, Antonio. *Meditations Through the Ṛg Veda.* New York : Nicolas Hays, 1976.

Feldhaus, Anne. *The Deeds of God In Rddhipur.* New York : Oxford University Press, 1984.

Gold, Daniel. *The Lord as Guru : Hindi Saints in North Indian Tradition.* New York : Oxford University Press, 1987.

Matilal, Bimal Krishna and Shaw, J.S., eds. *Analytical Philosophy in Comparative Perspective : Exploratory Essays in Current Theories and Classical Indian Theories on Meaning and Reference.* Dordrecht : D. Reidel, 1985.

Matilal, Bimal Krishna. *Perception : An Essay on Classical Indian Theories of Knowledge.* Oxford : Clarendon Press, 1986.

Panikkar, Raimundo. *The Vedic Experience : Mantramanjari.* Berkeley : University of California Press, 1977.

Minor, Robert N. *Radhakrishnan : A Religious Biography.* Albany, New York : State University of New York Press, 1987.

Phillips, Stephen H. *Aurobindo's Philosophy of Brahman.* Leiden : E.J. Brill, 1986.

Radhakrishnan, Sarvepalli. *Eastern Religions and Western Thought.* London : Oxford University Press, 1939.

───────. *The Hindu Way of Life.* New York : The MacMillan Company, 1927.

───────. *Indian Philosophy.* Vols. I and II. London : George Allen and Unwin, 1923.

───────. *The Reign of Religion in Contemporary Philosophy.* London : MacMillan, 1920.

───────. *A Source Book in Indian Philosophy.* Princeton : Princeton University Press, 1957.

Taber, John A. *Transformative Philosophy : A Study of Śaṁkara, Fichte, and Heidegger.* Honolulu : University of Hawaii Press, 1983.

7
Radhakrishnan's Contributions to Western Thought

TROY ORGAN
Ohio University

How few articles Sarvepalli Radhakrishnan wrote on Western philosophy! He wrote one article comparing the ethics of the *Gītā* and Kant in 1911, four articles on Bergson between 1917 and 1919, and two articles on James Ward in 1919. Robert N. Minor notes, "Though his education in philosophy was almost exclusively in Western thinkers including modern philosophers such as A.S. Pringle-Pattison, James Ward, and A.E. Taylor, his interests quickly turned to his own traditions, which he attempted to defend, but with many of the ideals of his Christian education as the basis of that defense."[1] Radhakrishnan was certainly not ignorant of Western philosophy. But, as bridge-builder between East and West, he worked more from the Eastern end of the East-West bridge.

Radhakrishnan constructed no system of philosophy. In his first book, *The Philosophy of Rabindranath Tagore*, he describes Tagore's works as "a sigh of the soul rather than a reasoned account of metaphysics : an atmosphere rather than a *system* of philosophy."[2] He confesses in the introduction of the book that he is open to the charge of confusing his own views with those of Tagore.

To state that Radhakrishnan did not build a *system* of philosophy is not a condemnation. Few philosophical systems have been built in the last one hundred and fifty years. I would say that Hegel's is the last in the Western world and that among Indian philosophers the last great system builder was Bsant Kumar Mallik (1879-1959). Radhakrishnan in the little volume about Mallik, written "by those who knew him best," wrote that in his opinion Mallik was ahead of his time. He also said the tragedy of Mallik's life was that few believed the cosmos to be as he described it. Mallik in the Schilpp volume on Radhakrishnan describes Radhakrishnan as "one almost lost in a dream."[3] It is amusing to find two great philosophers accusing each other of being out of touch with reality!

It is inappropriate to compare Radhakrishnan with Plato, Spinozaz, Hume, Dewey, and Royce. Rather he should be compared with Goethe, Matthew Arnold, and Emerson. He was an essayist. He gives the impression of being more concerned with fine phrasing than with precise meaning. For example, he wrote in the introduction to *The Reign of Religion in Contemporary Philosophy*, "It is my opinion that systems that play the game of philosophy squarely and fairly, with freedom from presuppositions and religious neutrality, naturally end in absolute idealism."[4] That sounds fine in an essay, but not in a philosophical treatise. "Systems" do not "play the game of philosophy." Philosophy is not a "game." One cannot philosophize "with freedom from presuppositions." The expression "religious neutrality" borders on meaninglessness. And philosophies do not "naturally end" in anything.

My approach to Radhakrishnan is based on the conviction he was an essayist who wrote apologies for Hinduism, for a modified form of Advaita Vedānta, and for India and Indian nationalism. He was capable of writing also first rate scholarly works, for example, *Indian Philosophy, The Principal Upaniṣads, The Brahma Sūtra,* and *The Bhagavad Gītā.* But even in these Radhakrishnan-the-essayist often predominates.

His defense of Hinduism appears to be a reaction against the attacks on Hinduism to which he was exposed in his twelve-year attendance at Christian educational institutions. He seems to have thought of himself as the discoverer of a lost *mārga*. Certainly for him philosophy was a discovery of his roots. Agehananda Bharati says his Hinduism is "the old stuff dressed up in impressive, up-to-date language."[5] Sometimes his defense of Hinduism is amusingly uncritical. For example, in *Religion and Society* he says that the erotic work, *Kāma Śāstra*, helps make life "full and poignant."[6] I suppose instructing a man how to kiss, bite, and copulate may do that; but surely he goes too far when he adds that these erotic works also provide ways to an oxymoronic condition which he describes as a "passionate spiritual serenity."[7] His Vedāntism falls somewhere between that of Śaṁkara and Rāmānuja, since he partially rejects the Śaṁkarite interpretation of *māyā* and partially accepts the theism of Rāmānuja. His defense of Indian culture and Indian nationalism often has the aroma of a politician running for office. He has been described as Plato's philosopher-king. I'd add that he illustrates the dilemma of being such a person. For example, he wrote in 1929, "There can never be a just war."[8] I was in India in 1965 during the Indian-Pakistan War. Radhakrishnan at that time was President of India. He did not condemn that war as unjust. He defended it as a just defense against aggression. I should add, however, that in his Independence Day broadcast on August 26, 1965, that is, only a few days before the beginning of hostilities, he said, "All forms of violence are symbols of human failure."

Radhakrishnan is classified philosophically as an idealist, even as an absolute idealist, although I think that term suggests a greater concern for metaphysics than he had. P.T. Raju has written that Radhakrishnan is best classified as a humanist. He was not a naturalistic humanist like Dewey, nor a self-sufficient humanist like Schiller, nor a scientific humanist like Julian Huxley. He was a spiritualistic humanist.[9] I would say that he was an idealist who put the letter "el" back into the term after Berkeley had altered idealism to what might better be called "idea-ism." He wrote in 1953, "Philosophy is an essential aid to life."[10] That, it seems to me, is an Indian view. Philosophy in the West, as Karl Marx complained, has become merely an intellectual interprise - even an intellectual pastime - with the distinct odour of the scholar's lamp. Radhakrishnan wished to restore Western philosophy to its Socratic motivations : the theory and practice of the examined life.

S.K. Ray begins his book, *The Political Thought of President Radhakrishnan* with this line : "The key words of Radhakrishnan's philosophy are spirit, intuition, and religion."[11] This could have been lifted from a sentence Radhakrishnan wrote exactly fifty years previously when he was twenty-eight years old : "Our knowledge aspires to something more than knowledge, viz., an intuitive grasp of the fundamental unity; our morality to something more than morality, viz., religion, our self to something more than personality, viz., God or the Absolute."[12] I find in these three words Radhakrishnan's contribution to Western thought :

1. His emphasis on the subjective.
2. His emphasis on intuition.
3. His emphasis on the spiritual.

Subjective

The first of Radhakrishnan's three chief contributions to Western thought was his emphasis on the subjective world rather than the objective world. Radhakrishnan was a worthy member of the great line of seers who beginning with Śvetakatu taught the *tat tvam asi* doctrine. I have long believed we mistranslate *tat tvam asi* as "*That* you are." The emphasis is better exhibited as "*You* are that." The introversive aspect of Indian thought is constantly stressed in Radhakrishnan's works. "Self-finding is the essence of all perfection," he wrote in *Kalki*.[13] "The whole history of philosophy may in a sense be regarded as the criticism of the category of substance," he noted in *An Idealist View of Life*.[14] And in *Eastern Religions and Western Thought* he declared, "The supreme task of our generation is to give a soul to the growing world-consciousness."[15] Physical unity, economic interdependence, and easy communication are not enough to create a universal human community. When he became the Spalding Professor of Eastern Religions and Ethics at Oxford University in 1936, he chose as the title of his inaugural lecture "The World's Unborn Soul." He said on that occasion that he was motivated by "a desire to lift Eastern thought from its sheltered remoteness and indicate its enduring value as a living force in shaping the soul of the modern man."[16]

According to Radhakrishnan the great need of the West is not for more knowledge of the external world, but for more awareness of and cultivation of the internal world. The West needs to regard knowledge as a change of the subject from nonknower to knower rather than change of the object from unknown to known. The West needs to discover the pure subject "whose existence cannot be ejected into the external or objective world."[17]

Radhakrishnan was not opposed to the natural and physical sciences, but he was very much opposed to those who believed that the expirical method is the only way to truth. He was particularly incensed by modern philosophers who regard scientific verification as the sole criterion of meaningfulness, and who would limit philosophy to language analysis. He wrote, "Philosophy is not a mere factual exposition of scientifically ascertained facts. It is not a list of propositions which are treated as meaningful because they can be sensibly verified."[18] I suspect one of the great intellectual satisfactions Radhakrishnan had was bearding Logical Positivism in its own den. He wrote, "The view that problems of philosophy are linguistic is itself a hypothesis. The verification principle is a metaphysical statement, neither a tautology nor an empirical fact. It is a synthetic *a priori* statement of exactly the type that Logical Positivism intends to exclude. Logical Positivism is itself a kind of metaphysics, a sceptical metaphysics."[19]

Intuition

Radhakrishnan's second contribution to Western thought was his emphasis on intuition. He recognized three forms of cognition : "sense experience, discursive reasoning, and intuitive apprehension."[20] Intuition, he said is self-validating. So intuitions have priority over shareable experiences and logical reasonings. The term *intuition* always had value connotations for Radhakrishnan. Whereas we in the West might refer to a moral person as "a person of principle," Radhakrishnan would refer to such a person as "a person of intuition." I detect in the writings of Radhakrishnan at least five meanings of the term *intuition* : (1) the direct understanding of ideas; (2) the use of the sense without an effort to identify the object of sensing; (3) the feeling of another's condition as though it were one's own; (4) the unanalysed grasping of values in morals, art, and religion; (5) the identifying of the self and totality in the *tat tvam asi* experience. In all intuitions the distinction between subject and object is eliminated. A philosopher, said Radhakrishnan, is "an intuitive seer."[21] Philosophy, he said, "is not so much a conceptual reconstruction as an exhibition of insights."[22] He claimed that as long as human beings are bound by the intellect and by discursive reasoning they "are lost in the world of the many."[23] They "seek in vain to get back to the simplicity of the one."[24] He claimed there is a vast difference between having an opinion about reality based on the subject-object dichotomy and having contact with reality,[25] or, as the Zen masters say, between water as H_2O and as cold wet staff thrown in one's face.

The reality of *Brahman*, according to Radhakrishnan, cannot be forced into intellectual categories. He wrote, "The whole, the Absolute, which is the highest concrete, is so rich that its wealth of content refused to be forced into the fixed forms of intellect. The life of the spirit is so overflowing that it bursts all barriers. It is vastly richer than human thought can compass. It breaks through every conceptual form and makes all intellectual determination impossible. While intellect has access to it, it can never exhaust its fulness."[26] Since the ultimate end of philosophy is to understand *Brahman*, philosophy must be "neither purely conceptualistic nor merely empiricist, but intuitional."[27] "A mere thinker cannot understand the nature of reality . . . We must become sensuous-intellectual-intuitional to know reality in its flesh and blood and not merely its skin and bone."[28] "Intuition is the crown of reason."[29]

I am bothered by two questions with respect to Radhakrishnan's claims for intuition : (1) If intuition is important, why did he say so little about art? (2) If conceptualization is inadequate, why did he talk and write so much?

The Spiritual

Radhakrishnan's third contribution to Western thought was his constant emphasis on the spiritual. The words *spirit, spiritual, spiritual reality, spiritual values,* and *religion of the spirit* appear again and again in his writing. In 1918 when he was appointed Professor of Philosophy at the University of Mysore at age thirty, he said he was persuaded that philosophy leads us "to a spiritual view."[30] In 1936 he submitted as his contribution to the volume on *Contemporary Indian Philosophy* an essay titled "The Spirit in Man" in which he lamented the "spiritual chaos" of the time.[31] He added, "The need of the world today is for a religion of the spirit, which will give a purpose to life."[32] It is the idealist tradition of Plato and Śaṁkara, he wrote, that "has asserted the supremacy of the spirit in man."[33] In 1939 he contended in *Eastern Religions and Western Thought,* "A reborn living faith in spiritual values is the deepest need of our lives."[34] In 1951 in the volume presented in honour of his sixtieth birthday the editors stated that "the ever-recurring theme of practically all his books and lectures" is "the primacy of spiritual values, the lack and necessity of the spiritual note in modern civilization, the logical inevitability of a spiritual absolutism in philosophy, the undeniable truth of our inner life or spirit."[35] And in 1952, when he was asked to sum up his thinking for the volume on him in *The Library of Living Philosophers,* he wrote, "Though I have not a sense of vocation, a sense that I was born to do what I am now carrying out, my travels and engagements in different parts of the world for over a generation gave me a purpose in life. My one supreme interest has been to try to restore a sense of spiritual values to the millions of religiously displaced persons."[36]

But what did he mean by *spirit* and *spiritual?* Alas, Radhakrishnan-the-essayist supersedes Radhakrishnan-the-philosopher. When he tells his readers that key ideas such as *spirit* and *spiritual* are "born of spiritual experience,"[37] I want to shout the exasperation William James once threw at Josiah Royce : "You must study logic! You need it so badly!" What did he mean by *spiritual?* I suppose that one can answer in *neti, neti* fashion that he meant nonmaterial, nonsecular, nonscientific, nonlogical, nonlinguistic, nonanalyzable, nonrational, nonepressible, etc. If one wishes to attempt a positive statement, terms such as *ascetic, religious, austere, sober,* and *dutiful* come to mind. Practises such as vegetarianism, teetotalism, celebacy, and pacifism are included in the denotation of *spiritual* as Radhakrishnan used the term. His abstinence from meat and liquor creating interesting situations for his friends at Oxford University. On one occasion he confided to Hindu friends that he wished to impress the luxurious British by his austerity.[38]

I think what Radhakrishnan usually had in mind when he spoke of "the spiritual" is what most people mean by *religion*. But the word *religion* appears to have bothered him, perhaps because for the majority of Western readers - and do not forget, he wrote in a Western language - the word *religion* has been preempted by Christianity. He did not like to call Hinduism a religion. For him Hinduism is not a religion among religions but the religious in religions. In his writings *Hinduism* denotes the religion of religions and designates the spiritual values in all religions. He wrote that Hinduism is "a fellowship of all who accept the law of right and earnestly quest for the truth."[39] Vedānta, he said, is "not a religion, but religion in its most universal and deepest significance."[40] The thrust of Indian thought, he said, is to wean human beings from secularity and to make them spiritual : "With its profound sense of spiritual reality brooding over the world of our ordinary experience, with its lofty insights and immortal aspirations, Indian thought may perhaps wean us moderns from a too exclusive occupation with secular life or with the temporary formulations in which logical thought has too often sought to imprison spiritual aspiration."[41] What this means, says M.N. Roy, is that Radhakrishnan was a theologian : "In his conception, philosophy . . . is not differentiated from religion. As a matter of fact, if he expounds any philosophy, it is admittedly the philosophy of religion; that is to say, theology, which tries to rationalize the belief in God."[42]

Those who criticize Radhakrishnan for his supposed confusion of religion and philosophy should take into account that he, as one who regarded all Indian philosophy as footnotes to the *Upaniṣads* and who regarded Śaṁkara as the greatest of all Indian philosophers, affirmed the inseparability of the highest value and the truly real. *Sat*, after all, designates both the *being* and the *worth* of things. Śaṁkara found it impossible to think of value except in the context of reality. The Advaita aspect of Vedānta is not only the nontwoness of *Ātman* and *Brahman* and of *puruṣa* and *prakṛti* but also of reality and value. Being is good. It is good to be. The ultimate *ānanda*, that is, joy, happiness, bliss, value, is the realization that existence, consciousness, and value are one in *Brahman. Brahman* is *saccidānanda*.

Radhakrishnan was teacher, philosopher, essayist, administrator, and statesman. But he was something else. He was a prophet. He agonized over the condition of human civilization in this century. He warned of disaster. But he also pointed the way to salvation. This he did most effectively in his "Concluding Survey" in *History of Philosophy : Eastern and Western* : "If we are to be saved from mounting chaos, we must find a new human order, where we do not reduce the human individual to a mere object of scientific investigation, where we recognize him as a subject of freedom. We must make the basic concepts of our civilization illumine, guide and mould the new life. If our civilization is to function, we must cease to be blind and thoughtless. We must not allow the values of spirit to recede beyond the horizon of man. We must strive to be human in this most inhuman of all ages. It is the task of philosophy not merely to reflect the spirit of the age in which we live but to lead it forward. Its function is creative, to state the values, to set the goals, to point the direction and to lead to new paths. It must inspire us with the faith to sustain the new world, to produce the men who subordinate national, racial and religious divisions to the ideal of humanity. Philosophy is nothing if not universal in its scope and spirit."[43]

Humanity is still in the making. The ideal is to make human beings perfectly human. In human beings living matter seeks to realize itself through self-discovery, self-knowledge, self-fulfilment, self-perfection. This was the insight of the *Mahābhārata* : "There is nothing nobler than humanity."[44] The life and works of Radhakrishnan make all of us proud to be human.

References

1. Robert N. Minor, *Radhakrishnan : A Religious Biography* (Albany : State University of New York Press, 1987), p. 14.
2. S. Radhakrishnan, *The Philosophy of Rabindranath Tagore* (London : MacMillan, 1918), p. 6. Italics are mine.
3. B.K. Mallick, "Radhakrishnan and Philosophy of the State and Community," in *The Philosophy of Sarvepalli Radhakrishnan*, Ed. Paul Arthur Schilpp (New York : Tudor, 1952), p. 753.
4. S. Radhakrishnan, *The Reign of Religion in Contemporary Philosophy* (London : MacMillan, 1920), p. vii.
5. Agehananda Bharati, "Radhakrishnan and the Other Vedānta," in *The Philosophy of Sarvepalli Radhakrishnan*, p. 465.
6. S. Radhakrishnan, *Religion and Society* (London : George Allen and Unwin, 1947), p. 149.
7. *Ibid.*
8. S. Radhakrishnan, *Kalki or The Future of Civilization* (London : Kegan Paul, Trench, 1929), p. 65.
9. P.T. Raju, "Radhakrishnan and Indian Thought" in *The Philosophy of Sarvepalli Radhakrishnan*, pp. 520-521.
10. "Concluding Survey" in *History of Philosophy : Eastern and Western*. Sponsored by the Ministry of Education, Government of India (London : George Allen and Unwin, 1953), p. 439.

11. S.K. Ray, *The Political Thought of President Radhakrishnan* (Calcutta : Firma K.L. Mukhopadhyay, 1966), p. 1.
12. S. Radhakrishnan, "The Vedāntic Approach to Reality," *The Monist*, Vol. 26 (April 1916), p. 219.
13. S. Radhakrishnan, *Kalki or The Future of Civilization*, p. 64.
14. S. Radhakrishnan, *An Idealist View of Life* (London : George Allen and Unwin, 1929), p. 234.
15. S. Radhakrishnan, *Eastern Religions and Western Thought* (London : Oxford University Press, 1939), p. viii.
16. *Ibid.*, p. 20.
17. S. Radhakrishnan, *The Bhagavad Gītā*, Second Edition, (London : George Allen and Unwin, 1949), p. 21.
18. S. Radhakrishnan, "Concluding Survey" in *History of Philosophy : Eastern and Western*, p. 442.
19. *Ibid.*
20. S. Radhakrishnan, *An Idealist View of Life*, Second Edition (London : George Allen and Unwin, 1957), p. 134.
21. S. Radhakrishnan, *The Philosophy of Rabindranath Tagore*, p. 152.
22. S. Radhakrishnan, "Reply to Critics," in *The Philosophy of Sarvepalli Radhakrishnan*, p. 791.
23. S. Radhakrishnan, *Indian Philosophy*, Vol. 1, Revised Edition (London : George Allen and Unwin, 1929), p. 36.
24. *Ibid.*
25. S. Radhakrishnan, *Eastern Religions and Western Thoughts*, p. 23.
26. S. Radhakrishnan, *The Reign of Religion in Contemporary Philosophy*, p. 440.
27. *Ibid.*, p. 441.
28. *Ibid.*, pp. 434-435.
29. *Ibid.*, p. 438.
30. S. Radhakrishnan, "My Search for Truth" in *Religion in Transition*, Ed. Vergilius Ferm (London : Geroge Allen and Unwin, 1937), p. 24.

31. S. Radhakrishnan and J.H. Muirhead, *Contemporary Indian Philosophy* (London : George Allen and Unwin, 1936), p. 265.
32. *Ibid.*, p. 266.
33. *Ibid.*
34. S. Radhakrishnan, *Eastern Religions and Western Thought*, p. 114.
35. W.R. Inge, L.P. Jacks, M. Hiriyanna, E.A. Burtt, P.T. Raju, Eds. *Radhakrishnan : Comparative Studies in Philosophy Presented In Honour of His Sixtieth Birthday* (London : George Allen and Unwin, 1951), p. 4.
36. *The Philosophy of Sarvepalli Radhakrishnan*, p.14.
37. S.Radhakrishnan, "Fragments of a Confession," in *The Philosophy of Sarvepalli Radhakrishnan*, p. 10.
38. Robert N. Minor, *Radhakrishnan : A Religious Biography*, p. 63.
39. S. Radhakrishnan, *The Hindu View of Life* (London : George Allen and Unwin, 1927), p. 77.
40. *Ibid.*, p. 23.
41. S. Radhakrishnan, "Fragments of a Confession," in *The Philosophy of Sarvepalli Radhakrishnan*, p. 7.
42. M.N. Roy, "Radhakrishnan in the Perspective of Indian Philosophy," in *The Philosophy of Sarvepalli Radhakrishnan*. p. 546.
43. S. Radhakrishnan, *History of Philosophy : Eastern and Western*, p. 448.
44. *Śānti Parva*, p. 300.

8
Radhakrishnan's Contributions to Philosophy

KRISHNA MALLICK
Salem State College

Radhakrishnan's Background

Sarvepalli Radhakrishnan was born in South India. During his time, South India assimilated the Dravidian culture with the orthodox Hindu culture. Though he was born in an orthodox Brahmin family, he was educated in Christian Missionary schools. He was taught the Christian Scriptures in his childhood. The Christian ideas were instilled in his mind very strongly. Later on, when he joined a missionary college, there also he was taught Western philosophy by competent Christian teachers. Being born of an orthodox Brahmin family, he had a strong sense of religion. So there arose a conflict and challenge in his mind. In a situation like this, it is easier to give up the orthodox religious belief and accept the glamour of Western culture. But Radhakrishnan did not take the easier alternative. He analyzed both the Western and Eastern thought and assimilated from each what was essential and valuable. As he wrote in *My Search for Truth*:

"The challenge of Christian critics impelled me to make a study of Hinduism and find out what is living and what is dead in it."[1]

On the one hand, he continued reading more Western philosophers. On the other hand, as a proud Indian, with the help of some orthodox teachers, he read the original texts of Indian Philosophy. It was an incredible task for him as he had to rationally understand both Western and Eastern thoughts and critically comprehend it at the philosophical level. Due to his keen interest in the history of human civilization, literature, art, politics and society as a whole and due to his great concern for ultimate values, Radhakrishnan was able to integrate both the Western and Eastern thought.

From this point of his life, he has written different books on comparative philosophy. Some of his earlier works were *Ethics of the Vedānta* and different articles that he wrote in philosophical journals like *International Journal of Ethics, The Monist* etc. In these works, Radhakrishnan was greatly influenced by the absolute idealism and monism of Hegel because he believed that this kind of absolute idealism is closer to Vedānta. He also showed in his earlier works how Vedāntic viewpoint can be practised in life also. In these earlier works, Radhakrishnan's method was to defend his own view without hurting his critics. In India, religion and philosophy are related to each other and it has a history of about five thousand years. As a result, there are different creeds and practises, different systems of thought which led to the emphasis of different principles at different times to suit the changing conditions. In all of his writings, Radhakrishnan takes this kind of comparative historical view of Indian philosophy. And he emphasizes those points which will be beneficial to the progress of India and also will be beneficial to the Western cultures. For Radhakrishnan, not only the Indian civilization but any civilization goes through this kind of gradual process of evolution of thought and culture.

Radhakrishnan's Philosophy

In this paper, I like to evaluate Radhakrishnan's contribution to philosophy by analyzing his view in two of his later works *An Idealist View of Life* and *Eastern Religions and Western Thought*. Radhakrishnan's idealism is influenced by Śaṁkara, Hegel and Plato. His idealism is different from the above philosophers. It is basically Upaniṣadic idealism. He accepts the monistic and theistic view of the Upaniṣads but he does not subordinate theism to monism.

In his work, *An Idealist View of Life*, the central concept is Spirit and how it is manifested in matter, life, mind and self. The Spirit is not homogeneous entity like the Brahman of Śaṁkara. It is not the substance of Hegel. It is a dynamic energy. It is something which is real in itself. In Radhakrishnan's words, "We know it, but we cannot explain it. It is felt everywhere though seen nowhere. It is not the physical body or the vital organism, the mind or the will, but something which underlies them all and sustains them. It is the basis and background of our being, the universality that cannot be reduced to this or to that formula."[2]

Creativity, order, change and progress are the characteristics of Spirit which is present at all the levels of existence in an ascending order, each representing a higher level than what precedes it. It is due to the Spirit that matter develops into life, life develops into consciousness and consciousness develops into self-consciousness. The development in evolution is not only continuous but along with its development new levels emerge. Reality is a general unity or continuity, running through the different levels. The Spirit is not only immanent but also transcendent. The Spirit is the Absolute as it has infinite possibilities present to it. One actual manifestation of the Spirit is the world. But the Absolute is not exhausted in the world. God and souls are the other aspects of the Absolute. Creation is a free act. The Absolute is not dependent on the world in any way. The

Absolute is the ground of the world in the sense that the possibility of the Absolute is the logical basis of the world. Here we see the strong influence of Śaṁkara's *vivartavāda* in Radhakrishnan's idealism.

In the cosmic context, God is the Absolute. He is organic with the world and He endures as long as the world lasts. The world is relatively real. There is no dualism of God and the world. God is not appearance of the Absolute but it is the very Absolute in the context of the world. When all the souls attain the conscious realization of unity with the Spirit, God and the world, that is the Absolute.

Human self is an organized whole, according to Radhakrishnan. Man and Spirit are similar. It is through religious purity and ethical perfection that man acquires the necessary merit for spiritual realization. Spiritual experience is realized fully in religious intuition.

According to Radhakrishnan, spirit is the symbol of the unity of man both as an individual and as a national and international community. It is in this spirit that the world with all its multiplicity is unified and feels itself as one. Radhakrishnan's main objective is to outline the philosophy of Spirit which is at once a Philosophy of Religion and a religious philosophy, a world-faith and a world-perspective. Radhakrishnan's view is similar to the great tradition in philosophy both in the East and the West which is characterized by the view that an intelligible world is in a deep sense beyond the sensible and the phenomenal. Radhakrishnan calls it the world of Spirit. He gives a new turn to the tradition as he develops Vedānta not only as a philosophy of personal salvation but also as the foundation for the fellowship of man in a world-community, for the solidarity of the human race. At every level of human existence, liberated life can be led.

In *Eastern Religions and Western Thought* Radhakrishnan has the same philosophical outlook. But this is a book on comparative religion from historical perspective rather than a book on comparative philosophy. The main point of this book is that the meeting of the East and the West is not an ideal which has never been realized. On the contrary, there actually have been such meetings of the East and the West in history. As a result of this meeting, Radhakrishnan shows that what we call the Western culture has many elements of the East and the Eastern culture, in turn, has many elements of the West. Through historical evidence Radhakrishnan shows that Eastern, particularly Indian elements, had entered in the early Greek thought and in the medieval, Christian thought. Also, different races and religions of the world met in India and lived side by side with mutual toleration. In Radhakrishnan's word, "The supreme task of our generation is to give a soul to the growing world-consciousness, to develop ideals and institutions necessary for the creative expression of the world soul, to transmit these loyalties and impulses to future generations and train them into world citizens."[3]

Through his elaborate analysis of the East and the West, Radhakrishnan showed that the Western civilization, dominated by the Greeks and the Romans, "has for its chief elements rationalism, humanism, and the sovereignty of the state."[4] Though Christianity accepted the Eastern elements of inner spirituality, renunciation, and toleration, it did not make that much impression in the West. In the West, political ends dominated over religion. The power of real unity, based on spiritual unity of man, toleration and renunciation, was lacking in the West. Because of this absence of real unity, the Greeks and the Romans were destroyed within eight or nine hundred years. According to Radhakrishnan, Indian and Chinese civilizations marked by their inner spirituality have survived and lasted for five thousand years or more. Eastern civilization has been able to adjust to the changes and continue living. But Radhakrishnan does not ignore the fact that Eastern people are not self-sufficient. They are inefficient and suffer from the weakness of age. Eastern people can benefit by taking the best thinking from Western humanism, rationalism and practical enthusiasm. This kind of assimilation of the spiritual and the worldly will benefit both the East and the West. As Radhakrishnan asks : "May we not strive for a philosophy which will combine the best of European humanism and Asiatic religion, a philosophy profounder and more living than either, endowed with greater spiritual and ethical force, which will conquer the hearts of men and compel peoples to acknowledge its sway?"[5]

Through his own life-long labour in comparative philosophy and religion, Radhakrishnan has answered the above question. He has brought out the best points from all the systems of Eastern and Western philosophy and incorporated them into a world-philosophy which benefits everyone, both East and West.

Radhakrishnan was not so much concerned with the sensible level of knowledge and life as with the ideal and spiritual level of knowledge and life. For this spiritual level of knowledge and life, intuition is very important.

The common source for his epistemology and metaphysics is the Vedas. The knowledge derived from the Vedas is obtained by the intuition of those who wrote the scriptures and those who achieved the spiritual depth to understand them. As Radhakrishnan writes, "The Ṛsis are not so much the authors of the truths recorded in the Vedas as the seers who were able to discern the eternal truths by raising their life-spirit to the plane of the universal spirit."[6] What Radhakrishnan here refers to as the discernment of eternal truths might be called intuition. So knowledge is derived from intuitive experience. Radhakrishnan presupposes the Upaniṣadic and Vedāntic conception of the oneness of reality, and equates intuition with the kind of spiritual experience which the Vedic seers had and which he claims to be possible only on "the plane of universal spirit." Radhakrishnan's theory of intuition is consciously derived from his understanding of the Veda. According to Radhakrishnan, only the spiritually advanced personality can experience the total of reality. And this is the same thing as intuition. Though he emphasizes the spiritual or mystical experience so much, he believes that intuition is effectively though not perfectly mediated by intellect. As Radhakrishnan writes in his "Replies to Critics" :

"The immediacy of intuitive knowledge can be mediated through intellectual definition and analysis. We use intellect to test the validity of intuition, and communicate them to others. Intuition and intellect are complementary. We have, of course, to recognize that intuition transcends the conceptual expressions as reality does not fit into categories."[7]

Radhakrishnan insists that intuition both transcends conceptual expression and complement intellect. This seems to be incompatible. Radhakrishnan is not very explicit with regard to this conceptualization of intuition but what he is basically saying is that spiritual or mystical intuitive experience has been expressed many times but these expressions are inadequate. So the process of conceptualization limits the immediacy and depth of intuitive experience but the mediation of concepts is the only way to preserve anything from intuition.

But then the next question is, is there anything cognitive in philosophical or mystical intuition independent of intellect? To this, Radhakrishnan's reply is that whereas philosophical intuition functions mainly within the terms of knowledge and truth, mystical intuition has its meaning primarily in terms of specifically religious ideals which are only incidentally cognitive.

From the above, it is clear that Radhakrishnan's conception of the nature of philosophy and the prerequisites for creative philosophizing are formed on the ideal of religious experience. Radhakrishnan's conception of intuitive knowledge, both philosophical and intuitive, is religious.

One of the more important implications of Radhakrishnan's philosophical synthesis is his vision of a world community.

Radhakrishnan was aware of the fact that the world will not achieve the ideal of genuine spiritual existence. But he emphasizes the point that man must still strive for this goal by contributing in every possible way to the creation of a world community. As Radhakrishnan writes :

"The most significant feature of our time is the growing realization of the dream of ages, the creation of one world. The Kingdom of God of which the prophets spoke is not this or that particular religious organization, but it is the world community. This ideal has ceased to be a Utopian dream and has become an attainable goal."[8]

So for Radhakrishnan, this vision of the world community for the first time is an ideal which can be realized. This vision of the world community follows from his metaphysical viewpoint and not from an analysis of the contemporary world.

Radhakrishnan's Contribution to Philosophy

It is because of Radhakrishnan that the veil of mystery from Indian philosophy with which it was always associated in the Western mind was cleared. That there is a rational basis to what appears mystical and magical, that there is an adequate appeal to reason also in Indian philosophy and that Indian thought does not ask for blind faith and acceptance but correct and awakened insight - all this has been clearly brought out by Radhakrishnan in his writings and lectures. In all this Radhakrishnan has not only done service to India but also to the West because he helped the

Western mind to discover their similar spiritual roots in their own tradition by citing proper parallels from their history. Radhakrishnan's extensive and profound knowledge in Western religion, philosophy and science placed him in the position of authority before them to say all this before Western people.

Another contribution that Radhakrishnan has made to the West is that he has bridged the gap between science and religion and has provided the opportunity for fresh religious experience undogmatically. Revelation is not opposed to reason. Reason serves to reconfirm spiritual experience in a systematic form. Reason brings order into what is revealed by intuition. This has been the case in science as well as in religion. Greatest discoveries in science have been made through the same process of struggle and hardship as in religion. There is no mystery in mysticism. It is as open and empirical as any scientific experience. Only a very one-sided, prejudiced and dogmatic mind can find mystical experience unscientific. In emphasizing the return to Spirit, by preserving the tradition and voicing the need of the time, Radhakrishnan has played a great role in bringing the East and the West to understand each other.

Many critics are dissatisfied with Radhakrishnan's view because they do not find any systematic 'ism' in Radhakrishnan's writings. But this is not a good criticism because if someone does not find in someone's philosophy what one is looking for, then it is not necessarily bad. Further, unlike Western philosophy, Eastern philosophy cannot be classified under specific schools.

Critics have also pointed out that Radhakrishnan applies to the rest of the world the standards defined by the epistemology and specific philosophy of the Eastern culture. They claim that the task of relating Eastern and Western cultural values is much more difficult than Radhakrishnan claims it to be.

It is true that it is very difficult to relate Eastern and Western cultural values. Radhakrishnan himself was aware of the fact. But I think that Radhakrishnan is one of the first philosophers who proposed such a meeting of the East and the West in systematic philosophical form. That itself is the greatest contribution of Radhakrishnan to philosophy. Now it is our, the present generation's, task to find out correct methods that are workable.

One can also criticize Radhakrishnan's view by saying that his idealistic viewpoint does not do justice to the non-idealist school of Eastern and Western traditions. I agree with this criticism to a certain extent because Radhakrishnan's view is essentially idealistic. So it has the strengths and weaknesses of any idealist viewpoint. But on the other hand, Radhakrishnan's idealistic viewpoint is more successful as a synthesis than any other contemporary philosophical system based on more than one culture. Also, Radhakrishnan has showed us the first step towards the progress of comparative philosophy.

As P.T. Raju in his article "Radhakrishnan's Influence on Indian Thought"[9] says that comparative philosophy has been approached in three different ways.

First, different philosophers are studied in relation to their environment and estimated in terms of their functions.

Second, comparison is made of different schools, systems or philosophers, not necessarily of different traditions, but even within the same tradition. Every philosophy is a philosophy of supposedly the same universe and in its own way aims to be a rounded-out system. Any concept in a philosophical system gets its significance from the place it occupies in that system and is, therefore, practically a function of that system. Thus, though a concept is apparently the same in two systems, it might have a very different import in each. Comparative philosophy thus assumes the form of the study of the comparative significance of concepts with reference to the various philosophical systems.

As P.T. Raju says, the above two ideas of comparative philosophy are mutually interdependent and useful.

But there is also a third idea of comparative philosophy which is considered as the study and evaluation of similarities and dissimilarities between the philosophies of the two main philosophical currents of the world, the Western and Indian, with the main purpose of coordinating and synthesizing the basic values of life which those two great traditions are taken to represent.

Radhakrishnan was concerned with comparative philosophy in the third sense above. The first two kinds of comparative philosophy are concerned with disinterested inductive study but this third kind of comparative philosophy is interested in human life and its values. With this kind of comparative philosophy, Radhakrishnan was able to bring the East and the West closer to each other.

As Dale Riepe in his article "Reflections on Comparative Philosophy"[10] asks, "What qualities of mind should one expect to find among those who claim to be comparative philosophers?" His answer is that a comparative philosopher should be curious, open-minded, skeptical, independent, should have love of adventure, should enjoy listening to others, should have drive towards integration and should be able to understand. If we keep this in mind, we will be able to understand each other without any difficulty.

References

1. S. Radhakrishnan, *My Search for Truth,* Shiva Lal Agarwala & Co., India, 1946, p. 2.

2. S. Radhakrishnan, *An Idealist View of Life*, George Allen & Unwin, 1932, p. 205.
3. S. Radhakrishnan, *Eastern Religions and Western Thought*, Second Edition, Oxford University Press, 1940, p. viii.
4. *Ibid.*, p. 260.
5. *Ibid.*, p. 259.
6. S. Radhakrishnan, *An Idealist View of Life*, p. 89.
7. Paul Arthur Schilpp, ed., *The Philosophy of Sarvepalli Radhakrishnan*, Tudor Publishing Co., New York, 1952, p. 796.
8. S. Radhakrishnan, "Religion and World Unity," *Religion and the Modern World*, Foreword, Louis Arnauld Reid., Allen & Unwin, London, 1962.
9. P.T. Raju, "Radhakrishnan's Influence on Indian Thought," in *The Philosophy of Sarvepalli Radhakrishnan*, edited by P.A. Schilpp, pp. 526-527.
10. Dale Riepe, "Reflections on Comparative Philosophy," in *Dr. S. Radhakrishnan : Souvenir Volume*, edited by B.L. Atreya, Darshna International, Moradabad, India, 1964, p. 380.

PART II

RADHAKRISHNAN AND RELIGIOUS PLURALISM

PART II

RADHAKRISHNAN AND RELIGIOUS PLURALISM

9

Radhakrishnan's Conception of the Veda

GEORGE CHEMPARATHY
University of Utrecht

Acceptance of the authority of the Veda has been the most basic criterion of orthodoxy in classical Hindu thought. Whatever the theory concerning the source or the ultimate reason for this authority, whatever the degree of importance or validity attached to the different Vedic texts, whatever the interpretation given to them by the different schools, a formal recognition of the infallible authority of the Veda was considered an indispensable condition for remaining within the fold of orthodox Hinduism. All the teachings concerning the Dharma, or the religious and social duties of a Hindu, were believed to be derived, in the ultimate analysis, from the Veda. Hence the importance of the authoritative nature of the Veda, which classical Hindu thinkers of all schools sharply distinguished from all other texts, religious or otherwise.[1]

In the following pages an attempt is made to examine the view of S. Radhakrishnan, undoubtedly the most distinguished representative of modern Hindu thought, on the nature and the authority of the Veda. This is done against the backdrop of the Advaita Vedāntic conception of the Veda; for, however much Radhakrishnan may have deviated from the traditional doctrines of Śaṁkara's Advaita, that is undoubtedly the Hindu system of which he was an ardent exponent and in which he would best see himself placed. After a brief exposition of the Advaitic view of the nature and the authority of the Veda, we shall set forth our author's conception of these issues and draw a few conclusions.

But, before we broach the theme of our study, it is necessary to point out some of the difficulties and limitations that go with it. In the first place, Radhakrishnan was a prolific writer, who left behind him a vast mass of philosophical and religious works, several of which contain statements on the Veda or on themes closely related to it. Even after collecting the relevant passages form these works, one does not find it easy to make an evaluation of them; for the tenor of these passages is not always the same, nay, at times they even seem to contradict each other. Secondly, our philosopher was a voracious reader of works on philosophy and religion, not only Indian but also non-Indian, notably Christian. A perusal of his works goes to show that his views underwent considerable changes in the course of his search after truth on account of his vast reading. In his earlier works, composed mostly during his academic career in India, he was, generally speaking, an exponent and defender of traditional Hinduism. By contrast, the works he composed after his appointment as Spalding Professor of Eastern Religions and Ethics at the University of Oxford in 1936 evince a new approach to Hinduism based on Western religious and philosophical ideas. Endowed with a keen intellect ever open to new ideas and with a will strongly determined to give a rational foundation to the form of Hinduism he had in mind, he incorporated freely and liberally foreign - especially Christian - ideas, as the numerous footnotes and quotations in his works amply testify. To limit ourselves to the theme of the Veda, the Holy Scripture of the Hindus, we come across in his works terms such as 'inspiration,' 'revelation,' or 'Word of God' which are borrowed from Christian theology of the Bible, where they have a specifically circumscribed meaning, and consequently would not fit in, or would fit in only with the necessary qualifications and reserves, when applied to the Veda. However, to do justice to Radhakrishnan, it should be added that such a procedure is almost inevitable for any Hindu writer, who wants to express teachings of his religion or philosophy in any European language. Thirdly, taking into account the limited space allotted to this contribution, only a few selected statements of our author on the Veda will be quoted and the evaluatory observations on them will be reduced to a minimum.

Advaita Conception of the Nature of the Veda

According to the Advaitins, there is only one Reality, the Brahman, one without a second, and the empirical world of multiplicity and diversity has only an illusory and relative reality. The Veda contains statements which presuppose multiplicity and diversity. Though it contains guidelines and instructions for man to attain liberation (*mokṣa*), these are related to the world of illusory reality. Moreover, one who realizes liberation realizes also the illusory nature of the Veda. In other words, viewed from the standpoint of absolute truth, the Veda has its reality and its validity only in the domain of the illusory empirical world of multiplicity and diversity.[2]

Even though the Veda has only a relative reality, it is conceived by the Advaitins as being eternal (*nitya*) and authorless (*apauruṣeya*). It is, however, to be kept in mind that, despite terminological identity, the Vedāntins do not understand 'eternity' and 'authorlessness' of the Veda in exactly the same manner as the Mīmāṁsākas do. No doubt, like the Mīmāṁsākas, the Vedāntins understand the eternity of the Veda to consist in the permanence and the unchangeability of the particular sequence (*ānupūrvī*) of the words in the Veda. Like them, the Vedāntins maintain also that the particular sequence of words in the Veda is not determined or fixed by any person, and in this sense the Veda is authorless. The order of words in any work which is known to have an author, such as the *Raghuvaṁśa*, is determined by the free choice and decision of the author himself. By contrast, the sequence of words in the Veda is not determined by any person, divine or human, but it is eternally self-determined. But here ends the agreement of the Vedāntins with the Mīmāṁsākas; for the Advaitins recognize also a certain kind of non-eternity and authorship of the Veda, more akin to the standpoint of the Nyāya-Vaiśeṣikas. For, though the Veda, inasmuch as it constitutes a particular sequence of words is eternal in the sense of being self-determined, it is non-eternal inasmuch as it is orally transmitted. The Mīmāṁsākas deny the theory of repeated cycles of originations (*sarga*) and dissolutions (*pralaya*) of the universe, and thereby they avoid the possibility of an interruption of the Vedic transmission at the time of every cosmic dissolution. The Vedāntins, by contrast, accept these cycles, and therefore they are constrained to admit that the transmission of the Veda is interrupted at the time of every cosmic dissolution. Thus, considered from the point of view of its transmission, the Veda is subject to periodic disappearance, and in this sense it is non-eternal. Likewise, although the Veda has no author in the sense that no person has determined or fixed the sequence of words in it, in other words, from the point of view of its existence, it has indeed an author (*pauruṣeya*) from the point of view of its transmission at the beginning of every new creation of the universe, in the person of Īśvara, who is none other than the personal aspect of Brahman. This Īśvara is author only in the limited sense of being the author of the transmission of a self-existing eternal Veda; he does not determine the sequence of words in the Veda, but merely reveals it, as it is in its eternal form, to the first human beings at the beginning of every new creation.

While giving a double interpretation of *Brahmasūtra* I, 1,3 : *śāstra-yonitvāt,* Śaṁkara brings out the reciprocal relationship between Brahman and the Veda. According to the first interpretation, Brahman is the source (*yoni*) of the Veda; for only an omniscient being like Brahman could be the source of the Veda, which is itself 'almost omniscient' (*sarvajñakalpa*) and 'the mine of all knowledge' (*sarvajñā-nākara*). At the time of creation, the Vedic scriptures are 'breathed forth' (*niḥśvasita*) 'after the manner of sport, without any effort at all, like the breathing out by a person' (*aprayatnenaiva līlānyāyena puruṣaniḥśvāsavat*).[3] Thus the Veda has an ontological relationship to Brahman as to its source. In the second interpretation, Śaṁkara asserts an epistemological relationship between Brahman and Veda; for the Veda is the source (*yoni*), that is to say, the cause (*kāraṇa*), or more accurately, the means of knowledge (*pramāṇa*), of Brahman as it is in its own nature. For it is *only* from the Vedic scriptures or by means of them (*śāstrād eva pramāṇāt*) that Brahman can be known as the cause of the universe. In short, the reality of the Veda goes back to Brahman for its source; at the same time, the Veda serves as the only (*eva*) means to our knowledge of the true nature of Brahman.

Like the other Hindu thinkers, Śaṁkara believed that supersensuous realities (*atīndriyārtha*) can be known only through the Scriptures (*śruti*).[4] It is therefore understandable that, being a supersensuous reality, Brahman can be known only through the testimony of the Veda, which is the source of our knowledge of supersensuous realities. Śaṁkara states time and again that Brahman can be known only through the Veda.[5] For none of the other means of knowledge can serve as our source of knowledge of Brahman. Being devoid of colour etc. (*rūpādi,* i.e. colour and other perceptible qualities), Brahman cannot be the object of sense perception (*pratyakṣa*). In the absence of a characteristic mark (*liṅgābhāvāt*) which would serve as a 'middle term' (*hetu*), Brahman cannot be known through inference (*anumāna*). Other means of knowledge such as comparison (*upamāna*), presumption (*arthāpatti*) and non-apprehension (*anupalabdhi*), based as these are on perception and inference, cannot be the means of our knowledge of Brahman.

On the other hand, Śaṁkara does not altogether rule out the role of reasoning (*tarka, anumāna*) in man's attainment of the knowledge of Brahman. However, he insists that reasoning, by itself alone (*kevalaḥ tarkaḥ*), that is to say, independent of the Veda (*nirāgama*), cannot lead to the knowledge of Brahman. For such a reasoning is a 'dry' (*śuṣka*) reasoning, that is to say, ineffective or unproductive of the knowledge of Brahman. In order to be an effective means to the knowledge of Brahman, reasoning should not be in contradiction with the Vedāntic statements (*vedāntavākyāvirodhi*); rather it should necessarily be supported by Śruti (*śrutyanugṛhīta eva*) and in conformity with the Scriptures (*āgamānusāri*) in order to be able to produce the knowledge of Brahman. In other words, Scripture alone - for the Vedāntin 'Scripture' means especially the Upaniṣadic statements (*vedāntavākya*) declaring the identity of one's own self with Brahman - can really lead to the knowledge of Brahman. Reasoning can at best be a help (*upakurvan*) in our attainment of the knowledge of Brahman, playing only a role that is subsidiary of Scripture, with which it must be in conformity. Reason should conform itself to Scripture, not Scripture to reason.[6]

Here a word must be said about the role of *anubhava* or *anubhūti* meaning 'intuition' or 'direct experience' - a term of capital importance in Radhakrishnan's thought - in our knowledge of Brahman. Śamkara admits that not only Scripture and reasoning but also intuition can be a source of knowledge of Brahman. This is because, he says, the knowledge of Brahman terminates in an intuition (*anubhavāvasānāt . . . brahmajñānasya*) and because, in contrast to things that are to be effected (*kartavye viṣaye*) - where knowledge does not have an object that is already existent but rather an object that is to be accomplished - the knowledge of Brahman leads to an object that already exists (*bhūtavastuviṣayatvāt*).[7]

Important to note here is the fact that, in the view of Śamkara, *anubhava* or intuitive experience is the culmination or the last stage of the process leading to the knowledge of Brahman. It is preceded by the 'hearing' (*śravaṇa*) of the words of the Veda from a qualified teacher, followed by reflection (*manana*) and meditation (*nididhyāsana*) - the three successive stages mentioned in the Upaniṣadic statement : *śrotavyo mantavyo nididhyāsitavyaḥ* (Bṛh. Up. II, 4, 5) and accepted by the traditional Vedāntins as the logical order of the mental processes leading to the knowledge of Brahman. For Śamkara, *anubhava* is nothing else than the culminating stage in the soul's search after liberation, which consists in the realisation that one's own self is identical with Brahman (*brahmasvabhāva*). For such a person, who has attained an intuition of Brahman, the Veda loses all reality and authority.

As regards the authority of the Veda, Śamkara recognized, like all the orthodox Hindu thinkers, that the Veda is absolutely infalliable. However, this does not mean that one should accept the validity of the Vedic statements, if these were to contradict valid knowledge gained by perception or inference. Commenting on a verse of the *Bhagavad Gītā* (XVIII, 66), Śamkara states that not even a hundred scriptural passages stating that 'fire is cold' or that 'fire does not illumine' can make fire cold or deprive it of its luminosity, the heating power and luminosity of fire being established by perception. But he immediately adds : "It should not, however, [be assumed] that it (namely, *śruti*) is contradicted by other means of knowledge or that it contradicts its own statements." Were Scripture to contain such statements that *prima facie* contradict the knowledge that is gained through other valid means of cognition, then they should be understood as having another meaning than the immediately apparent one. In other words, the Veda is absolutely infallible. However, if its statements seem to be untrue, it is not because they are untrue, but only because they have another meaning which we have not grasped. Let it be said here in passing that such a principle of Vedic interpretation is not something peculiar to Śaṁkara or to the Vedāntins but common to all Hindu schools.[8] Further, it may be useful to recall here that, just like the reality of the Veda, its validity too is restricted to the domain of empirical existence, in other words, only as long as one remains in the cycle of transmigratory existences, not after one has attained the true knowledge leading to liberation.

According to Śaṁkara and the Advaitins, the Veda is not only absolutely valid, but its validity is also intrinsic (*svataḥ prāmāṇya*), just as the capacity of the sun's rays for illumining colour in objects is intrinsic to the sun's rays. Reasoning (*tarka*) does not effect, or add to, the intrinsic validity of the Veda, but it only serves as a help for us in understanding or confirming the validity of the Veda, which is intrinsic and independent of any other factor.[9]

Concluding this section of our study we can say that for the Advaitins the Veda has only a relative reality in the sense that it is only a part of the illusory world of transmigratory existences. Nevertheless, in this limited domain of reality, its validity is absolute. Moreover, though it is self-existent, and not produced by the activity of any person, it is revealed by God at the beginning of every new creation.

Having thus examined the Advaita standpoint on the nature and authority of the Veda, let us now turn our attention to Radhakrishnan's views on the same.

Radhakrishnan's Conception of the Authorship of the Veda

Concerning the authorship of the Veda, we can distinguish two kinds of statements in Radhakrishnan's writings : one wherein the Veda is conceived as having a human author, and the other wherein a certain role is ascribed to God as inspirer of the Vedic seers.

(a) *Veda as having a human origin*

When we speak of Radhakrishnan's conception of Veda as having human origin or a human authorship, we have in mind his statements according to which the Veda is the record of the spiritual experience of the Vedic seers (*ṛṣi*).

In his book, *The Hindu View of Life,* our author writes :

> The chief sacred scriptures of the Hindus, the Vedas, register the intuitions of the perfected souls ... They record the spiritual experiences of souls strongly endowed with the sense for reality. They are held to be authoritative on the ground that they express the experiences of the experts in the field of religion.[10]

Elsewhere he observes :

> The Vedic statements are āptavacana, or sayings of the wise, which we are called upon to accept, if we feel convinced that those wise had better means than we have of forming a judgment on the matter in question. Generally, these Vedic truths refer to the experience of the seers ....[11]

The two passages cited above speak of the Veda as registering 'the intuitions of perfected souls,' as 'the sayings of the wise,' as truths which refer to 'the experience of the seers' — statements that indicate the human origin of the Veda. There is no mention of the transcendental nature of the Veda or of its having a divine author or inspirer. The human origin of the Veda is suggested also by his statements that the experience of the seers, which forms the content of the Veda, is the fruit of intellectual inquiry, and that any one who is willing to follow a certain course of discipline can have the experience of the seers. Thus, in his book, *Indian Philosophy*, our author maintains that the intuitional experiences of the seers "are within the possibility of all men if only they will to have them."[12] Elsewhere, he speaks of the Veda as the result of the intellectual inquiry of man :

> The name *Veda* signifying wisdom suggests a genuine spirit of inquiry. The road by which the Vedic sages travelled was the road of those who seek to inquire and understand. The questions they investigate are of a philosophical character.[13]

Likewise,

> The *Śāstras*, or Scriptures, are the records of the experiences of the seers who have grappled with the problem of Reality . . . . The experience [of these seers] may be gained by anyone who is willing to undergo a certain discipline and put forth effort.[14]

Similar passages could be multiplied. But the two quoted above leave no doubt that in Radhakrishnan's view the Vedic wisdom is the fruit of rational inquiry, accessible to every human being.

Radhakrishnan's conception of the Veda as having a purely human origin can also be seen in his description of the texts that constitute the Veda. After characterizing the Vedas as "the earliest documents of the human mind we possess,"[15] the author of *Indian Philosophy* speaks of the different texts that constitute the Veda. Of these the hymns in the Saṁhitās are said to be the "first efforts of the human mind to comprehend and express the mystery of the world."[16] The Ṛgvedic collection is "a work representing the thought of successive generations of thinkers and so contains within it different strata of thought . . . ."[17] Among the hymns of the Ṛgveda "there are some, especially in the last book, which embody the mature results of conscious reflection on the meaning of the world and man's place in it."[18] Such descriptions of the Ṛgvedic hymns seem to make them products of the human mind seeking to understand and express the mystery of the world. This is confirmed by the following statement wherein our author excludes any divine influence on the composers of the Vedic hymns :

> In the Ṛgveda we have the impassioned utterances of primitive but poetic souls which seek some refuge from the obstinate questionings of sense and outward things. The hymns are philosophical to the extent that they attempt to explain the mysteries of the world not by means of any superhuman insight or extraordinary revelation, but by the light of unaided reason. The mind revealed in the Vedic hymns is not of any one type. There were poetic souls who simply contemplated the beauties of the sky and the wonders of the earth, and eased their musical souls of their burden by composing hymns.[19]

Such is Radhakrishnan's conception of the origin and nature of the Ṛgvedic hymns. He has similar views also as regards the other Vedic texts :

> The Āraṇyakas come between the Brāhmaṇas and the Upaniṣads, and as their name implies, are intended to serve as objects of meditation for those who live in forests. The Brāhmaṇas discuss the ritual to be observed by the householder . . . . While the hymns are the creation of the poets, the

Brāhmaṇas are the work of the priets, and the Upaniṣads the meditations of the philosophers.[20]

As regards the Upaniṣads which constitute the most important Vedic texts for the Vedāntins, Radhakrishnan observes :

> They contain the earliest records of Indian speculation.... The Upaniṣads are essentially the outpourings or poetic deliverances of philosophically tempered minds in the face of the facts of life. They express the restlessness and striving of the human mind to grasp the true nature of reality.[21]

Elsewhere, our author states that "the Upaniṣads embody the experiences of the sages."[22]

Space does not permit us to cite more passages of the same tenor. But the passages cited above seem enough to indicate that in them Radhakrishnan conceived of the Veda as the record of the religious experience of the Vedic seers or as the expression of the fruit of reflection of these seers on the nature of reality and on the mysteries of life. In other words, the Veda is said to have a purely human activity to account for its origin. If this conclusion is right, it is indeed a far cry from the conception not only of Śaṁkara and the Advaita, but also from that of the traditional Hindu thought in general, which always claimed for the Veda a superhuman or transcendent character. Traditional Hindu thinkers have sharply and consistently distinguished Śruti (Veda) from the Smṛti texts on the ground that the former are of non-human origin or nature, wheres the latter are known to have human authors.

(b) *Veda as being inspired by God*

Along with statements which, as we said, seem to indicate that Radhakrishnan believed in the purely human origin of the Veda, there are other passages, fewer in number but unambiguous in expression, which seem to suggest that - at least occasionally - he ascribed to God a role of an inspirer of the sages which these were composing the Veda.

In the "Introduction" to his work, *The Principal Upaniṣads* our author observes :

> As a part of the Veda, Upaniṣads belong to *śruti* or revealed literature.... Their truths are said to be breathed out by God or visioned by the seers... They are not reached by ordinary perception, inference or reflection, but *seen* by the seers, even as we see and not infer the wealth and riot of colour in the summer sky.... The fruits revealed to the seers are not mere reports of introspection which are purely subjective. The inspired sages proclaim that the knowledge they communicate is not what they discover for themselves. It is revealed to them without effort. Though the knowledge is an experience of the seer, it is an experience of an independent reality which impinges on his consciousness. There is the impact of the real on the spirit of the experiencer. It is therefore said to be a direct disclosure from the 'wholly other', a revelation of the Divine.... Symbolically, the Upaniṣads describe revelation as the breath of God blowing on us. 'Of that great being, this is the breath, which is the Ṛgveda.... The Vedas were composed by the seers when they were in a state of inspiration. He who inspires them is God.[23]

In this passage quoted at some length because of its importance in the present context, Radhakrishnan seems to have attempted to incorporate the Christian conception of the inspiration of the Bible into the traditional Upaniṣadic-Advaitic conception of the origin of the Veda from Brahman. In the Upaniṣadic texts (*Bṛh. Up.* II, 4,10; IV, 5,

11) the four Vedas are said to have been "breathed forth by the Great Being" (*mahato bhūtasya niḥśvasitam*). Śaṁkara (on Br. Sūtra I, 1, 3) explained, as we saw, the term 'breathed forth' in the sense that the Vedas have come forth from the Great Being or Brahman "without any effort at all, in the manner of sport, like the breathing out by a person." In the Upaniṣadic passages and in Śaṁkara the expression `breathed forth' (*niḥśvasitam*) was employed to suggest the spontaneity or the effortlessness of the process of the origination of the Veda from Brahman. In Radhakrishnan, on the other hand, the expression is not applied to the process of the origination of the Veda, but rather to the seers, when he writes : "It is revealed to them [i.e. seers] without *their* effort" [italics added].

That Radhakrishnan was here trying to apply the Christian conception of biblical inspiration to the Veda seems to be indicated also from the following fact. After stating that "the Vedas are composed by the seers when they were in a state of inspiration," he quotes in a footnote a passage from the *Apologia* of Athenagoras, wherein the Christian apologist describes how the Divine Spirit, by inspiring the prophets of the Bible, made use of them as instruments in order to utter only those words which the Divine Spirit himself wanted them to utter.

In one of the passages quoted earlier in this study, where the Vedic statements were said to be *āptavacana*, or sayings of the wise, Radhakrishnan interprets the word *āpta* (i.e. 'trustworthy,' 'credible') in the plural and applies it to the seers, who are conceived as the authors of the Veda. But, in another passage, where the inspired seers are spoken of as having been illuminated by God's inspirational influence, our author interprets the term *āpta* in the compound *āptavacana* in the singular and applies it to God, as though to make God's inspiration on the Vedic seers similar to the Christian conception of God inspiring the human authors of the biblical texts. Thus he writes :

The scriptures register the experiences of seers, they are *āptavacana*, the sayings of the inspired men, who have time and again been illuminated by the light of God, *āptena* [note the singular!] *praṇītaṃ vacanam āpta-vacanam*.[24]

Even though Radhakrishnan speaks of the Vedic seers as being "illuminated by the light of God," in other words, as being divinely inspired, this divine activity is conceived as subordinated to the nature of truth : "Even when the Scriptures are traced to divine authorship, it is said that God is not free [in his authorship] but has to reckon with the nature of truth."[25] In fact, Scriptures would be scriptures, even without any divine authorship; for the Scriptures are nothing but "the records of the experiences of the great seers who have expressed their sense of the inner meaning of the world through their intense insight and imagination."[26] The ultimate authority of the Veda rests not on its superhuman origin or transcendent nature, but on its being the record of the experiences of the seers, who had personal experience of the truth. In the light of this idea, one can easily understand Radhakrishnan's repeated emphasis on religious experience as the ultimate basis of religion rather than on a divine revelation.

Closely associated with the conception of 'divine inspiration' of the Veda is also Radhakrishnan's conception of the Veda as revelation. But, however interesting it may be, this issue has to be set aside here for lack of space.

Concluding our brief inquiry into Radhakrishnan's conception of the nature or the origin of the Veda, we may state that fundamentally our author seems to have looked upon the Veda as having solely a human authorship. The few statements, wherein God is said to be the inspirer of the Vedic seers are, to judge from their context, merely incidental remarks made in the context of dealing with other Scriptures, especially the Bible, for which a divine authorship, in the sense of a divine inspiration of the authors of the biblical books, was recognized.

Radhakrishnan's Conception of the Authority of the Veda

Let it be stated at the very outset that Radhakrishnan nowhere explicitly denies the authority of the Veda as such. Nevertheless, as a few of his statements quoted below seem to indicate, he formally acknowledges that the Veda is not infallible in all that it states. In a way, such an acknowledgement is not, really speaking, substantially different from the standpoint of the traditional Hindu thinkers; for while formally confessing the infallible validity of the Veda in principle, these interpret some Vedic statements as they want and as they need, giving them a meaning different from what those statements seem to mean at first sight. Every interpretation, however different from or even contradictory to each other, is accepted as authoritative. Radhakrishnan's stance differs from that of these thinkers in this that, whereas they formally accept that the Veda cannot contain any error, Radhakrishnan accepts formally that the Veda contains error.

The denial of the absolute infallible nature of the Veda is but an extension or application of his general view that Scriptures in general are liable to error. In his work, *An Idealist View of Life*, while advocating the need of a critical approach to all Scriptures, our author observes:

> The scriptures which affirm absolutism of religions and announce themselves as infallible, such as the Vedas and the Tipiṭaka, the Bible and the Qu'ran, are treated today in the same critical and historical spirit as the Dialogues of Plato or the Inscriptions of Aśoka. They are all human documents written by human hands and liable to

> error. Not merely religious scriptures but codes of custom and laws of society, all these are supposed to have come from the gods.... We know now that they all originated in the discordant passions and the groping reason of human beings.[27]

In this passage we have not only one more testimony to Radhakrishnan's conception of the purely human origin of the Veda but also the reason why the Scriptures of religions are liable to err : being products of fallible human mind, they participate in the fallible nature of their cause. In sharp contrast to the traditional Hindu view that the Veda is infallible *in toto,* our author is willing to concede the fallible nature of some parts of the Veda if these are found to be incompatible with reason or the scientific spirit :

> The scriptures are the products of history and some of their parts are forgeries.... Every revealed scripture seems to contain in it a large mass of elements which scientific criticism and historical knowledge require us to discard and there is no reason why we should accept it at all. Truth is greater than any revelation.[28]

In his book, *The Brahma Sūtra,* our author is more explicit : "Scriptures are not infallible in all they say."[29]

If the Veda, which is the Scripture of the Hindus, is not infallible in all that it says, one should not accept in blind faith all that it teaches, but rather one should cultivate a critical attitude towards them, as he observes :

> The Hindu attitude to the Vedas is one of trust tempered by criticism : trust because the beliefs and forms which helped our fathers are likely to be of use to us also; criticism because, however valuable the testimony of past ages may be, it cannot deprive the present age of its right to inquire and sift the evidence.[30]

Such is, of course, not the general Hindu attitude towards the Veda, in any case, not of traditional Hinduism; but it can be said to be the stance of Neo-Hinduism or Neo-Vedantism, of which Radhakrishnan is undoubtedly the most typical and outstanding representative.

The attribution of errors in the Veda as well as the advocacy of a tempered trust in the inerrance of the Veda and of a critical attitude towards it was the outcome of Radhakrishnan's concern to apply the method of science to the study of religion. The method of science is opposed to, what Radhakrishnan calls, dogmatism and authoritarianism, which, in his view, are the dominant features of religion. The method of science is empirical, critical, open to inquiry, and willing to modify or eventually discard traditionally accepted views if these are found to be not in conformity with the data of science. The scientific spirit is characterized by "its reluctance to accept anything on trust.... It does not accept any view without scrutiny or criticism and is free to ask questions and doubt assertions.... For science, all judgments are provisional and subject to revision in the light of fresh knowledge."[31] The consequences of the application of such a method to Veda, or for that matter to the Scriptures of any religion, need no further elaboration.

Radhakrishnan was the apostle of a religion that is not attached to unchangeable dogmas or beliefs based on revelation or accepted on faith. "We need a religion," he writes, "which is both scientific and humanistic.... Truth is not opposed to reason..., but to dogma and fossilized tradition. We cannot rest the case of religion any more on dogmatic supernaturalism."[32] The infallible authority of the Veda, on the other hand, is based on faith, and it is not susceptible to scientific scrutiny. Consequently, if their statements are not altogether inadmissible, they are at least open to doubt:

Each religion claims that its scripture is, in a unique sense, the word of God and so infallible. The inerrancy of the scriptures is inconsistent with the spirit of science.... The scriptures give us the impact of revelation on the fallible minds and hearts of those who respond to or receive the revelation. Their utterances cannot be regarded as infallible.[33]

Averse to all dogmatism and authority, even of the Scriptures, our author claimed that "Belief in authority... depersonalizes the human being."[34] Moreover, he was convinced that "no religion can hope to survive if it does not satisfy the scientific temper of our age."[35] What he wanted was "to present a reasoned faith which deals justly with the old tradition and the demands of modern thought,"[36] a religion which is "scientific and humanistic."[37]

Radhakrishnan maintains that "Hinduism adopts a rationalist attitude in the matter of religion. It tries to study the facts of human life in a scientific spirit.... Religion is not so much a revelation to be attained by us in faith as an effort to unveil the deepest layers of man's being and get into enduring contact with them."[38] In fact, when he speaks of the rationalist attitude of 'Hinduism' in the matter of religion, it applies only to the type of Neo-Hinduism as advocated by him as an ideal religion, and not to the historical or actual Hinduism; in any case, it is not applicable to the traditional Hinduism with its traditional thinkers.

The path of scientific method is a path of movement, growth and progress. If the Scriptures of Hinduism are subjected to the laws of movement and progress, then Hinduism itself will undergo the same process. In fact, Radhakrishnan takes up such a stance : "Hinduism is a movement, not a position; a process, not a result; a growing tradition, not a fixed revelation."[39] In this process of movement and growth, in which the continuity with the past in kept up, there is also progress. Every succeeding stage in this process is an improvement of the preceding. Thus, "the Upaniṣads are the products of a perfectly spiritual movement which implicitly superseded the cruder ceremonial religion of the Vedas."[40]

Being in a continuous process of evolution, Hinduism and its Scripture will undergo change, always for the better or the more perfect. The ideal religion to be realized at the end of the process, the one, universal and absolute religion of which Radhakrishnan is the staunch apologete and a fervent apostle, is nothing other than the Vedānta, which is "not a religion, but religion itself in its most universal and deepest significance."[41]

Concluding Remarks

An evaluation of the stance taken by Radhakrishnan concerning the nature and the authority of the Veda cannot be attempted here. We shall content ourselves with only a few remarks wherein his views will be briefly placed against the standpoint of Śaṁkara and of the traditional Advaita.

In the first place, according to traditional Advaita, Brahman is the source of the Veda and Iśvara, the personal aspect of Brahman, its revealer to the human beings. Man has nothing whatever to do with the being or the origin of the Veda or its revelation. In Radhakrishnan's view, by contrast, despite a few remarks wherein a divine influence on the seers in spoken of, the Veda is essentially of human origin; for the Veda is the record of the religious experiences of the Ultimate Reality by perfect souls, the seers (*ṛṣi*), an experience that is within the reach of every man.

Secondly, though the traditional Advaita admits experience (*anubhava*) of the Ultimate Reality or Brahman, it is declared possible *only through* the Veda. Śaṁkara was never tired of stating that Brahman can be known in his own nature only through Śruti, though a subsidiary role is allotted to reasoning in attaining the knowledge of Brahman as the cause of the universe. The direct experience of Brahman is preceded by the Veda; in other words, the Veda is prior to, and is the cause of, our knowledge of Brahman. Radhakrishnan, on the other hand, reverses this order, making the knowledge of the Ultimate Reality by the seers take precedence over the Veda, by declaring the Veda to be the record of the experience of the seers.

Thirdly, as regards the authority of the Veda, the traditional Advaita, like all systems of Hindu thought, unambiguously defended the absolute authority (*prāmāṇya*) of the Veda. If the *prima facie* sense of some Vedic statements seemed to contradict valid knowledge gained by other means of cognition, the Vedic statement in question was not to be considered as an error and discarded; rather, one should assume that it has a sense other than the apparent one. The Veda was, as a whole and in all is parts, declared to be true. Radhakrishnan gives up this very fundamental thesis and admits explicitly that the Veda is not true in all that it says and that those parts of it which are found to be in contradiction with the data of science should be discarded as erroneous. Although such a thought is quite in conformity with his conception of the nature of Veda and of religion, it is a far cry from the teaching of the traditional Advaita.

Finally, traditional Advaita admits that the authority of the Veda does not come from outside itself; rather, it validates itself (*svataḥ, prāmāṇya*). In applying the method and the data of science, which are completely foreign to the domain of the Veda, as criterion to test the validity of Vedic statements, Radhakrishnan not only gives up the Advaitic stance that Śruti alone is the means to our knowledge of supersensuous realities (*atīndriyārtha*), but strikes at the very roots of Vedic authority.

These differences of views on such an important issue as the nature and the authority of the Veda leads us to draw the conclusion that Radhakrishnan's Advaita is radically different from the traditional Advaita. His statements must be evaluated not in terms of the traditional Advaita, but rather in terms of his own Neo-Vedāntism. Such a stance seems to correspond to his own confession :

> Although, I admire the great masters of thought, ancient and modern, Eastern and Western, I cannot say that I am a follower of any, accepting his teaching in its entirety. I do not suggest that I refused to learn from others or that I was not influenced by them. While I was greatly stimulated by the minds of all those whom I have studied, my thought does not comply with any fixed traditional pattern. For my thinking had another source and proceeded from my own experience, which is not quite the same as what is acquired by mere study and reading. It is born of spiritual experience, rather than deduced from logically ascertained premises.[42]

References

1. Although the *Bhagavad Gītā* has at all times exercised an enormous influence on the Hindu thought, far above that of the Vedic texts in general, it enjoyed only an authority inferior to that of the Veda. This is because, whereas the Veda or the Śruti was held to be superhuman, the *Bhagvad Gītā*, belonging as it does to the class of Smṛti, had a human authorship.

2. See Śaṁkara's *Brahmasūtrabhāṣya* (hereafter abbreviated BSBh; edition used is : The *Brahmasūtrabhāṣya*, ed. by Nārāyan Rām Ācārya, Nirnaya Sagar Press, Bombay, 1948. Numbers within brackets indicate the page(s) and the line-number from top), II, 1,14.

3. BSBh I, 1, 3 (= p. 9 : 15-10 : 1)
4. BSBh II, 3, 1 (= p. 262 : 17-18): *śrutiś ca naḥ pramāṇam atīdriyārthavijñānotpattau*. See also BSBh II, 1, 1 (= p. 181 : 5-7) : *na cātīndriyān arthān śrutim antareṇa kaścid upalabhyata iti śakyaṃ sambhāvayitum*).
5. BSBh, I, 1,4 *passim*, p. 11-6-7 : *brahma sarvajñaṃ sarvaśakti jagadutpattisthitilayakāraṇaṃ vedāntaśāstrād evāvagamyate*.
6. See BSBh I, 1, 2 (= p. 7 : 25-8 : 5; II, 1, 11 (= p.194 : 14-16)' II, 1, 13 (= p. 184 : 5), etc. From the large number of contributions on the position and role of reasoning in Advaita we may mention : M. Hiriyanna, "The Place of Reason in Advaita," in his *Indian Philosophical Studies*, Vol. I, Kavyalaya Publishers, Mysore, 1957, pp. 45-52; K. Satchindananda Murthy, *Revelation and Reason in Advaita Vedānata*, 1959, reprint, Motilal Banarsidass, Delhi, 1974, esp. pp. 140-165; W. Halbfass, *Studies in Kumārila and Śaṁkara*, Dr. Inge Wezler Verlag, Reinbeck, 1983, pp. 27-84.
7. BSBh I, 1, 2 (= pl. 8 : 6-19).
8. For similar interpretations by the Nyāya-Vaiśeṣikas, see G. Chemparathy, "The Nyāya-Vaiśeṣikas as Interpreters of Śruti," in *The Journal of Dharma* (Bangalore), Vol. III, No. 3, July-Sept., 1978, pp. 274-294.
9. BSBh II, 1, 1 (= p. 182 : 10-11) : *vedasya hi nirapekṣaṃ svārthe prāmāṇyāṃ, raver iva rūpaviṣaye*.
10. *The Hindu View of Life*, George Allen & Unwin Ltd., London, 1931, p. 17.
11. *Indian Philosophy*, Vol. I, George Allen & Unwin Ltd., London, 1941, p. 51.
12. *Ibid.*, p. 51. Our author refers, in a footnote, to BSBh III, 2, 24, where the Yogins are said to be able to "see" (*paśyanti*) Brahman, thanks to their devotion (*bhakti*), meditation (*dhyāna*) and deep contemplation (*praṇidhāna*).
13. *The Principal Upaniṣads*, George Allen & Unwin Ltd., London, 1953, p. 29.
14. S. Radhakrishnan, "The Indian Approach to the Religious Problem," in Charles A. Moore (ed.), *Philosophy and Culture - East and West*, University of Hawaii Press, Honolulu, 1968, p.

260. See also our author's "Reply to Critics," in Paul A. Schilpp (ed.), *The Philosophy of Sarvepalli Radhakrishnan,* The Tudor Publishing Company, New York, 1952, p. 795: *The Hindu An Intealist View of Life,* George Allen & Unwin Ltd., London, 1951, p. 89 : "The Veda, the wisdom, is the accepted name for the highest spiritual truth of which the human mind is capable."
15. *Indian Philosophy,* Vol. I, p. 63.
16. *Ibid.,* p. 66.
17. *Ibid.,* p. 69.
18. *Ibid.,* p. 69.
19. *Ibid.,* p. 71.
20. *Ibid.,* p. 65.
21. *Ibid.,* p. 138.
22. *The Hindu View of Life,* p. 22.
23. *The Principal Upaniṣads,* pp. 22-23.
24. *The Brahma Sūtra,* George Allen & Unwin Ltd., London, 1971, p. 113.
25. *Ibid.,* p. 113.
26. *Ibid.,* p. 113.
27. *An Idealist View of Life,* p. 38.
28. *Ibid.,* pp. 38-39.
29. *Op. cit.,* p. 115.
30. *The Hindu View of Life,* p. 18.
31. *Recovery of Faith,* George Allen & Unwin Ltd., London, 1956, pp. 10-11.
32. *Eastern Religions and Western Thought,* Oxford University Press, London, 1940, p. 294.
33. *Recovery of Faith,* p. 12.
34. *East and West in Religion,* George Allen & Unwin Ltd., London, 1933, p. 116.
35. *Recovery of Faith,* p. 10; see also *Eastern Religions and Western Thought,* p. 61; *The Hindu View of Life,* p. 15.
36. *The Brahma Sūtra,* p. 11.

37. *Eastern Religions and Western Thought,* p. 294.
38. *Ibid.,* pp. 20-21.
39. *The Hindu View of Life,* p. 129; see also his *Religion and Society,* George Allen & Unwin Ltd., London, 1947, p. 54.
40. *The Hindu View of Life,* p. 129.
41. *Ibid,* p. 23.
42. S. Radhakrishnan, "Fragments of a Confession," in Paul A. Schilpp (ed.), *The Philosophy of Sarvepalli Radhakrishnan,* p. 10.

10
Radhakrishnan's Approach to Yoga : Its Inter-disciplinary Concerns and Implications

S. GOPALAN
National University of Singapore

It is perhaps a truism to state that Radhakrishnan's contribution to philosophy is particularly noted for the *comprehensive treatment* of the subject and for the *deep analysis of man* it offers. Even a brief reference to these two aspects of Radhakrishnan's methodology would be helpful in appreciating his approach to Yoga, the theme of the present paper.

The need for a 'manifold approach' could best be indicated by recounting that before the specialized disciplines (new classified as the physical, the biological and the social sciences) began to grow autonomous, they were all *aspects of philosophy* and noting the fact that even long after they branched off, their analytical-reflective aspects are distinctly evident.

The analytical aspect of Radhakrishnan's method of doing philosophy signifies that while the empirically observable aspects of man *are* important, the non-empirical dimensions too are vital. Implicit in this approach is the whole-hearted acceptance of inter-disciplinary studies for philosophy insofar as arriving at a concept of man is an integral aspect of *philosophizing* itself.

We shall attempt to show that Radhakrishnan's reflections on the Yoga system clearly point to his applying inter-disciplinary approaches to the study of man and that such an approach is a sequel to his recognition of the comprehensive scope of philosophy. Since Yoga is mostly treated as a system of philosophy intent on portraying the spiritual ideal as the culmination of higher forms of meditation, it is interesting to see how Radhakrishnan, without denying those aspects, offers us insights into the secular (here understood as standing for the physiological and psychological) aspects of Yoga.

Personality : A Structural Analysis

A brief reference to Radhakrishnan's statement of the classical Yoga theory of man (as espoused by Patañjali, the founder of the Yoga system of philosophy) as a complex of the triumvirate, - body, mind and self - is necessary to set the stage for highlighting his multi-disciplinary approach to Yoga.

The three-fold aspect of personality accepted by Patañjali is referred to succinctly by Radhakrishnan thus : "In the human organism we find the physical body, the vital dynamism (and) the psychic principles, in addition to the *puruṣa*. The *puruṣa* is hidden behind veils of corruptible flesh and restless mind . . . ."[1] He explains the physiological basis of Yoga by pointing to the detailed study of nerves (*nāḍis*) discernible even at an early stage of the history of Yoga; and, by referring to the theory of psychic centres (*cakras*) and potential energy (*kuṇḍāliniśakti*) stored at the base of the spine, he elucidates the psychological aspects of Yoga.[2] The wealth of material found in Yoga literature is fully utilized by Radhakrishnan to explain the psycho-physical aspects of personality. For he writes :

> The human body has two main parts, the upper and the lower. The head, trunk and limbs form the upper, and the legs and feet, the lower part... The nerves and the ganglionic masses of nervous matter are arranged in two great systems, the sympathetic and the cerebro-spinal. The brain and the spinal cord contained within the bony cavity of the skull and the spinal column are the great centres of the cerebro-spinal system. Brahmāṇḍa or Merudaṇḍa of Hindu physiology is the spinal column. It is the seat of nāḍi-suṣumna, which extends from the Mūlādhāra or the root-support at the base of the vertebral column to the Sahasrāra lying within the cerebral region. The other four cakras (pelxus) are the Svādhiṣṭhāna, Maṇipura, Anāhata and Viśuddha.[3]

The point which needs attention here is that Radhakrishnan takes note of the fact that the 'psychical' is located in the 'physical' and indicates Yoga's recognition of the intimate relationship between the two aspects of human personality. Citing an important aphorism from Patañjali[4] Radhakrishnan observes : "The close connection of body and mind is insisted on, for, pain, despondency, unsteadiness of the body and inspiration and expiration are the accompaniments of distractions."[5]

Radhakrishnan indicates the Yoga idea of tridimensionality of personality by first pointing to the psycho-physical complex and then hinting at the third aspect, viz. the self which is regarded *not* as a mere adjunct but as *organic to the mind-body complex*. This is referred to as *puruṣa* in the yogic terminology and is to be found by an inner search ; "it is the search for what Novalis called 'our transcendental me,' the divine and eternal part of our being," observes Radhakrishnan.[6]

Personality : A Functional Analysis

It is important to reiterate that though the idea of personality can be understood in *structural terms* as outlined above, the study of it becomes complete only when the *functional aspects* are also dilated upon. This is perhaps the reason why whenever and wherever *personality* is analysed, the process of *personality-development* is considered to deserve equal attention and the Yoga system is no exception. For it maintains that the functional aspects of personality-development are rooted in the structural aspects of the self as the third dimension. Hence some reference to self is necessary for delineating the personality-development idea in the Yoga system.

The self as the third dimension of personality being identified with pure consciousness is an idea accepted by Yoga from Sāṁkhya, a sister-system which refers to the need for disengaging the self (*puruṣa*) from the non-conscious aspects of Reality (*prakṛti*).[7] However, the Yoga system is more concerned with suggesting a method of achieving such a consummation than with speculating about the origin and aim of human life, one of the major concerns of Sāṁkhya.

The line of thinking that the Yoga system takes is that consciousness as the desideratum of states of consciousness which can be analysed phenomenologically, represents the inner core of personality.[8] The identification of consciousness with the self understood in such terms signifies that in the ultimate analysis, achieving full personality-development consists in progressively intensifying 'states of consciousness' till consciousness as such, i.e. the inner core of personality as self is reached.[9]

The celebrated eight-limb (*aṣṭāṅga*) scheme proposed by the Yoga system is precisely designed to achieve personality-development as outlined above. The eight limbs (*aṣṭa aṅga*) proposed are the following : *yama* (restraint), *niyama* (observance), *āsana* (posture), *prāṇāyāma* (regulation of breath), *pratyāhāra* (withdrawal of the senses), *dhāraṇa* (fixed attention), *dhyāna* (meditation) and *samādhi* (concentration).[10] Suffice it to note here that these 'limbs' refer to the ethical, the physical-psychological and the psychological-spiritual steps.[11] The expression "the eight stages of Yoga" often used, is quite useful in pointing to the need for achieving personality-development in a methodical way.

It is now easy to appreciate the reason why Radhakrishnan was keen on explaining the physical basis of personality-development while elucidating the significance of the third stage of *āsana* or posture. His brief observation on the emphasis laid by Patañjali on disciplining the body as one of the preparatory steps in Yoga is this : "Yoga realises that our body has a dignity of its own, as much as the mind. "*Āsana* or posture is a physical help to concentration."[12] The clear implication is that even though the ultimate aim of personality-development is achievable only in the eighth stage of *Samādhi*, the physical aspects of life should not be disregarded either as unimportant or as insignificant.

The need for nurturing the physical aspects of personality arises from the fact that "the later stages of . . . Yoga demand great powers of physical endurance."[13] Radhakrishnan also reminds us that "cases are not wanting where the strenuous spiritual life strains the earthen vessel to the breaking point."[14] Hence the need to take due care of the body by means of practising the *āsanas*. No wonder, therefore, *haṭha-yoga* (physical culture) is regarded by him (following Patañjali) as aiming at "perfecting the bodily instrument, freeing it from its liability to fatigue and arresting its tendency to decay and age."[15]

Thus one should not consider the body a hindrance to personality-development and inflict pain on it. "Yoga asks us to control the body and not kill it," he writes[16] and adds : "Abstinence from sensual indulgences is not the same as crucifixion of the body."[17] Radhakrishnan seems to highlight the significance of the third step, *viz., Āsana*, with a view to indicating that the aim of Yoga is not *merely* achieving physical fitness.

While explaining the significance of *prāṇāyāma* (breath-control) too, he is keen on indicating its importance from the viewpoint of physiological well-being by a citation from an article in a medical journal. Part of the citation reads as follows:

> The remarkable improvement in the heart's nutrition and action is, I think, to a great degree, caused by the deep inspirations which are necessitated by the act of climbing, esp. steady and prolonged climbing. This consideration has led me to pay particular attention to respiratory exercises, which since then have been very useful to myself and many others, especially persons with weak heart muscles . . . .[18]

It is significant that Radhakrishnan takes due note of the fact that "breath-control is regarded as a steadying influence on the mind."[19] Here is an acknowledgement of the intimate and reciprocal relationship between the physical and psychological aspects of personality, the commonly accepted fact that happenings on the bodily side have their effects on the mental side and *vice versa*. This is also to suggest that what seems on the surface to have only physiological significance turns out, on analysis, to have a psychological significance as well. The further suggestion here is that Yoga is not to be understood as a mystical system merely but as empirically well-based (though normatively oriented) since the physiological well-being of man is pointed to as a *sine qua non* for erecting the metaphysical superstructure of an integrated personality.

Personality-development : Psychological and Metapsychological Analyses

The intimate relationship between the structural and functional aspects of personality and the reciprocal relationship between the mental and the self aspects should have become evident by now. For reasons which will become evident in the sequel, these can also be visualized as the psychological and metapsychological aspects of personality-development, when functionally considered.

Turning first to the psychological aspects, it should be noticed that Radhakrishnan acknowledges the Yoga view that the mind does not possess consciousness as its intrinsic property. In this connection he refers to the acceptance of the Sāṃkhya view by Yoga that *Citta*, the first product of evolution of *Prakṛti*, is a composite of the intellect, the element of self-consciousness and the mind. "It is essentially unconscious, though it becomes conscious by the reflection of the self which abides by it," Radhakrishnan observes.[20]

The logic behind this conception is that since *Citta* is a product of evolution of the non-conscious *Prakṛti*, consciousness is extraneous to it. Obviously, *puruṣa* (self) is, in its intrinsic nature, distinct from the mind-body complex. The distinction may also be referred to as that between *empirical personality* and *transcendent personality*. Personality-development, consequently, is to be understood as the process of transforming empirical personality into the transcendent personality. Since however consciousness is experienced also at the empirical level, i.e. at the psycho-physical level, the process of transformation of personality connotes purifying the quality of consciousness until the state of prestine purity is achieved ultimately.

Hence this may be referred to as laying the emphasis on the metapsychological aspects of personality. The point to note here is that this emphasis ought not to be mistaken as the deletion of the psychological aspects altogether. For, the Yoga system abounds in references to the empirically experienced, immediately verifiable mental states, what may also be described as 'empirical states of personality.'[21] Further, the reciprocal relationship envisaged between the psychological and the metapsychological aspects of personality would also point to the fact that since the two aspects intersect and interact, the emphasis on the latter is not to be understood as overlooking the former but as pointing to the need for identifying the inner core of personality, the self, which, as Radhakrishnan observes "is not to be found by means of an objective use of the mind but by ... penetration beneath the mental strata ...."[22] This in effect signifies that personality-development involves realizing, in *one's own experience,* the distinctness of the self from the *Citta.*[23]

It should be reiterated, however that in addition to the distinction between the mind and the self that Yoga draws, that between the bodily and mental aspects of personality is also considered quite significant. The distinction drawn is evident from the fact that the mind is visulized as itself redirecting the sensory and motor organs[24] (respectively being referred to as *jñānendriyas* and *karmendriyas*) and also as identifying itself with both.[25] It seems to me that by such a reference, Yoga offers us an insight into the reasons why the mind is at times identified (though mistakenly) with the body. The failure to draw the distinction is critically viewed by Radhakrishnan, perhaps bearing in mind the type of distinction drawn in Yoga. And from the viewpoint of interdisciplinary approaches to Yoga, his reference to researches in psychology is quite significant. He writes:

> The investigations of the Psychological Research Society ... have begun to shake the hardiest faith in the truths hitherto accepted in the name of science, that intelligence and memory are

> functions dependent on the integrity of the cerebral mechanism, which will disappear when that mechanism decays . . . . Psychologists tell us that the human mind has other perceptive faculties than those served by the five senses, and philosophers are slowly accepting the view that we have mental powers other than those of ratiocination and a memory conditioned by the brain.[26]

His critical observations on the Brain-mind identity theory are evident here and this is an indication of how the implications of the ancient Yoga view of personality are to be understood in the light of prevailing theories of the mind.

It remains for us to refer, in conclusion, to the way in which Radhakrishnan brings in comparative light even while interpreting the Yoga view of a transcendent state of being as a distinct possibility. An important reference he makes is to the reflections of a great literary figure like Tennyson :

> A kind of waking trance I have often had, quite from boyhood, when I have been all alone. This has generally come upon me through repeating my own name two or three times to myself silently, till all at once, out of the intensity of the consciousness of individuality, the individual itself seems to dissolve and fade away into boundless being; and this is not a confused state, but the clearest of the clearest and the surest of the surest, the weirdest of the weirdest, utterly beyond words, where death was an almost laughable impossibility, the loss of personality (if so it were) seeming not extinction, but the only true life.[27]

Radhakrishnan is not adopting an apologetic approach to the Yoga view of a transcendent state of man's being, but is pointing to a deeper dimension in man acknowledged 'elsewhere' too. It seems to me that if the Yoga tradition is not to be understood merely as a metaphysical system of thought but as incorporating deeper insights into the inner nature of man (as the drift and thrust of Patañjali's *magnum opus* indicates clearly), Radhakrishnan's creative-interpretative endeavour may be considered a concerted attempt at unravelling the deeper significance of the philosophy and psychology of Yoga.

It is worth noting that recent empirical studies on Yoga[28] have investigated the physiological no less than the psychological foundations of the system. Whether these research-pieces were inspired by Radhakrishnan's studies, it is hard to say. But the pioneering nature of Radhakrishnan's work seems to be that it has provided the world of scholarship with a cue to the way research in the humanities should proceed. And more specifically in regard to research in philosophy, his message is clear. Philosophy, as a humanistic study, should be considered to have its ramifications which lead a serious inquirer into other studies on man - biological, psychological, literary and social-scientific.

References

1. S. Radhakrishnan, *Indian Philosophy*, London: George Allen & Unwin Ltd., 1927, Vol. II, p. 352.
   The term *puruṣa* refers to the self, the third dimension of personality.
2. *Kuṇḍaliniśakti* is regarded as the highly concentrated psychic force and is esoterically described as *nāda-bindu* or the quintessence of cosmic energy which remains dormant - "asleep like a coiled serpent." (*Śiva-Saṁhita*, V. 80-83) at the sacrum (the triangular bone at the nether end of the spinal column). Once the psychic force is aroused with the

aid of *prāṇāyāma*) (regulated breathing) and other methods of self-culture, it passes through the median nerve (*Suṣumna-nāḍi*) threading through the spinal column and opening (via, *medulla oblangata*) into the Sahasrāra located in the brain. (*Śiva-Saṁhita*, II. 23-27, IV. 2-8 and V. 161-162, *Gheraṇḍa-Saṁhita*, III, 47-49). *Nāda-bindu* is the subtle *anāhata* (unstruck) sound-wave which manifests itself as consciousness in every living creature. It represents Cosmic Energy and is believed to get 'recorded' in a creature the moment *nāda* (ovum) and *bindu* (sperm) unite. See Shyam Ghosh, *The Original Yoga*, New Delhi : Munshiram Manoharlal Publishers Ltd., 1980, p. xvii.

3. The *cakras* referred to by Radhakrishnan are mentioned in *Śiva-Saṁhita* and Patañjali's *Yoga-Sūtra*. The *cakras* are points alongside the spinal column and the head. The *Mūlādhāra* is identified as located in the sacrum, at the bottom of the spinal cord. *Svādhiṣṭhāna* is located four centimetres above, at the sex centre, *Maṇipura*, near the navel, *Anāhata*, inside the heart, *Viśuddha*, inside the throat, *Ajñā*, between the eye-brows and *Sahasrāra*, in the brain-centre. The last one is considered the abode of consciousness or the self. Both *Śiva-Saṁhita* and *Yoga-Sūtra* emphasize the special role of these spots or pockets of psychic energy since concentrating on them helps converting potential energy into actual energy. (*Śiva-Saṁhita*, V. 63-74; 92-99 *et. seq.* and *Yoga-Sūtra*, III. 21-35).

4. *Yoga-Sūtra*, I. 31.

5. *Op. cit.*, p. 352.

6. *Ibid.*, p. 337.

7. The Yoga system does not have a metaphysics of its own. It accepts the metaphysical categories of *Prakṛti* (the non-conscious principle) and *Puruṣa* (the principle of consciousness) proposed by the Sāṁkhya system and, following the lead given by that system, is concerned to work out the practical means of regaining the state of purity of *puruṣa* which was lost, thanks to its contact with *prakṛti*. It is this emphasis on the technique of achieving the ultimate ideal through studying the various states of consciousness

that are generally experienced that makes for the psychological analysis that characterize the Yoga system.

8. *Yoga-Sūtra*, I. 5-11.
9. This may be truly referred to as self-realization; for, in it is involved the realization of the true nature of the self. It is obvious, persistent efforts are required to achieve the state of purity of consciousness.
10. *Yoga-Sūtra*, II. 29.
11. The hyphenated expressions, "physical-psychological" and "psychological-spiritual" made use of here need some explanation. The first expression signifies that even the physical exercises (*āsanas* and *prāṇāyāma*, for instance) have their psychological effects. Hence it would be inaccurate to consider them as pure forms of physical exercise. The second expression means that the ideals sought after is not something extraneous to the nature of man. It can be achieved only when the purely psychological level is transcended. This is the metapsychological level of personality-development, as we have described it in the text of the present paper; and, reaching out to this aspect of personality is referred to as "spiritual realization" or "self-realization."
12. *Op. cit.*, pp. 354-355.
13. *Ibid.*, p. 355.
14. *Ibid.*
15. *Ibid.*
16. *Ibid.*
17. *Ibid.*
18. *British Medical Jouurnal,* December 5, 1903.
19. *Op. cit.*, p. 356.
20. *Ibid.*, p. 345.
21. *Yoga-Sūtra*, I. 4-5.
22. *Op. cit.*, p. 351.
23. The emphasis laid on realizing the distinctive characteristic of the self in one's own experience signifies that an intellectual comprehension of the distinction between *citta*

and *puruṣa*, while it may be considered a *necessary condition*, is *not* to be regarded as a *sufficient condition* for achieving full personality-development.

24. The mind together with the five cognitive sense-organs (*jñānendriyas*) and the five conative sense-organs (*karmendriyas*) are known as the psychical evolutes. The cognitive organs are : the senses of hearing, touch, sight, taste and smell. The conative organs are : the senses of speech, prehension, movement, excretion and reproduction.
25. *Sāṁkhya-Sūtra*, II. 26.
26. *Op. cit.*, p. 336.
27. *Life of Tennyson*, Vol. I, p. 320.
28. R.K. Wallace, H. Benson and A. Wilson, "A Wakeful Hypometabolic Physiologic State" in *American Journal of Physiology*, September, 1971; Michael West, "The Psycho-Somatics of Meditation" in *Journal* of *Psycho-Somatic Research*, Vol. 24, 1980; and K.N. Udupa, *Stress and Its Management by Yoga*, Delhi : Motilal Banarsidass, 1985. These are just a few studies which have been cited. There are scores of others which are equally important.

11
Radhakrishnan and the Development of a Global Paradigm of Meaning

DAVID M. BROOKMAN
Hays State University

Since the publication of Thomas Kuhn's *The Structure of Scientific Revolutions* in 1962, it has become fashionable to refer to the emergence of paradigms in various fields of human endeavour. Accordingly, the term "paradigm shift" indicates a " . . . cultural and political shift from a mechanistic and patriarchal worldview to one informed by holistic, ecological, and postpatriarchal concepts and values."[1] A paradigm, then, is an accepted model or pattern. But, as Kuhn points out, a paradigm is rarely an object for replication. Rather, it becomes" . . . . an object for further articulation and specification under new or more stringent conditions."[2]

On the basis of Kuhn's multiple definitions of paradigm found in various parts of his book the following definition may be offered : "A constellation of achievements - concepts, values, techniques, etc. - shared by a scientific community and used by that community to define legitimate problems and solutions."[3] Fritjof Capra has extended this definition beyond science in order to define a social paradigm : "A constellation of concepts, values, perceptions and practises shared by a community, which forms a particular vision of reality that is the basis of the way the community organizes itself."[4]

The thesis of this paper is that Sarvepalli Radhakrishnan sought to articulate a paradigm of meaning that would transcend the limitations and distortions produced by extreme identification with a particular religious tradition or nationalistic ideal. In the final analysis such a paradigm would be created only through an act of interpretation that would synthesize the disparate yet complementary insights of East and West. Thus, when Radhakrishnan wrote in the Preface of his Brahma Sūtra commentary that the hopes of a better world lie with the creative interpreters,[5] he provided a succinct statement of his own intentions. For it is implied that the present state of the world requires change, that change is possible and that the work of the interpreter can contribute to it.

In his "Fragments of a Confession"[6] as well as in a 1955 address[7] he identified what for him was the root issue : the world, unified as a body, is groping for its soul. He recognized that material, economic and political processes shape the world. But he also held that the world could not endure without psychological unity and spiritual coherence. Ultimately, he thought that confusion in the world is a reflection of the confusion "in our own souls."[8] The panacea required is

> .... a free interchange of ideas and the development of a philosophy which will combine the best of European humanism and Asiatic Religion, a philosophy profounder and more living than either, endowed with greater spiritual and ethical force, which will conquer the hearts of man and compel peoples to acknowledge its sway.[9]

Throughout his writings Radhakrishnan sounds again and again the note of urgency which reflects the tensions of his

Indian milieu as well as the stresses of the international environment. As he explains in the Preface of his Brahma Sūtra commentary,

> This book is not a product of purely scholarly interests. It has grown out of vital urges and under the pressure of a concrete historical situation. We are in the midst of one of the great crises in human history, groping for a way out of fear, anxiety and darkness, wandering in search of a new pattern in which we can begin life over again.[10]

Radhakrishnan makes at least two assertions here based upon personal value judgments. First, a breakup of traditional patterns has occurred which requires reintegration. Second, this crisis is global in character and in scope. Elsewhere he maintains that the world is undergoing changes so vast that they are hardly comparable to changes which occurred in the past.[11] Previously, he says, civilizations collapsed from external attack. But today the malignant forces work from within.

The symptoms of this malaise are obvious : division, fighting, lack of discipline and absence of a common purpose.[12] But its cause is no less apparent. "The present unrest, it is clear, is caused as much by the moral ineffectiveness of religion, its failure to promote the best life as by the insistent pressure of new knowledge on traditional beliefs."[13] Here, in Radhakrishnan's most original work, is echoed the awareness that there is a causal link between the lack of a vital spirituality on the one hand and incoherence in cultural life and political affairs on the other. In this work and in others is articulated the nostalgia for a lost unity which organized religion is unable to restore. Even those people who do have contact with some form of religion may profess a creed merely for the sake of appearance, habit or convenience.[14] But organized religion, as it is presently constituted and practised, is, in Radhakrishnan's view, incapable of ameliorating the difficulty.

At the same time it is clear that what Radhakrishnan understood as philosophy, not the historical forms of religion, would contribute to the discovery of the factors needed to effect the reintegration process. Some indication of the parameters of this philosophy is provided in the following :

> It is the function of philosophy to provide us with a spiritual rallying centre, a synoptic vision, as Plato loved to call it, a samanvaya, as the Hindu thinkers put it, a philosophy which will serve as a spiritual concordant, which will free the spirit of religion from the disintegration of doubt and make the warfare of creeds and sects a thing of the past.[15]

Radhakrishnan proposed to use this "synoptic vision" to preserve the spirit of religion while at the same time jettisoning all that he regarded as parochial and divisive.

He complained that contemporary philosophy is detached and specialized, that it does not deal with transcendental things but with scientific and secular concerns only.[16] One need only peruse chapter two of his *An Idealist View of Life* to realize that his evaluation of many trends in twentieth century Western thought was essentially negative. Among these he included naturalistic atheism, agnosticism, scepticism, humanism, pragmatism, modernism and authoritarianism. None of them, he wrote, satisfy" . . . the primal craving for the eternal and the abiding. . . ."[17]

Philosophy for Radhakrishnan has, then, the negative task of critiquing all that does not contribute to the vital spirituality which he believed animated the historical forms of religion. But its positive function is the recovery of this vital spirituality from the traditions of East and West by disengaging it from historical forms and by synthesizing it into a new gestalt. "There are bits of knowledge here and there," he remarked, "but no visible pattern."[18] It is noteworthy that the trajectories present in Radhakrishnan's understanding of philosophy - the criticism of much of contemporary Western thought and the recovery of wisdom from golden ages of the past - correspond to the neo-Hindu reaction against Western "materialism" and the rediscovery of the glories of ancient India.

In sum the interpretive task of philosophy for Radhakrishnan is, therefore, to revitalize and synthesize for the purpose of creating a new pattern of meaning - a new paradigm - which could replace the ones that have been destroyed. Any contribution in this vein would presumably help to restore the psychological unity and spiritual coherence lacking in the contemporary world. Radhakrishnan set forth the vision of spiritual fellowship to be realized in a "city of God in and out of time"[19] as the ultimate symbol of reintegration. Philosophy accordingly places upon the interpreter an ethical demand to meet the present-day requirement for meaning in order that the metaphysical union of heaven and earth might be accomplished at some point in the future.

When one sets out to create a new pattern of meaning, what norms or set of rules should apply? Radhakrishnan always tried to link his own interpretation of texts to what he understood to be the needs of the present human situation. He contended that, at the foundation of all the major religions is "the recognition of a Transcendent Supreme, the freedom of the human individual as a manifestation of the Supreme and the unity of mankind as the goal of history."[20] Accordingly, *samanvaya* (reconciliation, harmonization) is the instrument which, when applied to the utterances of the masters of all sacred traditions, will make explicit this unity and thereby facilitate its realization. In the final analysis such unity is, for Radhakrishnan, grounded in the suprasensory experience of transcendent reality reported by the seers of all religions.

Whereas Śaṁkara restricted the application of *samanvaya* to *śruti*, Rāmānuja expanded the legitimate field for harmonization to include *smṛti* as that is defined in the Vaiṣṇava tradition. Rāmānuja conceived the commentator's task as one of finding " . . . a method of interpretation by which all conflicting statements can be reconciled and given their proper place in a consistent explanatory system."[21] Thus the whole Bhagavad Gītā was interpreted by Rāmānuja so that it formed a consistent whole. And the different parts which make up this whole were explained as consistently as possible. Radhakrishnan shared with Rāmānuja the assumption that all scriptures are equally authoritative although scripture obviously has a much broader meaning for Radhakrishnan than Rāmānuja could have imagined.

In fact Radhakrishnan found in the text of the Bhagavad Gītā a synthesis of idealism—the presupposition that ultimate reality lies in a realm transcending phenomena - and realization. These emphases, along with imagistic and symbolic representations, provide three basic trajectories according to which Radhakrishnan attempted to forge a global paradigm of meaning. In the following examples Radhakrishnan's translation of each Gītā *śloka* will be accompanied by discussion of the appropriate non-Indian text.

Bhagavad Gītā 2.53. *śrutivipratipannā*
yada sthasyati niścalā
samādhāu acala buddhis
tadā yogam avāpsyasi
When thy intelligence, which is bewildered by the Vedic texts, shall stand unshaken and stable in spirit

(*samādhi*), then shalt thou attain to insight (*yoga*).

Śloka 2.53 is situated in the midst of Kṛṣṇa's discourses on the merits of *buddhi-yoga*. Previously, he has counselled Kṛṣṇa that whatever he does must be done in a spirit of detachment (2.47). Not until the third *adhāya* will he suggest that it is better to work than to do nothing at all.

Radhakrishnan, in his commentary, points out that "*samādhi* is not loss of consciousness but the highest kind of consciousness." In a footnote he avers that "it is what Plato means when he exhorts the soul to 'collect and concentrate itself in its self'."[22] When *samādhi* has been achieved, according to Radhakrishnan, the mind is in communion with the Divine Self.

At the conclusion of section 82 of the *Phaedo* Socrates maintains that the soul views existence through the bars of a prison and not in her own nature. The captive soul, through desire, is led to conspire in her own captivity. But philosophy counsels the soul that the senses are full of deceit and so tries to persuade her to desist using them except when necessary. Thereby she might be "gathered up and collected into herself, and to trust only to herself and her own intuitions of absolute existence, and mistrust that which comes to her through others and is subject to vicissitude...."[23] Otherwise, pleasure and pain rivet the soul to the body so that she believes to be true that which the body affirms and so excludes herself from communion with the divine and pure and simple.

The question raised by Radhakrishnan concerns whether *samādhi* is what Plato means when he has Socrates say, in *Phaedo* 83 A, that the soul ought to be gathered up and collected in herself. Eliade states that the meanings of the term *samādhi* include "union, totality; absorption in, complete concentration of mind; conjunction."[24] He, however, prefers to translate it as "enstasis" or "stasis." The final result of all the ascetic's spiritual efforts and exercises is this state which is a modality peculiar to yoga. It is this state which makes possible the self-revelation of the Self (*puruṣa*). The passage from "knowledge" to "state" is, in Eliade's opinion, the characteristic feature of *samādhi* and, indeed, of all Indian meditation.

> The 'rupture of plane' that India seeks to realize, which is the paradoxical passage from *being* to *knowing*, takes place in *samādhi*. This suprarational experience, in which reality is dominated and assimilated by knowledge, finally leads to the fusion of all the modalities of being.[25]

Radhakrishnan, in asserting that *samādhi* is the highest kind of consciousness, receives some support from Eliade who says that non-differentiated enstasis implies consciousness which "is saturated with a direct and total intuition of being."[26] And there does appear to be some parallelism between the *samādhi* state and the state of the soul described in the *Phaedo*. Both have to do with reliance upon intuition, the overcoming of the prevarications of sense experience and the attainment of a divine state.

The sources of divergence between the *samādhi* state and Plato's description of the state of soul seem to lie, on the one hand, in the paradoxical state of yoga itself and, on the other, in the fundamental dualism which seems to structure Plato's thought. The yogin

> is in life, and yet liberated; he has a body, and yet he knows himself and thereby *is puruṣa*; he lives in duration, yet at the same time shares in immortality; finally, he coincides with all Being, though he is but a fragment of it, etc.[27]

The yogin overcomes the dualism between body and spirit by integrating them, not by ultimately separating them as is apparently the case in the *Phaedo*. Also, the yogin does not achieve a state of communion with the divine and pure and simple. He actually becomes all Being, eschewing divine communion as a conditioned state. It is these divergencies which Radhakrishnan does not attempt to reconcile in his identification of "spirit" with *samādhi* and of "soul" with *buddhi*.

Bhagavad Gītā 6.10.   *yogī yuñjīta satatam
atmānaṁ rahasi sthitaḥ
ekākī yatacittātma
nirāśīr aparigrahaḥ*
Let the yogin try constantly to concentrate his mind (on the Supreme Self) remaining in solitude and alone, self-controlled, free from desires and (longing for) possessions.

Radhakrishnan finds in the parable of the rich young ruler (Luke 18. 18-30) a resonance with the teaching of Gītā 6.10 to remain "self-controlled, free from desires and (longing for) possessions." The parable, from verse 22 through verse 25, follows :

And when Jesus heard it, he said to him, 'One thing you still lack. Sell all that you have and distribute to the poor, and you will have treasures in heaven; and come, follow me.' But when he heard this he became sad, for he was very rich. Jesus looking at him said, 'How hard it is for those who have riches to enter the kingdom of God! For it is easier for a camel to go through the eye of a needle than for a rich man to enter the kingdom of God.'

The remainder of the parable, verses 26 through 30, is a dialogue between Jesus and others present. In reply to their query, "Who then can be saved?" Jesus tells them that what men find impossible is not so for God. When Peter points out that they have abandoned their possessions to follow

Jesus, the latter responds that any who have abandoned possessions and family for the sake of God's kingdom will receive back many more times in this age and in the world to come.

It seems undeniable that in the Lukan parable as well as in Gītā 6.10 there is a common intentionality; namely, that possessions and family ties are impediments which must be cast aside if the spiritual life is to be practised with integrity. Indeed, Jesus' stringency on this point calls to mind the requirements of the life of the saṁnyāsin who, for all practical purposes, has died to society. But Jesus is even more radical because he calls upon his followers to sever their familiar ties before their worldly obligations to society have been fulfilled. So also the teacher of the Gītā - the yogin must remain aloof from desires and the longing for possessions. Radhakrishnan, therefore, has put his finger upon a common denominator of two of the world's religious traditions.

Ideologically, the matter is more complex. Success in yoga, at least in Patañjali yoga, is a matter of individual effort even with the superadded Īśvara. A positive result is contingent upon human will. That is, the demands for self-control and freedom from desires are continuous with the discipline of yoga and the eventual concentration and integration of the mind. In the broader context of the Gītā, however, the doctrine of grace enunciated by Kṛṣṇa introduces a discontinuity between the will of the devotee and the attainment of salvation. The realization of mokṣa is no longer contingent only upon the devotee's effort. In the Lukan parable attainment of God's kingdom is contingent upon His grace. That is, abandonment of worldly ties is necessary but not sufficient. In the parable of the rich young ruler, then, there is also an apparent discontinuity between the disciple's will and the attainment of the kingdom as there is between the aspirant's will and the attainment of mokṣa.

While recognizing that the grace of the divine is important in both texts, the end to be attained is different. The kingdom of God as the reign of righteousness and the attainment of *mokṣa* as deliverance from the prevarications of *māyā* are hardly identifiable, Radhakrishnan's implication notwithstanding : "We must get out of the slavery to things to gain the glad freedom of spirit."[28] Yet the act of relinquishing possessions and the dependence upon a gracious deity are features undeniably common to both Christian and Hindu spirituality.

Bhagavad Gītā 11.9. Saṁjaya uvāca
evam uktvā tato rājan
mahāyogeśvaro hariḥ
darśayām āsa pārthāya
paramaṁ rūpam aiśvaram

Saṁjaya said :
Having thus spoken, O King, Hari, the great Lord of yoga, then revealed to Pārtha (Arjuna), His Supreme and Divine Form.

Beginning with *śloka* 11.9 the text narrates the transfiguration of Kṛṣṇa whereupon Arjuna has a vision of all beings within the divine form. The awesomeness of this vision, described through the utterances of Arjuna (11. 13-31), is communicated through vivid imagery and simile. These devices serve to reinforce the numinous quality of Arjuna's encounter.

Since it is Radhakrishnan's intention to universalize the spiritual experience of Arjuna in the Gītā, he calls the reader's attention to other examples of visionary experiences. According to Radhakrishnan the vision that Arjuna experiences".... is not a mental construction but the disclosure of a truth from beyond the finite mind."[29] Apparently he assumes as much about the other experiences which are now briefly described.

The unspecified reference to Ezekiel's vision in Radhakrishnan's commentary almost certainly refers to the event which occurred when Ezekiel received his call to be a prophet. The climax of the vision, following the observation of four living creatures in human form and the wheels beside them, is detailed in 1.28^a where Ezekiel describes a fire with encircling radiance. It was "like a rainbow in the clouds on a rainy day . . . ; it was like the appearance of the glory of the Lord." Indeed, the uniqueness of the event is emphasized through the first chapter by the use of a word which could be translated "semblance" or "like(ness)." The overall impression is that the prophet declined to speak, except in veiled terms, of God's manifestation. One might say that "the appearance of his glory and all that accompanied it is described as an image or symbol of the reality itself."[30]

Equally vivid is the vision reported by John in the fourth chapter of Revelation. Also striking are certain elements which the visions of Ezekiel and John share in common. John reports "four living creatures, full of eyes in front and behind." The first of these was like a lion, the second like an ox, the third with the face of a man and the fourth like a flying eagle (Revelation 4. 6-7). However, Ezekiel's creatures all have the face of a man in front, the face of a lion on the right while on the left they bear the face of an ox and the face of an eagle at the back (Ezekiel 1. 10). John may have simplified the more complicated imagery of Ezekiel which was inspired by the winged sphinx of the ancient Near East.[31]

But John's vision is dominated by a symbol of divine sovereignty, the throne of God. There was, he says, one seated on the throne who " . . . appeared like jasper and carnelian, and round the throne was a rainbow that looked like an emerald (Revelation 4. 2-3)." John does not say that he has actually seen God. Rather, the appearance of God was like brilliant jewels. Here the impression is that John encountered a brightness which at once revealed and hid God's presence. Again, the imagery of the rainbow was most likely drawn from Ezekiel.

These passages have at least two features in common. The first is that the glory of God was made manifest in some way to each of the receivers of this special knowledge. The second common feature is that, while each of the receivers felt himself to be in God's presence neither claims that he actually beheld God. At first glance some interesting parallels between these visions and Arjuna's experience of Kṛṣṇa's transfiguration present themselves. Arjuna beholds Kṛṣṇa-Viṣṇu's form as a "mass of glory" (tejo-rāśi) "shining everywhere" (sarvato dīptimantam) in śloka 11. 17^a. Yet in 11. 17^b this divine form is also "hard to see" (durnirīkṣya). It will be recalled that John also encountered a brightness which at once revealed and hid God's presence. The supernal majesty of Kṛṣṇa-Viṣṇu, relates the charioteer Saṁjaya, might resemble a thousand suns blazing forth together (11. 12).

Other details that are comparable among the visions include the mouths and eyes of Kṛṣṇa-Viṣṇu, mentioned in ślokas 11. 10 and 11. 23. In 11. 24 the mouths are described as "wide open" (vyātta) and the eyes are blazing and distended (dīpta-viśāla). According to Revelation 4.8 the four living creatues are full of eyes all around and within. They continually praise God in song. In Ezekiel's vision the rims of the wheels which were beside the creatures were full of eyes (1. 18). But the eyes are not a feature of God himself. There are, of course, other details such as Kṛṣṇa-Viṣṇu's tusks which are not comparable. But these Radhakrishnan might explain as the result of historical and cultural conditioning.

In Arjuna's vision the glory of the Supreme was made manifest to him as it was to the seers and prophets of the Hebraic and Christian traditions. At the same time none of the latter claims to have seen God whereas the vision in the

Gītā is replete with details of Kṛṣṇa-Viṣṇu's infinite form (*ananarūpa*) which include celestial garlands and divine fragrance (11. 11). In the Gītā simile is used to augment the reader's understanding of Arjuna's direct and powerful confrontation with the numinous. In the Hebraic texts simile enhances the ultimately ineffable and transcendent character of the numinous. Arjuna's *darśana* of the Lord in his bodily form is, then, the fundamental difference. And it is this which precludes inevitable reconciliation among these texts.

The Bhagavad Gītā commentary provides, perhaps, the clearest examples of the way in which Radhakrishnan sought to generate a global paradigm of meaning. On the one hand Radhakrishnan, in choosing his Indian texts, attempted to set forth Hinduism as a way of life, well integrated throughout in its many aspects. Radhakrishnan would maintain that even certain archaic aspects could be revivified and adapted to the needs of both Indians and non-Indians alike in the twentieth century. On the other hand, in choosing his non-Indian texts, Radhakrishnan attempted to demonstrate how certain directions in Western thought could be reconciled with the Gītā.

Thus the text of the Gītā served Radhakrishnan as a lens by which details in the "seamless" tapestry of Hinduism might be more clearly defined and by which the scattered light of the non-Indian traditions might once more be gathered and reintegrated. In a word the Gītā for Radhakrishnan is the keystone that holds in place the overarching paradigm of meaning by which he defined the relationship between India and civilization at large.

During the foreseeable future, however, Radhakrishnan's world-view, rooted as it is in his idealistic view of life, will remain a world view. The present reality, of course, is that people who inhabit our multicultural world subscribe to different paradigms concurrently irregardless of the limitations of these paradigms. The world view which Radhakrishnan projected is not yet a paradigm because it is not yet shared by the global community. What must happen before this world view can be either confirmed as a global paradigm or rejected?

Radhakrishnan's world view rests upon an epistemological base consisting of three different types of knowledge : perceptual, conceptual and intuitive or contemplative. The data of each type corresponds to the sensory, mental and spiritual domains, respectively. Perceptual knowledge, produced by sense experience, provides information about the external world. Conceptual knowledge, which depends upon the processes of analysis and synthesis, is indirect and symbolic in character. At this level there remains a duality of distinction between knowledge of a thing and its being.

It is intuitive apprehension which makes possible an individual's capacity for existential understanding and which, according to Radhakrishnan, undergirds the philosophical tradition of idealism. His term for this third level of knowledge is "Integral insight" because it utilizes not merely a portion but, rather, the whole of one's conscious being. "Integral insight" implies that the knower is united in some fundamental way with that which is known. While it does not contradict logical reason it goes beyond it and, according to Radhakrishnan, can be neither verified nor disputed. Radhakrishnan's assertion is unusually dogmatic in tone and hardly represents the final word on the matter of proof.

Now scientists, as a community of investigators, use experiments to rebuff erroneous factual claims. Having apprehended data through sensory channels, the scientist engaged a community of scientists to verify his or her results.

Similarly, scholars, comprising a community of interpreters, "can generate the intersubjective basis for a set of criteria that might validate the truth claims forming a coherent interpretation."[32] Finally, in the domain of spirit, the members of a "community . . . whose cognitive eyes are adequate to the transcendent..." either affirm or rebuff the transcendental apprehensions of individuals.[33] A Zen master and participant meditators, for example, share the responsibility to either verify or reject the validity of an intuition or insight.

It will be recalled that a paradigm emerges from the shared life of a community. The present writer would suggest that no community now exists which can claim the appropriate transcendental methodology to either verify or reject Radhakrishnan's metaphysical truth claims. As Paul Ricoeur observes

> . . . we are drawing closer to the moment of a creative encounter and the reshaping of a memory based on the opposition of 'near' and 'far;' but we are not in a position to imagine what that will mean for the categories of our ontology and for our reading of the Pre-Socratics, Greek tragedy, and the Bible . . . . It will not cease to be true that we were born to philosophy by Greece and that as philosophers we have encountered the Jews before encountering the Hindus and the Chinese.[34]

As this creative encounter unfolds and as a concomitant reshaping of memory occurs, then, perhaps, a community or communities will emerge that can offer the intersubjective basis upon which to either validate or rebuff the truth claims of Radhakrishnan's world view. In the meantime one may approach his commentarial work in particular as a protracted effort to translate a world view into a yet to be realized global paradigm of meaning. The role of the prophet who would dare to discern the shape of things to come is one necessarily fraught with anxiety and uncertainty. But it is the role for which Radhakrishnan will be remembered.

Bibliography

Anderson, Walter Truett; Callenbach, Ernest; Capra, Fritjof; and Spretnak, Charlene. "Preface," *ReVision*, IX (Summer/Fall 1986), 5.

Buitenen, J.A.B. van. *Rāmānuja on the Bhagavad Gītā*. 'S-Gravenhage : N. V. de Ned. Boek - en Steendrukkerij V/H H. L. Smits, 1953.

Capra, Fritjof. "Paradigms and Paradigm Shifts," *ReVision*, IX (Summer/Fall 1986), 11-12.

Corley, Keith W. *The Book of the Prophet Ezekiel*. Cambridge: Cambridge University Press, 1974.

Eliade, Mircea. *Yoga : Immortality and Freedom*. Princeton : Princeton University Press, 1970.

Harrington, Wilfrid J. *The Apocalypse of St. John*. London : Geoffrey Chapman, 1969.

Jowett, B. *The Dialogues of Plato*. Vol. 1, Oxford : Clarendon Press, 1871.

Kuhn, Thomas S. *The Structure of Scientific Revolutions*. Chicago : University of Chicago Press, 1962, 1962.

Radhakrishnan, S. "The Religion of the Spirit and the World's Need : Fragments of a Confession." In *The Philosophy of Sarvepalli Radhakrishnan*. Edited by Paul Arthur Schilpp. New York: Tudor, 1952.

_____. *Recovery of Faith*. New York : Harper & Bros., 1955.

_____. *An Idealist View of Life*. London : George Allen & Unwin, 1957.

Radhakrishnan, S. "Inaugural Address to Union for the Study of the Great Religions (India Branch)." In *Occasional Speeches* and Writings (October 1952-February 1959). Delhi : Government of India, 1960.

_____. *The Brahma Sūtra : The Philosophy of Spiritual Life.* New York : Harper & Bros., 1960.

_____. "Traditional Values and Modern Knowledge." In *President Radhakrishnan's Speeches and Writings* (May 1962-May 1964). Delhi : Government of India, 1965.

_____. *Recovery of Faith.* Vol. IV of *World Perspectives.* Edited by Ruth Nanda Anshen. New York : Greenwood Press, 1968.

_____. *The Bhagavad Gītā.* New York : Harper & Row, 1973.

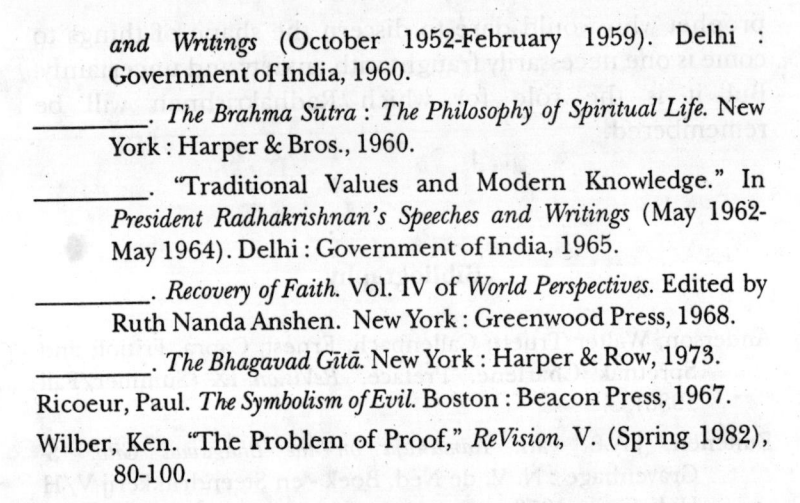

Ricoeur, Paul. *The Symbolism of Evil.* Boston : Beacon Press, 1967.

Wilber, Ken. "The Problem of Proof," *ReVision,* V. (Spring 1982), 80-100.

References

1. Walter Truett Anderson, *et. al.,* "Preface," *ReVision,* IX (Summer/Fall 1986), 5.
2. Thomas S. Kuhn, *The Structure of Scientific Revolutions* (Chicago: University of Chicago Press, 1962), p. 23.
3. Fritjof Capra, "Paradigms and Paradigm Shifts," *ReVision,* IX (Summer/Fall 1986), 11.
4. *Ibid.*
5. S. Radhakrishnan, *The Brahma Sūtra : The Philosophy of Spiritual Life* (New York : Harper & Bros., 1960), p. 8.
6. S. Radhakrishnan, "The Religion of the Spirit and the World's Need : Fragments of a Confession," in *The Philosophy of Sarvepalli Radhakrishnan,* ed. Paul Arthur Schilpp (New York : Tudor, 1952), p. 7.
7. S. Radhakrishnan, "Inaugural Address to Union for the Study of the Great Religions (India Branch)," *in Occasional Speeches and Writings* (October 1952-February 1959), (Delhi : Government of India, 1960), p. 303.
8. S. Radhakrishnan, "Traditional Values and Modern Knowledge," in *President Radhakrishnan's Speeches and*

Writings (May 1956–May 1964), (Delhi : Government of India, 1965), p. 141.
9. S. Radhakrishnan, "Fragments of a Confession," p. 7.
10. S. Radhakrishnan, *Brahma Sūtra*, p. 7.
11. S. Radhakrishnan, *Recovery of Faith* (New York : Harper & Bros., 1955), p. 3.
12. S. Radhakrishnan, "Traditional Values and Modern Knowledge," p. 141.
13. S. Radhakrishnan, *An Idealist View of Life* (London : George Allen & Unwin, 1957), p. 49.
14. S. Radhakrishnan, *Brahma Sūtra*, p. 9.
15. S. Radhakrishnan, *Idealist View*, p. 83.
16. S. Radhakrishnan, *Brahma Sūtra*, p. 10.
17. S. Radhakrishnan, *Idealist View*, p. 82.
18. S. Radhakrishnan, "Fragments of a Confession," p. 25.
19. S. Radhakrishnan, "Inaugural Address to Union for the Study of the Great Religions," p. 304.
20. S. Radhakrishnan, *Recovery of Faith*, Vol. IV of *World Perspectives*, ed. by Ruth Nanda Anshen (New York : Greenwood Press, 1968), p. 204.
21. J.A.B. van Buitenen, *Rāmānuja on the Bhagavad Gītā* ('S-Gravenhage : N. V. de Ned. Boek- en Steendrukkerij V/H H. L. Smits, 1953), p. 30.
22. S. Radhakrishnan, *The Bhagavad Gītā* (New York : Harper & Row, 1973), p. 122.
23. B. Jowett, *The Dialogues of Plato*, Vol. I (Oxford : Clarendon Press, 1871), p. 431.
24. Mircea Eliade, *Yoga : Immortality and Freedom* (Princeton : Princeton University Press, 1970), p. 77.
25. *Ibid.*, p. 82.
26. *Ibid.*, p. 93.
27. *Ibid.*, p. 95.
28. Radhakrishnan, *Bhagavad Gītā*, p. 195.
29. *Ibid.*, p. 272.

30. Keith W. Corley, *The Book of the Prophet Ezekiel* (Cambridge : University Press, 1974), p. 19.
31. Wilfrid J. Harrington, *The Apocalypse of St. John* (London : Geoffrey Chapman, 1969), p. 111.
32. Ken Wilber, "The Problem of Proof," *ReVision*, V (Spring 1982), 85.
33. *Ibid.*, 91.
34. Paul Ricoeur, *The Symbolism of Evil* (Boston : Beacon Press, 1967), p. 23.

12

Radhakrishnan and the Doctrine of Karma

NARAYAN CHAMPAWAT
California State University, Northridge

In this paper I shall argue that the doctrine of karma had a humble and reasonable beginning and as time went on it grew more complex and increasingly hard to justify rationally. Radhakrishnan recognized these difficulties and returned the doctrine to a more rationally defensible form.

Yjñavalkya, the first exponent of the doctrine of karma said, "Truly one becomes good by good action and bad by bad action."[1] Here he is enunciating a law of human nature which has wide empirical support. Indeed, a person's character is formed by his actions. A person does develop a virtuous character by doing morally right acts and he does become wicked by wrong acts. Let us call this the minimal doctrine of karma. So far no mention is made of rebirth. Nor does this doctrine require rebirth. But suppose you did believe in rebirth for some other reasons. Then it would be only natural to extend the doctrine and claim that a person inherits the character he developed in his last life. Thus he would inherit a propensity towards right or wrong acts, as the case may be, but he could overcome this propensity by his free choice.

The ancient thinkers also shared the scientific urge to seek explanations for natural phenomena. And it seemed to them that certain phenomena such as a person's natural life-span, his caste and certain other life experiences could only be explained by some features of that person's previous life.

Radhakrishnan himself develops this line of thought. "The self enters this life with a certain nature and inheritance. We commonly speak of talents that are inherited, an eye for beauty, a taste for music, which are not common qualities of the species but individual variations. So the self must have had a past history here and elsewhere."[2]

Note that this explanation is naturalistic, by which I mean, it makes no reference to any moral qualities. For example, in order to explain a musical child prodigy (Radhakrishnan refers to Yehudi Menuhin as a case in point) we need only postulate that he was a musician in his previous life; we need not claim that his being a musician previously was morally commendable and his being born a child prodigy was his 'reward.'

So far then we have two basis ideas : first, a person's character is inherited from his previous life and second, some of his unusual traits can be explained by reference to some features of his previous life. For all this, we need not go beyond one previous life.

How, then, do moral considerations come into the doctrine of karma. There seems to exist a need to believe that right actions (punya) result in happiness (sukha) and wrong actions result in unhappiness (dukha). Contrary to the law of character-formation, which we previously dubbed the minimal doctrine of karma, this moral doctrine is not based on any clear cut empirical data. In actual life, right actions often result in pain and wrong actions in pleasure. So the doctrine is a priori and the theory of rebirth is annexed to the doctrine to make it true. Perhaps this moral

Radhakrishnan and the Doctrine of Karma

version of the doctrine was considered a necessary motivation for moral behaviour.

Thus the doctrine was widened to explain both good fortune and misfortune by characterizing them as the consequences of right or wrong acts in a previous life. Hence, every benefit or harm that occurs to a person is the result of his own previous moral action.

At last, we have what I call the maximal doctrine of karma. Here is a paradigm case. Once, as the Buddha was walking through a forest with his disciples, his foot was pricked by a thorn. When asked to account for this painful experience, he replied that ninety-one kalpas ago he had struck a person with a spear.

As the example shows, the doctrine of karma asserts a theory of rebirth and a law of karma. A painful experience is seen as the consequence of a wrong act and the act and its consequence are separated by many lives. The doctrine is esoteric since we see no ordinary, natural connection between striking a person with a spear and being pricked by a thorn.

What exactly is the maximal doctrine of karma? It consists of a law of karma and a theory of rebirth :

Law of Karma

(1) Every right act results in a proportionately desirable consequence and every wrong act results in a proportionately undesirable consequence. In brief, every moral act has its appropriate *karmic consequence.*

(2) Every desirable event in a person's life is the *karmic consequence* of a right act previously performed by that person and every undesirable event is the *karmic consequence* of a wrong act previously performed by that person. In brief, every desirable or undesirable event has its *karmic antecedent.*

Theory of Rebirth

First Version

Karmic consequence of an act might occur in the same lifetime as the act or in the next lifetime. And, the karmic antecedent of an event might occur in the same lifetime as the event or in *the* previous lifetime.

Second Version

Karmic consequence of an act might occur in the same lifetime as the act or in some future life. And, the karmic antecedent of an event might occur in the same lifetime as the event or in any of the preceding lives.

For the maximal doctrine of karma, version one of theory of rebirth will suffice. For some unexplained reason, second version is always assumed.

Let us now look at some puzzles generated by the maximal doctrine of karma.

Here is a nice guy helping a blind lady across the street. He is happy that he is doing a good deed. We would say that his happiness is caused by his good deed and her happiness is also caused by his good deed. But, although the law of karma allows that the nice guy's happiness is caused by his own good deed, the blind lady's happiness cannot be caused by his good deed since a person's happiness can only be caused by that person's own previous right act. Soon, thereafter, comes the bad guy who trips the blind lady as she crosses the street and enjoys his mischief immensely. She of course is distraught. In this case too, we would say that his joy is caused by his bad deed and so too her sorrow. But not according to the law of karma. His joy cannot be caused by a wrong act so it must have been caused by some good act he had done before. Her sorrow too cannot be caused by his act but by her own previous bad act.

In fact, according to the law of karma no one can ever cause happiness or sorrow to anyone else. Everyone is a moral monad. Others can at best provide occasions for one to reap what one sows. Moral occasionalism does not appear any more intellectually satisfying than post-Cartesian mind-body occasionalism.

Another puzzle generated by the maximal doctrine of karma has to do with justice. By definition justice means giving a person what he deserves and injustice means a disharmony between a person's estate and his desert. But the doctrine of karma guarantees that everyone always gets what he deserves and nothing but what he deserves. So there can be no injustice, and all attempts to rectify individual or social 'injustice' are redundant.

Yet another puzzle comes from the existence of judicial systems which are central features of all states. These judicial systems aim at bringing about justice by attempting to punish all wrong doers or at least all criminals. However, if the doctrine of karma is true there is no injustice in the world; all wrong doers infallibly get their just deserts. This makes all judicial systems quite superfluous.

We need to dig deeper into the doctrine of karma to see if the puzzles can be solved.

Various discussions of the law of karma presuppose two different models : The Judicial Model and the Natural Law Model. The judicial model explains the operation of the law of karma as being analogous to the operation of a judicial system within a state. The natural law model compares the law of karma to physical laws such as laws of electricity and magnetism.

Let us first examine the judicial model. Ideally a judicial system includes clearly stated laws, an agent who intentionally violates the law, a judge who determines guilt and passes a sentence and a punisher who carries out the sentence. The criminal knows exactly what crime he committed and what his sentence is. The punisher knowingly and voluntarily carries out the sentence and his action is morally right, not wrong. If the law of karma functions on the judicial model, there must be a God acting as the judge and there are persons who do wrong and punishers who carry out the sentences.

How does this scheme apply to our puzzle about the bad guy tripping the old lady? The old lady is being punished for some past wrong. But she does not know what her 'crime' is. The bad guy is her punisher. But he is not carrying out the sentence knowingly or voluntarily. Moreover, his action is considered to be wrong, whereas a punisher in carrying out a sentence does no wrong. So he is unwittingly meting out karmic justice while doing wrong. Sounds like a world according to Kaffka.

A judge brings about the infliction of punishment by persuading the punisher that the punisher is obligated to mete out justice. How does God bring it about that the bad guy trips the old lady? Clearly, he does not persuade the bad guy to do it. God cannot cause it since actions, being free acts, cannot have external causes. Furthermore, if God caused the bad guy's action, the bad guy is no longer responsible for it.

The judicial model of the law of karma does make human judicial systems superfluous and does assure that there is no injustice in the world. Far from solving the puzzles generated by the law of karma, the judicial model seems to create new ones.

We conclude that the judicial model is not a satisfactory way of understanding the workings of the law of karma.

Let us turn, then, to the natural law model. This model is based on the idea that the connection between an act and its consequence is nomological i.e. based on laws of nature similar to laws of physics.

In order to understand this model, let us imagine a case where a person, A, breaks his leg. This could happen in three ways : (i) self-caused, as when he jumps; (ii) other-caused, as when he is thrown by another; or (iii) nature-caused, as when the branch of a tree falls on his leg. In general, we could classify all events that happen to a person as either *person-caused* or *nature-caused* So, here is an undesirable, painful event B (breaking a leg) in A's life. What according to the law of karma is the cause of B? Remember that the cause must be a wrong act done by A himself; so it cannot be A's jumping or another's throwing A or the branch falling on A's leg. In case (i), we must have a causal chain going from *the* wrong act, W, (whatever it may be) through A's jump to event B. In case (ii), there must be a causal chain from W through another's throwing A to event B and in case (iii) there must be a causal chain from W through the branch falling to B. However, if we allow that human beings have free will then there cannot be causal chains such that human actions form a link in the chain. For instance, there can be a causal chain from a switch being turned on to a bulb being lit, but if a signal being given leads to an operator lighting a torch, then the link from the signal to the lighted torch cannot be causal since the operator is free not to light the torch. If this reasoning is correct, the natural law model can only explain nature-caused events but not the person-caused ones. But this would be a very severe blow to the doctrine of karma, since most of our joys and sorrows are caused by others or ourselves. We would be left with a very restricted doctrine of karma.

We conclude that the natural law model of the law of karma is not satisfactory either.

It does not seem possible to combine the idea of human free will and moral responsibility with that of a perfectly just world in which every desirable or undesirable event is seen as the karmic consequence of the person's own right or wrong action. The maximal doctrine of karma is fraught with grave conceptual difficulties.

Radhakrishnan wisely eschews the maximal doctrine of karma in favour of a character-oriented doctrine of karma. His doctrine is much closer to the versions first expounded by Yajñavalkya.

> "In the moral sphere no less than the physical, whatsoever a man soweth that shall he also reap. Every act produces its natural result in future character. The result of the act is not something external to it imposed from without on the actor by an external judge but it is in very truth a part of the act itself . . . our mental and emotional make up is reborn with us in the next birth, forming what is called character."[3]

Our actions form our character. Our character determines our next birth. We take birth in circumstances best suited to realize our character. Our character and circumstances condition our actions but do not determine them. We have free will. Hence his famous metaphor :

> "Life is like a game of bridge. The cards in the game are given to us. We do not select them. They are traced to past karma but we are free to make any call as we think fit and lead any suit."[4]

Radhakrishnan's version of the doctrine of karma sounds eminently reasonable when compared to the extremism of the maximal doctrine of karma. Of course, as a consequence, we get no necessary connection between a moral act and its karmic consequences but only a probabilistic connection. Furthermore, this version of karma gives no moral explanation for nature-caused events, since karmic explanations always involve the agent's character. It is not often that a branch falling on one's leg can be explained as the consequence of one's own bad character.

It is difficult to find good arguments in favour of Radhakrishnan's doctrine of karma. The maximal doctrine of karma was based on the intuition that the Universe forms a just moral order. If the Universe is just, every moral act must have its appropriate consequence and every appropriate event its karmic antecedent. This evidently does not happen within one life, hence there must be rebirth. Such is the reasoning that yields the maximal doctrine of karma. But that intuition is much too strong for a probabilistic character-oriented karma theory. What Radhakrishnan does instead is fortify his karma theory with the intuition that the Universe is a stage upon which an individual plays out his drama of salvation. Since one life is not enough to attain salvation, a person must keep being reborn until he attains salvation. Karma links his character and circumstances from one life to another.

Radhakrishnan believes that it is possible for a person to attain salvation (mokṣa) and escape rebirth while engaging in action. This appears to be contrary to the doctrine of karma which states that your actions, good or bad, *must* bear their consequences in future lives. This problem is solved by the concept of niṣkāma karma (action without attachment) and the claim that niṣkāma karma does not have any karmic consequences. The idea seems quite reasonable. Only actions done with the desire for their fruit are reinforcing and therefore mold one's character. With niṣkāma karma a person has transcended conditioning and thereafter he is not obliged to be reborn although he may freely choose to do so for the benefit of humanity.

Radhakrishnan also believes that the drama of the cosmos will continue until everyone is redeemed. His doctrine of karma fits in with this idea too.

If a person starts on the path of virtue he will keep purifying his character until he reaches the state of niṣkāma karma and becomes a free spirit. There is no sliding back. On the other hand, if a person starts on the path of vice, his character will degenerate. But this is not irreversible. Sooner or later, given that a person has innumerable lives, he will turn around and embark on the path of virtue. Thus eventually everyone will be liberated.

Radhakrishnan's life goal was to revivify Indian philosophical heritage by discarding the untenable and the archaic and thus making it a viable philosophy of life in an age of science and rationality. His treatment of the doctrine of karma is a beautiful example of his method.

References

1. Brhadāranyaka Upaniṣad 3.2.13.
2. Radhakrishnan, S., *An Idealist View of Life* (London : George Allen & Unwin Ltd.), 1971, p. 289.
3. Radhakrishnan, S., "*Hinduism*" in Basham, A.L., *A Cultural History of India* (Oxford : Oxford University Press), 1975, p. 76.
4. Radhakrishnan, S., *An Idealist View of Life*, (London : George Allen & Unwin Ltd., 1971), p. 279.

13

On Having More than One Home

HARRY M. BUCK
Wilson College

A few years ago, near the end of October, we visited a family whose small son was planning his Hallowe'en costume. He persistently queried me : "What are you going to be?" While I fumbled for an answer, because I hadn't planned any trick-or-treat adventures, he insisted over and over, "But everybody has to be something." Everybody has to be something - some one thing. Robbie, at his young age, had thoroughly grasped the notion that has governed our social relationships for many centuries. We must wear some sort of mask - our *persona*.

I can pin on many labels. I am professor, an author, a husband of one wife, a father of two sons, a grandfather of four grand-daughters. I am a homeowner and tax payer, a card carrying member of several organizations including the American Association of Retired Persons, the National Association of Railway Passengers - even the ACLU. I could recite my social security number, my real primary identification these days.

But these labels — some more significant than others - tell you virtually nothing about my real selfhood, even though without them I am something of a no-person. I have no "belonging place," as my Madras friends so aptly refer to it.

We can hardly deal with someone we cannot classify : Jew, Arab, Tamil, Sinhalese, Sikh, Lingayat, Vaisnavite, Irish Catholic, liberal, feminist, conservative, Southern Baptist, white Anglo-Saxon Protestant. These identification tags are political, linguistic, religious, and nationalistic. Although you may display more than one label, rarely do they overlap, and they must not be contradictory. You must be something, living somewhere, belonging to this or that.

Before the days of routine air travel the mighty Himalayas insulated India from the rest of the world. Japan could close its ports to *guyjin* ("outside persons"), and Americans lived on a comfortable island separated by two vast oceans from the turbulence of Europe, smugly unconcerned about Asia. In those days we thought we knew who we were and where we lived. *We* belonged; *they* were foreigners.

Although the century that produced Sarvepalli Radhakrishnan was to change all this, political, social, and religious behaviour remained largely unaware. Colonizing powers used their military might to subjugate vast areas of the world, including India. Religious communities - particularly the monotheistic ones - strengthened the walls of their fortresses, reaching outside their boundaries only to gain converts. Most of us remained content within our fences; we were really afraid to step outside, to give up a secure identity. We preferred to live, as it were, in purdah. Such isolated luxury is inappropriate in the present age. Indeed, it may be suicidal, a warning signalled by Dr. Radhakrishnan half a century ago.

Don't Fence Me In

It was my privilege to meet Dr. Radhakrishnan in connection with the Third East-West Philosophers' Conference at the University of Hawaii in Honolulu in the summer of 1959. I shall never forget his thrilling plenary address[1] three decades ago where he stressed the need to give up certain pervasive ideas : (1) the militaristic approach, (2) nationalist sentiment, and (3) the feeling of helplessness on the part of the human individual. He called for a religious realization that can produce "the transformation of oneself, the transmutation of one's whole being so as to make it one integrated whole." He then extended this vision to the family of nations on this planet. No doubt Radhakrishnan's experience as a sensitive Indian helped him develop these insights, since India has more religious diversity than any other nation in the world, despite its predominantly Hindu patina.

As he spoke, a popular song from the forties ran through my head : "Don't Fence Me In." In India - as elsewhere - it was typical for religious communities to build fences around themselves to preserve the purity and integrity of their own institutions.

Walls and Barriers

We build our barriers higher and higher, echoing the words of the Reformation hymn, "A mighty fortress is our God." Biblical religion has conditioned our actions and even dictated the character of warfare with its sharp choices between "truth" and "falsehood" ("abomination."). "If 'Moses' God *is* God,' as Pharaoh Yul Brynner complained in *The Ten Commandments,* 'then everyone else's god . . . isn't.' Over the long haul this basic principle can lead to, certainly lends itself to, intolerance."[2] If I accept this judgment and live by it, I can have only one "belonging place." Here I stand; from this position I speak. You stay on your side, and I'll stay on mine, for "good fences make good neighbours."

The rejoinder that such a posture presents only what the sixties called "organized religion" ignores the fact that by definition religion is organized. Except in most unusual cases, we do not explore concerns of ultimate Reality on our own as solitary individuals. Information does not just "float around the universe at random; information to *be* information has to be codified, channelled, protected, and received. Between humans, it can then be shared and transmitted from one life, or from one generation, to another."[3] Although religion in its varied forms has been one of the most important creative impulses in the world, we cannot deny that much of it is dangerous. When used as the legitimators of corporate or national power plays, the religions of the world have even been called "licensed insanities,"[4] exhibiting precisely those characteristics that Dr. Radhakrishnan urged be removed from our thinking.

Adherents regard their accumulated information as so important that it must be preserved and transmitted. This requires boundaries - to keep the faithful in and the infidels out. What is being protected is not words and ideas only; it is behaviour patterns, costume, language, social organizations, the regulation of sexual conduct, and so on; most of it communicated by techniques far more powerful than mere words. Since these information banks have developed over such a long period of time, we can understand a reluctance to change. In times of tension—and our lives are full of it—strong "fundamentalism" will have wide appeal. It provides a safe harbour, a place where I can know I belong. Religious leaders, popes, imams, sheiks, pundits, evangelists, bishops, and gurus, remain "boundary-minded," and their adherents want just that kind of secure home. It is only a creative minority in any religious system—be it Hindu, Buddhist, Sikh, Jewish, Muslim, or Christian—that has broader vision.

Experience or Tradition

Patriarchal religion lives in tension between experience and tradition. Theologians tend to hold their legacy of faith and practice as normative. Human expereinces that would suggest otherwise must, then, be suspect. Nonetheless, in our own day we hear more and more voices crying out to insist that if repeated experience is at variance with tradition, the tradition may be in need of revision—a truth the Buddha knew well some 2,500 years ago. "Eho passika" he said to inquirers : "Come and see for yourself."

Radhakrishnan stressed this as early as 1926 in his Upton Lectures at Manchester College, Oxford.[5] Perhaps his view of Hindu-ism is overdrawn, but what he said then continues to have universal application :

> Religion is not the acceptance of academic abstractions or the celebration of ceremonies, but a kind of life or experience. It is insight into the nature of reality (*darsan*), or experience of reality (*anubhava*). This experience is not an emotional thrill, or a subjective fancy, but is the response of the whole personality, the integrated self to the central reality. Religion is a specific attitude of the self, itself and no other, though it is mixed up generally with intellectual views, aesthetic forms, and moral valuations (p. 13).

The life of truly sensitive persons, then, will go well beyond any religion or even beyond religion itself, for the goal will never be the protection of the integrity of any institution. Nor do we meet the issue by simply repudiating our past. Indeed, we cannot jump out of our skins. It rarely suffices to leave one house completely and move into another. Conversion is usually not the answer to a problem; it simply substitutes one set of boundaries for another.

We cannot expect that the great religions of the world will abandon their high walls in our time, but we do not need to remain inside. Instead of crouching in the shadow of any particualr tradition, we can stand firmly on it and reach beyond it. Then we can even be comfortably at home in more than one house. In time we may want to give up all our religious fortresses so that the real spirituality that underlaid them in the first place can be rediscovered, that is, to give up religion for God's sake. "It is not healthy," Sister Joan Kirby maintains, "to protect religious security within a high and impenetrable wall. If your search for God is a threat to my faith, then that sets a wall between us, and that is not good." She sees a paradigm in the Christian Jesus, who

> surrendered power and prestige. He avoided solidarity with a group of religious insiders. He went outside the walls, in order to express his compassion and love for the poor and oppressed . . . . He was required to move beyond the fence. In fact, he so scandalized his contemporaries that he was put to death beyond the walls.[6]

Where, Then, Is Home?

This is the heart of a central problem facing us in the latter days of the twentieth century, perhaps the latter days of Western civilization. Dr. Radhakrishnan knew it, and he was not alone in sounding this note on his prophetic trumpet.

Beyond the Meridian, to the Omega Point

Pierre Teilhard de Chardin believed that as the human race evolved, separation and specialization produced the fruits of modern culture, including science and education. He likened human progress to longitudinal lines moving upward on a globe, ever expanding and diverging from each other. But, he cautioned, we have passed the meridian. It is time to see these discrete elements move back toward each other, toward what he called the "Omega Point,"[7] to recognize our human unity in the midst of developed diversity, drawing on the unique contributions each of these diverse ways can provide.

The words of W.C. Smith[8] have stayed with me for many years. Writing about Christians he asserted that "God does not give a fig for Christianity. God is concerned with people, not with things. We read that God so loved the world that He gave His Son. We do not read anywhere that God loved Christianity." Today the comfortable island or the mighty fortress, containing all truth, is clearly an illusion. Those we call heathen are not there for the purpose of being converted to the Truth - which, of course, we believe we possess in abundance and with certainty.[9] Dr. Radhakrishnan's reply to such a point of view was simple and direct:

> Hinduism repudiates the belief resulting from a dualistic attitude that the plants in my garden are of God, while those in my neighbour's are weeds planted by the Devil which we should destroy at any cost.[10]

Planet Earth Is Our Home

We have been searching for the wrong guru. If the needs of the late twentieth century cannot be served by converting from one system of faith to another, in the illusion that at least one of them can provide a safe refuge, we may need to go beyond them all, striking out in courage, beyond Hinduism, beyond Christianity, beyond Judaism or Islam, Sikhism or Buddhism. This may be the best way for each tradition to maintain its integrity and yet be part of a harmonious whole.

This is not repudiation, neither is it thoughtless amalgamation or syncretism. It is a series search for ultimate

Reality amid the myriad partial loyalities clamouring for attention. When the gopis sported with Lord Kṛṣṇa they did not repudiate their human loves. Two strings sounding together produce music neither could perform alone. When each string remains true, a violinist can play on two or even more at the same time. If we learn to participate fully in more than one tradition, the result exceeds the sum of its parts.

The arrogance that marks our religious life has been intensified in recent decades with an unparalleled arrogance toward all of creation. The West has sold its soul to the illusion of progress, which, put in its simplest terms, has meant primarily the invention of more efficient means of converting irreplaceable raw materials to nondegradable trash. In its sense of guilt at being dubbed underdeveloped, the East has been rushing to catch up on this suicidal race. Our arrogant posture has reified our religious traditions, isolating us from each other and separating us from the world in which we must live if human life is to survive.

Dr. Radhakrishnan's concern to give up the militaristic approach, nationalist sentiment, and the feeling of helplessness must not only heard again in our day but strengthened and carried beyond what he was able to see in Honolulu in 1959. For survival we need more than one home, or to put it another way, our only real home is this entire planet. "The human is less a being on the earth or in the universe than a dimension of the earth and indeed of the universe itself," as Thomas Berry observes.[11]

Religion transformed to serve in this period can provide the integrative force that will draw our disparate competitions together to celebrate the wholeness of the universe, a holy living whole. We cannot succeed by pitting one system of faith and life over against another nor by looking at other ways of life only through the window of our own fortress. "The supreme need of our times is to bring about a healing of the earth through this mutually enhancing human presence to the earth community."[12] In this task there is no religious system extant that can completely fill the need, but there are many that can contribute. To contribute means just that, to be a part of the whole.

K.R. Sundararajan recalls that the traditional world is isolated, but the modern world is interdependent. All major religions grew up, he said, in a world where outsiders did not matter, and we could fence ourselves in with impunity. But, he continues, "we cannot meaningfully ignore 'outsiders.' The time has come for all world religions to develop some kind of global theologies to deal adequately with those 'outsiders,' now neighbours, instead of attempting to convert them, or simply closing their eyes and ignoring their presence."[13]

Such a realization cuts deeply into the psyche of most religious people. "Our Father who art in heaven" has become a repository for the projection of our petty human strivings to dominate the universe and each other. We have not succeeded in solving what Reinhold Niebuhr called the human dilemma, the conflict between knowing that we are part of the whole created world and the conviction that somehow we are apart from it.[14]

Gods, in whatever tradition, project human values into the heavens. In monotheistic traditions, this is carried to extremes. Yahweh, who manifested himself to Elijah by his absence from earthquake, wind, and fire - the very places deity had been sought until that time - followed by commanding the military defeat of his people's enemies as service to God. Sukumari Bhattacharji has shown how Hindu solar deities eclipsed earthly ones.[15] It is an old pattern, allowing the patriarchal structures of religion to grow rapidly.

Territoriality soon followed, along with the assumption that each of us must belong to a particular tradition or community. Without labels to classify us we are nobodies. Dr. Radhakrishnan, although remaining an Indian and a Hindu, knew better. Not only can there not be among the whole range of humanity any chosen people, preferred by God above all others, even humanity itself cannot be seen as a chosen species. We are one among many. Just as various dharmas were assigned to castes, varnas, and jatis, human dharma and that of a dog or a palm tree differ from each other. One is no more important than another, and we do not condemn a palm tree for not being an oak, although both are nourished by the same soil and watered by the same rains. This is what is meant in Buddhism by *suchness*.

It is hard for us to think of ourselves in such a world. We are separated by language, colour, custom, and particularly religion. What separates persons who speak different languages - particularly when these languages are from radically different sources - is not a simple matter of vocabulary; it is frequently an expression of entire value systems. The same is true of what we call religion or its plural *religions*. We are not dealing, then, with ideas that matter only in our own solitariness. The transcedence of walls and fences is a matter of survival. Ultimate loyalties to partial truths can destroy us.

What, Then, Does It Mean to Belong?

The early chapters of Genesis tell of two trees, a tree of life and a tree of discrimination, called "knowledge of good and evil." Our forebears ate of the one and not of the other, learning to put labels on all aspects of human activity. We need discrimination, else we should know very little in our age, but now we must learn to eat of the tree of life. Many little streams flow into the mighty Ganges, and all rivers merge in the sea. Many grains of wheat and other crops are fused together in a loaf of broad. Many seekers after Truth must have beyond their concern for specific identities toward the reality that truly is God. Chandran Devanesen caught this spirit in his little poem :

> As a little bird
> flies into the leafy vastness
> of a tree,
> as a little rivulet
> flows into the swelling vastness of a sea,
> as a little seed
> sinks into the spreading vastness
> of the earth,
> Lord,
> let me come
> to Thee.[16]

To realize that because I am human I am heir to all human traditions is not a matter of simple eclecticism or syncretism, words that have become far more pejorative than they should be. It is rather an intelligent choice that transcends boundaries.

For many of us, there is a dilemma : What does it mean to belong? Is it a matter of place, ownership, description, or classification? Frequently one hears an Indian person ask another, "Where is your belonging place?" Rare is the person who will claim more than one. Yet, in the spiritual realm, it may be necessary; and I think that Dr. Radhakrishnan would agree were he addressing an audience today, for despite the deep-seated animosities among India's various communities, there is within the Indian spirit something that supports this approach.

We like to classify : He is a Buddhist; she is a Christian; they are Muslims; those people are Hindus; and over there are the Jews. This is convenient, like putting a name on a dog's collar if you don't wnat your pet to get lost. But the dog isn't Fido, and my name doesn't describe me. They are labels given by someone else.

Many of us would like to participate—to participate fully, to "belong"—in more than one context, and we often wonder just what it means to belong. It may be time to find a different word, for the whole sense of the word *belong* may be at the root of our problem.

Robbie was right in a sense, "Everyone has to be something." But he was dead wrong in believing that by donning a costume a person can be defined. I believe that the real defining act in human life is to love, to live, and to learn, to eat of the tree of life more than of the tree of judgment, to participate fully in the ultimate Reality of all there is - and by whatever human means there are.

I am not suggesting a spiritual smorgasbord, but I am suggesting that when we drink of the waters of spirituality we may use more than one spring. Then we can see that Jesus is not only for Christians, or Gautama only for Buddhists, or Moses only for Jews, or Kṛṣṇa only for Hindus. This would indeed be unfortunate.

References

1. His plenary address, "The Present Crisis of Faith" was reprinted in Charles A. Moore, ed., *Philosophy and Culture*: *East and West* (Honolulu : University of Hawaii Press, 1962), pp. 754-761. This same volume contains his conference paper, "The Indian Approach to the Religious Problem," pp. 255-262.
2. Stanley N. Rosenbaum, "Monotheism and the Roots of Intolerance," in Louis J. Hammann and Harry M. Buck (eds.), *Religious Traditions and the Limits of Tolerance* (Chambersburg PA: Anima, 1988), p. 7.

3. J.W. Bowker, "The Burning Fuse : The Unacceptable Face of Religion." *Zygon,* 21/4 (December 1986), pp. 415ff.
4. Idem.
5. Published as *The Hindu View of Life* (New York : The MacMillan Co., n.d.).
6. Hammann and Buck, chap. 20.
7. See, for example, Pierre Teilhard de Chardin, *Man's Place in Nature* (New York : Harper & Row, 1966).
8. *Meaning and End of Religion* (New York : MacMillan, 1963).
9. I cannot help recalling a missionary prayer service I happened to stumble into in Kathmandu, where one of the laides prayed earnestly and almost pathetically, "Lord, help us to love these Nepalese."
10. *Hindu View,* p. 89.
11. Thomas Berry in an unpublished address at the Riverdale Center, New York, February, 1988.
12. Berry, *ibid.,*
13. Dr. K.R. Sundararajan, "Progress allows for world spirituality," *The Bona Venture,* February 5, 1988.
14. Reinhold Niebuhr, *The Nature and Destiny of Man : A Christian Interpretation* (New York : Charles Scribner's Sons, 1943), Vol. 1, chap. 1.
15. Sukumari Bhattacharji, *The Indian Theogony* (American Edition, Chambersburg PA : Anima Press, 1988), passim.
16. Chandran Devanesen, *The Cross is Lifted* (New York : Friendship Press, 1954), p. 1.

14
Radhakrishnan's Approach to the Problem of Religious Diversity

J.G. ARAPURA
McMaster University

1. Introduction

Radhakrishnan belongs to the company of philosophers who have thought that the problem of religious diversity is important enough for philosophical attention. Hegel certainly belongs to this company. This problem is only a part of the philosophy of religion, and it is a part only if a particular philosophy of religion allows it to become a theme. In Radhakrishnan's thought it is a matter consciously dealt with, and it occupies a place of importance. But it does not get aired often though it deserves to be.

His approach to religious diversity accords completely with his idealistic metaphysics on the whole, especially with his interpretation of the Absolute. [Parenthetically, I may simply characterize his idealism as idealism of the spiritual life, with emphasis on both 'spiritual' and 'life'.] In this respect, the first thing that seems most noteworthy is his contention that, since religion signifies a universally available knowledge-and-experience relation to the absolute (the word relation not to be taken literally), it is necessary that religion as such, not to say any particular religion, be not thought of absolutistically.

Religion's proclivity to become absolutistic, Radhakrishnan seems to suggest, comes about in two ways : One, in terms of its tendency to regard the knowledge of the absolute it possesses as final, with the inevitable result that it gets formalized and then petrified. Accordingly, he criticizes it, and recommends the example of science, which sees its truths as "provisional and tentative,"[1] as relevant to the religious quest too. The other, in terms of the utter pre-eminence that one religion may feel towards the others, Radhakrishnan describes it as "religious absolutism which attempts to legislate for the whole universe and believes in an isolated supernatural revelation"[2] for itself. He adds that this is due to "the dualistic philosophy" which insists that God is "distinct and separate from the world." [The logic of this is not explicit but is valid in an implicit way, nonetheless.] And, in a sentence to follow, he advances the Advaitic consciousness of "those who are anchored in the centre of all being" as a surety against this error inasmuch as they "know that every religion is a response to a divine condescension that has uplifted us." [It would appear that the postulate of the divine condescension as the origin of religion, i.e., of the *religions* (plural), might bear being stated independently as well, because it is an independent one, with very many implications.] Radhakrishnan suggests that different religious traditions are "like different languages" which convey a set of very special facts but which have an underlying unity embedded in "the same spirit."[3] [This is mainly based on the romantic view.]

At this point, his mind deftly moves to show that if we can cure religion's proclivity to be absolutistic - in the two respects discussed -, the diversity in which religion appears and functions among human beings can itself be turned around and be used to demonstrate the existence of the absolute Being. This is especially the case in respect of the facts of religious experience as they are stored and conveyed through concepts. But Radhakrishnan contends that such conceptual frames must be treated as tentative and provisional, exactly in the manner he had said previously in respect of our outlook on all religious truths, in wholesome emulation of science's attitude towards its own truths. But in the present case the point is different, which is to argue that the tentativeness and provisionality of conceptual expressions - and other types of expressions - of the facts of religious experience furnish evidence to the existence of the absolute Being, rather than to the opposite. It is thus that Radhakrishnan is able to say : "After all, conceptual expressions are tentative and provisional, not because there is no absolute but because there is one."[4] The point further is to argue that these characteristics of religious expressions, conceptual as well as other, are the vindication of religion's inevitable - and thoroughly wholesome - diversity. This understanding must go hand in hand with the belief in the existence of the absolute. So then, if diversity bears testimony to the absolute, the absolute vindicates diversity. This reciprocality of logic between the two seems to me to be adroitly conceived and consistently carried out throughout Radhakrishnan's writings on the subject.

It will be instructive to see how Radhakrishnan's view is in stark contrast with the well-known speculative formulation of Hegel. For Hegel, the spiritual principles underlying the life and the vogue of the religions as living manifestations of the spirit exist in a vertical succession in history, i.e., arranged in progressive stages, each, however, annulling and also preserving as well as exalting all the previous ones (expressed by his celebrated Concept of *aufheben*).[5] Hegel saw the unity of all successive spiritual forms, embodied in their respective stages, from the speculatively presumed end-point of the *Weltgeist*'s march, where stands "a religion (that) has the absolute concept of the spirit as its principle."[6] That religion for him is Christianity, centred on "the incarnation of the divine being," and it is absolute religion. Thus he writes :

> This incarnation of the Divine Being, its having essentially and directly the shape of self-consciousness, is the simple content of Absolute Religion. Here the Divine Being is known as Spirit. This religion is the Divine Being's consciousness concerning itself that is Spirit .... In this form of religion the Divine Being is, on that account, revealed ....[7]

What precisely did Hegel mean by absolute religion, i.e., Christianity in what sense, is a matter of debate. Is it a spiritual form comprehended in speculation and at the same time the actual Christianity of history transfigured speculatively? Emil Fackenheim, in his excellent book, *The Religious Dimension in Hegel's Thought*, demonstrates convincingly that the Christianity presumpposed and transfigured by Hegel, especially in the *Philosophy of Religion*, "is astonishingly close to the Christianity of History."[8] Also, this Christianity is, specifically, modern Protestant Christianity," adds Fackenheim.[9] Suffice it to say, in short, that for Hegel, diversity in religion reaches - has reached - an end-point at which it has been spiritually subjected to *aufheben* by one absolute religion. What happens between that "absolute religion" and the "absolute philosophy" is beyond our purview, and beyond our call to discuss. But we cannot be oblivious of the suggestion that that religion too is transfigured by philosophy, for which, however, spirit is the basic term (of correspondence).

Further, in fairness to Hegel, it is needful and useful to know what he was reacting to while struggling with the subject of religion and the religions. It should be clear that he was fighting on three fronts - firstly, against the Enlightenment doctrine of a natural or rational religion in general; secondly, against the romanticists' acceptance of the truth claims of all religions, along with their naive view of unity in this very plurality; and thirdly, against Schleirmacher's oblique Christian apologetics, but without a sense of historicity, put forward as "religion of religions" and consequently ending up as a sheer doctrine of universal intuitionism.

Hegel seems to find the solution in breaking down pluralism to concrete particularities, assigned for their genuine life-vogue to successive states where each religion in its own rightful stage must confront others and then absorb them. The process comes to its fulfilment in the *"revealed"* religion. But as Fackenheim points out, "comprehensive is that 'revealed' means."[10] Again, this concretely particular religion, for which the claim of absoluteness is made, sheds some of the offensiveness acquired because of the claim, in light of Hegel's view typified by the following statement:

> The Christian religion will emerge as "the religion of Truth and Freedom. For Truth consists of not being related to the objective as something alien. Freedom expresses the same as Truth, with the determination of negation .... Here the negation of distinction of otherness is stressed, hence Freedom appears in the form of reconciliation.[11]

The equation of the concretely particular religion with the particular form of the spirit is such that when read in opposite directions the meaning and the implications would profoundly change. So then, one may also wonder whether religion, at the point of the concretely particular Christian religion, is not so internalized in the Spirit that it is not only speculatively transfigured but actually speculatively transcended. Many orthodox Christian theologians have had this suspicion, and they may be right.

Now, returning to Radhakrishnan, I may call attention again to certain matters. Firstly, he saw the significance in the fact of religious diversity itself as evidence of the inadequacy of any and all expressions, and therefore, felt no need to break it down into particularities, with all the Hegelian implications of doing so, not did he, for that matter, subscribe to the solutions of any of the three views against which Hegel himself had striven. There is no evidence for that. Secondly, as pointed out earlier, Radhakrishnan rejected any suggestion of the absoluteness of religion *per sec*, whichever way religion is viewed, and with whatever end, for the absolute alone is absolute.

'Experience' is the key word in Radhakrishnan's thought. He explicity declares that philosophy of religion "must become empirical and found itself on religious experience."[12] And as he works it out, experience is profoundly concrete and personal too in character, especially at the height.[13] And yet the object experienced — the Absolute — is beyond personality. At the summit it is a mystical "apprehension of the real and an enjoyment of it for its own sake."[14] Radhakrishnan has worked it out in detail, taking into account all its complexities, under the name "integral experience." His choice of experience, or *integral* experience, as the ground of the whole structure is the main reason why he rejects Hegel's view of religion as a form of knowledge,[15] grounded, we might add, in speculative thought. The difference is epochal. Radhakrishnan has an extremely effective way of juxtaposing the reality of experience and the reality experienced and then elevating the former to the level of the highest veracity so long as it is uniquely juxtaposed with the latter as absolute reality, i.e., *qua sat-cit-ānanda*, which he translates as "reality, consciousness and freedom," [i.e., *ānanda* as freedom instead of bliss].[16] "The experience," he writes, "is real though inarticulate."[17] "The real was there actually confronting us."[18]

From experience conceived in this manner **expression has to be distinguished**, but also seen as related in these crucial ways : (1) As body to soul - "If experience is the soul of religion, expression is the body through which it fulfills itself."[19] The word 'body' is a direct translation of *śarīra*, as used in Advaita, signifying all kinds of media, or forms, at once necessary and dispensable : religions, and religious texts too would be called 'body.' And "all forms," Radhakrishnan adds, "according to Śaṁkara, contain an element of untruth, and the real is beyond all forms."[20] But then, this position too must, because under the species of absolute reality *qua sat-cit-ānanda* it can, be turned around such that the diversity of forms may be approached positively under the principle of one truth, many expressions. From Radhakrishnan's point of view, this is a thoroughly positive dialectical turn around entirely worthy of the subject-matter of religion's diversity.

2. The Principle of One Truth, Many Expressions

A. As Embedded in the Indian Religious Tradition

Radhakrishnan rightly sees this principle of one truth, many expressions which he has laid as the corner-stone of his approach to religious diversity, actually to have been also derived from the Indian tradition. He reflects the critical wisdom of that tradition, often turned towards itself, when he writes : "No god seems to be final and no religion perfect .... The history of religion is the record of the conflicts of contradictory systems, each of them claiming dogmatic finality and absolute truth, a claim made apparently absurd by the plurality of claimants .... Spirit is growth, and even while we are observing one side of its life, the wheel is turning and the shadow of the past is twining itself into it."[21]

Again :

> The symbols and dogmas are not definitive. Eastern forms of religion hold that differences of interpretation do not affect the one universal truth any more than the differences of colours

affect the uncoloured light which is transmitted. Western forms of religion are inclined to hold that one definition is final and absolute and others are false. In India, each definition represents a *darśana* or viewpoint. There are many ways of viewing one experience. The different *darśanas* are different viewpoints which are not necessarily incompatible. They are pointers on the way to spiritual realization. If religious truth is seen by different groups in different ways it is not to deny the truth is ultimately one.[22]

"Every expression of truth," he observes subsequently "is relative. It cannot possess a unique value to the exclusion of others. It cannot be the only possible expression of what it expresses."[23] Many-ness is not only numerical, but a qualitative *apriori* condition for the relation of expression to the one truth.

This whole position ultimately rests upon the famous statement in the *Ṛg Veda* (1.164.46): "One is the truth, the sages speak of it diversely" - *ekam sat viprāḥ bahuthā vadanti.* We also can perceive that these words did not come out of the blue but were uttered in the context of an existing theological controversy, as the rest of the passage says "they speak of/call upon [him/it] as Agni, Yama or Mātarīśvan" - *agniṁ yamaṁ mātarīśvānam āhuḥ.* It is apparent that the *Ṛg Veda* too was resolving a pluralistic religious situation although, there only bordering between "polytheism" and its own inner destiny. The word *ahuḥ* (from *a + hve*) has the double meaning of speaking and invocation or worship. Various gods have been mentioned in different places as the true deity to be worshipped, for which a resolution is indicated in *Ṛg Veda* 3.55.1 in the words *mahat devānām asuratvam ekam,* which M. Hiriyanna happily translates as "the worshipful divinity of the gods is one."[24]

Sayings bearing the same idea can be found scattered throughout old Indian sacred literature, upon which Radhakrishnan draws profusely. Some of these may be cited here. The *Yoga-vāsiṣṭha* has the following : "Sages have called it by many names, such as *Ṛta, Ātman,* supreme *Brahman* and Truth, for the sake of our empirical consciousness."[25] Elsewhere, "To the Sāṁkhyans it is the Person, to the Vedāntins it is *Brahman*, to *Vijñāna-vādins* it is the alone holy *Vijñāna*, to the *Śūnya-vādins* it is *Śūnya*, to the Worshippers of Eternal Light it is the Illuminator. It is the Speaker, the Thinker, *Ṛta*, the Enjoyer, the Seer, the Maker, all these."[26] [We can not fail to note parenthetically, that various *darśanas* are introduced here.]

The *Bhāgavata* also has something especially interesting to say : "Just as one and the same object residing in many qualities become manifold as perceived by the different senses, so also it is (the same God) known in different ways through different scriptures."[27] [The interesting aspect of this passage is that the notion of the different scriptures (*śāstras*) as the media of the same God/Truth is brought into play. But for us now this is by the way.]

There is a famous verse in the *Bhagavad Gītā* (4.11), which Radhakrishnan translates thus : "As men worship me so do I accept them; men on all sides follow my path, O Pārtha."[28] This is used by Radhakrishnan as well as several modern writers as a text for "one truth, many expressions," and also for "one spiritual goal, many paths." This is a new use of this verse which seems to have started with Vivekananda. Radhakrishnan himself cites it as a text bespeaking "the (same) transcendent spiritual aim of all historical religions."[29] Actually, classical interpretations by Śaṅkara and others do not allow this wide meaning, but that is not a point to be pressed here. However, within the given tradition itself, it does have a great metaphysical bearing as to the relation between one goal and the many paths; and in a purely deductive way, it could be interpreted to have a bearing on the relation between truth and its expressions. However, Radhakrishnan sees it somewhat more directly and puts it more categorically : "The Hindu thinkers are conscious of the amazing variety of ways in which we may approach the Supreme, of the contingency of all forms.... From the stand-point of metaphysics (*paramārtha*), no manifestation is to be taken as absolutely true, while from the stand-point of experience (*vyavahāra*) every one of them has some validity."[30]

Besides the Indian tradition, Radhakrishnan dips deep into much of the world's literature, Western, Islamic, Chinese, in that order, to find support for his view of one truth, many expressions; one God, many symbols (forms); and one goal, many paths. Thus, just one example here from Meister Eckhart : "God never tied man's salvation to any pattern.... One good does not conflict with another ... for not all people may travel the same road."[31]

B. *The Principle Carried Through on the Basis of Mysticism*

The part of the Indian tradition Radhakrishnan has appealed to in support of the principle, being largely also the source of its inspiration, is pointed in the mystical direction. And it is further buttressed by the appeal to mystical writings from other traditions. And he recognizes mysticism as that part of religion, present universally, which is apt to give flesh and bone to the principle. So he fastens the principle on to it. I am not suggesting, however, that the extraction of the principle is the sole reason why he explores mysticism. But I am suggesting that it is one, and in comparison with various other studies of mysticism his is unique and original.

As a rule mysticism has been approached with either of two diametrically opposite assumptions, accordingly reaching similar conclusions. Thus, at one end stands the belief that somehow mysticism is a kind of inner religion subtly pervading all the religions, obliterating all distinctions or at least rendering them totally insignificant and trivial. This belief has strong affinities with certain trends in romanticism. Without going that far, however, Radhakrishnan too has reached the conclusion that "a study of the classic types of mystical experience discloses an astonishing agreement which is almost entirely independent of race, clime or age," but cautions that "an ultimate inward similarity of the human spirit does not mean absolute identity of mystical experience."[32]

At the other end, there is the tendency to make strong distinctions on the basis of religious or theological determination of types of mysticism, that is where mysticism is accepted as significant at all, more specifically between Christian and Eastern, prevalent among some theologians and philosophers of religion. Radhakrishnan severely criticizes this predilection "to distinguish Eastern mysticism from that of the West, or to be more precise, Hindu mysticism from Christian, by contrasting the immense ethical seriousness of the latter with the ethical indifference of the former."[33] [The reference is mainly to Albert Schweitzer's *Indian Thought and Its Development*, and F. Heiler's *Prayer* (*Das Gebet*).]

Radhakrishnan's criticism would be based on his own view that even though in terms of the mystic's apprehension of the absolute - and consequently in terms of communication -, there will be room for religious determination, the truth that underlies the apprehension still transcends the mode of it and hence the form by which the truth is communicated. This is what really makes a mystic mystic. "It matters not," he writes, "whether the seer who has the insight has dreamed his way to the truth in the shadow of the temple or the tabernacle, the church or the mosque."[34] So in mysticism "one truth, many expressions" is still the rule. As

Radhakrishnan sees it, "truth wears many vestures," and these "vestures" are also of the nature of "intellectual representations."[35] As mysticism by definition is the sole act *within* religion which can revolt against all forms this rule still holds. For, "those who have the radiant vision of the divine," he remarks, "protest against the exaggerated importance attached to outward forms."[36] [But this is not any social protest.]

However, this principle validates variety within mysticism, as surely as it testifies to unity of the truth. For, "the mystic," Radhakrishnan observes, "is convinced of the inexhaustibility of the nature of God and the infinite number of its possible manifestations."[37] But it runs along lines of individual and cultural variations as much as along lines of religious diversity. The last is overlaid by the others. But the mystic must be able to see the variety as but expressions of the one truth. This truth is the reference of what Radhakrishnan speaks of as "the universality of mystic experience," being so despite the by-no-means unimportant "differences in the formulations of it."[38] And it is on account of that (and of nothing else) that "the mystics of the world, whether Hindu, Christian or Muslim, belong to the same brotherhood and have striking family likeness."[39]

Now, Radhakrishnan would inquire as to the way by which the often-missed one-truth focus of mystic experience, especially in its historically attested variety be illuminated. What he seems to suggest is that while in other aspects of the religions the one-truth focus is apt to be blurred on account of the diversity, in the mystical aspect it is recoverable, though that still does not imply that the variety of expressions will have to go. Radhakrishnan's argument is that mysticism alone has this capacity whether we are speaking of possibilities within religion or outside.

The theoretical framework in which he gathers all this, with the truth-focusing mysticism as the ground and model, is of the essence of what he has called "integral experience." The emphasis of course, is on the integrating rather than on the analytic method. The possibilities here are, I think, tremendous and are worth exploring.

The concept of 'integral experience' as used by Radhakrishnan has some difference compared to the way it was used by others before him - Bergson mainly, inasmuch as behind his use stands the great Indian tradition of *Jñāna*, or gnosis (not of course in the Gnostic sense).

At one time, however, **Radhakrishnan** preferred the word *anubhava* to *jñāna*[40] for conveying his meaning of integral experience. The reason seems to be that the sense of experience, which as a religious experientialist he wanted to stress, is too concealed in *jñāna*. *Anubhava* he says is "a vital spiritual experience."[41] It is "to know and to see in oneself the being of all beings, the Ground and the Abyss."[42]

As for *jñāna*, I am one who feels that in whatever way it can be brought to bear on modern thought it will be to the good. But then each way will always have to be specified as being pointed to some particular end. Radhakrishnan laid special emphasis on the "experience" (*anubhava*) and the "integrating" aspects of it and pointed it in the direction of spiritual life, anchored to mysticism, which in turn lives within religion. So then the burden of the whole project here under consideration is something peculiarly human that man does, called religion, which he does diversely.

3. The Spiritual Uses of Religious Diversity

I began this discourse with the statement that Radhakrishnan belongs to the company of philosophers who have thought that the problem of religious diversity is important enough for philosophical attention. Now we have reached a point at which we may consider the other side of the matter, namely how Radhakrishnan speaks of that diversity as a positive resource for our spiritual good.

At the background stands something very unique, namely, Radhakrishnan's vision of the future of the human race, and the role that religion (in its diversity, of course) may play in it. "There is no future for man apart from the religious dimension," he declares.[43] This stance is entirely different from Auguste Comte's positivism, or even Hegelian idealism, not to speak of the more radical views of our time; different also from the one-religion views of thinkers with a definite theological bias, who see the future in terms of their own particular (usually Christian) faith and its prophetic modes. Here then is another kind of prophetic vision - profoundly human too - which looks upon future as somehow to be mediated by religion in its character of diversity "which enshrines precious spiritual gift,"[44] as Radhakrishnan puts it. However, Radhakrishnan also seems deeply to believe that the essence of the historically conceived future depending for its advent upon mediation by the objective reality of religion in its diversity has for that reason a universal religion that goes with it, which he characterizes as "religion of the future" and as "experiential." 'Experiential' in this context would mean that is of the nature of immediacy. As we have seen, experience of this kind is the source of religion in the historical sense. The experience is the undifferentiated experience of the seers in primordial terms. Differentiation is due to the individual adaptation of it, attended by the advent of systems, dogmas and rituals. Thus Radhakrishnan writes : "When we find that the great seers of religion do not prescribe definite systems or dogma or ritual. They invite the soul to its lonely pilgrimage and give it absolute freedom in the faith that a free adaptation of the divine into oneself is the essential condition of spiritual life."[45] The undifferentiated is the pre-differentiated. Now, at the other end, i.e., in the future, what we should hope for is a post-differentiation "unity of religions,"[46] which, however, because of religion's passage through diversity, consequent upon the differentiation of primordial experience, is "not featureless" : so Radhakrishnan states. As I understand Radhakrishnan's thought here, diversity itself would signify mediation from the one end to the other, carrying the *telos* of immediacy *a la* experience, and unity. In that sense, again, it is both necessary and yet dispensable : these two terms, in a way of thinking are basic to any historical creativity.

Here we notice the framework for a very hopeful outlook. And it can be translated into a number of practical prospects of utilizing religious diversity such as we have, now that we have it. These I shall outline as follows :

(i) *The Meeting of the Religions.* This is the title of Chapter VIII of *Eastern Religions and Western Thought*. "The different religions," Radhakrishnan writes at the opening, "have now come together, and if they are not to continue in a state of conflict or competition, they must develop a spirit of comprehension which will break down prejudice and misunderstanding and bind them together as varied expressions of a single Truth."[47] "Every historical view is a possible, perfect expression of the Divine, capable, not in spite of but because of its peculiarity of leading us to the highest. The distinctiveness has a special appeal to the group."[48]

(ii) *Inter-religious Friendship.* This is the title of Chapter VIII of *Recovery of Faith*. Radhakrishnan visualizes all the varied religions as individual edifices erected on a common foundation of limitless dimensions. "There is," he writes, "a common element in all religious experience, a common foundation on which it rests its faith and worship. But the building that is erected on this foundation differs with each individual. God's architecture is not of a standard pattern."[49] Radhakrishnan believes that this inter-religious reality is a creative thing. It entails laying stress on diversity rather than on unity and it is capable of being undertaken, no doubt, under the already existing conviction of unity - for unity does not fall under the category of creativity : it is beyond it. Hence in inter-religious fellowship, the principle of one truth, many expressions is obverted (but, no doubt, to be held side by side). Accordingly, he writes : "This dynamic fellowship is based on the principle of diversity in unity which also has the quality of creativity."[50] [This comes out as a little twist in the process of his writing. There are many such. Actually, such twists are most important for understanding a great thinker's mind.] Here it would seem that each of the many expressions of the one has a destiny, which, however, in order to be realized has to be joined up with all the other expressions. Accordingly, it is remarked, as the very conclusion of *Recovery of Faith* : "We can so transform the religion to which we belong as to make it approximate to the religion of spirit. I am persuaded that every religion has possibilities of such a transformation. We must look upon Hinduism or Christianity as part of an evolving revelation that might in time be taken over into the larger religion of the Spirit."[51]

(iii) *The Fellowship of Religions*. This is the title of Chapter VI of *Religion in a Changing World*. Here and in other places (especially in "The Fragments of a Confession" (*The Philosophy of Sarvepalli Radhakrishnan*),[52] he interweaves Hinduism's traditional comprehensiveness with the new Christian-ecumenism, pointing to a larger, universal ecumenism, of the religions. At several points here as elsewhere, especially in *Religion and Society*, he integrates into this the spiritual basis of democracy, and the freedom of conscience. "The

Vedas," he writes, "ask peoples of the earth to walk together, to talk together and think together to secure peace on earth."[53] Pages are filled with quotations from the Buddha, the *Talmud*, the *New Testament*, and the *Qur'an*, admonishing their respective followers to honour other religions.

(iv) *The Fellowship of the Spirit.* This is the title of his address, opening the Centre for the Study of World Religions at Harvard in 1961.[54] The idea of fellowship of the spirit directly follows from Radhakrishnan's over-all theory of the religion of the spirit, which, while not a super-religion, seems to grant one a spiritual vantage point from which to criticize the religions for their failure to accomplish their mission, and at the same time provides also with the vision to see their yet higher, common destiny lying out there in the future. The dispensation of the religions, with all their short-comings is not finished, he rightly believes. They are the means by which man plugs into his own spiritual destiny, which is never going to be out of date as a goal. For, "In the depths of his (man's) consciousness he feels that he is incomplete, that he has to be surpassed, that he has to enter a larger life of spirit and freedom, that he is still in the making, that he has to make himself. Religion has been the discipline used by man to achieve the goal of Spiritual ascent."[55] It is conceivable, however, that the religions themselves, unless they turn, and join together in a fellowship of the spirit, could be left behind, rendered irrelevant; and man's spiritual destiny, which will never become obsolete, will seek other directions for its self-realization, as it certainly is already marching to other trumpets. But then the loss of religion will be an irrecoverable one for spiritual life.

A Concluding Note

Radhakrishnan's philosophy, essentially, is the articulation of a vision of the spiritual life; and as such it is based very much on religion. But then, religion implies the religions. However, the reverse is also correct for him : the religions imply religion as well. The plural and the singular cannot be separated. And they are related in the manner of one truth, many expressions.

He approached the religions as they present themselves in the world, and yet with reference to an ability that human beings possess universally by virtue of "the spirit in man," which alone can identify and exalt something as religious. By religion, therefore, he means both a universal that is within the spirit in man and a number - any number - of concrete particulars. The universal is essentially experiential, and in that sense is really timeless. But recast in the mode of particularities, i.e., fundamentally, forms of expression, we can speak - as indeed we think - of genesis as well as *telos* (though not *eschaton*, to be sure), that is to say, the past beginnings and the future transformation, or *theosis*, or realization.

There are, no doubt, things in the particularities, i.e., in the religions as they are, that need to be corrected. But then particularity itself is not one of such things. We should not throw away the baby with the bath-water. The fact we have different kinds of religion is not an impoverishment; on the contrary, if we had only one kind of religion in the world our spiritual life would have been infinitely poorer. In Radhakrishnan's thinking there is no place for the idea of a monolythic, totalitarian, all-embracing religion. Accordingly, he writes : "To obliterate every other religion than one's own is a sort of bolshevism in religion which we must prevent . . . . For almost all historical forms of life and thought can claim the sanction of experience and so the authority of God. The world will be a much poorer thing if one creed absorbed the rest. God wills a rich harmony and not a colourless uniformity."[56]

The things in the particularities, i.e. in the concrete religions, that need be corrected can be corrected. But there is no guarantee that they will be. For, although religion is, in principle self-correcting, being self-critical, in actual fact is not automatically so - there is no automaton guiding the moral evolution of the religions. The correction must come from the spirit in man, which is dispenser of the one truth and its distributor into the diversity of expressions, and therefore the only judge of what is right. The spirit in man is also in the deepest sense personal, which, however, should not be construed to mean that it is *a person*. It is rather the basis of the personhood of persons; therefore in a profound sense it is corporate and social - and historical. It is what Radhakrishnan often calls "the whole man," who reacts "to the whole reality."[57] Religious individuals and communities must learn to criticize and correct themselves according to the spirit in man, and hence they must be ever vigilant.

Radhakrishnan believes that for these things to happen everything in religion must be out in the open. In fact he would, as had Henri Bergson before him, call for an "open religion,"[58] so that every religion becomes a common human possession, a common human heritage.

In this context, it strikes one that Radhakrishnan does not speak about what is currently in the air, i.e., the so-called dialogue among the religions. Dialogue for him, it appears, is what takes place between human persons; and between a human person and the religions, any or all, on the basis of the spirit in man. The much touted dialogue of the religions seems to suffer from want of a basis. The theological ends of one participating religion cannot be that basis. Besides a person who internalizes the relation with "the other," which is possible only in terms of the spirit in man, is both the actor and the theatre of such a transaction. But then that transaction is also an invitation to other persons to do the same. This procedure, however, will lead only to a dialogue between persons and between a person and the religions on the common basis of the spirit in man, not on the wholly fallaciously presumed basis of the persons concerned either representing or embodying the respective religions, as such a thing is impossible. What we really have then is a common spiritual effort, a deeply philosophy-assisted one. Radhakrishnan would settle for that. That is the call we hear from his utterances. What we have then at best is a dialogue *with* the religions, not dialogue of, or between the religions. Even so, Radhakrishnan does not consider it to be exclusive but as the comprehensive essence of what he speaks of as "a dialogue with the world."[59]

The concept 'dialogue' is also where I should end this discourse. For, it too has been nothing more than an effort to hold dialogue with a great mind on a matter of some importance to him and great importance to me in the perspective of things philosophical. Accordingly, it has been, admittedly, largely expository. Not that there are not some points on which I may disagree, but that does not mean that I will agree with his critics, especially when the criticism comes due to philosophical allegiances that are totally at variance with what has moved Radhakrishnan and humbler persons like myself to philosophy.

References

1. Cf. S. Radhakrishnan, *An Idealist View of Life,* London, George Allen & Unwin, 1961, p. 13. *Note*: This is the edition to be used throughout for all references to this book; others have different pagination.
2. *Ibid.*, p. 94.
3. *Loc. cit.*

4. *Loc. cit.*
5. *Note* : The concept of *aufheben* has been traced back to Luther's translation of the *Epistle to the Romans*, 3.33, where he used *heben* . . . *auf* ("fulfilled" as well as "set aside") in reference to the Old Testament Law under the Gospel.
6. Hegel, *Lectures on the Philosophy of World History*, Trans. H.B. Nisbet, London, Cambridge University Press, 1975, p. 111.
7. Hegel, *The Phenomenology of Mind*, Trans. Sir J.B. Baillie, London, George Allen & Unwin, Sixth Impression, 1964, p. 758.
8. Cf. Emil L. Fackenheim, *The Religious Dimension in Hegel's Thought*, Bloomington and London, Indiana University Press, 1987, p. 119.
9. *Ibid.*, p. 22.
10. *Ibid.*, p. 127.
11. Hegel, *Werke*, XII, pp. 208 f.; here cited from Fackenheim, p. 129 fn. Cf. Hegel, *Lectures on the Philosophy of Religion*, trans. E.B. Spiers and J.B. Sanderson, London, Kegan Paul, Trench and Trubner, 1895, p. 346.
12. *An Idealist View*, p. 66.
13. *Ibid.*, p. 70 f.
14. *Ibid.*, p. 69.
15. *Ibid.*, p. 69.
16. *Ibid.*, pp. 11, 80.
17. *Ibid.*, p. 78.
18. *Ibid.*, p. 74.
19. *Ibid.*, p. 70.
20. *Ibid.*, p. 76.
21. *Ibid.*, p. 28.
22. S. Radhakrishnan, *The Recovery of Faith*, New York, Harper (*World Perspectives*), 1955, p. 155.
23. *Ibid.*, p. 157.
24. M. Hiriyanna, *Outlines of Indian Philosophy*, London, George Allen & Unwin, 1956, p. 39.

25. ṛtam ātmā param brahma satyammityādikā budhaiḥ; kalpitā vyavahārārtham tasya samjñā mahātmanaḥ., *Yogavāsiṣṭha of Vālmīki*, with the Commentary *Tātparya prakāśa*, ed., W.L.S. Pansikar, Vol. I, 3rd edition, Bombay, Pandurang Jawaji, 1937, iii, 1.12, p. 129.

26. yaḥ pumān sāṁkhyadṛṣṭinām, brahma vedānta-vādinām; vijñānamātram vijñānavidām-ekānta-nirmalam. yah śūnyavādinām śūnyo bhāsako yo'rkatejasām; vaktā mantā ṛtam bhoktā draṣṭā kartā sadaiva ca., *Ibid.*, iii., 5.6.7, p. 240.

27. yathendriyaiḥ pṛthak-dvāraiḥ artho bahuguṇāśrayaḥ eko nāneyate tadvad bhavagān śāstravartmabhiḥ, *The Bhāgavata*, iii.32.33.

28. ye yathā māmprapadyante tāṁs tathaiva bhajāmyaham mama vartma anuvartante manuṣyā pārtha sarvasaḥ. See S. Radhakrishnan, *The Bhagavad Gītā* (text, trans. and notes), London, George Allen & Unwin, 1963 edition, p. 158.

29. *The Recovery of Faith*, p. 156.

30. S. Radhakrishnan, *The Bhagavad Gītā*, Trans. with Introduction and Notes, London, George Allen & Unwin, 1948; 1970, p. 158.

31. *The Recovery of Faith*, pp. 156-7 fn.

32. S. Radhakrishnan, *Eastern Religions and Western Thought*, London, Oxford University Press, 1940, p. 79.

33. *Loc. cit.*

34. S. Radhakrishnan, *The Hindu View of Life*, London, George Allen & Unwin, 1956 reprint, p. 35.

35. *Ibid.*, p. 36.

36. *Ibid.*, p. 35.

37. *Ibid.*, p. 34.

38. *Loc. cit.*

39. *Ibid.*, p. 35.

40. S. Radhakrishnan, *Indian Philosophy*, Vol. II, London, George Allen & Unwin, 1927, p. 510.

41. *Ibid.*, p. 1518.

42. *Ibid.*, p. 512.

43. S. Radhakrishnan, *Religion in a Changing World*, London, George Allen & Unwin, 1987, pp. 133-4.
44. *Loc. cit.*
45. *An Idealist View*, p. 161.
46. *Religion in a Changing World*, pp. 133-4.
47. *Eastern Religions and Western Thought*, p. 64.
48. *Ibid.*, p. 327.
49. *The Recovery of Faith*, p. 188.
50. *Ibid.*, p. 202.
51. *Ibid.*, pp. 204-5.
52. P.A. Schilpp, Editor, *The Philosophy of Sarvepalli Radhakrishnan (The Library of Living Philosophers)*, New York, Tudor, 1952, pp. 72, ff.
53. *Religion in a Changing World*, p. 129; Cf. *The Hindu View of Life*, pp. 58-59.
54. *Note* : The booklet, *Fellowship of the Spirit*, was published by the Center for the Study of World Religions at Harvard; distributed by Harvard University, Cambridge, MA.
55. *Ibid.*, p. 4.
56. *The Hindu View of Life*, pp. 58-59.
57. *An Idealist View of Life*, p. 69.
58. *The Fellowship of the Spirit*, p. 63.
59. *Religion in a Changing World*, p. 13304.

15
Radhakrishnan as the Exponent of the Advaitic Approach to the Question of Encounter of Religions

ANINDITA N. BALSLEV
Aarhaus University

The Indian renaissance - as it is often described - witnessed ideological clashes on all planes. Radhakrishnan's concern for religious questions, having direct bearing on socio-political issues, stems from this awareness of conflicting ideologies. His reflections, scattered in many of his writings and speeches, exerted considerable influence on those who read him or listened to him thereby shaping their opinion, sometimes provoking controversies.

Radhakrishnan was acutely sensitive to the role that religion plays in all cultures and societies, and especially to the question of religious pluralism. His views are particularly valuable for several reasons. To begin with, an early exposure to another major religious tradition, apart from his own, viz. Christianity was a challenge, emotional and intellectual. Being born and brought up in a Hindu home and a considerable number of years of education in a Christian institution was an experience which quickly enabled him to see what meeting of religions entails in a concrete day-to-day situation. He has not hesitated to record the emotional reaction of his early youth.

Later, as a philosopher and a stateman, throughout his long career, he expressed his deep intellectual concern and tried to indicate of action in the face of a global situation which is plural in every sense. His words are a fair demonstration of the conviction that the question of religion is not confined only to the domain of contemplation. Religion is a power, an influence which guides human action, shapes human history. In the course of years he became a distinguished exponent of a philosophy of religion, fighting on two major issues which are still relevant viz. (a) how to and why combat anti-religious movements or ideologies based on secularism, (b) how to resolve conflicts of world religions. These are issues which no conscientious theologian of the twentieth century can afford to evade. Although it is the second issue which is the main concern of this paper, a few general observations may be made regarding the first Radhakrishnan's intellectual struggle with world-views based on secularism of one sort or another is illuminating in more than one way. Firstly, it clearly shows that his spiritual conviction about the role of religion in society was not born of any uncritical acceptance of an unexamined set of dogmas. He was fully conscious of the trends and tensions that dominated the minds of his contemporaries - that they had no more confidence in 'the simple consolation of religion' and that "it has become sign of good breeding to avow disbelief in traditional religion." But what is remarkable is to note with what searching mind he examined the assumptions and arguments hat led to disbelief, to which extent they could be justified and how much of these were due to "material success and intellectual conceit."

He certainly observed the slow but inevitable dissolution of many of the social codes and sanctions which formerly owed their support to religious beliefs. Many of these, he recognized, were welcome.

On a theoretical plane, he was aware of all forms of scepticism and gave full hearing to the repudiation of the dogmas of established religions.

He was aware of the plight of the fundamentalists and why it could not satisfy the modern man, let alone persuade the non-believer. He saw through the limitations of causal, moral and teleological arguments and why they could not convince.

He was equally mindful to the different schools of thought which were becoming influential, supported by sociologists who analyzed religion as a social phenomenon or by the scientists who held a mechanistic view of the universe and projected an altogether different image of the place of man in such an universe. A detailed and a careful survey of a sufficiently broad area of investigation made him familiar with alternative models which all departed from the views of traditional religions; these however, left him unconvinced. Radhakrishnan, on the contrary, saw in this critical and scientific temper of his days the assurance and the inevitability of a universal religion, as distinguished from established religion, about which he wrote and spoke tirelessly. Radhakrishnan realized that lack of faith has generated a sense of crisis in modern man, just as he recognized that much of the beliefs of established, organized religion have lost their value and validity. He expressed his view in the Preface of his book *"Religion in a Changing World"* in the following words :

> "We need a faith that is reasonable, a faith that we can adopt with intellectual integrity and ethical conviction, a large flexible faith for the whole human race to which each one of the living religions can bring its specific contribution.

We need a faith which demands loyalty to the whole of mankind, and not to this or that fraction of it...."[1]

It is an important perception that many of the ideals which are sought to be expressed in socio-political terms need first to be conceived clearly, without any ambivalence on the level of religious consciousness. On the other hand, once so conceived, their relevance is not only for the meditative mind. Radhakrishnan wrote :

"The religious soul must seek for divine fulfilment not only in heaven above but on earth below."[2]

In other words, the insight is to be understood as a realisable goal and not merely as an ideal to be admired in an abstract framework of contemplation.

Let's now focus on the question of religious pluralism as an issue for both sociological and theological concerns.

Conflict of religions is not a story of a by-gone era. The reports of the contemporary global situation still justifies the famous utterance of Jonathan Swift - "we have enough religion to hate one another but not enough to love one another." Deeply aware of what socio-political mischiefs could be supported in the name of religion, Radhakrishnan strove to use his philosophical insights to combat these. "Religions," he wrote, "hitherto have been building walls between one another instead of breaking down barriers." He emphasized that a genuine comprehension and appreciation of one religion by members of another is the need of the day. There is a stamp of authenticity when he remarked that "no one is so vain of his religion as he who knows no other," and observed that advocates of religion sometimes become missionaries of hatred towards other religions. Who can question the fact that ignorance of the other man's belief makes us intolerant and that "hatred is the product of intolerance, and persecutions are born of hatred...."

Confrontation with this social reality as is to be expected, provokes various reactions and responses. There is a trend in modern mind, which looks aghast at the contemporary scene of religious conflicts scattered throughout the globe, and wishes to efface all religions from the face of this earth. Some again, in vain have pronounced this age to be a post-religious era. Evidences show, on the contrary, that much unrest, social and political, still centres around the issue of religion.

Radhakrishnan, however, never sought a solution of this sort. He was convinced that world - religions have a practical mission. The vision of a universal religion, supporting and promoting the idea of a universal brotherhood, is indispensable. 'Faith in solidarity of the human race' is not something which can be abandoned. Religions have to fight injustice on socio-political level, across national frontiers. He wrote :

> "A civilization based on injustice cannot last long. It is a welcome sign of the times that a religion which does not make social reform and international justice are essential part of its teaching has no appeal to the modern mind. Religion is not a simple spiritual state of the individual. It is the practise of the divine rule among men."[3]

Obviously, a mere rejection of secularism, however convincing, is not enough. How does one bring it on surface that there is an unity of purpose that the religious traditions have, despite their differences? This is intimately related to the question. How should the presence of diverse religious traditions be perceived? Is there a philosophy of religion which can be said to provide an answer to the question of raison d'être for religious pluralism? Is the presence of different world-religions defensible in a manner that their conflicts can be overcome through a more profound insight into their ultimate purpose?

Radhakrishnan drew his inspiration from the philosophy of Advaita Vedānta. It goes to his credit that time without number he expressed boldly and eloquently the implications of the Advaitic approach in the context of encounter of religions.

At this point it needs to be emphasized that when we describe Radhakrishnan as an exponent of the Advaitic approach to the question of religious pluralism, the significance of the Advaitic attitude in the context of encounter of religions must be captured authentically.

Some misgivings from certain quarters have been expressed regarding this matter. Some ponder whether Advaita itself is not one of the contending traditions and thereby one among the competing creeds? Or, is by acknowledging the presence of others it only seeks to create a hierarchy where it supersedes all? Some consider this as a clever move and react to it by an outright denial that any other religion except the one they hold has any claim to equal legitimacy. In this connection it is well worth emphasizing that the exponents of the philosophy of Advaita Vedānta did not spare any effort to give a bold rational expression to the basic thesis. This implies that the views which are not in harmony with the Advaitic insight have been dealt with in accordance with the accepted methods of philosophical disputations. To take this as an example of violation of the spirit of non-violence or as a threat to religious pluralism is to miss out the main thrust of the Vedāntic tradition. Moreover, the established thesis could then become a powerful device for interpreting and appreciating the plurality of world religions.

It seems that now time is ripe to make open inquiries regarding these issues. Need be, polemics should not be discouraged. As a matter of great contemporary significance the question of encounters of religions should be taken up seriously. A mere lip-service to the cause of religious pluralism when no genuine effort for greater comprehension is made has little value.

It still is a puzzle, especially when the declared and the overt goal of any world-religion is peace, love and service to humanity, why does it become a medium for violence and hatred? How can a religion be taken as giving sanction to kindle hatred towards members who do not belong to the same fold, while it is considered as preaching love among its adherents? Is this embedded in the core of the religious insight itself or is it due to the failure of adequate theological formulations of the message received from any specific tradition? It can hardly be doubted that there is an unresolved theological task which is a source of constant threat. It is obvious that the challenge of religion has by no means lost its relevance at this age of science. Does the contemporary global situation not point to the issue of religious pluralism as a vulnerable one, prone towards disastrous political and military consequences? In the framework of modern technological development, the demand for a cooperation of theologians of various traditions emerges to be all the more urgent.

The following is an attempt to summarize the basic rudimentary ideas which can be taken as consequences of the Advaitic treatment of encounter of religions, noting at the same time how S. Radhakrishnan expressed them.

For Advaita Vedānta the Ultimate Real is non-dual (ekamevādvitīyam) and it is inexpressible (yataḥ vāco nivartante). Consequently, religion itself is not the goal but is to be viewed as a means (*marga*) a path, an expression. Any representation of the Ultimate Real is only symbolic, technically *mayic*. Hence, it is pointless to insist on the exclusive truth-claim of one path or one symbol alone. There is no way to maintain the legitimacy of only one approach and deprive others of similar claim. It is however important to emphasize that conceptually speaking this position should not be confused with *anekantavada* as will be noted shortly.

Radhakrishnan puts the message in this manner: "The illogical idea of a single religion for all mankind, one set of dogmas, one cult, one system of ceremonies which all individuals must accept on pain of persecution by the people and punishment by God, is the product of unreason and the parent of intolerance."[4] Thus, to put it more sharply, the Advaitic message in the context of religious pluralism is to acknowledge it as inevitable and natural. Advaita, on the other hand, would deny the claim of exclusivity on the part of a specific religion. As a philosophy of religion, Advaita spares no pain to work out a system of concepts which supports the view that Real is one and that the sages call it by many names (*ekam sat viprāh bahudha vadanti*). Any description, determination of it is only an ascription (*upacāra*). This holds true even when personality is attributed to it, as theistic systems invariably do.

The influence of the notion of Nirguna Brahman, as Advaita Vedānta understands it, is evident on Radhakrishnan, where he wrote :

"While we cannot conceive of the Supreme Spirit except in terms of our personality, we should admit that personality is only a symbol which is inadequate to the reality which is too large and too complex for us to grasp entire. The history of religion refers to a series of ideas by which the human being attempts to satisfy its innate sense for the infinite."[5]

Needless to say that this attitude demands an appreciation of the fact of difference of spiritual temperament as legitimate, a undeniable. To refuse to admit this is eventually to pave way to fanaticism.

But, once this idea is considered as realizable, an important step in the sphere of encounter of world-religions will be achieved. No religious tradition can then be made a vehicle by propagation of hatred and violence towards members of another denomination of the same or of any other tradition. It will indeed be a great accomplishment when the theological expressions of specific traditions will attain such clarity on a conceptual level that it will be impossible to find any justification for hatred in the name of religion.

It breeds humility to recognize that the highest idea of Ultimate Reality that we have is but a symbol, a suggestion of the ineffable.

If the Indian soil has supported the major world-religions, stemming from its cultural frame or not, one could say that it is to a very large extent due to the Advaitic character of the Indian culture.

In the socio-political context of present India, this eternal message still needs to be expressed. What Advaita sought on a conceptual plane is non-violence in the profundest sense.

Now, before closing this paper, the following question may be raised :

Is it only the *sanatana dharma* which can propagate this message? Obviously, any such claim of exclusivity will be self-defeating. The Advaitic perceptions in the context of encounter of religions are not tied to any particular tradition. Radhakrishnan's writings are strewn with quotations and references from sources other than the Indian tradition which indicate similar perceptions. He considered especially the messages of the mystics. Within the Indian cultural context itself, one could cite equally powerful perceptions by the Buddhists and the Jaina philosophers.

The Jaina conceptual world, for example, focused on a many-sided view of Reality : 'anekantavada.' This view supported by *syādvada* or a theory of standpoints repudiated all one-sided views of Reality (*ekantavada*), emphasizing that no statement about anything is absolutely valid but is so only under certain conditions. This position can also be fruitfully explored in the context of religious pluralism. It becomes an intellectual demand to understand the other points of view as each of them contains an aspect of ultimate truth. To reject outright, without grasping the insight which is valid from a certain standpoint would be a form of violence. In other words, it is both a moral and an intellectual obligation. *Anekantavada* can make room for distinctly different views, where no view has to yield to any other, but can coexist with the other. In brief, the Jaina perception, following the idea that reality has infinite aspects (*anatadharmatmakam vastu*), would be that all religions, like all points of view, are true, subject to appropriate conditions (*syad*).

Again, another marvellous example of transcending the particularity of one's own tradition can be seen in the Madhyamika school of Buddhism. Here unlike the Jaina, is not to be found a philosophy which seeks to justify the presence of other views of Reality as valid from different standpoints, but one motivated to demonstrate that all perspectives (*drsti*) are false, since they all involve self-contradictions. But to say this does not amount to claiming all views, excepting their own, to be inadequate. The Madhyamika dialectic is not designed to overthrow any specific view of an opponent but is a call to give up all *drsti* whatsoever. The Madhyamika Sunyavada is an interpretation of the silence of the Buddha about any categorial characterization of reality. The rigorous dialectic did not make any exception to the Abhidharmika position, but exposed the logical contradictions inherent in it just as much as in any view stemming from non-Buddhistic sources. To understand the falsity of all views is to transcend all *drsti* and to realize that reality cannot be grasped through discursive thought.

The Madhyamika philosophy, in rejecting all views as fallacious, and the Jaina philosophy, in accepting the validity of all views, each from its own standpoint - are bold intellectual adventures. These are to be considered as important sources of ideas, which when fully explored, can contribute immensely valuable and profound insights, providing alternative conceptual solutions to the context of religious pluralism.

The Advaitic conceptual experience is yet distinct from these two. Here too, all that which belong to the domain of plurality, including all religions, is to be understood as *mayic* where not one can claim legitimacy - even if provisional, which is to be denied to others.

The technicalities of the conceptual systems will bring out the differences in the Advaitic and the Madhyamika understanding of 'falsity'. Omitting details, it may be mentioned that the logical contradictions, paradoxes and incoherencies form the essential core of the notion of falsity in Madhyamika. While late Vedānta, largely influenced by Buddhism, has also used similar methodology, the 'false' in early Vedānta is that which is experientially contradicted. Moreover, the false always implies a ground (*adhisthana*), unlike the Madhyamika.

These can all be seen as various attempts which seek to resolve the conflict of different views by adopting a higher standpoint. The method adopted for this purpose, often playing on the idea of Reality as Inexpressible, varies from one conceptual system to another. This is an intellectual enterprise which bears witness to the utmost concern for arriving at an understanding which can grant or deny truth-claim, as the case may be depending on the system, to other views without claiming any partial treatment for its own tradition. Needless to say, that when the conceptual growth in the self-understanding of a tradition reaches such a level that it can see itself as one sees others, it also has a deep impact on a social level. It increases critical awareness not only on a theoretical plane, but influences our attitude in the practical day-to-day encounter with other faiths.

I will end by presenting before you the following lines of Paul Tillich as an example of what a Christian theologian sees in the present encounter of world-religions. " . . . . The way to achieve this he is not to relinquish one's religious tradition for the sake of a universal concept which would be nothing but a concept. The way is to penetrate into the depth of one's own religion, in devotion, thought and action. In the depth of every living religion there is a point at which the religion itself loses its importance, and that to which it points breaks through its particularity, elevating it to spiritual freedom and with it to a vision of the spiritual presence in other expressions of the ultimate meaning of man's existence."[6]

There must not be any doubt that what an exponent of the *sanatana dharma* understands by the Advaitic vision is not by any means tied to any particular religious persuasion, nor does it require relinquishing one's own faith. On the contrary, Advaitic insight in the presence of religious pluralism is one which grants freedom to approach the question of Ultimate Reality in any form or without a form.[7] It is in a set up impregnated with such a spirit that the question of encounter of world religions can be seriously approached. The theological task would be, to being with, to arrive at an understanding on a purely conceptual level which will expose the futility of suppressing diversity, or of promoting any sense of hierarchy amongst the various traditions. Each religious tradition has to work this out using concepts that are intrinsic to its own conceptual structure, and come to terms with the presence of other faiths. This will then undoubtedly open up dialogue touching upon various issues of technical nature. Polemics and exchanges which will eventually ensue can only enrich the intellectual traditions, as ancient India has witnessed over centuries.

The practical consequences could then be that finally the unexplored resources of specific traditions can hopefully be utilized for the good of all mankind - which now sounds utopaic.

The question of encounter of world religions cannot be underplayed as long as we recognize the fact that there are "enough religions to hate one another." The impact of religious traditions in the present day meeting of cultures is subtle and yet profound, despite its overt secular appearance. The socio-political frictions are much too often indicative of the unresolved tension which call for a theological solution. It is singularly important for world peace.

References

1. S. Radhakrishnan, *Religion in a Changing World* (London : George Allen & Unwin, 1967).
2. *Ibid.*
3. S. Radhakrishnan, *The Religion We Need* (London : Ernest Benn, 1928), pp. 24-25.
4. *Ibid.*
5. *Ibid.*
6. Paul Tillich, *Christianity and the Encounter of World-Religions* (New York, 1963).
7. Anindita Balslev, *Religious Tolerance or Acceptance* (Calcutta : The Ramakrishna Mission Institute of Culture, 1987).

16

Radhakrishnan : The Prophet of the 'Religion of the Spirit'

ISHWAR C. HARRIS
The College of Wooster

Writing in 1964 for *Radhakrishnan Souvenir Volume,* edited by J.P. Atreya, William A. Shimer stated, "God must place a high value on a creative spirit such as Dr. Radhakrishnan. His words should be added to our sacred scriptures as revealing much of eternal truth."[1] William Shimer's tribute needs to be recalled at the occasion of the 100th anniversary celebration of Dr. Sarvepalli Radhakrishnan. Indeed the words of Radhakrishnan have a prophetic character, for they are spoken from the depth of his being, pointing to a universal quest of all humankind - the quest for the Absolute - manifesting in the form of religion. In spite of his concern for politics, education, philosophy, psychology, etc., it was religion that preoccupied his mind. The prophetic nature of his writings on religion begins to manifest when throughout his writings and speeches he is determined to focus on what he terms, "The Religion of the Spirit." He views it as a universal religious phenomenon that transcends the boundaries of the historical religious traditions, and yet pervades at the core of all the world's great religions. For him the *Recovery of Faith,* the title of his 1955 book, is the recovery of this universal dimension of religion, which is overshadowed and often forgotten due to the preoccupation with the particularities in a given religion. He firmly believes that such a recovery of a universal religion will provide a solution to many ailments that beset humanity.

Within the parameters of this essay I intend to exegete Radhakrishnan's understanding of "religion" in general and his views on "the Religion of the Spirit" in particular.

The Meaning and Function of Religion

In most of his scholarly writings, it is "religion" that demands Radhakrishnan's attention. He attempts to study the phenomenon objectively, also relying on the subjective experiences of the ancient sages he finds himself in agreement with. Since he does not relate publicly to his own religious experiences, one is drawn to his writings to find an explanation. What one finds there is a scholar's careful attempt to delineate what is hidden and obscure. Thus, he relies on various disciplines to inform us how religion can be perceived, studied, and explained. He informs us that the root meaning of the word "religion" suggests a binding force, akin to the Latin "religio." But, for Radhakrishnan this has two different meanings. Internally, religion as a binding force can perform a psychological function, bringing integration, wholeness, and togetherness to a broken life. Spiritually it means to find unity within, to be united with the God-head as suggested in Vedānta Hinduism. Externally, it means that "religion" functions as a binding force socially, bringing people together for the betterment of humankind. Of course, Radhakrishnan will deduce that the true religion is that which brings all of humanity together. It is on this issue that he is different from some ancient Indian seers. He is more concerned about the social applicability of religion to make it more relevant for our times. It is not the purpose of his religion to withdraw one from society, rather to encourage participation in it. Here his religious thought is similar to such modern Indian religious thinkers as Vivekananda, Tagore, Gandhi, and Vinoba Bhave.

Radhakrishnan often appeals to the esoteric dimension of religion. Although he recognizes the exoteric function of religion, he labels it incidental, external, the particular which could be transcended. However, the transcending of the particulars is not viewed as their denial. It is their affirmation, as much as the universality of a faith cannot be apprehended without its particularity. In his later writings, Radhakrishnan was quite clear on this issue. Perhaps his Western critics had made him aware of the significance of the particular nature of religion. Consequently he took the historicity of religions more seriously than in his earlier writings. None-the-less, it is the universal in a religion that preoccupies Radhakrishnan's attention. Such an analysis stems from the fact that he belongs to the tradition of a "perennial philosophy" that has had a long history of appealing to the mystical element in religion. Thus, he defines religion as an insight into the nature of reality, and calls it "the direct apprehension of the Supreme.[2] It is "a personal encounter of the individual with the Supreme,"[3] it is "Seeing God face to face,"[4] and a direct vision of Reality."[5] Such a description of religion earned him the title of a "Neo-Vedāntist" for it is unmistakably akin to the Vedānta Hinduism. Regardless of its similarities with Vedānta, Radhakrishnan informs us that "religion is an autonomous form of experience which cannot be confused with anything else."[6] It is trans-cultural because "there is an insistent need in the human soul to come to terms with the unseen reality."[7] Therefore, the roots of religion lie "in the spirit of man deeper than feeling, will, or intellect."[8] It exists at the depth of the human spirit as the fountainhead of all creative activities. As such, religion is not a creation of humans, but a discovery they make upon transcending reason and logic. When religion becomes a creation it produces *religions* that vary from culture to culture. Preoccupation with *religions* results in adherence to the dogmas and doctrines. When taken to be the ultimate (while they are proximates), they confuse the real with the relative. The consequence is fanaticism and religious exclusivism.

The function of religion is to cleanse our inner being and thereby cleansing the world.[9] It is quite clear that Radhakrishnan does not promote a mystical religious experience that has no relevance to the human activity in the world. Much has been written on his treatment of the concept of Maya to suggest that unlike many Vedāntists, Radhakrishnan takes the world quite seriously. This being the case, religion is highly functional for him. In an individual "the endeavour of religion is to get rid of the gulf between man and God and restore the lost sense of unity."[10] On a collective level it is to transform humanity to bring about the creation of *Brahmaloka* (the Kingdom of God). Of course the religion that can genuinely perform these functions is a universal religion free from parochial interests and blind loyalties to dogmas and doctrines. It is Radhakrishnan's contention that the world desperately needs this kind of religion if we are to pull ourselves from the pit of conflicts, wars, and strife into which we have fallen. The function of religion then is to create responsible selves, the *bodhisattvas* of Buddhism, the suffering servants of Christianity, who can help restore the health to an ailing humanity. The name of this religion, which produces such beings is *Sanatana Dharma*, the Eternal Religion, which is found in many religions but transcends them as well. Radhakrishnan calls it "The Religion of the Spirit."

The Vision of "The Religion of the Spirit"

Radhakrishnan's rebellion against the missionary Christianity is sometimes viewed as the cause for his interest in the religion of the spirit. Although it is true that he has many harsh words against a certain type of Christian exclusivism, his pen did not spare criticism of other religions, including his own, e.g. Hinduism. As a philosopher of comparative religions, he was well versed in the developmental history of religions, and his keen eye was observant of religious exclusivism wherever it surfaced, Consequently in his formulation of "the religion of the spirit" it is the exclusivity of the religious claim that he condemns in favour of a universalistic position. He believes the exclusivism breeds intolerance, while universalism promotes tolerance. He sees the lack of tolerance as one of the reasons for world conflicts, and wishes to heal the wounds of an ailing society through the medium of "the religion of the spirit." Radhakrishnan is sensitive to global problems and concludes that all of humanity is suffering from many crises, may they be political, religious, social, or economic. Although not pessimistic about the fate of the world, he feels that the situation is grave and demands immediate attention. Radhakrishnan lived through two world wars and numerous other political crises. As a political leader he was more concerned about peace and international cooperation in order to bring about a new world order in the future. What is significant is that he attributes all problems to the lack of religious concern. For him the crises of the world are basically spiritual. The inward expression of the crisis is anxiety, tension, loss of meaning and purpose. This is the anguish of the human soul wanting to find tranquillity. The outward expression is manifest in various human institutions and the conflicts they produce. The consequence is human suffering. Radhakrishnan feels that the world is looking for a spiritual religion that will address itself to the situation. Here his optimism is quite remarkable. Whether he has accurately diagnosed the cause of human problems or not is debated by various scholars. It is certain that he launches a severe criticism of existing religions for not meeting the needs of humanity and proceeds to formulate the basis of his own universal religion.

In his vision of the religion of the spirit, Radhakrishnan is quite clear as to what this religion is not. For example, he insists that this is not a new religion. More than once he writes, "we do not want a new religion but we need a new enlarged understanding of the old religions."[11] Inherent in this idea is the belief that the religion of the spirit already exists within the existing religions. Therefore, it is a matter of a new awareness rather than the creation of a new faith. Furthermore, his universal religion does not seek religious syncretism which lapses into a shallow spirituality and abstractness. He insists, "no one need give up one's own religion and engage in a syncretism. We can learn from other religions in a spirit of mutual respect."[12] He realizes that there are bound to be differences among religions. These differences should be recognized and used "to strengthen and enrich partnership."[13] He is against undifferentiated universalism or an easy indifferentism. Thus, the goal of the religion of the spirit is fellowship not the fusion of religions.[14] He also condemns obscurity and abstractness that are often relegated against religious universalism. He writes, "Religions must be cured of their provincialism and made to reveal their universality. This does not mean spiritual vagueness or ambiguity."[15] A significant point to be noted is that his religion does not disregard the particularities of a given religion. It is often thought that in the enthusiasm of universality, the particularity is often negated. It may be so, but Radhakrishnan is quite aware of this problem and categorically states, "we do not wish to eliminate the particular elements in different religions. Beliefs are codified expressions of experience ... rites and ceremonies do not grow in void."[16] In contrast to the "religion of authority" which is often linked with an institution, "the religion of the spirit" is not an organized religion. It is not subjected to the dogmas and doctrines, though it recognizes their relative position within religion.

If "the religion of the spirit" is not a new religion, and is not a synthesis of religions, then what is it? It is the discovery of the essence of one's own religion. He once wrote, ".... our aim should be not to make Converts, Christians into Buddhists or Buddhists into Christians, but enable both Buddhists and Christians to rediscover the basic principles of their own religions and live up to them."[17] This is confirmed by what Radhakrishnan calls a life of the Spirit. It is marked with the development of a spiritual consciousness within an individual, which brings a total transformation in life devoid of egotism and desires. With the transformation springs a new sense of freedom. Radhakrishnan affirms, "an individual is free when he attains universality of spirit."[18] This is akin to a conversion experience, a rebirth, and being awakened to a new perspective with the fullness of meaning and purpose. It is reflected in love. He writes, "true universality of spirit consists not in knowing much but in loving widely."[19] Love is not seen as an emotional experience which is privatized in a mystical experience. Rather, with love comes social responsibility and a bodhisattva like temperament to suffer for the sake of others. The religion of the spirit is the religion of service because, "the soul that has attained unity of spirit and strength has to spend itself not in self-satisfaction . . . but active service."[20] For Radhakrishnan the examples of this kind of life in the spirit are found in different religious traditions. It is his hope that humanity will hold on to this essence of religion and let religions go.

A crucial aspect of Radhakrishnan's "religion of the spirit" is the understanding of the term "spirit." Does he attribute to it the same qualities as St. Paul does to the "Holy Spirit?" Is his notion of the spirit more akin to the Hindu concept of "Atman"? His critics are bothered by the fact that he makes no distinction between the Christian and the Hindu views of the spirit. For that matter, he sees all religions as expressions of the same spirit. Not only that, the human creativity as expressed in art, literature, music, etc. is also due to the working of the spirit in human beings. The universality of the spirit is explained by its power. It can be deduced that for Radhakrishnan spirit is a "power" - a creative power - which has a spiritual quality in as much as it transcends human limitations. He does not hesitate to call it "the Spirit of God," since God represents that element of transcendence. The religion of the spirit then is the essential religion which points to the inherent spiritual presence in all human beings.

A Critical Evaluation

So far in this essay I have presented the "thesis" of Radhakrishnan's prophetic voice. Now I shall deal with the "antithesis" and a possible "synthesis." A comprehensive analysis of these matters has been presented elsewhere.[21] Here I shall simply outline the issues involved. First, let us look at some of the views of Radhakrishnan's critics which constitute the antithesis of his Universalist position. Among his critics are some Christian Theologians and the philosophers of religion.

The basic position of the Christian theologians is that Radhakrishnan's universal religion relativizes the particular nature of Christianity and robs it of its uniqueness.[22] Here his monistic idealism is brought into question and dismissed as a form of Hindu mysticism. Consequently, the religion of the spirit is seen as Hinduism in disguise. For Christianity, monism denies the personality of God, devaluates the world, negates revelation, and "empties the concept of Grace, Forgiveness, Sin, etc. . . . ."[23] It promotes and sanctions a certain type of religious liberalism which could be called, "spiritual latitudinarianism."[24] Radhakrishnan's emphasis on "religious experience" is also brought into scrutiny. While "integral experience" can bring peace, tranquility, and harmony, Christianity sees the heart of its faith as salvation from sin. Here the role of Jesus becomes unique in the form of a particular revelation transcending all general types of revelation. What Radhakrishnan sees as a point of religious exclusivism, Christianity views it as the very cornerstone on which the entire edifice of the Christian faith rests. Radhakrishnan's "intuitive experience" is viewed as a creation of the human mind, which remains tainted with sin, and therefore incapable of liberating itself. Furthermore, the Christian concern with ethics and morality is seen as given the secondary role under the monistic vision of religion as in the religion of the spirit (or Hinduism). For, the monistic view of religion which sees religious experience as the basis of truth, "reduces all forms of religious and moral expression and endeavor, metaphysically speaking, to mere instruments, to mere ends, to an end."[25] As for the nature of the world is concerned, in spite of Radhakrishnan's efforts to show that the world is real and needs to be taken seriously, under the monistic scheme Christianity finds the reality of the world a logical absurdity. As a result the whole Judeo-Christian axiom that "God acts in history" loses its meaning, leaving history to chance rather than submitting it to a divine purpose.

As far as the philosophical attack on Radhakrishnan's views on religion is concerned, the entire matter of "the essence" as the core of all religions is brought under question. Some phenomenologists of religion continue to point out that religion is a particular historical phenomenon. This raises a serious dilemma for religious universalism. Scholars like William E. Hocking and Wilfred C. Smith have given ample attention to this problem in their writings.

Hocking maintains that religions are always concrete, and without it they are given to abstractions. For him " . . . communication is never to human beings in general; it is to specific human beings, having specific languages and histories . . . with specific ethical and social questions to meet."[26] W.C. Smith insists that the very quest for the essence of religion should be given up. He believes that religion is a process and no living religion ever ceases to evolve.[27] Consequently, one can never come to an essence or core of a religion which can be considered as being the same in all religions. A most recent critic of the universalistic position is Professor Steven T. Katz, who has launched an intellectual war against the "perennial philosophy." He insists that there are no pure unmediated experiences, therefore, no essential mystical experience that could be perennially acceptable.[28] Like other contra-perennial philosophy thinkers, Katz calls for the recognition of the differences rather than similarities that separate religions from each other. For him, "perennial philosophy" which insists on the universality of the oneness of the mystical experience is false in its approach. "It is, in reality, a grand tautology. Nothing can count against it. Non-disconfirmable premises and postulates are paraded as explanatory keys to reality while, in fact, the details of reality are ignored with alarming casualness."[29] Although not directed towards Radhakrishnan, Katz remarks in general dismiss the validity of the religion of the spirit propounded by Radhakrishnan.

Having looked at the antithesis of Radhakrishnan's position, it is only expected that we discuss the "synthesis" which either he provides or is present elsewhere. In this discussion of the viability of the existence of the religion of the spirit, there are three issues that need to be dealt with. First, is there a universal essence (an absolute) that can provide a unity among all religions? Second, is there a universal religious experience which is the same in different cultures? Third, is it possible to envision a universal religion that can heal the wounds of an ailing humanity? It seems that Radhakrishnan deals with all of these questions in his writings, attempting to provide a synthesis between the opposing point of views. In regard to the issue of "essence," it is clear that he holds a Vedāntic position. Even his critics cannot deny that all religions allude to the existence of an ultimate force, a reality, identified as God, Spirit, or Transcendence. The debate is over the fact whether it is the same in every religion. If the critics deem a tension between the monistic and the theistic interpretations of this reality, Radhakrishnan resolves that tension within his religion of the spirit. The quarrel is not over what attributes are given to this reality as long as one accepts that there are many ways to approach the Real. Radhakrishnan's religion of the spirit allows this possibility. In other words, he does not insist that one has to be a radical monist or a theist to practise the religion of the spirit. The beauty of his religion is that it permits these differences to exist as long as one allows the Real to shine through whatever medium it chooses. His insistence on the Real as "One" raises the issue of the relationship between the One and the many. For Radhakrishnan, the many are the manifestations of the One. Thus, his position is akin to the Upaniṣadic dictum that the 'Real is One, but the sages speak of it in many ways.' This is confirmed by the religious experience. His affirmation of the oneness of the Real is the same as the Truth being one. Truth might wear vestures of many colours, but it remains the same. Thus, for Radhakrishnan, the religion of the Spirit is the Truth of a particular religion. It is that which unities all religions, whatever names might be given to them. If this position appears to be Vedāntic, for him it is not confined to India or Hinduism.

As to the question of a universal religious experience, the critics object to such a possibility. It should be pointed out that there are those who would side with Radhakrishnan on this issue. Karl Jung with his notion of the "archetypes" has given us the possibility of entertaining the thought that the phenomenon of a universal religious experience does exist. This approach is well reflected in the works of such phenomenologists of religions as Rudolf Otto and Mircea Eliade. Even if we agree with Katz that all mystical experiences are mediated, and therefore particular, it does not repudiate the fact that some mediated experiences are similar, and therefore raise the possibility of some mystical experiences that are universally valid. The religion of the spirit appeals to these similarities. The differences are recognized but the emphasis is laid on the similarities. This is a matter of placing the value on the life lived in the spirit, which in a manner of speaking confirms the validity of the Universalist position.[30] Thus, for Radhakrishnan, universally valid religious experiences do exist, and in no way eliminate the differences of experiences. The important question to be asked is: why is this similarity of religious experiences an important factor in the religion of the spirit? For Radhakrishnan, this similarity is one of the keys to the unity of humankind. First, the genuine religious experience brings peace and harmony. It produces tranquillity and eliminates strife. Second, it naturally pulls people together and attracts them to the value of harmony. It engenders a quality of life that seeks co-operation with others to enhance the meaning of life. Such a vision needs to be promoted and differences minimized. Radhakrishnan does not deny that the religious experiences might be different. However, he consciously does not want to dwell upon the differences. It is his firm belief that insistence upon differences will divide humankind, whereas his mission is to bring it together. Such is his idealism.

The third and the final question raises the possibility for the existence of a universal religion. The critics object to it because it is seen as denying the particularities of religions. Perhaps the critics have failed to read Radhakrishnan properly. I have already given several quotes from his writings where he accepts the particularities of religions. Furthermore he insists that he is not seeking a colourless synthesis of religions. Also, it is not a new religion that he is formulating. In his later writings, Radhakrishnan suggests that the religion of the Spirit is inherently present within a given religious tradition. Therefore, it is the matter of discovering the universality of faith within one's own religion rather than turning to other faiths. His synthesis between the universal and the particular is the very point that separates him from the classical Vedāntists such as Śamkara. Perhaps the critics would appreciate his religion more if he had called it "the religion of the concrete spirit" as done by Paul Tillich.[31] But that to me is a matter of semantics. For when one compares Tillich's notion of the *concrete* spirit with Radhakrishnan's understanding of the religion of the spirit, remarkable similarities between the two appear. Tillich speaks of the experience of the "Holy" as a universal phenomenon like Radhakrishnan. He appeals to "mysticism" like Radhakrishnan. He also lifts up the dimension of the "ethical" like Radhakrishnan. Furthermore, he claims that "the inner aim of the history of religions is to become a Religion of the Concrete Spirit."[32] Like Radhakrishnan, Tillich also suggests that the way to achieve universality is "to penetrate into the depth of one's own religion."[33] Tillich proposes a universal religion while remaining within the fold of his Christianity. Radhakrishnan does the same by remaining a Hindu. That is living proof that the universality of the spirit exists at the depth of one's own religious tradition as Radhakrishnan claims.

The question remains as to how can this universal religion heal the wounds of an ailing humanity? The answer lies not so much in its metaphysics, but in its ethics. Radhakrishnan is aware that his Western critics have taken Hinduism to task on the issue of ethics. He is quite emphatic in showing that Hinduism, particularly Vedānta does not lack ethics. When it comes to the religion of the spirit, he maintains the same rationale. Furthermore, he argues that it is the universal ethic of love, which is at the heart of his universal religion, that can heal the wounds of the ailing humanity. He does not resist invoking the Christian and Buddhist imageries of love and compassion within the matrix of the religion of the spirit. As a true Universalist he finds such an exercise quite appropriate, since the ethics of love and compassion are not confined to Christianity or Buddhism. The life in the spirit requires a conscious effort on the part of the believers to love the neighbour, and to serve humanity in order to bring peace and harmony on earth, thereby healing the wounds of an ailing humanity.

Assessment

When evaluating the nature of the Universalist position that Radhakrishnan attempts to uphold, it is evident that three clear perspectives appear. First, that the religion is always *particular*. The champions of this position seem to adhere to the "cultural-linguistic" approach, which seems to be prevalent in certain academic circles today.[34] If taken to an extreme, " . . . cultural conditioning becomes, first, cultural subjectivism, and finally cultural solipsism."[35] I have previously pointed to this danger as "religious exclusivism" with all its pitfalls. Second, that the religion is always *universal*. Most recently this has been labelled as the "experiential-expressive" approach to religious experience.[36] When taken to an extreme this approach can result in religious abstractness, vagueness, and simplemindedness. On the other hand, it can take on the garb of particularity and end up as "exclusive universalism." The third position acknowledges that a religion has both its universal as well as the particular nature. This seems to be the position that Radhakrishnan holds. He recognizes that religion cannot be universal without being particular, and that particularity without the ideal of universality can turn demonic (to use the Tillichian imagery). Needless to say that to maintain this critical balance requires dedication as well as creativity in religious life.

If religion is a process as Whitehead would have us believe, then the issue of the universal vs. the particular nature of religion takes on an entirely different meaning. First and foremost neither the universality nor the particularity can be prioritized. Both become part of a dynamic process in the evolution of religion. As religion (spirituality) moves ahead and goes through the inevitable condition of change, various dimensions of its nature play out their role in the arena of history. They are part of a link (dependent co-origination of the Buddhists) and neither are independently significant. Their relative nature indicates that one needs to accept a holistic view of religion, which is non-dogmatic. Radhakrishnan seems to have felt that the Western religious traditions have taken a one-sided approach to religion. They have overly emphasized the particularity (through dogmas and doctrine) of their faith. Here he has been keenly observant of the religions of "authority," which he contrasts with the religion of the "spirit." Through the religion of the spirit he wishes to counter balance the excessive emphasis on the particular nature of religion. He wishes to put the process of religious development back into order. It is in this spirit that he points out that even the Western religions have the universal dimension to them. Consequently, the religion of the spirit is not a product of the East. It resides within each religion regardless of the geographical boundaries. There is no doubt, however, that in this enthusiasm for a universal religion he is unduly critical of Christianity and praiseworthy of Hinduism. Perhaps, that is his greatest weakness. He could not separate his emotional ties to his own faith as a scholar of the history of religions.

In spite of his shortcomings, it would be wrong to label Radhakrishnan as "reductionist," who reduces the complexities of religious phenomena to his brand of universalism. He is a creative thinker, who has given systematic attention to the philosophical and religious intricacies when dealing with the discipline of comparative religions and philosophies. He favours the Universalist position because he finds it logical and comprehensive. More than that, he believes in the *value* of the religion of the spirit for the purpose of the unity of humankind. He would agree with Huston Smith that perennialists are attracted to unity as moths to the flame. But in the unity of the absolute (which includes as well as transcends everything) the particulars are integrated and the absolute/relative distinction disappears.[37] One can argue that there is nothing new here that has not already been discussed in the various schools of Vedānta. Although it may be true, Radhakrishnan's is the applied Vedānta. He has taken it out of the realm of thought and applied it within world religions, enlightening those traditions that lack such an insight to find it within themselves. Hence comes his claim that all religions can proximate themselves to the religion of the spirit. If there is a dogma in his claim it is that his opinions on religion are definite, embracing the universal dimension of religion. The absolute is no longer mysterious, an incomprehensible Real, but manifest Being whose attributes can be experienced. The critics cannot accept that a scholar will sacrifice his objectivity and become so subjective in his claims. But, are not the world's great religions based on subjective experiences of a few individuals, elevated to the claim of objectivity? What saves Radhakrishnan from being dogmatic is that he did not leave a blueprint for his religion of the spirit. He founded no institutions and initiated no disciple. Rather he left it up to the creative genius of an interested individual to delve deeply in his/her own religious tradition to find, to create, and to manifest the religion of the spirit.

In light of the growing interest in 'religious pluralism' which seeks to foster an attitude of religious tolerance and openness, the significance of Radhakrishnan is self-evident. Religious diversity which was once under theological attack is now beginning to be accepted. The channels of dialogue between Christianity and other religions have been opened.

Serious Christian theologians are attempting to do theology in the context of world religions. Such developments are indicative of the fact that in the West there is a growing recognition that we live in a religiously pluralistic society. Needless to say that when Radhakrishnan expounded the religion of the spirit a few decades ago, he had the similar changes in mind. However, his dream went beyond such developments. He envisioned that all historical religions will so transform themselves as to approximate the religion of the spirit. It would seem that the growing sense of religious tolerance is leading humanity in that direction. None-the-less, religious exclusivism is by no means dead. There are renewed signs of intolerance, fundamentalism, and separatism. It would seem that the message of Radhakrishnan is still valid and timely.

In spite of Radhakrishnan's optimism for his religion of the spirit, the problem remains that it is grounded in mysticism. It appeals to the esoteric dimension of spirituality which is not easily accessible to the masses. For the majority, it is the exoteric aspect of religion that seems functional. How then can this mysticism be made public? Radhakrishnan seems to leave the responsibility on the particular religious tradition to transform itself into the religion of the Spirit. He must realize that within a given religious tradition, only a few can have the insight or the inclination toward a deep religious experience. Furthermore, he must also realize that a mystical experience doesn't necessarily promote unity. It can instill a sense of separatism and aloofness as evidenced by the history of religions. How then can humanity be joined together through a universal religion as Radhakrishnan proposes to do? Doesn't it become a wishful thinking rather than a concrete reality? He must be aware of all of these issues since he categorically stated that unless all of humanity achieves the universality of spirit, the faithful have much work to do. It is here that Radhakrishnan the philosopher, turns

Radhakrishnan the theologian, and his thought turns prophetic.

The prophetic quality of Radhakrishnan can be seen in many ways. First and foremost, in its true intentionality of being a prophet, he is a mouthpiece for the "perennialist tradition." His religion of the spirit is not his creation, but a discovery of a spiritualist tradition that has survived within many cultures. Like a prophet, he is a reformer, who sees the pitfalls with a given faith and warns the believers against them. He cannot compromise with religious exclusivism and chauvinism in the name of religion. His reformation is not limited to theological matters, but spills over into the social, political, and cultural spheres. His political and academic career was divested in seeking links between spirituality and secularity, bridging the gap between the two. For he saw most of human creativity as an expression of the spirit. His prophetic voice can be heard today as challenging humanity, informing us and thereby seeking to transform us.

References

1. William A. Shimer, "Dr. Radhakrishnan, Man, and the Universe," in J.P. Atreya, editor, *Dr. Radhakrishnan Souvenir Volume*, 429.
2. S. Radhakrishnan, *Religion in a Changing World*, p. 102.
3. *President Radhakrishnan's Speeches and Writings*, May, 1962-64, p. 34.
4. *Ibid.*, p. 34.
5. S. Radhakrishnan, *Our Heritage*, pp. 82-83.
6. _____, "My Search for Truth" in McDermott, *Radhakrishnan*, p. 41.
7. _____, *Kalki on the Future of Civilization*, p. 37.

8. _____, "My Search for Truth," p. 41.
9. _____, Fragments of a Confession" in Paul A Schillp ed., *The Philosophy of Radhakrishnan*, p. 81.
10. _____, *An Idealist View of Life*, p. 87.
11. _____, *Recovery of Faith*, p. 204.
12. _____, *Religion and Culture*, p. 68.
13. *Ibid.*, p. 43.
14. S. Radhakrishnan, "Fragment of a Confession," in Schilpp Vol., p. 74.
15. _____, *The Present Crisis of Faith*, p. 24.
16. _____, Fellowship of the Spirit, p. 9.
17. _____, "Fragments of a Confession," in Schillp Vol., p. 74.
18. *Ibid.*, p. 43.
19. _____, *The Present Crisis of Faith*, p. 52.
20. _____, *Kalki on the Future of Civilization*, p. 45.
21. See the author's *Radhakrishnan : Profile of a Universalist* (1982).
22. Among those who hold this position, the names of Hendrik Kraemer, Thomas Urumpackal, and Stephen Neill stand out.
23. Hendrik Kraemer, *Religion and the Christian Faith*, p. 112.
24. *Ibid.*, p. 112.
25. *Ibid.*, p. 111.
26. William E. Hocking, *Living Religions and a World Faith*, p. 36.
27. Wilfred C. Smith, *The Meaning and End of Religion*, p. 179.
28. Steven T. Katz, *Mysticism and Philosophical Analysis* (1978), also *Mysticism and Religious Traditions* (1982).
29. Steven T. Katz, "On Mysticism" (Reply to Huston Smith), *Journal of the American Academy of Religion*, Winter 1988, Vol. LVI, No. 4, p. 751.
30. Professor Huston Smith gives a different interpretation to this idea. For him the universality of mysticism is not proven by the experiences that the mystics have, but on the

assertions of metaphysical intuition they make (Huston Smith, "Is there a perennial philosophy," *Journal of the American Academy of Religion*, Fall 1987, Vol. LV, No. 3.

31. Paul Tillich, *The Future of Religions*, p. 80.
32. *Ibid.*, p. 88.
33. Paul Tillich, *Christianity and the Encounter of World Religions*, p. 97.
34. Huston Smith, "Is there a Perennial Philosophy?" *Journal of the American Academy of Religion*, Fall 1987, Vol. LV, No.3, p. 559 (footnote no. 8).
35. *Ibid.*, p. 560.
36. *Ibid.*, p. 559 (footnote no. 8).
37. *Ibid.*, p. 562.

17

Radhakrishnan's Eternal Religion (*Sanātana Dharma*) and the Religions : His Contributions to Religious Dialogue

DONALD R. TUCK
Western Kentucky University

An important strain in Radhakrishnan's writing, if not the most important theme to which he returned in many of his writings, formulated, illustrated and compared his vision for the religious quest of society - an eternal religion (*sanātana dharma*), behind, beyond as well as manifested within the historical religions of mankind.[1]

In this essay, we will refer to Radhakrishnan's vision of a unified Religion by using capitalization, and will refer to the historic religions in the lower case and plurally. The context in which Radhakrishnan referred to Religion and the religions clarified his inquiry as he sought to sketch and colour various characteristics of this timeless tradition.

Lecturing at the Center for the Study of World Religions, Harvard Divinity School, Radhakrishnan concluded :

> The world will give birth to a new faith which will be the old faith in another form, the faith of all ages, the potential divinity of man which will work for the supreme purpose written in our hearts and souls, the unity of mankind.[2]

Radhakrishnan called for a scholarly investigation characterized by cooperation and mutual respect, in which the inquiry pressed the manifestations of Religion within the religions of mankind to bring into focus the pattern, purpose and meaning of the eternal Religion.[3]

When P.A. Schilpp, who edited *The Philosophy of Sarvepalli Radhakrishnan,* asked Radhakrishnan to write an autobiographical sketch, Radhakrishnan reviewed his own life through his published works, and concluded that the eternal Religion had guided his search for truth.

Drawing upon the insights of seekers after truth from the ancient to modern times, in both the Eastern and Western civilizations, Radhakrishnan showed that classical writers at their best have attempted to let the divine in man manifest itself. When that divine has revealed itself through their rational inquiries, the results have offered to the consciousness of humankind a striking similarity at the deepest level of spirit or the ground of being - a likeness which Radhakrishnan called the crown of the different religions.[4]

Radhakrishnan pointed out that man has lived through the period of infancy on earth, during which diversity of thought reigned, but as human society matures, humans will work toward a higher integration of thought and experience, which will progress toward a higher fellowship of faiths, and will produce men and women, whose quest will include the whole rather than culturally confined parts of the religions of mankind.[5] Radhakrishnan found fragments of this central core of Religion among the great writers of Indian literature, e.g. the *Upaniṣads* and Buddhism, as well as among the thinkers, who interacted with the Greek mysteries, Platonism, the Gospels and Gnosticism. Radhakrishnan proposed that the aspects of truth, which such thinkers found isolated from each other, unfertilized by deep cross-examination, and which lead each of the thinkers to develop a partial self-satisfaction, could have, if they had worked cooperatively, developed into a harmony of religions, and would have produced the parameters of the eternal Religion behind the concretized religions.[6] Radhakrishnan recognized within the different religions a unity of spiritual aspiration, which coupled with disciplined endeavour, attempted to ascend to the highest level of religious concern, e.g. the top of the mountain of humankind's highest desire. As true exponents of the religions continue their upward climb, they begin to show a remarkable agreement - signs that the ascending paths lead to the *sanātana dharma* conceived by the Hindus.[7] Radhakrishnan built his vision on an hierarchical pattern of the religious quest. He based his ideas on the Indian-Hindu model, but found these perceptions homologized in the other major religions, which favoured nondualism and intuitional experiences.

Radhakrishnan's biography and writings show that from his early training, he had interacted with the missionary, Christian religion.[8] Challenged by the negative criticisms from Christian scholars, Radhakrishnan felt impelled to scrutinize his own Hindu tradition, in order to examine and adapt those elements which fostered wholeness. In his scholarly work as an historian of philosophy,[9] he engaged in research not as a mere mechanical ragpicker, but as a critic and interpreter of the Indian system of religion. He determined to excise, whenever necessary, those aspects, which like dead fossils could not substantiate the best presentation of the living, Hindu religion.[10] His M.A. thesis, *Ethics of the Vedānta* indicated the contours of his later thought. The eternal Religion, like the roots of a tree, gave life to the religions - its trunk and branches.[11] When Religion expressed itself through the religions, the resulting high code of morality included reasonable thought, fruitful action, and right social institutions.[12] The Hindu religion sought to discipline individuals as part of the integral society to reach the desired end—to discover the world's potential for virtue and to derive happiness from the world. The complete vision, the eternal Religion, will incorporate the reflections of integration displayed, though sometimes, minimally in the religion of the Hindus.[13]

Within the various religions, which Radhakrishnan had researched, he also found articulate, experienced, spiritual people searching for Religion. Whether they identified their particular search within the Hindu, Buddhist, Christian or Muslim religions, these comrades in a joint enterprise sought the best solutions to common problems through peaceful, coexistent means. The pressing issues of international welfare, justice, racial equality and political independence have brought together representatives from these different religions to seek the best means to understand, formulate and apply the eternal Religion to humankind. Working cooperatively, they will unite the parts into a complete whole, and participate in a common heritage. Radhakrishnan's plan envisioned a reconstructed Religion, which the world's best representatives will build together from the different shapes of the available materials extant within the religions.[14]

In his voluminous writing spanning an academic career of sixty-one years, Radhakrishnan has proposed that the classical religious thinkers of the major religions have attempted to formulate an eternal Religion (*sanātana dharma*), united in essence, but plural in its manifestations as the religions. Through inter-religious dialogue and interdependent research, Radhakrishnan has articulated many characteristics of this Religion. He thought and wrote primarily from the Hindu perspective, but attempted like few other philosophical-religious thinkers to show that the eternal Religion manifested its qualities through the differing religions. This research will not attempt to exhaust the whole of his vision of a unified Religion, but will examine three of the characteristics of his vision of the eternal Religion.

The first aspect of Radhakrishnan's *sanātana dharma* emphasized that Religion manifests itself among humans as a fellowship of faiths - a unity within variety. Teachers about ultimate matters aim neither at training others exclusively in their own way of thought and life, nor at substituting one form of religion for another. As instructors of the eternal Religion, they investigate the progress of the devotee, and help him comprehend his own faith more deeply. By means of a cooperative search, all teachers and learners need to learn humility and charity toward others en route to the fullness of being. The repentance and conversion, which they all must experience will not take them from one religion to another, but lead them from a surface understanding of the religions to the depths of the eternal Religion.[15]

The fellowship of the faiths, based upon religious experience, will not bring forth a fusion of the religions. But those aspects of the religions, whether they represent doctrines or practises, which do not impair a spiritual fellowship will remain.[16] Radhakrishnan reviewed the diverse religions, and found that at their best each, rather than developing in isolation, drew upon and affected other religions with which it came into contact, e.g. Judaism, Christianity, Hellenism and Islam drew from each other in western Asia; likewise, the Hindu tradition benefited from its encounter with Buddhist and Jain religions. The result, which emerged from the interactions, made each religion stronger, and together represented aspects of the quest for inward spiritual life. Each religion attempted to provide the means to experience the ineffable, and to teach its followers a rational means to comprehend its inexplicable end. The intellectualization of the ways to truth varied, but each way lead to the complete experience within the human spirit, and directed the worshipper to reunion and integration. Those who creatively contribute to the highest Religion find a cooperative communion with those of similar purpose.[17] Radhakrishnan's own experience, as well as his observations of like-minded men caused him to write :

> A study of other living religions helps and enhances the appreciation of our own faith. If we adopt a wider historical view, we obtain a more comprehensive vision and understanding of spiritual truth.[18]

Such a larger vision requires that those who travel on the pilgrimage respect the religion of their fellows, understand their different cultural backgrounds, and include them as walkers on a common path.[19] The eternal religion demands neither syncretism of intellectual perspectives nor fusion of cultural variations, but requires a sharing of a common end.[20]

The unity of purpose and means, which Radhakrishnan discovered in his research of the religions, caused him to criticize the barriers set by both conservative and radical interpreters of the Hindu religion. Against the conservatives, who held tenaciously to the glories of the ancient past, while bemoaning the irreligion of modern times, Radhakrishnan proposed an openness to change. He viewed the conservative, exclusively past-oriented perspective as perverting to the whole spirit of the Hindu tradition. Faithfulness to the past, although partially helpful, prevents conservatives from seeing the more complete, changing tradition. The method Radhakrishnan chose disentangled the eternal Religion from its past tentacles, and freed Religion from the tangled network of its historic form. He mused regarding the historical manifestations of the Hindu religion, "One cannot tell what flowers may yet bloom, what fruits may yet ripen on hardy old trees."[21] Eternal Religion partially revealed in the Hindu religion will emerge as the end toward which it has historically aimed. Conservatives understood the ancient pattern, but failed to ascertain the changing tradition.

Radhakrishnan also put the progressives under the searching light of his criticism. The radical extremists, diametrically opposed to the conservatives, developed an intolerance for the ancient tradition. When they rejected the whole of the ancient Hindu system, they had no pole star; lacking the historical basis, they substituted a naturalistic rationalism for the religion. By throwing aside the past manifestations of eternal Religion, they also deprived themselves of the quest for the eternal Religion behind the historic accretions. The radicals contributed a much needed critique of the past tradition by unmasking its unfounded appearance, but they need to penetrate surface layers to the ground of man's being - the eternal spirit in man. Progressives emphasized the need for change in the modern period, but failed to understand the enduring continuity of the eternal Religion encased in the Hindu religion.

Radhakrishnan proposed a balanced use of tradition, which rejects both the conservative and radical extremes. A more complete view returns to traditional values, roughly encountered in the writings of the great minds of the Indian past, and combines them with their modern reassessments by men like Vivekananda, Gandhi and Tagore. When the best of the Indian tradition has combined with the most balanced view of the Western contributions, men will confront the possibilities of a fellowship of faiths. Such a cooperative spirit need not demand fusion, but involves a sharing short of syncretism. Then, the religions of man will flower and bear fruits of the eternal Religion.[22]

Radhakrishnan's eternal Religion contained a second characteristic, which he proposed as religious experience or mystery.[23] he maintained that the dominant theme of Indian thought has stressed its spiritual tendency. Radhakrishnan founded eternal Religion upon spiritual experience—a mysticism, which insisted that the realization of the spiritual demanded a disciplined inquiry.[24] Systematic Indian thinkers based religion on intellectual knowledge, but pressed beyond its limitations to an intuitive apprehension of the inner truth, that which lies beyond appearance (the six *darśanas*).

Not only have scholars like the proponents of nondualism (Advaita Vedānta) adopted this way of apprehending Ultimate Reality, but even illiterate Hindus have caught this vision, for they, too, have learned that symbols or images reflect ultimacy beyond the confines of the rational mind. Although he conceded that many Hindus have become victims of paralyzing thought, even superstitions, and archaic social institutions, Radhakrishnan's acquaintance with their highest aspirations kept him from relegating the common followers of the Hindu tradition to a level devoid of a higher religious sense. The Sanskritic and Sanskritized religions have at least taught the common man to act in ways conscious of a higher end, and to live a nobler life, based upon "the contemplation of eternal ideas, to struggle to behold the divine with the eye of the mind, and to feed on the shadow of perfection."[25]

Mystery pervades Radhakrishnan's perception of the Ultimate Being, and his writings have explored deeply this dimension of eternal Religion. Radhakrishnan understands the Supreme as one reality under two aspects, the concept Absolute-God. As the Absolute, the Supreme manifests itself impersonally, non-relationally, namelessly and formlessly. The Hindu tradition identified this transcendent Absolute as *nirguṇa* Brahman. The Advaita Vedānta view has influenced this aspect of Radhakrishnan's exposition of Hindu religion. But *nirguṇa* Brahman does not exhaust the knowledge of the Supreme, for the second aspect perceives the Ultimate as personal, actively involved with human seekers, named and formed (*mūrta*). The theistic tradition of India contributed the personal God to the two-part conception, and called the divine Īśvara or reified it to one of the gods or goddesses as the chosen deity for devotion. Balancing the concept, the Supreme manifested itself to human comprehension with creative freedom and love. Thus, Radhakrishnan offers an eternal Religion, which does not choose from either the system of Śaṁkara or Rāmānuja, but combines both of their best insights as simultaneous poises of being.[26]

The direct experience of eternal Being involves human awareness in three kinds of consciousness, which Radhakrishnan often paired more simply as intellect and intuition. In an attempt to respond to criticism of his ideas and to clarify ambiguities within his earlier writings (articles by Wadia, Brightman, Phillips and Browning in Schilpp), Radhakrishnan replied that the inquirer begins by perceiving with his sense-mind (*manas*). The knowledge he has acquired from empirical data helps him perceive the objective world. But the sense-mind does not stop or find fulfilment at this level of observation, for perception progresses hierarchically to logical intelligence or rational reflection (*vijñāna*). What the sense-mind observes outwardly, the intellect/reason attempts to formulate with principles governing the empirical data - a second step in perceptual knowledge. The sense-mind affords the first step, and intelligence builds upon and incorporates what external observation has acquired; both combine to produce perceptual, outward knowledge. The third kind of human consciousness leads sense-mind and intelligence to a deeper realm of awareness. From perception and reason, intuition (*ānanda*) takes the human consciousness to a non-intellectualized apprehension, which Radhakrishnan called integral insight. Intuition examines and reflects upon observation in depth; it involves the whole consciousness and brings man to a direct, immediate, and highest experiential knowledge.

When applied to the mysterious aspect of eternal Religion, Radhakrishnan taught that perception understands the various religions, separating the mind (subject) from the object; it observes their beliefs, practises, symbols, and social institutions in partial forms. Intelligent reflection isolates principles within the religions; it's fragmentary understanding proves inadequate, though not necessarily false. Intuition explores the religions in depth, reveals their partial truths, but, most importantly, presses knowledge to an experience of fullness. Without the direct, immediate experience, the observer remains only partially satisfied, but through intuitive insight, the subject and object unite in the mysterious wholeness of being. The Religion of the spirit integrates intuitively what other forms of human consciousness apprehend in part. Without the mysterious aspect of Religion, Hindu man grapples with either the Absolute or God, follows either Śaṁkara or Rāmānuja, dividing the whole into truncated parts. Mystery allows a coincidence of seeming opposites, and unites the Ultimate Being as the compound Absolute-God, the unity revealed in two aspects.[27] Eternal Religion does not set itself against sensual observation or rational analysis, but transcends both in experience. From the spiritual, experiential level, intuition verifies the partial knowledge of sense and mind by offering coherence and harmony to the patterns articulated by rational investigation.

Intuition passes the test of verification by cross-examination with the intellect. Religious thinkers who allow intellect to transcend itself, know by experience the complementary kinds of consciousness of eternal Religion. Those who will not or cannot apprehend mystery fall short of the eternal Religion; their inability to experience this highest consciousness does not invalidate it, but indicates the barriers they have built against it. However, another who can apprehend the larger or deeper dimension breaks through those barriers of inexperience and verifies by individual interaction that the Eternal being is the Absolute-God.[28] Radhakrishnan reasoned :

> Intellect cannot repudiate instinct any more than intuition can deny logical reason. Intellectual preparation is an instrument for attaining to the truth of the spirit, but the inward realization of the truth transcends all intellectual verification, since it exists in an immediacy beyond all conceivable mediation.[29]

What Radhakrishnan claimed as the foundation of the Hindu tradition, he found homologized in the intuitive experiences and writings of Western Christians, e.g. Augustine, St. Bernard and St. John of the Cross.[30] Christian writers, like their fellow Hindus, have taught that spiritual experience or mystery engages the whole person, and have related man to the whole transcendent-immanent Ultimate Being.[31] Integral experience results in a unity of spirit, which indicates that the eternal Religion satisfies the highest aspirations of spiritually conscious humans in both the Eastern and Western religions. Radhakrishnan compared the mystical experience to the love of the lover for his beloved, a theme particularly emphasized by theism, and an integral part of eternal Religion.[32] Autobiographically, Radhakrishnan has exposed his own life an example of the highest religious quest. Intellectually, but more importantly intuitively, he has known that the Absolute-God showed interest and care by guiding his own life and work. Such a complete being wooed him with love to an experienced reality, which contained both rational and nonrational elements, and which involved both mediated and immediate means.[33]

Moreover, Radhakrishnan observed the mysterious aspect of eternal Religion among spiritual Hindu women. He noted that in the midst of a Hindu wife's performance of her routinized duties, she realizes that a truer meaning of life beckons her. If she pierces the veil of mediocrity or contingency, she perceives reasons, and intuits a deeper more fulfilling meaning to her life. Separated from her husband, her devotion to him deepens; like Rādhā, she discovers an eternal love, which waits more patiently and unwearily for the return of the Supreme to satisfy her deepest longings.[34] Both the symbolic human and the divine loves contain sensual, rational, and intuited elements; both loves manifest personal and abstract means to the fulfilling end. Whether sophisticated or simple, the Hindu woman expresses dignity, tenderness, and magnanimity - intuitive characteristics found neither among her merely sensually oriented nor often intellectually, rigorous contemporaries. The mystery pervading the eternal Religion's relationship between humans and the Absolute-God, reflects itself figuratively in the relationships between caring human beings, and in the interdependent transactions of a woman's relationship with her husband.

Freedom from dogma identifies the third characteristic of Radhakrishnan's eternal Religion. Thinkers within the separate religions have expended great effort to describe their particular experience of integral insight. Their attempts at verbalization have exhibited both intellectual rigour and intense emotion.[35]

Radhakrishnan has researched classical writers within several religions, and has approached them as tolerantly and appreciatively as possible to compare them with Hindu religious thinkers. He has elicited more adverse criticism and emotional attacks by conservative thinkers in the religions over his characteristic of freedom from dogma in the expression of eternal Religion than any other of his proffered characteristics.

Radhakrishnan observed that the most vociferous criticisms of eternal religion come from those who narrowly isolate their thought to their own tradition. They have failed to admit that their religion has affected and been influenced by surrounding religions, and have little researched knowledge of religions besides their own.[36] Such thinkers vainly and ignorantly generalize specifics drawn only from within their narrow persuasions. Against these aggressive dogmatists, he warns :

> The greatest of the temptations we must overcome is to think that our religion is the only true religion, our own vision of Reality is the only authentic vision, that we alone have received a revelation and we are the chosen people, the children of light and the rest of the human race lives in darkness.[37]

Rather than confining his research only to the Hindu religion, his extension study of the classics of religious literature opened his vision to admire, respect and even share their gratest insights. He exhibited a tolerant appreciation of other religions, a willingness to reexamine his own religion, and to incorporate a broad spectrum of creative contributions from other religions into his vision of the eternal Religion.[38]

Addressing the issue of doctrine, Radhakrishnan argued that no singular verbal formulation could delimit a single religion, much less the eternal Religion. His research in the Upaniṣadic, Buddhist and Confucian literature, revealed that the writers did not insist upon adherence to dogma. Those who emphasized experience as the end of essential knowledge of the Ultimate showed reticence toward a fixed formula whether simple or complex. The experiencers could not adequately describe the inexpressible; in fact, their faltering attempts to expose their highest accomplishments reduced fixed formulations to epithets, aphorisms or silence to indicate the overwhelming experience. Their ultimate silence symbolized their relational satisfaction with Ultimate Being, and that the fulfilling experience of the whole transcended both discursive knowledge and the subject-object model.[39]

Radhakrishnan regarded rational knowledge as secondary reflection, and dogmatic ideas as impediments to the holistic experience. Radhakrishnan clarified his thought in relation to eternal Religion : "Doctrines about God are only guides to the seekers who have reached the end. They represent God under certain images, as possessing certain attributes and not as He is in Himself."[40] When verbal images hardened into doctrines and ossified as dogmas, teachers proposed exclusive claims. When confronted by other religious claims, the dogmatists retreated from dialogue, and set up their own formulations as the primary, most valuable, and finally, the only truth. Instead of correlating the outward, secondary forms of one's religion with other comparable ideas, the dogmatists hardened their exclusive views; the history of dogmatism has shown that it has not only precipitated highly divisive quarrels and fostered debilitating pride, but has energized fanaticisms and destructive aggressions.[41]

Eternal Religion grounds the adherent in the experience of Ultimate Reality. The learned believer attempts to preserve the memory of his experience and to convey it's meaning to the inexperienced through rational discourse.[42] Once experienced, the Absolute-God brings vitality to the human spirit, and although known partially through observation and reason, the Supreme exists beyond concept or image.[43] If the intellect becomes self-sufficient, the mind cripples the human spirit by thinking, that

> truth has been found, embodied, standardized and nothing remains for man but to reproduce in his feebleness some treasured feature of an immutable perfection which is distinct from him.[44]

The learned teacher of eternal Religion recognizes linguistic limitations, and presses the intellect toward an experience beyond "the word of tongue or concept of mind." Filled with the highest spirit, the believer in eternal Religion presents more than arguments about the Supreme, and seeks the common ground in the experience of an unseen reality. The experienced common ground unites fellow searchers, who cooperate and engage in inter-religious dialogue and interactive understanding.[45]

According to Radhakrishnan, when the proponents of the religions relinquish their myopic views, they will open themselves to the vision of the eternal Religion. With corrected insight, they will no longer stop at the boundaries of any one religion, and will cease claiming that any solitary perspective represents the final, absolute and only truth - a normative proposition, which cannot pass the historical test for any one tradition. The integral insight gained from experience of eternal Religion, questions all exclusive claims, and suggests that no single, systematic formulation can satisfy the quest of all men. Confronted by this broader perspective, the seeker rejects the option of conflict, because it proves debilitating, and chooses the way of cooperation with men of like inclination, because it enriches spiritual life by offering freedom from over-restrictive dogma, and an inter-relational understanding of truth gained from cross-fertilization.[46]

The resulting Religion, free from doctrinal conformity will adopt the approach of respectful tolerance of differences. To illustrate tolerance within the Indian experience, Radhakrishnan chose the religious reign of the Buddhist King Aśoka, who fostered inclusive, interactive, and joint participation in the mystery of being among the various religions in his kingdom. Aśoka developed an intellectual posture, which treated the various religions under his rule with respect. Incised in his rock edits, Aśoka reminded the religious leaders to tolerate each other, and warned them against the disparagement of another's religion. One edict read, "By dispraising other religions, we hurt our own," and a second advised, "An injustice done to others is an injustice done to oneself."[47] Aśoka demonstrated the spirit of cooperation, respect and tolerance among the diverse religions—a quality of eternal Religion.

Radhakrishnan maintained that those who hold these qualities of eternal Religion, and maintain comparable respectful and tolerant attitudes, "have more in common with each other than with the bulk of adherents of their own religions."[48] The inter-relational experiences of the tolerant bind them with cords of ultimacy beyond the intellectual productions of the scholars or the rigid ceremonials of the priests. The tolerant no longer set up the boundaries of the quest for eternal Religion within either their own or a single religion. Proponents of a narrowly confined system of belief and practise may satisfy a few followers for a short time, but they cannot satiate the thirst for truth for all people over a lengthy time period, because they have isolated their formulations from the greater pursuit of the eternal Religion. Radhakrishnan included in his writing many characteristics of the *sanātana dharma*. This research has examined three qualitative aspects : first, that eternal Religion includes a fellowship of faiths, secondly, that *sanātana dharma* grounds itself upon religious experience or mystery, and finally, the highest Religion produces freedom from over-constricting verbalizations or dogma, and fosters an openness of mind to experience the highest aspiration of humankind.

References

1. S. Radhakrishnan, "Reply to Critics," in P.A. Schilpp, ed., *The Philosophy of Sarvepalli Radhakrishnan*, (New York : Tudor Publishing Co., 1952), 789 ff.
2. _____, *Fellowship of the Spirit* (Cambridge : Harvard University Press, 1961), 40.
3. *Ibid.*, 1-2.
4. _____, "Fragments of a Confession/The Religion of the Spirit and the World's Need," in Schilpp, *The Philosophy...*, 80f.
5. *Ibid.*, 82.
6. *Ibid.*, 73, where he quoted A.L. Whitehead's similar idea.
7. *Ibid.*, 77.
8. _____, "My Search for Truth," in V. Ferm, ed., *Religion in Transition* (London : Allen and Unwin, 1937), 15; Radhakrishnan attended German Lutheran High School, Voorhees College and Madras Christian College.
9. _____, *Indian Philosophy*, Vol. I (London : Allen and Unwin, 1923), 672.
10. Radhakrishnan reexamined the caste system, cycles of time, "Fragments . . .," 42-46, as well as corrected misunderstandings regarding the Hindu religions as world-denying, *Ibid.*, 65, *māyā* as illusion, "Reply . . .," 800-802, *karma* as fate, *An Idealist View of Life* (London : Allen and Unwin, Ltd., 1932), 274ff., and the renunciation and freedom of the *sannyāsin*, *Eastern Religions and Western Thought* (London : Oxford University Press, 1939), 380 ff.
11. _____, *Eastern Religions . . .*, 347.
12. _____, "Fragments . . .," 20; within the Hindu religion, Radhakrishnan found traces of the eternal Religion, see his discussions of *dharma*, the four-fold objective for life, *aśrama*, the stages of life as gradual accomplishment, and *varṇa*, the four-fold order of society in *Hindu View of Life* (New York : The MacMillan Company, 1926), 45-92, *Eastern Religions . . .*, 349ff., and *Idealist View . . .*, 222ff.

13. Radhakrishnan, *Eastern Religions* . . ., 349-385.
14. _____, *Fellowship* . . ., 39.
15. _____, "Fragments . . .," 74.
16. *Ibid.*, 75.
17. _____, *Fellowship* . . ., 76.
18. _____, "Fragments . . .," 73.
19. _____, *Fellowship* . . ., 73.
20. _____, "Reply . . .," 812.
21. _____, *Indian Philosophy*, II, 776.
22. _____, *Indian Philosophy*, I, 24.
23. _____, "Fragments . . .," 79; see also *Indian Philosophy*, I, 27, 41.
24. _____, *Indian Philosophy*, I, 41.
25. _____, "My Search . . .," 16-17.
26. _____, "Reply . . .," 796ff.
27. *Ibid.*, 790-795.
28. *Ibid.*, 794.
29. _____, "Fragments . . .," 61.
30. *Ibid.*, 62.
31. *Ibid.*, 63.
32. _____, *Idealist View* . . ., 108-109, 139, 142; "Fragments . . .," 60-63.
33. _____, "My Search . . .," 13.
34. *Ibid.*, 14.
35. _____, "Fragments . . .," 79.
36. _____, *Religion in a Changing World* (London : Allen and Unwin, 1967), 117.
37. _____, "Union for the Study of Religions," Address to the Meeting of the Indian Branch of the Union, 26 December, 1956, in *Occasional Speeches and Writings : October, 1952-February, 1959* (Delhi : Ministry of Information and Broadcasting, 1956), 368.

38. Hyde credited Radhakrishnan with tolerance, but accused him of failure to incorporate elements from other religions into his own religion, P.A. Schilpp, *The Philosophy of Sarvepalli Radhakrishnan*, New York: Tudor Publishing Co., 1952, 25.
39. Radhakrishnan, "Fragments . . .," 78f.; for further references to Radhakrishnan's opposition to conservative, Christian views of their unique, definitive and absolute claim to truth, e.g. K. Barth and H. Kraemer, and Radhakrishnan's appeal to more tolerant writers, e.g. Justin, Origen and Clement, see *Eastern Religions* . . ., 343ff., *Recovery of Faith* (London : Allen and Unwin, Ltd., 1956, 56, 64ff., "Fragments . . .," 74, *Occasional Speeches*, 379ff., and "Reply . . .," 808.
40. _____, "My Search . . .," 17.
41. _____, "Fragments . . .," 72.
42. _____, "Inter-Religious Understanding," Newton Baker Lecture, Cleveland Council on World Affairs, Ohio, 27 March, 1958, in *Occasional Speeches* . . ., 377-378.
43. _____, "Religion and Its Place in Human Life," Address given at Rishikesh, 12 August, 1954, in *Occasional Speeches*, 285f.
44. _____, "The Ancient Asian View of Man," Broadcast Address for the Columbia University Bi-Centennial Celebrations, October, 1954, in *Occasional Speeches* . . ., 291.
45. _____, "The Social Message of Religion," Address at the Marian Congress, Bombay, 4 December, 1954, in *Occasional Speeches* . . ., 294.
46. _____, "Indian Religious Thought and Modern Civilization," Presidential Address at All-India Oriental Conference, Annamalai University, 26 December, 1955, in *Occasional Speeches* . . ., 335f.
47. _____, "Inaugural Address," International Congress of World Fellowship of Faiths, 3 October, 1956, in *Occasional Speeches* . . ., 355.
48. _____, "Inter-Religious Understanding . . .," in *Occasional Speeches* . . ., 377.

18

Sarvepalli Radhakrishnan's Use of Christian Scripture : An Introduction

BOYD H. WILSON
Hope College

In the Spring of 1975 I was introduced to the writing and thinking of Sarvepalli Radhakrishnan. Perhaps it was the fact that just as I was learning about this amazing man's life I also learned of his death that I remember the occasion. I recall being impressed with the writing of Radhakrishnan on every subject but his interest in the comparative study of religion is what caught my attention. Again, it may have been the serendipity of timing that caused me to be impressed with Radhakrishnan : I was first embarking on my own study of comparative religion in the Spring of 1975. Whatever the reason, I have had a personal affinity for and interest in the writings of Sarvepalli Radhakrishnan for many years.

As I read the works of Radhakrishnan, one of the things that impressed me the most was his use of scripture. Although he used the scriptures of India thoroughly, it was his knowledge and usage of Christian scriptures in his writings that I noted. I was particularly impressed with the unusual and refreshing approach he brought to the interpretation of the passages he cited. In my subsequent studies I witnessed the same tendency to employ Christian scriptures in the course of an argument in other modern Indian writers, such as Gandhi, Aurobindo, Ram Mohun Roy, and even the recorded sayings of Ramakrishna. But none of these other writers demonstrated the same breadth of knowledge of the Christian scriptures, nor depth of interest in them. Radhakrishnan stands alone in this arena; or perhaps it is two arenas in which he stands simultaneously. His knowledge of Christian scriptures sets him apart from most modern Indian thinkers and his familiarity with Indian scriptures sets him apart from most Western thinkers.

There is no doubt that Radhakrishnan is well-versed in the Christian scriptures and interested in employing them in his works. In the eighteen works that I was able to research, I discovered over 700 references, both direct and indirect, to Christian scriptures.[1] This brief introduction should be seen as a first step toward a much larger undertaking. I envision several results following from this introduction. First, I trust that it will lead to further work on my part in the development of a much larger project on the use of Christian scripture in Radhakrishnan's writings. Second, I hope that it will encourage other scholars who have an interest in Radhakrishnan and an interest in the field of comparative religion to pursue this particular angle of the investigation. Third, I trust that it will contribute to the on-going dialogue between religions.

Radhakrishnan's Religious Background

Sarvepalli Radhakrishnan was born into a family that was Telugu Brahmin; his father was a priest in this rather small and insignificant caste.[2] Although he was raised in the context of a devout family, worshiping the Lord Kṛṣṇa with his family, much of his formal religious training and education came from the schools he attended. Most of his young life was spent in boarding schools operating under the aegis of Christian missions. He attended a high school run by the Hermannsburg Evangelical Lutheran Mission, an intermediate school, Voorhees College, supported by the Reformed Church of America, and Madras Christian College, founded by the Church of Scotland (Presbyterian).[3] This education is singularly important in an understanding of Radhakrishnan's early introduction to and consequent knowledge of Christian scripture. The Bible was employed in missionary schools as the primary text-book, thereby teaching students reading and writing while also teaching them the basic doctrines and texts of Christianity.

Through this education Radhakrishnan received thorough familiarity with the scriptures and doctrines of Christianity. Along with this education, however, came a critique of Hinduism. Those things with which the Christian missionaries found fault in Hinduism were the very things that later troubled Radhakrishnan about his own tradition. He was particularly stung by the criticisms of Hinduism as a theologically incoherent and philosophically inchoate religion. He also learned that it was a false religion and a particular affront to God because of its polytheism. But the most telling criticism that he encountered was the castigation of Hinduism as "world and life negating" - that it was a religion that had no serious basis for an ethic of personal or social activism. These criticisms were taken to heart by the sensitive young philosopher and they occasioned serious conflicts in his religious outlook.

Although he had problems with Hinduism, Radhakrishnan was never able to feel comfortable with the Christian position either. He had some serious reservations about the Christian religion, not the least of which was its exclusivistic stance. He felt it was a position of arrogance and pride that was unbecoming of a religion. So he was in a sort of religious parenthesis : unable any longer to embrace the religion of his birth and unwilling to accept the religion of the missionary. From his studies in philosophy, however, he was able to resolve some of his conflicts. The teachings of

Professor Hogg suggested to him that the ethical and philosophical value of a religion could be separated from the doctrinal and theological packaging. This allowed Radhakrishnan to identify himself with Hinduism while retaining the value and strength that he found in Christianity.

He also found inspiration in the writings and lectures of Swami Vivekananda who gave a philosophical legitimacy to Hinduism that had been lacking before in Radhakrishnan's mind. He learned to be round to be a Hindu, and set about to defend this faith from the unfortunate and uninformed attacks of the missionaries.[4] As he identified himself with Hinduism, though, he began to develop a vision of just what Hinduism really was. Naturally part of the problem was that he had inherited the reified concept of "Hinduism" from the missionaries and had no real definition of it. But from Vivekananda he derived the idea (as did much of the Western world) that true Hinduism was synonymous with "Vedānta," so Radhakrishnan set about defending Vedānta. Perhaps persuaded by his own logic, Radhakrishnan later identified Vedānta with the "Hindu Ideal" or the "Hindu View." But even this designation eventually gave way to the concept of the "religion of the spirit" and finally to the "Sanatana Dharma" or the Eternal Religion. The changes, however, were mainly titular : Radhakrishnan never seemed to move from his position that Hinduism in the form of Vedānta was the ideal religion.

Radhakrishnan's View of Religion

Throughout his long career, the topic of religion was never far from the centre of Radhakrishnan's thought. He was constantly trying to come to terms with what he thought about religion in general and where he stood in relation to a specific religion. One does not need to search very long or sift very carefully through the writings of Radhakrishnan to encounter his view of religion. In this section, however, what is being entertained is an overview of Radhakrishnan's view of religion as it is presented through and supported by citations and allusions to Christian scriptures. This does not necessarily narrow the view but it draws the perspective into sharper focus.

Radhakrishnan seemed fascinated with the question of the basis of religion : he experiments throughout his works with theories that explain the phenomenon of religion. In one context, he suggests that the basis of religion is the satisfaction of needs, particularly the need to believe that there is more to life than the temporal physical and that there is a final justice in the world in which innocent meet with reward and the guilty are punished. He does not necessarily feel that this is a positive basis and contrasts what the prophetic seers of religions proclaim as a creed that unifies people with what the "traders in religion" turn into exclusivistic visions that torture the foreigner outside the camp.[5]

In a different context, and on a more positive note, Radhakrishnan cites the writer of *Ecclesiastes* to conclude that the sense of the Infinite, which is placed in the human soul by God himself, is the basis of religion: " 'God has put eternity into the heart of man,' says the Preacher."[6] Religion is the outward expression of this inner consciousness of the Infinite and the Divine. Then drawing on a more human image, Radhakrishnan asserts that love is the very foundation of all religions : love for one another, love of neighbour and even love of our enemies. Although love is the principle taught by all religions, in these contexts he cites the First Epistle of John, the Epistle of James, and the Gospel of St. Matthew to support his assertion.[7] He elaborates on this idea by expounding the virtues of selfless love as articulated by the Apostle Paul in his Epistle to the Corinthians. Love, he reminds us, "is patient and endures all things ... wears out conceit and cruelty ..." and is the law of being for those dwelling in the Spirit of God.[8] The love that all religions demand must demonstrate itself in compassion to the suffering :

> Christianity, for example, asks us to do good to them that hate us and despitefully use us. There is nothing special in loving those who love us or who are themselves lovable. Jesus asks us to love our enemies in the hope of awakening the humanness, their potential capacity for love.[9]

Behind all these suggestions, though, lies the overwhelming conviction of Radhakrishnan that religion is based primarily and fundamentally on personal experience. This personal experience is the common ground of all religions, and while most emphasized by the Eastern religions this experience is essentially the same in Hinduism, Buddhism, Christianity and Islam.[10] This experience generally comes in the form of a beatific vision which is seen only through the eye of the spirit.[11] It is a direct spiritual apprehension of the Supreme which closes the gap between knowledge and experience."[12] This rather lengthy quote best illustrates Radhakrishnan's use of Christian scriptures to support his contention that all religion is based on visionary experience :

> Moses saw God in the burning bush, and Elijah heard the still small voice. In *Jeremiah* we read : 'This is the covenant which I will make with the house of Israel after those days, saith of Lord. I will put my hand in their inward parts, and in their heart will I write it.' Jesus' experience of God is the basic fact of Christianity : 'As he came up out of the river he saw the heavens parted above him and the spirit descended like a dove towards him : and he heard a voice sounding out of the heavens and saying, "Thou art my beloved son. I have chosen

thee".' According to St. Mark, the baptism in the Jordan by John was to Jesus the occasion of a vivid and intense religious experience, so much so that he felt that he had to go for a time into absolute solitude to think it over. He obviously spoke of the ineffable happening, the sudden revelation, the new peace and joy in words that have come down to us . . . . The vision that came to Saul on the Damascus road and turned the persecutor into an apostle is another illustration.[13]

Even though Radhakrishnan thinks that all religions have the same basis, he discerns significant weaknesses in some religions. The most egregious of weaknesses in religion is the fault of exclusivity. He feels that this particular flaw was invented by the Hebrews and inherited by Christianity. Both religions subscribe to the detrimental vision of the "chosen people" and the "jealous god." This leads to the sin of "sacred egoism" and the religious flaw of national identity with religious reality.[14]

Another weakness that Radhakrishnan finds in religions is the idea of predestination. He rejects the idea that the doctrine of karma in Hinduism is at all related to the idea of predestination supported by the Calvinistic interpretations as well as the words of St. Paul who refers to some "vessels of wrath fitted to destruction." He feels that the idea of God that envisions him creating some things for the express purpose of punishing and destroying them is an unethical concept and an assault on true religious spirit.[15] A similar flaw is the negation of life, or at least the separation of life into the realms of the sacred and the profane, the religious and the social or political. Again, it is not Hinduism that is prey to this fault, but Christianity. The division of those things which are Caesar's and those things which are God's has led to a divisive and separative spirit in religion. Similarly, the Apostle Paul's obsession with separating the "things of the flesh" from the things of the spirit has contributed to an unhealthy advocacy of celibacy and mendicancy in Western religion.[16]

The greatest weakness of religion is the sin of pride and the sense of superiority. Any missionary religion expresses both implicitly and explicitly that "We are the only possessors of truth; you are hopelessly lost in ignorance." These same religions that glory in their own strength also possess the weakness of exalting their founders from the status of mere holy men and teachers to divinity.[17] This leads to the two sins of pride and proselytizing. Actually, the one implies the other, for there is no proselytizing without the sin of pride.

These weaknesses notwithstanding, Radhakrishnan is still able to argue for a universal essence of religion. There are many dimensions to this essence, but this does not detract from the essential unity of religions. The over-riding essence is found in the universal aspiration for "potential sonship" or the realization of one's divine status.[18] All religions emphasize the divine character of human-beings and aim at directing one to the fulfilment of this divinity. The specific religions differ only on the means by which the realization of this divine destiny is enjoined.[19] All religions lead to the renewal of life which is perceived as a perfection that is interpreted as a "rebirth." This experience is realized as a purification of the heart and soul and causes one to find fulfilment in this life.[20]

This renewal of life contributes to another dimension of the essence of religions - the emphasis on the ethical. All religions intend to lead to a state of ethical perfection which is the first step toward the realization of the divine. Even though the ethics of a religion may reflect transcendent values, the immediate legitimacy and applicability is the standard upon which the ethics are judged.[21]

The ethical standards upon which all religions are judged can be the same because the nature of the Supreme, the same nature of the same Supreme, is manifest in all religions.[22] This essential manifestation is ethereal, not ephemeral. The experience of the Supreme is an ecstatic phenomenon and cannot be quantified or tested. It is self-validating, known only in the religious consciousness of the depths of the soul.[23] Since this phenomenon is neither quantifiable nor verifiable the Western world does not know how to accept it, or even how to measure it. Nevertheless, the membership of this religion of the Supreme constitutes the invisible church of the spirit, recognized and represented wherever there are people of goodwill and basic goodness.[24]

This vision of the shared essence in all religions naturally leads Radhakrishnan to conclude that there is a basic unity of all religions. This understanding of the basic unity is found throughout much of his writing :

> When the Upaniṣads proclaim the great truth "That art thou," when the Buddha teaches that each individual has in him the power to grow into a Buddha or Bodhisattva, when the Jews say that the "spirit of man is the candle of the Lord," when Jesus tells his hearers that the Kingdom of Heaven is within them and when Muhammad affirms that God is nearer to us than the very artery of our neck, they all mean that the most important thing in life is not to be found in anything external to man but is to be found in the hidden strata of his thought and feeling.[25]

This basic unity, couched in all religions, seems best expressed in Hinduism, or Vedānta. Many pages in his writing are devoted to indicating the ways in which the teachings of Hinduism are not in conflict with the teachings of Christian scriptures. Often he is careful to draw a clear distinction between the teachings of Christian scriptures and the teachings of Christianity. It is in these contexts that Radhakrishnan makes the most frequent usage of Christian scripture.[26]

Radhakrishnan's View of Scripture

Radhakrishnan's view of religion both derives from and contributes to his view of scripture. He asserts that scriptures are human documents that are liable to error while also describing them as products of revelation directly from God. The revelatory process is a steady, on-going process, though, not merely a past event.[27] This apparent disjuncture between the human and divine aspect of revelation is resolved by the distinction that Radhakrishnan draws between the revelatory action of the divine in self-manifestation and the human experience of receiving it and recording it. Revelation is timeless and always true; reception and interpretation is time conditioned and capable of error. For this reason, scriptures are not infallible in all that they say, nor are they absolute and final in their apprehension of truth. There is no finality in any one scripture.[28]

Revelation is primarily an internal experience whereas scripture is the outward expression of this experience. Radhakrishnan considers the source of revelation, though, to be the presence of the Divine that is in all human beings so that every individual is a potential prophet or receptor of revelation. One need only be conscious of and attuned to the silent voice of the infinite within.[29]

Since revelation is dynamic and scripture is static, it is incumbent on each individual to renew and reaffirm the truths of revelation. The truths contained in scripture are even hidden, in a sense, by the scripture itself.

> Every scripture has two sides, one temporary and perishable, belonging to the ideas of the people of the period and the country in which it is

produced, and the other eternal and imperishable, and applicable to all ages and countries.[30]

It is the duty of the interpreter to bring to life the eternal truth while sorting through and discarding the perishable container. It is the task of the interpreter of scripture to make the timeless truth speak with a fresh voice to the current times.[31]

The purpose of scripture itself becomes a little ambiguous for it is to convey truths that are eternal in vehicles that are temporary. Because of that ambiguity Radhakrishnan suggests that some of the greatest prophets in the history of religion have chosen silence over speech in order to communicate the truth. The nature of truth itself often overwhelms one into the silence of reverence. Radhakrishnan says that Lao Tzu, the Buddha, and Jesus all recognized the power of silence in the communication of truth.[32] Similarly, when the silence is broken, the language of scripture is rarely the language of daily discourse. It is more often the language of poetry or passionate love communicated in symbolism and allegory.[33] The purpose of scripture is to describe what cannot be described, to teach what cannot be taught, to speak about the ineffable.

With this view of the nature and purpose of scripture, Radhakrishnan is not perplexed by the relationship between scriptures - those of the same tradition as well as those of divergent and disparate traditions. On the one hand, all scriptures bear testimony to the same truth and are inspired by the same fire. On the other hand, there are special and specific revelations, such as those claimed by the Jews, Christians, and Muslims. That is the nature of scripture - to put into specific form the general truth. But the claim of a special revelation is not and cannot be seen as a final or complete revelation. All scriptures, as well as all revelations, are necessarily limited and provisional. Even the writers of the Christian scriptures recognized that God had spoken in diverse ways to many people in the past and that He has never left Himself without a witness. The message is universal, the medium is localized.[34]

Inasmuch as no one scripture is infallible or final, Radhakrishnan is willing to assert that some scriptures are more true than others. Some come closer to communicating the truth behind the scriptures, or do so in a more lucid fashion, than others. Scripture, then, can be used to judge and measure other scriptures.[35]

Radhakrishnan's Use of Christian Scripture

The matters covered thus far have all been indirect examples of the way in which Radhakrishnan uses Christian scriptures to his work. This section promises to be more direct in cataloguing and analyzing the way in which scriptures are cited, the occasions and manner in which scriptures are cited, the purpose for his use of scripture and the reason behind his employment of Christian scriptures in his writing. Whereas this section does not promise to be encyclopaedic in its coverage, it does attempt to be comprehensive. That is, although every type of usage will be noted, certainly not every single use of scripture will be cited.

When Sarvepalli Radhakrishnan's works are read it is evident to even the most casual reader that the author is well-versed in the literature of the world; not only the religious literature, but the philosophical and belletristic literature as well. If the reader is familiar with the Christian scriptures, she may well be amazed at the knowledge of this literature displayed in Radhakrishnan's writings. The knowledge demonstrated by Radhakrishnan is clearly more than a cursory knowledge; it is one that has been the outcome of many years of intimate interaction with the Christian scriptures. Although much of his knowledge surely derives from his many years at Christian missionary institutions of learning, it also seems that he carried a personal interest in these scriptures throughout his life.

His familiarity with and knowledge of Christian scriptures is sufficient to arouse the envy of the most conservative Christian. Many of the texts to which he makes reference are so obscure that I am vaguely aware that they are "biblical" but cannot even place them within the limits of the Old or New Testament, much less the specific book and chapter. He is not drawing on the old favourites and the standard texts that any preacher on any Sunday may be speaking on in his sermon. Radhakrishnan seems to have an extensive and deep knowledge of the Christian scriptures.

Ways of Citing Scriptures

The ways in which Radhakrishnan cites these scriptures can be characterized in many ways. I have catalogued the ways in which he quotes Christian scriptures in his writings according to the following categories :

    a. unconscious references
    b. conscious, cited references
    c. conscious, semi-cited references
    d. conscious, uncited references
    e. self-conscious references
    f. unconscious and/or self-conscious references

By the first category, the unconscious references, I intend those references to Christian scripture that are apparently not meant as references but it just happens that the phraseology of some texts has become a part of Radhakrishnan's vocabulary. In several contexts when he is trying to demonstrate the need for spiritual sustenance in human life, Radhakrishnan affirms that "man does not live by bread alone."[36] Although he uses this phrase frequently he never cites it as a quotation from Deuteronomy 8:3 (or

Matthew 4:4 or Luke 4:4). Apparently he is unaware of the biblical source of this phrase, having adopted it as his own.

In a similar fashion, when he is trying to underscore the importance of the spiritual matters in life over the material, Radhakrishnan asks in several contexts, "what shall it profit a man, if he shall gain the whole world and lose his own soul?"[37] Again, he is so accustomed to employing this particular phrase and it fits so well into his world view, Radhakrishnan seems to have lost sight of the source. It is so much a part of his thinking and speaking that it has become what I call an unconscious reference to the Bible.[38]

The second category, the conscious and cited references, designates those times when Radhakrishnan quotes a passage from the Christian scriptures, indicates that it is a citation by setting it off in quotation marks, and then either in the text or a footnote gives the precise location of the passage. This is probably the most common method of scriptural quotation by Radhakrishnan and is sufficiently self-explanatory to require no specific examples.[39]

The third category, the conscious and semi-cited references, is distinguished from the second only by the fact that Radhakrishnan does not give a precise location for the quotation. He designates it as a direct quotation by the use of quotation marks, but only gives a vague reference to the source. He may only credit the Apostle Paul without citing the specific epistle, refer to the epistle by name but not the author, or refer to what Jesus said, what the Psalmist said, etc., without specifying the exact location of the statement.[40] Similarly, Radhakrishnan may set off a citation with quotation marks and then follow with a vague reference to the source in parentheses. In at least one context, he is content to allow the citation to be as general as "The Hebrew Bible."[41]

In all of these contexts it seems that Radhakrishnan is conscious that he is citing scripture from the Christian tradition (and the Hebrew tradition), even aware of the general location of the text in the scriptures. But he does not give the precise location or the full citation of the reference. It could be that he knows the location but does not consider it important to communicate since it is not his purpose to teach the Christian scriptures. Or it could be that he is only vaguely aware of the location of the text and does not deem it to be of sufficient significance to track it down (again, for the reason that it is not his purpose to teach Christian scriptures). Since these are speculations on the purpose for citing Christian scriptures, they will be dealt with more fully below.

One more use of the third category merits particular consideration. In at least two contexts, Radhakrishnan employs an awkward circumlocution in introducing the quotation; he indicates that he knows it is in a scriptural tradition, but seems to go out of his way to avoid naming the tradition. When he wants to introduce the words of Jesus which teach that "by their fruits you shall know them," Radhakrishnan tells us that this is the observation of "one of the greatest religious geniuses of the world." Likewise, when he wants to indicate that women are often held blameworthy for many of the world's ills, he points to the narrative that ends with the accusation that "the woman tempted me." Rather than citing this narrative as being found in the book of Genesis, or the Torah, or the Hebrew canon, Radhakrishnan tells us that this narrative is "according to a great religious tradition."[42] It seems that he wants to give credit to a source but is reluctant to name the source.

This usage leads into the fourth category, the conscious uncited references to scripture. By this category I intend those times when Radhakrishnan sets off a phrase in a sentence or a paragraph with quotation marks, indicating that he is borrowing this phrase from an outside source, but does not give any general or specific citation to a source.

Sometimes the context suggests that the uncited quotation is from Christian scriptures. For example when discussing the history of the Christian church Radhakrishnan says that a conflict could be found between the impulse to "render unto Caesar the things that are Caesar's" and the belief that "the powers that be are ordained by God."[43] But in other contexts it is not nearly so clear. For example in a chapter on the philosophy of the Upaniṣads, Radhakrishnan indicates that traditions are founded on revelations but the followers trust the revelations rather than receive them. To substantiate this assertion, he adds the quotation, "Blessed are they that have not seen and yet have believed." Although he sets it off in quotation marks, indicating that it is derived from an independent source, he gives no indication what that source may be.[44] For the reader unfamiliar with the Christian scriptures there is no clue that this is a quotation from the Bible. It could just as easily be from the Upaniṣads or a Buddhist Sūtra, and it often is. In some contexts it is not clear if Radhakrishnan is aware of the fact that he is using a biblical quotation or if he is simply aware that the words are not his. Some of these "conscious, uncited" references may be close to his "unconscious references;" he is aware only that the phraseology is borrowed but is so familiar with the phrase that he has lost the origin, having made the phrase his own.

A similar overlap between categories one and four can also be found in category five, the self-conscious references. I call this category the self-conscious references because it is clear that Radhakrishnan is aware that he is quoting Christian scripture by citing it either directly or indirectly. But it seems equally clear that he is aware that he is employing it in a way that would not be considered orthodox by the average Christian, or at least recognized as a non-standard interpretation. In *An Idealist View of Life*, for example, Radhakrishnan quotes or cites ten passages from the New Testament in just six pages in order to show that

Jesus, the disciples, and the Gospel writers taught, or at least believed in, the doctrine of karma and the idea of reincarnation. In a comparable manner, in *Indian Philosophy* (vol. 1) Radhakrishnan quotes biblical passages when describing Indian principles : "give us this day our daily bread" was the spirit of the Vedic Aryan; "blessed are the pure in heart for they shall see God" describes the Vedic ṛṣis (seers); "become perfect even as your Father in heaven is perfect" defines the spirit of the ethics of the Upaniṣads.[45]

The sixth category, the unconscious and/or self-conscious references, reflects some of the ambiguity that surrounds the way in which Radhakrishnan quotes and cites Christian scripture in his writings. This category designates those usages that are not set off by quotation marks, and therefore give the appearance of being unconscious references, but which are also rather familiar texts used in quite non-standard (or as I call, self-conscious) ways. For example, Radhakrishnan says that all avataras claim that they are the truth, the way and the life. He does not put this in quotation marks, nor does he cite it as a biblical reference, but it is unmistakenly drawn from a very familiar text in the Gospel of John (14:6, "Jesus said . . . 'I am the way, the truth, and the life . . .'"). In another context, Radhakrishnan says that for the Hindu mind, religion has been a lamp unto its feet and a light unto its path. Though no reference is made and no quotation marks are used, this is clearly drawn from a popular passage in the Psalms of the Hebrew canon (119:105, "They word is a lamp unto my feet, a light unto my path"). Likewise, when Radhakrishnan says that the pinnacle of religion is found in the injunction to do justly, to love beauty, and walk humbly with the spirit of truth, it is difficult not to see the connection to the well-known affirmation of the Hebrew prophet Micah (6:8, "what does the Lord require of you but to do justice, and to love kindness and to walk humbly with your God?"). But Radhakrishnan does not draw this connection.[46]

It seems clear that all of these passages teach something other than what Radhakrishnan is drawing from them, but by not using quotation marks or giving any citation he is not even directing attention to the fact that these are biblical quotations. Are these unconscious usages, and therefore rightfully placed in the first category or are these self-conscious usages, and therefore placed in the fifth category? Because neither category seems adequate for these particular usages, I have created this sixth category.

Occasion and Purpose of Scripture Citations

We turn now from an examination of the way in which Radhakrishnan cites Christian scripture to a cursory survey of the occasions and purposes of these citations. Although this was the initial intention of this study, constraints of length cause it to be little more than an appendix. This segment of the study, though, is the most significant aspect of the question of Radhakrishnan's use of Christian scriptures and merits far more investigation and analysis. This section, then, will prove to be more suggestive than conclusive but will also provide the basic material necessary for a more serious pursuit of the question. I have summarized the principles that Radhakrishnan uses when quoting Christian scriptures according to the following categorical outline :

1. Statements of Basic Truths
   a. basic human truths
   b. basic religious truths
   c. basic moral truths

2. Explanations
   a. assist in explanation of a point
   b. a parallel statement to a truth already asserted
   c. confirmation

3. Demonstration of Similarity

    a. similarity with other religions
    b. similarity with Indian religions
 4. Interpretation
    a. indicate a new way of interpreting a text
    b. indicate an Advaitin interpretation of a text
 5. Expression
    a. employ a well-turned phrase

Radhakrishnan is interested in the nature of truth and the variety of sources of truth that can be found in the world, especially the world of religion, so it is natural that he would look to Christian scriptures for statements of basic truths. When he wants to show the basic human truth that common people tend to follow leaders, he quotes Jesus. Jesus speaks of the leaders of the community as the "salt, the light, and the leaven" of that community; it is these few that lead and influence the many. When he wishes to demonstrate the basic human truth that the cause of war and strife in the world can be traced not to social, political, or economic problems but to human problems of greed and lust, he quotes the apostle James.[47]

Radhakrishnan also quotes Christian scripture in order to exemplify basic religious truths. This is particularly evident when he makes statements that he considers to be true for all religions. Radhakrishnan quotes Christian scriptures as examples of the basic religious truth that all religions are based on : personal experience, love, love of neighbour, love of God, self-denial, and/or compassion to the suffering.[48] Another example of a basic religious truth is the fact that spiritual insight begins with prayer for a divine vision; for support of this truth, Radhakrishnan cites the Bhagavad Gītā, the Saddharmapundarikasūtra, and four biblical texts. In another context supporting the same basic religious truth, Radhakrishnan quotes the Vedas, Plato Augustine, Aquinas, the Qur'an, and five biblical texts.[49]

Statements of basic moral truths are also supported by quotations or references to Christian scripture. Radhakrishnan refers to the parable of the talents told by Jesus in the Gospel of Matthew in order to illustrate the truth of the principle of dharma which teaches that everyone must do their own part to the best of their abilities. He quotes a passage from the apostle Paul when illustrating the truth of the doctrine of karma which teaches that if you sow to the flesh you will reap in the flesh, i.e., you reap what you sow.[50]

Radhakrishnan also draws upon Christian scripture in order to provide explanations in his writings. Possibly this is done in order to assist the Western/Christian reader in finding a point of contact between what they already know and that which Radhakrishnan is trying to teach. Radhakrishnan's commentary on the Bhagavad Gītā provides numerous examples of the quotation of biblical passages for the purpose of assisting in the explanation of a point. For example, when addressing the question, "How can we identify an historical individual with the Supreme God," that is, how can Kṛṣṇa be God, Radhakrishnan quotes six passages from the Gospels that relate to the divine consciousness and divine status of Jesus. This does not answer the question as much as it puts it in a context that can be understood and appreciated by a Western/Christian reader. Similarly, when explaining what is meant by action done without any desire for reward, he quotes passages from the New Testament that speak of God or Christ working in and through the individual.[51]

Another way that Radhakrishnan employs biblical passages for explanatory purposes is to follow a statement about Indian religion or philosophy with a parallel statement from Christian scriptures. For example, he cites a Hindu text which asserts that humans are immortal and then quotes a biblical text which declares the same thing. In another context he follows a quotation from a Sanskrit proverb that teaches the mysterious way of the spirit with a quotation from Jesus that suggests a similar teaching : "the wind bloweth where it listeth . . . ."[52]

Radhakrishnan's use of Christian scripture for confirmation of a truth previously asserted is analogous to the manner just noted; it differs only in that the quotation does not seem to elucidate an obscure or foreign notion. Rather, the quotation seems to be used merely to lend additional support to the proposition. When Radhakrishnan says that God is in us, he quotes a passage which says "the body is the temple of the Holy Spirit." When he states that Śaṁkara finds nothing worth pursuing in this life, Radhakrishnan quotes a lengthy passage from the New Testament which begins, "love not the world . . . ."[53]

Since Radhakrishnan concludes that all religions have the same bases and derive from the same premises, it is no surprise that he frequently quotes Christian scriptures in order to demonstrate the similarity between other religions and Christianity, specifically the similarity between Christianity and Indian religions. The quotation itself asserts the point he is trying to make; all religions are similar.

To show the similarity of Christ's experience with that of the Buddha, Radhakrishnan cites two passages from the Epistles of Paul that speak of rebirth, revelation, and development of spiritual wisdom, and a passage from the Second Epistle of John that speaks of overcoming the world. To demonstrate that all religions teach that silence is the best way to approach the ultimate, Radhakrishnan quotes Lao tzu, the Buddha, and Jesus. To establish the fact that all religions and philosophies teach that victory over evil comes through suffering, Radhakrishnan quotes a passage from Jesus that summarizes the experience of the Buddha and Socrates.[54]

It is more fundamental to the concerns expressed in Radhakrishnan's writings, though, that he be able to demonstrate the similarity of Christianity with Indian religion, specifically Hinduism. This theme is interwoven throughout several of his major works, including *Bhagavad Gītā, East and West in Religion,* and *Eastern Religions and Western Thought.* Only a few examples of this dominant theme will suffice. He seems particularly interested in demonstrating the similarity of the Hindu doctrines of karma, samsara, and mokṣa to doctrines taught or suggested in passages from Christian scriptures. In many contexts he quotes passages from the teachings of Jesus and Paul which teach, or at least imply, a belief in something very similar to these central doctrines of Hinduism.[55] He quotes many passages from both the Old and New Testament that he feels teach the doctrine of maya as he understands it and he finds the equivalent of "tat tvam asi" taught in passages from both the Old and New Testaments.[56]

Whenever Radhakrishnan cites Christian scripture, for whatever reason, he is implicitly interpreting the texts that he cites. But there are instances when an innovative interpretation is clearly the intention of the quotation; these are what I consider the demonstration of a new way of interpreting old texts. Naturally these new ways of interpreting are roughly synonymous with the fifth category of ways of citing scripture, the self-conscious references. Radhakrishnan tells us that when Jesus said "destroy this temple and I will raise it again in three days" he is asserting the truth that the spirit within is mightier than the world of things. He feels that Peter's testimony in Acts 10 confirms the fact that missionaries are not necessary. When the Gospel of John says, "the word becomes flesh," it refers to meditation on truth or the internalization of teaching. When Jesus says, "no one knows the father but the son," it teaches that only those who truly love know God. When the apostle Pauls says that Jesus is the first-born of many (Rom 8.92), he teaches that others like him are to come.[57] These are just a few of the fresh interpretation that Radhakrishnan has given to Christian scriptures.

A specific class of novel interpretations can be found in Radhakrishnan's derivation of Advaitin teachings from biblical texts. Again, example of this particular usage abound. Radhakrishnan considers the passage about the image of God in man (Gen, 1.27) to be about the unity of Atman/Brahman; the statement of Jesus, "I and the Father are one" teaches the same thing. Likewise, the statement in I John 5.21, "Greater is he who is in us than in the world," also teaches the inter-penetration of Atman/Brahman. The fact that the ultimate principle of the universe, Brahman, is within accounts for the fact that Jesus taught that "the Kingdom of God is within you." So that when Jesus declares that "the truth shall make you free," he was referring to the spiritual apprehension of the supreme within. This is the eternal, internal truth that was spoken of by the prophet Jeremiah, who tells us that God said, "I will put my law in their inward parts and write it on their hearts." That is why ultimate truth can be found through introspection.[58]

The last occasion that I note for Radhakrishnan to quote Christian scriptures is in his affection for employing a well-turned phrase. Naturally there is some overlap here with the first category that I noted in the way in which he uses scripture, the unconscious reference. Many times Radhakrishnan will use just a few words from a biblical text which have a nice ring to them or that sound particularly poetic. There is no interpretative or illustrative intention; it is just for the way in which the words come together and communicate a good sound or image that Radhakrishnan uses them. He says Hindus think of religion as a lamp unto the feet, a light unto the path. He speaks of Indian thinkers pouring new wine into old bottles. When referring to the transitory nature of the physical world, Radhakrishnan says that our body is dust returning to dust. He tells us that true faith is the evidence of things not seen.[59] These are all images and phrases found in Christian scriptures, but Radhakrishnan seems to be using them not because of their source but because of their sound.

After recognizing the manner in which Radhakrishnan quotes scripture one is tempted to draw some conclusions about the purpose for his employment of Christian scripture. But the data is not there to support any solid conclusions. It is my impression, though, that it is not for an ulterior purpose of subverting Christianity and subsuming it within Hinduism. It is rather a natural result of his view of religion. Since he finds common bases to all religions and sees as essential unity of all religions, it follows that he would quote scripture from any religion to support truths in all religions. His use of Christian scriptures follows from his assumptions about the nature of religion rather than trying to lead to a conclusion about the place of Christianity or Hinduism within these religions.

Similarly, his reason for quoting scripture is not altogether clear, but it is probable that it results from his view of scripture. Although no one scripture is final or complete, every scripture has truth in it. So it is natural that Radhakrishnan would feel compelled to quote from as many different scriptures as possible, thus ensuring a full coverage of the field. Furthermore, there is a universal message behind and within all scriptures, so it is almost irrelevant which particular scripture is employed. It does happen, however, that Radhakrishnan's background instilled a knowledge of Christian scriptures that he drew upon throughout his life.

Conclusions

This study is meant to be an introduction to the question so the possibility of conclusions at this point is a bit tenuous. Everything that was reviewed in this study is necessary for a complete investigation into the question of Radhakrishnan's use of Christian scripture, but none of it is sufficient. In combination, though, it stands as a necessary propaedeutic. To understand how Radhakrishnan uses Christian scripture, or any scripture for that matter, it is necessary to establish his view of religion as well as his view of scripture. But that alone does not explain the way in which he employs Christian scripture, nor his reasons and purposes for using it. These are scintillating questions that press themselves upon me as I continue my study of Radhakrishnan's writings.

Several things can be learned from this study nevertheless. First of all, it is clear that Radhakrishnan has more than just a passing familiarity with Christian scriptures. Furthermore, his interest in them seems to be more than academic. He seems to have some affinity for them and even, perhaps, a commitment to them. It is surely not a mistake or a coincidence that he happens to call upon the texts of the Christian scriptures so often in his writing. From his unconscious usage to his self-conscious usage, Radhakrishnan weaves Christian scripture throughout his writing.

But what interests me even more than how or why Radhakrishnan uses Christian scriptures in his writing is what can be learned from his usage. That is, to every employment of Christian scripture, Radhakrishnan brings an interpretation, whether implicit or explicit. I think a great deal can be learned from a study of his interpretation of Christian scripture. The study itself would be of sufficient academic value to warrant the effort, but I see a more pressing relevance. I think that Christianity could benefit from the insights offered from a learned "outsider" of the Christian tradition. The shibboleth of contemporary comparative religion is "dialogue;" such a dialogue is available through the writings of Radhakrishnan. An important aspect of this dialogue is hearing what one's own religion sounds like to the ears of a believer in a different religion. Radhakrishnan has given us this in his usage of Christian scripture.

The presuppositions and the world view that Radhakrishnan brings to the texts he quotes and interprets are unencumbered by the baggage of the Western world view that has held Christianity captive for so many centuries. This is not to say that he is not bringing his own peculiar baggage, but at least it is different baggage. His interpretations often sound strange, but not necessarily false. Rarely does he do violence to the text; the interpretations he extracts can often be seen as a legitimate reading of the text. These radically new interpretations are not necessarily wrong; but even if they are wrong, it is important to see the Bible through the eyes of another reader. This provides fresh insights on texts that have become too familiar to Christianity. It would be a great contribution to the arena of East-West dialogue if the interpretations that Radhakrishnan brings to the texts of Christian scripture were assimilated and systematized. I trust this study has been an important introduction to that undertaking.

Working Bibliography

Sarvepalli Radhakrishnan. *An Idealist View of Life,* Bombay : George Allen & Unwin Ltd., 1971, (first edition, 1929).

———. *Bhagavad Gītā.* London : George Allen & Unwin Ltd., 1948.

———. and J.H. Muirhead, eds., *Contemporary Indian Philosophy.* London : George Allen & Unwin Ltd., 1952 (second edition, first edition 1936).

———. *East and West in Religion.* London : George Alen & Unwin Ltd., 1967 (fifth edition, first edition 1933).

_____. *Eastern Religions and Western Thought*. London : Oxford University Press, 1940 (second edition, first edition 1939).

_____. ed. *History of Philosophy Eastern and Western*, Vol. I. London : George Allen & Unwin Ltd., 1952.

_____. ed., *History of Philosophy Eastern and Western*, Vol. II. London : George Allen & Unwin Ltd., 1953.

_____. *Indian Philosophy*, Vol. I. London: George Allen & Unwin Ltd., 1929 (second edition, first edition 1923).

_____. *Indian Philosophy*, Vol. II. London : George Allen & Unwin Ltd., 1930 (second edition, first edition 1927).

_____. *Indian Religions*. Delhi : Orient Paperbacks, 1983 (edited collection of essays and articles).

_____. *Recovery of Faith*. New York : Harper and Brothers, 1955.

_____. *Religion and Society*. London : George Allen & Unwin Ltd., 1959 (fourth edition, first edition 1947).

_____. *The Brahma Sūtra*. London : George Allen & Unwin Ltd., 1959.

_____. and P.T. Raju, eds., *The Concept of Man*. London : George Allen & Unwin Ltd., 1968 (first edition 1960).

_____. *The Hindu View of Life*. London : George Allen & Unwin Ltd., 1927.

_____. "My Search for Truth," in Vergilius Ferm. *Religion in Transition*. Freeport, New York : Books for Libraries Press, 1969 (first printed 1937).

Sarvepalli Gopal. *Radhakrishnan : A Biography*. Oxford; Oxford University Press, 1989.

Robert Minor. *Radhakrishnan : A Biography*. Albany : State University of New York Press, 1987.

Paul Schilpp, ed. *The Philosophy of Radhakrishnan*. New York : Tudor Publishing Company, 1952.

Robert McDermott. *Basic Writings of S. Radhakrishnan*. Delhi : Jaico Publishing House, 1972.

References

1. See bibliography for the works by Radhakrishnan that have been researched. These 700 references actually indicate far more individual texts cited; I noted only when Christian scripture was cited, and many times several texts were cited at the same time. This does not mean that over 700 individual texts were cited, but that in over 700 specific locations, texts were cited. An actual analysis of the texts cited would indicate that the same text or texts were cited many times.

2. I am indebted both directly and indirectly in nearly everything I say about Radhakrishnan's youth, upbringing and education to works by Robert N. Minor of the University of Kansas : Robert N. Minor, *Radhakrishnan : A Religious Biography* (Albany : State University of New York Press, 1987) and "The Christian Education of Sarvepalli Radhakrishnan : A Resource for His Defense of Hinduism," a paper presented at the National Convention of the American Academy of Religion in Atlanta, Georgia, November, 1986. See also Sarvepalli Gopal, *Radhakrishnan : A Biography* (Oxford : Oxford University Press, 1989).

3. It is noteworthy that all of these institutions are considered "reformed" in origin, and the last two are specifically Calvinist in their orientation. I also must note that Radhakrishnan's educational background deepens my affinity for him : there is a dormitory two buildings down from my office on the campus of Hope College (also an institution supported by the Reformed Church of America) named Voorhees Hall, funded by and named after the same Voorhees family that founded and funded Voorhees College.

4. Again the reader is referred to an excellent work by Robert Minor on this stage in Radhakrishnan's life in which he was called on to defend Hinduism, but realized that first it must be defined : "Sarvepalli Radhakrishnan and 'Hinduism' Defined and Defended," in *Religion in Modern India*, Robert D. Baird, editor, New Delhi : Manohar, 1981.

5. *Eastern Religions and Western Thought*, p. 39.
6. "My Search for Truth" in Vergilius Ferm, *Religion in Transition*, p. 21.
7. *East and West in Religion*, p. 111; *The Principal Upanishads*, p. 24, cited in McDermott, *Basic Writings of S. Radhakrishnan*, p. 111; *An Idealist View of Life*, p. 92.
8. *An Idealist View of Life*, p. 92.
9. *Recovery of Faith*, p. 26.
10. *East and West*, "Creative Religion," cited in McDermott, *Basic Writings of S. Radhakrishnan*, pp. 300-305.
11. *Bhagavad Gītā*, pp. 272 and 284; commenting on BG XI.8 and XI.42, Radhakrishnan cites II Kings, Ezekiel, Exodus, Revelations, Isaiah and I Samuel to support his idea of the special vision required for religions experience. Cf. *Religion and Society*, p. 45f, where Radhakrishnan cites Deuteronomy, the Psalms and II Corinthians to support this idea of a spiritual eye.
12. *History of Philosophy Eastern and Western*, Vol. II, p. 446; here R. draws the visions of the Upaniṣadic seers, the Buddha, and Jesus into the same circle. Cf. *Bhagavad Gītā*, p. 270; here Radhakrishnan analogizes the visions of the Hindu seers with the transfiguration of Jesus and the vision of Saul on the road to Damascus.
13. *An Idealist View of Life*, p. 71; citations are noted from Jeremiah 31.37; Mark 1.10; Matthew, 11.11, Acts, 9.1-9. Radhakrishnan argues that the religious experience is self-validating (*ibid.*, p. 176), it is internal (*East and West in Religion*, p. 98, *Recovery of Faith*, p. 75) and personal (*Bhagavad Gītā*, pp. 154 and 193).
14. *Eastern Religions and Western Thought*, pp. 10, 324; *An Idealist View of Life*, p. 226; *Religion in a Changing World*, cited in McDermott, p. 325.
15. *An Idealist View of Life*, p. 222.
16. *Ibid.*, pp. 32-35. It is interesting to note at this point how Radhakrishnan turns the "world and life negating" criticism back on Christianity.

17. *The Brahma Sūtras*, pp. 112, 172; *Recovery of Faith*, p. 36; *East and West in Religion*, p. 124.
18. *An Idealist View of Life*, p. 165; *East and West in Religion*, pp. 24, 32, 37. For purposes of expedition, I am no longer drawing specific attention to the Christian scripture being cited in support of these assertions. But the reader is reminded that the references to works by Radhakrishnan draw attention to those locations where Christian scriptures have been cited for support.
19. *Religion in a Changing World*, in McDermott, p. 328; *An Idealist View of Life*, p. 217.
20. *Recovery of Faith*, p. 14; *Bhagavad Gītā*, pp. 158, 196.
21. *East and West in Religion*, p. 66; *East and West*, in McDermott, p. 303; *Indian Philosophy*, Vol. I, p. 52.
22. *Bhagavad Gītā*, p. 38; *Contemporary Indian Philosophy*, p. 498; *Indian Religion*, p. 17.
23. *Bhagavad Gītā*, p. 195; *Recovery of Faith*, p. 23; *Eastern Religion and Western Thought*, p. 79; *Recovery of Faith*, p. 92; *Eastern Religion and Western Thought*, p. 295.
24. *An Idealist View of Life*, p. 172.
25. *Recovery of Faith*, p. 149.
26. See especially chapters V and VI of *Eastern and Western Thought*. Cf. "Hindu Thought and Christian Doctrine" in *Indian Religions*.
27. *An Indealist View of Life*, p. 28f; *Bhagavad Gītā*, pp. 152-153; "My Search for Truth" in *Religion in Transition*, V. Ferm, ed., p. 18.
28. *The Brahma Sūtra*, pp. 112, 113, 115; *An Idealist View of Life*, pp. 28f; *Indian Religion*, p. 142.
29. *An Idealist View of Life*, pp. 81f, 111; *Bhagavad Gītā*, p. 179. Radhakrishnan tries to connect this spirit of the divine with the great "I am" proclaimed by Yahweh and affirmed by Jesus.
30. *Bhagavad Gītā*, p. 6.
31. *Bhagavad Gītā*, pp. 6-7; *The Brahma Sūtra*, p. 11.
32. *Bhagavad Gītā*, p. 21.

33. *An Idealist View of Life,* pp. 73, 77.
34. *East and West in Religion,* pp. 30f, 38, 106; "My Search for Truth" in *Religion in Transition,* V. Ferm, ed., p. 18; *Indian Religion,* p. 142; *The Brahma Sūtra,* p. 113. Radhakrishnan cites many Christian scriptures on this point : John 16.12; Acts 10.34 35; and several other passages which he cited but did not identify.
35. *An Idealist View of Life,* p. 251.
36. *Religion and Society,* p. 23, *The Hindu View of Life,* p. 58, "My Search for Truth" in Ferm, *Religion in Transition,* p. 16.
37. *Hindu View of Life,* p. 64; *Religion and Society,* p. 59. These two references are particularly interesting because there is no indication that this phrase is biblical. In *Hindu,* it leads into a quotation from a Sanskrit text; in *Society,* it follows after a quote from the Mahābhārata and a footnote to this phrase quotes a poem by Cowper.
38. Other examples of this manner of usage can be found in : *Eastern Religions and Western Thought,* pp. 43, 44, 51; *Indian Philosophy,* vol. I, pp. 85, 659; *Indian Religion,* p. 21; *Religion and Society,* p. 47; *The Hindu View of Life,* pp. 27, 37, 46, 54.
39. See for example *Eastern Religions and Western Thought,* p. 8 (a passage is both quoted and cited by book, chapter, and verse in a footnote); p. 10 (a passage is quoted in the body of the text and the book, chapter, and verse is provided in a footnote); p. 70 (a passage is quoted in the body of the text by book or author and a footnote provides the details of chapter and verse); p. 224 (a passage is quoted in the body of the text introduced by book and chapter, with no further citation in a footnote); p. 264 (a passage is quoted in the body of the text introduced by book, chapter, and verse). These seem to be all the possible variations of conscious citations and examples of these can be found in virtually every work written by Radhakrishnan.
40. *Indian Philosophy,* Vol. I, p. 196 (introduces a passage with the words, "St. Paul says;" *Bhagavad Gītā,* p. 157 (refers to a quote from "the book of Romans"; *Bhagavad Gītā,* pp. 140, 152 (introduces a passage with the words, "Jesus says;"

Eastern Religions and Western Thought, p. 90 (introduces a passage with the words, "the Psalmist tell us."

41. *Indian Religion,* p. 38 (follows a quotation with the simple notation (Psalms)); p. 42 (follows a quotation from the book of Acts which records a sermon of the apostle Paul with the notation (Paul)); p. 38 introduces a quotation from the book of Exodus with the citation "The Hebrew Bible tell us."

42. *Indian Philosophy,* Vol. II, p. 652; *Religion and Society,* p. 143.

43. *Eastern Religions and Western Thought,* p. 10; cf. *Recovery of Faith,* p. 35.

44. *Indian Philosophy,* Vol. I, p. 231; cf. p. 241.

45. *An Idealist View of Life,* pp. 218-220 (for teaching about karma) and pp. 227-229 (for teachings about reincarnation). *Indian Philosophy,* Vol. I, pp. 108, 128, 208. In *Indian Religions,* he say that early Hinduism taught "an eye for an eye, tooth for tooth" (p. 67) and the Hindu doctrine of ahimsa is summarized as "thou shalt not kill" (p. 87).

46. *Bhagavad Gītā,* p. 158; *Eastern Religions and Western Thought,* p. 20; *Religion and Society,* p. 47. Perhaps the ambiguity of this category derives from my assumption that these particular uncited references are popular and well-known by even those unfamiliar with Christian scriptures. If this assumption is incorrect, then this category is unnecessary. Cf. *Bhagavd Gītā,* p. 159f; *Indian Philosophy,* Vol. I, pp. 77, 245, 246; *The Hindu View of Life,* pp. 58, 63, 64.

47. *Bhagavad Gītā,* p. 140; *Religion and Society,* p. 21. Cf. *Bhagavad Gītā,* p. 21; *East and West in Religion,* p. 94; "My Search for Truth" in Ferm, *Religion in Transition,* pp. 21, 47.

48. *An Idealist View of Life,* p. 71; *East and West in Religion,* pp. 111, 112, 123; *Indian Philosophy,* Vol. I, p. 204; *Indian Religions,* p. 189; *Recovery of Faith,* p. 26.

49. *Indian Philosophy,* Vol. 1, p. 556 and *Religion and Society,* pp. 45f. Cf. *East and West in Religion,* p. 108; *Indian Religion,* p. 164; *Recovery of Faith,* p. 23.

50. *Bhagavad Gītā*, p. 147; *The Hindu View of Life*, p. 53. It must be noted here, though, that in both of these instances, the scripture reference would fall under the category of unconscious reference or unconscious and/or self-conscious because there is no indication that these are biblical quotations.

51. *Bhagavad Gītā*, pp. 31, 31n, 71, 71n, *passim*. Cf. *An Idealist View of Life*, p. 267; *East and West in Religion*, p. 37; *Indian Philosophy*, Vol. II, p. 641; *Recovery of Faith*, pp. 15, 22; *Religion and Society*, p. 77; *The Hindu View of Life*, p. 53.

52. *An Idealist View of Life*, p. 244, *Indian Religions*, p. 74; Cf. *Bhagavad Gītā*, pp. 153, 196; *East and West in Religion*, pp. 73, 93; *Indian Philosophy*, Vol. I, p. 421; *Indian Religions*, pp. 37, 87; *Recovery of Faith*, p. 24; *The Hindu View of Life*, p. 21.

53. "My Search for Truth" in Ferm, *Religion in Transition*, p. 45; *Indian Philosophy*, Vol. II, p. 631. This particular usage by Radhakrishnan is so common that it is unnecessary to list all the occurrences.

54. *An Idealist View of Life*, p. 165; *History of Philosophy Eastern and Western*, Vol. II, p. 445; *Bhagavad Gītā*, p. 21; *East and West in Religion*, p. 124.

55. *An Idealist View of Life*, pp. 218ff, 227, 234; *Indian Philosophy*, Vol. I, p. 244; *Indian Religions*, pp. 145, 155f.

56. *Eastern Religions and Western Thought*, p. 85; *Indian Religions*, p. 103.

57. *An Idealist View of Life*, p. 219; *East and West in Religion*, pp. 30f, 82, 111; *Indian Religion*, p. 140.

58. *An Idealist View of Life*, pp. 81, 82; *Indian Religions*, pp. 103, 74, 138; *History of Philosophy Eastern and Western*, Vol. II, p. 446; *Eastern Religion and Western Thought*, p. 49.

59. *Eastern Religion and Western Thought*, p. 20; *Indian Philosophy*, Vol. I, pp. 52, 536, 659; Cf. *An Idealist View of Life*, pp. 82, 187; *Bhagavad Gītā*, pp. 36, 159f; *Indian Philosophy*, Vol. I, pp. 26, 35, 77, 245, 246. It is worth noting at least in passing that by misquoting the passage about new wine (into old wine *skins*, not bottles), Radhakrishnan indicates that he missed the point of the biblical image.

19
Radhakrishnan and Tolerance in Hinduism

S.S. Rama Rao Pappu
Miami University

Tolerance is the homage which the finite mind pays to the inexhaustibility of the infinite.

S. Radhakrishnan
Eastern Religions and Western Thought

It is generally said that Hinduism is a very tolerant religion. Indian and Western scholars alike state that whereas a minimal tolerance was achieved in "Western" religions rather late in history after a long struggle, a maximal tolerance was evident in Hinduism throughout its history. Jawaharlal Nehru, for example, says that the religion of the ancient Hindus was amazingly tolerant, and "by their extreme tolerance of other beliefs and other ways than their own, they avoided the conflicts that have so often torn society asunder . . ."[1] According to A.L. Basham, the "capacity for toleration contributed to the characteristic resiliency of Hinduism and helped to assure its survival."[2] In several of his works, Radhakrishnan not only lends support to this position but also provides philosophical foundations for tolerance in Hinduism. I shall explicate in this paper Radhakrishnan's analysis of Hindu tolerance.

Let me, at the outset, explain four categories I shall use to analyze the concept of religious tolerance. Religious tolerance may be (a) internal or (b) external; (c) maximal or (d) minimal. From an *internal* point of view, religious tolerance is a function of the concessions of freedom which a religion grants to the non-conformists within its fold and from an *external* point of view, it is a function of the attitudes which one religion adopts towards other religions, the State and other secular institutions.

From an *external* point of view, religious tolerance is *maximal* if one religion accepts the truth of other religions as of equal value with one's own. *Minimally*, an externally tolerant religion is not hostile to other religions and not at war with the State and other secular institutions. It "puts up" with another religion because it cannot destroy it. Some intermediate degrees of tolerance between the maximal and the minimal is possible here. Thus one religion's attitude to another religion may be "live and let live" or it may take the attitude of *primus inter pares*, "first among equals."

From an *internal* point of view, religious tolerance is *maximal* if a religion tolerates every kind of non-conformist belief and action, especially with regard to its metaphysical foundations. Internal religious tolerance is *minimal* if a religion tolerates some deviance sometimes in what it considers to be non-essential matters, e.g. in the performance of rites and rituals and in following socio-religious mores and customs.

According to Radhakrishnan, Hinduism is maximally tolerant, both externally and internally. "The Hindu attitude is one of positive fellowship, not negative tolerance."[4] Regarding Hinduism's external tolerance, several examples can be given about the warm welcome and reception given to other religions on Hindu soil. As early as the first century A.D., the Jews who fled the persecution of the Romans came to India. "Two races of Jews, white and dark, have for long been established on the south-west coast of India and received charters granting them freedom of worship from the Hindu princess."[5] It is also believed that in 52 A.D. the apostle Thomas came to India and converted the local population to Christianity. "There are copper plates now in Kottayam granted by the king of Cranganore, which confer on Christians privileges of the highest caste and freedom of worship. The first Christian Church in Travancore was built by generous grants from the Hindu king."[6] In the eighth century, likewise, the Zoroastrians who fled to India to escape Persian persecution were given hospitality, and through the generosity of a Hindu prince, they have even built their fire temple. Hindu attitudes to Islam was also one of toleration. The Hindus have permitted the Muslims to build mosques and preach their message. As testimony to this tolerant attitude, Radhakrishnan quotes Abdul Razak, the Ambassador from the court of Persia about the middle of the fifteenth century. Abdul Razak says "the people (of Calicut) are infidels; consequently I consider myself in an enemy's country, as the Muhammadans consider every one who has not received the Quran. Yet I admit that I meet with perfect toleration, and even favour; we have two mosques and are allowed to pray in public."[7] Hinduism's tolerance from an external point of view can be appreciated by the non-Hindu religions if they look at the history of their own encounters with other religions elsewhere and compare how easy it was for them to feel at home in the land of Hinduism.

Hinduism is tolerant internally also. History does not record any Inquisitions within Hinduism and no "heretics" have been sent to the torturer's rack in India. In fact, Hinduism does not have a doctrine of heresy. "Heresy hunting, the favourite game of many religions, is singularly absent in Hinduism."[8] For example, the very existence of divergent "schools" of Hindu philosophy (*darsanas*), ranging from the socalled "heretical" school of Cārvākas to the Absolutism of the Advaita Vedāntins is evidence for maximal tolerance in Hinduism. Aśoka and Dasaratha have patronised the Ajivakas who are atheists.[9] After "defeating" several religious sects in Hinduism, Śaṁkara, the greatest of the Hindu philosopher who lived in the eighth century A.D. has again reestablished six of them, and hence he is called "*sanmathasthāpanācārya.*" Jayantha, a ninth century philosopher states that everyone believed during his time that all religions are equally true. Appayya Dikshita, a famous Vedāntic philosopher, says : "I do not find any difference in essence between Śiva the lord of the world and Viṣṇu the spirit of the universe. Yet my devotion is given to Śiva."[10] Hindu lawgivers like Manu and Yajñavalkya also require and recognize that the heretics' customs must be held and recognized.[11] This toleration in religious beliefs has resulted in Hinduism becoming a mosaic. In religious practise too, it has led to such morally unacceptable customs as the *Devadasi* and the *suttee*. K.M. Panikkar, for example, says : "In Hindu society alone no limit seems ever to have been set on the principle of toleration. Nude men can walk about freely in the streets of India and will even be permitted to ride on elephants amidst wide acclamation in the streets on the pretext of religious sanctity. In fact, this abuse of tolerance is one of the reasons for the elevation of fantastic practises to the position of religious customs."[12] Hindu religious sects, here and there, were fanatical about their point of view, but Radhakrishnan justifies the occasional conflicts between religious sects on the analogy of the Oxford University which is constituted of different colleges, competing with each other, but always aiming at obtaining the same knowledge and truth.

Why is this maximal tolerance exhibited in Hinduism (and its offshoot Buddhism) but not in Semitic religions? I shall delineate from Radhakrishnan's writings four philosophical reasons. It should however be borne in mind that Radhakrishnan is not establishing here a logical but a factual connection between a religion like Hinduism possessing these four characteristics and a tolerant attitude.

A. First, Hinduism is, for Radhakrishnan, an "experiential religion," and not a "belief religion." "Hinduism is not bound up with a creed or a book, a prophet or a founder, but is persistent search for truth on the basis of continuously renewed experience."[13] Elsewhere he says : "As religion is experience of reality, there is less concern with religious doctrine than with religious feeling, religious life."[14] Tolerance is the essence of an experiential religion, but for a belief religion tolerance at best is an accidental attribute. A belief religion consists of a set of beliefs which are *believed* to be true. Right believing and believing the right things are the most important things. In addition, a belief religion may hold that believing a religion to be true also implies the belief that all other religions are false. Intolerance in a belief religion may thus arise at two levels : (a) From an internal point of view, an individual who holds a belief different from the "true" (i.e. authoritatively held) belief is holding a false belief. Since a belief religion is defined by the truths of the beliefs it holds, a person holding a false belief cannot belong to that religion. Hence problems of intolerance arise leading to heresy, excommunication of members, etc. (b) Externally also a belief religion cannot accept the truths of other religions, since it is a part of the acceptance of the beliefs of a belief religion that truths of other religions are not truths but falsehoods. Therefore, when a belief religion confronts another religion, the attitude of tolerance that it exhibits may at best be minimal, i.e. it may put up with it out of necessity.

Experiential religions like Hinduism, however, are different. The important thing in an experiential religion is not what one believes, but what one experientially encounters. In an experiential religion, an individual is not enjoined merely to *believe* in the truths of a religion but should "realize" the truths of the religion. In a belief religion, the emphasis is on the *truth*, in an experiential religion the emphasis is on *experience* of the truth. Diversity and self-validation are closely related to the concept of experience. Minimally, even if my experience is a false experience, what is false in a false experience is not the experience but the object of my experience. If I have experienced X, even if there is no X, I have still *experienced* X. An experiental religion thus tends to be tolerant in two ways : (a) Internally, it recognizes that the individual's experiences of the truth are different; and (b) externally it holds that religion itself is the experience of the truth which different religions may experience differently.

B. "The religions of the world can be distinguished into those which emphasize the object and those which insist on experience. (Religion) is more than a transforming experience than a notion of God."[15] Radhakrishnan's second argument is when a theistic God, a "God-with-attributes," is postulated as the highest reality, disputes may arise concerning the nature of God and His attributes. Absolutistic religion, on the other hand, places the Absolute beyond all human description and comprehension. If nothing specific can be *said* concerning the Absolute, no disputes can arise on the nature of the Absolute! Hinduism is the absolutistic religion par excellence where the highest Reality, Brahman, is the pure Absolute, which can only be experienced, but not stated. The argument developed in (A) above that Hinduism is tolerant because it stresses experience should not be interpreted to mean that the Hindu experience is a purely subjective, personal thing and therefore it is foolish not to accept as true another person's experiences. Religious experiences which are recognized in Hinduism are neither subjective (like feeling sad), nor objective (like experiencing a house or a tree). Brahman experience is unique, beyond the subjective-objective polarity. The experience is unique because Brahman, the

One, is unique. Brahman does not have any predicates and therefore cannot be pinpointed as the "this."

Given this uniqueness of Brahman and the uniqueness of the religious expereince of Brahman, tolerance becomes the only rational attitude towards another's *anubhava* or experience. Internally, it rules out the possibility of someone being a "heretic" and therefore the problem of tolerating the heretics is dissolved. Externally, given the uniqueness of Brahman or the Absolute, one absolutistic religion cannot be intolerant of another, since all absolutist religions seem to say the same thing, viz. the impossibility of characterizing the Absolute. However, when an absolutistic religion encounters a theistic religion, it is not intolerant to it either, since it views different religions as diverse ways of grasping the same Absolute. Theistic religions, from the absolutist's point of view, are attempts to comprehend the Absolute by giving it qualities (*guṇas*) or predicates. To put the same point from the Hindu context, different conceptions of Absolute as *Saguṇa Brahman* are compatible with the Ultimate conceived as *Nirguṇa Brahman*. In the *Bṛhadāraṇyaka Upaniṣad* (3.9, 1-9), when Yajñavalkya was asked to state the exact number of gods, he starts with 3306 and reduces them to One Brahman. Using this analogy in a reverse way, we may say that the One Brahman who is *nirguṇa* may be conceived as 3306 *saguṇa* (theistic) gods.

C. Theistic Hinduism also, due to the influence of Absolutism, breathes an air of tolerance in matters of worship and in their encounters with other religions. In matters of external tolerance, for example, Kṛṣṇa says in the *Bhagavad Gītā* that "Even those who are devoted to other deities and worship them, filled with faith, they too really worship Me ... For I am both the recipient and the lord of all worship .... But they do not know Me alright."[16] In the *Gītā* conception, therefore, there are no "wrong gods" whom we may worship. There are also no "wrong paths" of worshipping God. *Jñāna*, *Bhakti* and Karma *mārgas* are all equally valid, and each individual ought to adopt that path which best suits his nature. Radhakrishnan says that "the *Gītā* recognizes that different men are led to the spiritual vision by different paths, some by the perplexities of the moral life, some by the doubts of the intellect, and some by the emotional demands for perfection."[17] When we consider that one of the reasons for one religion to be externally intolerant of other religions is that they worship the "wrong gods" and internal intolerance arises because their followers worship in the wrong way, the *Gītā* attitude to God breaths an unparalleled tolerance by stating that there are no wrong gods and no wrong paths to worship God.

Hinduism has become a religion of six million gods because of the same attitude of tolerance. It has developed, says Radhakrishnan, "an attitude of comprehensive charity instead of a fanatic faith in an inflexible creed. It accepted the multiplicity of aboriginal gods and others which originated, most of them, outside the Aryan tradition, and justified them all."[18] Historically polytheistic religions have been more tolerant than monotheistic religions that have insisted on the dogma that belief in a particular religion, in a particular conception of God, in a particular prophet, etc. are necessary for salvation. Commenting on the Greek polytheism, Radhakrishnan says that "if the fair name of Greece is not stained by any religious wars, it was due to its polytheism. The Greeks do not insist that if we call Zeus by some other name, we will suffer eternal perdition."[19]

D. Last but not least, problems of intolerance arise with "organized religions," where the religious authority is centralized in a person or a body of persons. Thus we have problems of external intolerance between the church and the state, church and other religions, and internal intolerance between the church and the dissidents. "When religion becomes organized," says Radhakrishnan, "man ceases to be free."[20] "An organized religion or a church is hostile to every belief which is opposed to its own creed ... A church cannot allow liberty of thought within its borders or, for that matter, even without. It is obliged to enforce beliefs and persecute unbelief on principle."[21] Hinduism has avoided problems of intolerance because it is unorganized. There is no central authority in Hinduism which imposes on its followers what they should believe concerning the nature of God, the path to salvation, the divine law, etc. Brahman in Hinduism is impersonal, the Scriptures are *apauruṣeya* (no personal author), and the Divine Law is nothing more than the *sanātana dharma* or the eternal tradition.

References

1. Jawaharlal Nehru, *The Discovery of India*, ed. by Rober I. Crane (New York : Doubleday Co. Inc., 1959), pp. 60-61.
2. A.L. Basham, *The Wonder That was India* (New York : Grove Press, Inc., 1959), p. 345.
3. I owe this distinction between "internal" and "external" point of view to H. L.A. Hart's *The Concept of Law* (Oxford : Oxford University Press, 1961), pp. 66-100.
4. "The Hindu attitude is one of positive fellowship, not negative tolerance." *Eastern Religions and Western Thought* (Oxford : Oxford University Press, 1939), p. 335.
5. *Eastern Religions and Western Thought*, p. 311.
6. *Ibid.*, pp. 310-311.
7. S. Radhakrishnan, *East and West* (London : George Allen & Unwin Ltd., 1956), p. 31.
8. S. Radhakrishnan, *Hindu View of Life* (London : George Allen & Unwin Ltd., 1927), p. 37.
9. S. Radhakrishnan, *Religion and Society* (London : George Allen and Unwin Ltd., 1947), p. 55.
10. *Eastern Religions and Western Thought*, p. 311.

11. *Religion and Society*, p. 55.
12. K.M. Panikkar, *Hindu Society at Cross Roads* (New York : Asia Publishing House, 1961, pp. 75-76).
13. *Religion and Society*, p.54.
14. *East and West*, p. 24.
15. *Eastern Religions and Western Thought*, p. 21.
16. *The Bhagavad Gītā*, IX. 23, 24.
17. S. Radhakrishnan, *Indian Philosophy* (London : George Allen and Unwin, 1923), Vol. l, p. 554.
18. *Hindu View of Life*, p. 37.
19. *East and West in Religion* (London : George Allen & Unwin, Ltd. 1933), pp. 50-51.
20. *East and West*, p. 41.
21. *East and West in Religion*, p. 50.

20
Radhakrishnan's Philosophy of Religion : Some Methodological Considerations

JOHN M. KOLLER
Rensellaer Polytechnic Institute

I. Introduction

Can Radhakrishnan's philosophy of religion meet the challenge posed by skeptics of comparative philosophy? Further, can his philosophy of religion incorporate recent insights of philosophers, historians, theologians and anthropologists? One of the principal concerns of the contemporary study of religion is how we can admit the legitimacy - even the truth - of differing religious faiths - doctrines, values and norms - without committing ourselves to a thoroughgoing relativism, reducing ourselves ultimately to abandoning all claims to truth and reality. Can Radhakrishnan admit the plurality of religious ways that empirical and historical studies reveal? And can it admit this plurality without sinking into relativism?

As a comparativist, Radhakrishnan was acutely aware of the tension between the (presumed) universality of philosophy's canons (its criteria of truth), and the local and relative nature of a given culture's canons (its norms of reality and action).

Not only did Radhakrishnan inherit a cultural and religious tradition which saw plurality and diversity as a manifestation of the underlying unity of being - thus being able to admit the truths of local cultures and traditions and to see their relations to each other in terms of a shared ground, but at an early age he encountered Christian claims that Christianity was the one true religion, forcing him to work out a view which reconciled his experience of the truth of his own faith with the truth of Christian faith. This provided the groundwork for a lifetime of comparative work in which he constantly encountered different views of reality and truth, each claiming to be unique or exclusive. His distinction between the universal transcendent ground of existence and the local conditions which mediate the growth and expression of existence points the way to resolving this tension by recognizing the difference between what is shared by people across cultures and what is peculiar to individual cultures, and indeed, to individual persons. But before examining how Radhakrishnan's philosophy can meet recent philosophical challenges, we need to sketch his view of religion and religions.

Radhakrishnan referred to his philosophy of religion as "philosophy of the spirit," which he saw as a universal philosophy, applicable to all religions, not merely to Hinduism, or Hinduism and Christianity. In his opening essay in *The Philosophy of Sarvepalli Radhakrishnan*, entitled "The religion of the spirit and word's need : fragments of a confession," he recognizes that the world badly needs a common philosophy, or at least a common world outlook.[1] The recognition of this need and his own personal experience shaped what he called his "search for a spiritual religion, that is universally valid."[2] He saw this need as urgent and the quest imperative. Without religion or spiritual values, he said, "All that remains for man to do is to be born, to grow up, to earn and to spend, to mate, to produce offspring, to grow old, and at last to sleep forever, safe in the belief that there is no purpose to be served in life except the mechanical processes."[3]

Although he blamed science and technology for their role in the development of the modern mechanistic world view, he saw the decline of religious life "due to dogmatic religion as much as to mechanistic science."[4]

The "confession" he refers to in his title is that his life-long ambition was to show, philosophically, that all life is ultimately grounded in spirit and that to live fully as human beings we all must respond to the spiritual dimension of life. As he says, "My one supreme interest has been to try to restore a sense of spiritual values to the millions of religiously displaced persons."[5]

"Spirit" is a word Radhakrishnan uses to refer to the ultimate reality recognized by different names in the different religious traditions, God, Allah, the Dharma, the Tao, etc. He says, "The Upaniṣads believe that the principle of Spirit is at work at all levels of existence, moulding the lower forms into expression of the higher. The spendour of Spirit, which in Greek philosophy was identified with the transcendental and timeless world of Ideas, or in Christian thought is reserved for the divine supernatural sphere, is making use of natural forces in the historical world."[6]

Probably the closest to a definition of religion (religion of the spirit) that Radhakrishnan comes is the following : "The function of the discipline of religion is to further the evolution of man into his divine stature, develop increased awareness and intensity of understanding. It is to bring about a better, deeper and more enduring adjustment in life. All belief and practise, song and prayer, meditation and contemplation, are means to this development of direct experience, and inner frame of mind, a sense of freedom and fearlessness, strength and security. Religion is the way in which the individual organizes his inward being and responds to what is envisaged by him as the ultimate Reality."

Central to this view of religion is the insight that "The fundamental truths of a spiritual religion are that our real self is the supreme being, which it is our business to discover and consciously become, and [that] this being is one in all."[7] It may be tempting to interpret this as a view peculiar to Hindu Vedānta, taking the statement "our real self is the supreme being" to be a paraphrase of the Upaniṣadic identity affirmed in the great sayings, *Aham Brahmasmi*, or *Tat tvam asi*, which identify Atman, the indwelling self of the individual with Brahman, the indwelling self of reality itself, and thereby to dismiss it as parochial, but I think this would be a mistake. It would also be a mistake to assume that the way Radhakrishnan sees to discover and become this true being is limited to the practise of yoga. I propose that we try to understand how the claim that the supreme being is "one in all" can refer to not merely a Vedāntic view of the unity of existence in Brahman, but an underlying universality of all religious faiths - characteristic of all religious persons. What all religious persons have in common is a conviction that their own being is grounded in a being or reality that transcends their individuality, their own time, and place, and their own immediate history or society. Indeed part of the reason, at least, why many religions make exclusive claims, e.g., why it is claimed that "there is no God but Allah," or "through Christ alone is salvation possible," is that the supreme reality is held to be universal - it grounds all existence, the existence of all people, and indeed, all existence. When, however, the religious faith that affirms the universality of the supreme reality which grounds all existence, becomes aware of other faiths, there are basically two types of response available. The first response is to regard the other as somehow ignorantly or willfully believing in a false supreme reality, or of not having yet attained to faith in a supreme reality (making such persons candidates for conversion). The second response is to see that the supreme reality can be recognized in diverse forms; that is culture that differentiates into diverse forms what is in itself is undivided. This later, of course, is the view taken in the Vedas where it is said, "the one called by many different names."

What is the relationship between the single, shared ground and the diverse manifestation of existence from this ground? How do we know that what is called by many names is the same reality and not different realities?

Here we come to the challenges the skeptics present to the comprativist. (1) The first challenge begins with the observation that empirical and historical studies reveal many different religions, each changing over time, each with its own world view, teachings and practises. No universal religion which could provide a vantage point from which to judge the truth or adequacy of particular religions has yet been discovered, nor does it seem logically possible that there could be such a "super" religion. To talk about religion in the singular is an empty abstraction, as is talk about a single reality which the diverse traditions designate in their different ways. (2) The second challenge accepts the plurality of religions, pointing out that each consists of a culturally unique set of symbols, making it impossible for us ever to understand them in their own context, from the inside, as it were, since this would mean living in this other culture, rather than our own. (3) The third challenge asks, How does a comparativist ever know if his view, as an observer of another's way of life, is correct? This challenge assumes that being shaped by our own cultural context, we can never enter the cultural context of the other, but it raises the additional question of whether any world view can be compared with another. This latter question can be looked at as a separate, though related, challenge. (4) This fourth challenge asks, How can we ever judge a world view to be true, for to determine its truth requires comparing it with reality itself. But this requires yet another view in which they can be compared. However, the truth of this second world view requires yet another view, and so on, in an infinite regress. In truth, aren't we locked into our own world view, forever separated from reality itself?

II. Religion or Religions?

The first challenge suggests that we should talk about "religions" in the plural, since we recognize many religions. In a sense this is true, for we certainly do recognize that different people have different ways of being religious. My concern is with what "religion" refers to. Since I take religion to be a convenient term to refer to the most fundamental faith by which a person orients her/his life, it is not the sort of thing we can easily say a person *has* - certainly not "has" in the sense of having a car or house, or even a set of concepts or ideas; A religious person *is* religious; does not *have a religion*. There is something very strange about asking someone - or being asked by someone - "do you have a religion?" To think about religion as an object, an "it" which you can add or delete from your repertoire of techniques for managing your life is to seriously misunderstand the religious life, the life of faith. Radhakrishnan was not willing to concede that there are many different religions, although, of course, he recognized that people are religious in different ways; not only are Buddhists religious in different ways from Catholics, but Catholics are religious in different ways from each other; and so are Buddhists. Why, if the different ways of being religious that characterize Catholics - or that characterize Methodists, Lutherans, and Catholics - do not prevent us from seeing them - and they from seeing themselves - as members of one on-going Christian community, should the fact that Hindus are religious in different ways from Christians prevent us from seeing all of them as participating in one on-going religious community?

Perhaps the difference is primarily historical - we are aware of the historical schisms that have taken place, and are aware of the parting of the ways of being religious within the Christian community. But today, as we become increasingly conscious of the fact that we all share the same eco-system, that we are indeed one human family sharing our life on this planet with each other, can't the historical process of joining in our self-consciousness with the self-consciousness of others count as an important historical fact enabling us to recognize our sameness in being religious as well as our diversities in the ways in which we are religious? The key is to see religion in its many forms, and in these forms find what makes them different forms of religion. The historic mistake was to think that different forms of religion were different religions, analogous to the mistake in going from different world views to different worlds.

III. Understanding in Context

The second challenge suggests that full understanding of a religion other than one's own is impossible because of the inaccessibility of its context. The appropriate response to this challenge is to recognize that in a sense, all thought is comparative, for knowledge or information is essentially awareness of differences, and we become aware of differences only through comparing different things. But difference always presupposes sameness; unless we can bring different things within the same view we cannot compare them; and to compare is see what they have in common as well as how they differ. Difference and sameness are thus complementary opposites that function only in relation to each other. But the explicit method of comparative philosophy is to compare views, arguments, analyses, and ways of thought across cultures. This has tremendous advantages in that it allows - even forces - us to overlook the many subtleties and nuances - the incredible density - of the things we are comparing, enabling us to look at only the more general features; by overlooking the minute details of the individual trees and the interrelations between them we are able to see the entire forest. At the same time, it has risks, for by overlooking the details of our subjects and all the subtleties of the contexts in which our subjects are located, we miss the richness and colour of the subjects. If we have no sense of individual trees, and of relations between individual trees and other plants, and of various forms of life that have as their home the environment of the forest - then our comparisons of one forest with another are relatively shallow and insignificant. We see only relative shape, density and size, for example, but don't see what these differences mean to the trees and to the rest of forest life. Thus, the comparative method requires both detailed study of our subject in relation to its context and more general studies of the subject located in a larger context of the metaphors and hypotheses of comparative thought. Although sensitive to the context of the subject being studied, comparativists recognize that to think about something is always to take it out of its original context and place it in the context of thought. Trying to understand how different cultural traditions have thought about reality and human life, we try to think about thought in terms of categories broad enough to embrace several cultures.

As Scharfstein points out : "To understand the density of human beings is to preserve one's modesty in characterizing them. No one has a full grasp of the working of even a single cell in a human body, let alone a human's philosophical views; and it does not usually help us to understand his philosophical views if we insist on confining our study to the single cells of his body. It is necessary for us to be clear about context and to try sometimes to come as close as we can to being sufficient. At the same time, we should not allow our interest in context to stand in the way of distant and radical comparison. Contextualism is too easy a refuge from analysis. It prevents a more than instinctive understanding of even individuality and context. The parochialism it encourages is itself a form of misunderstanding, intellectually little but myopia raised to the status of a virtue.

He goes on to comment that "The fullest attempt to understand distant thought may be, in effect, both to insert it into and extract it from context. Local detail and nuance make an object rich in texture but may obscure its shape against its background and make it difficult to compare. If we disregard its nuances and extract it, so to speak, from its context, we get a clear but sparsely textured shape."[8]

Typically, and this is what this second challenge assumes, when we try to understand another person's religion we make that person's world view - the doctrines of his religion or the principles of her metaphysics - part of the data that we are organizing, that we are organizing according to our own world view. Is this the best we can do? Or can we learn to see *through* that person's world view; use that person's frame to see the world, and then compare the world we see using our traditional world view?

Morris Augustine (*Buddhist-Christian Studies,* Vol. 6, 1986), shows us one way to enter another's context in our studies of other religious ways. Noting that "purely intellectual research into ideas, world views . . ." does not necessarily lead to any deep understanding or any real feeling of equality and respect for the people studied, he suggests that we need to share human experience as well as ideas. "Performance," he says, "shared performances, provide a basis for comparing one anothers most beloved cultural treasures - including religion."

Although Augustine doesn't elaborate on idea of religion as performance, it seems an important suggestion. My first question is, if we take religion as performance, what is performed? What does religion perform - or better, what does the religious person or the religious community perform? Is religious activity the performance of life itself? Is it the co-creation and expression of life in response to experienced promptings or urgings of ultimate reality - experienced as the divine or sacred ground of existence? If so, we can look at religion as the making of life; this is why it makes sense to look not at religion but at religious activity, for here we naturally focus on the dynamic, on the creative aspects that constitute the making of life religiously. The religious person's calling is to respond to the sacred, creative force, shaping his life in accord with its demands.

We might say that the religious person performs the sacred dance of life in beat with the sacred rhythm of ultimate reality itself, in the style or manner the cultural community has shaped as an appropriate response to the music of the sacred, simultaneously shaping his style in accord with the traditional style of the culture, and shaping that continuing tradition with his unique response and style, thus contributing to the ongoing tradition even as he receives from it. (If this analogy works, it should be possible to substitute the appropriate cultural terms into the formula without doing violence to the deepest convictions about human relation to the sacred).

Augustine's thinking about a comparative philosophy of religion is informed not only by intellectual thought about religion by theologians, philosophers, historians, anthropologists and sociologists, but by inter-faith participatory practise. He was one of the group of seventeen Catholic monks and nuns who lived as Zen monks with Japanese monks in a Zen monastery in Japan for a month in 1983, and who earlier, in 1979, had shared Benedictine monastic life with some fifty Japanese practioners who had come to Europe to live as Benedictine monks for three weeks. According to the author, Professor Anzai Nobru's sociological study of the participants sharing their religious life with each other showed that almost all reported greatly increased respect and admiration for their host's tradition and were greatly impressed with the common ground uniting the two religious traditions - despite the many differences between them. Augustine's task - and ours - is to try to construct a theoretical account of religious activity that will account for ground of both the differences and similarities found in the various religious traditions considered, relying on both shared experience and thought.

IV. Getting it Right

The third challenge to the comparativist philosopher of religion asks how we can ascertain that our view, as observer of the others' view is correct. Part of the answer was suggested above : Don't remain merely an observer, become a participant as well. While this may be sound advice, we still need ways to verify the correctness of our categories of thought and analyses. Surely one appropriate test is to ask the other about the correctness. If our view cannot be accepted by the other, then we have it wrong. When dealing with historical issues, for example, whether our view of Śaṁkara's view is correct, we need to translate our language into the language Śaṁkara used, and look at the appropriate texts to see if he actually talked the way we are claiming he talked; or the way he would have talked if he held the view we are ascribing to him.

According to W.C. Smith, "Radhakrishnan's interpretation of Christianity, some Christians may feel, will become valid only when Christians adopt a Hindu attitude to religion and to Christ."[9] The issue is whether a Hindu theology subordinates all other religions; whether a Christian theology subordinates all others, etc. How can Radhakrishnan be a Hindu (Vedāntic Hindu) and not take this faith to be true, and to have priority over any other faith? Can a theology which does not give priority to the Muslim faith possibly be acceptable to a Muslim? In working out a philosophy of religion we must be sensitive to such questions, for a philosophy of comparative religion which is not acceptable to the religions explained is ultimately not acceptable. In addition to getting its understanding right, this means that somehow the philosophy must make clear that its statements are on a different level (of a different type) than the statements of a Christian theology or an Islamic theology; and that these theological statements are themselves on a different level than the statement of faith that provide the framework through which the religious person views the world. (A framework looked through is different than a framework looked at; these are of different types or levels; the second is a metastatement about the first.)

A comparative philosophy of religion must articulate the forms and dynamics of faith in a way that people who are religious in different ways can accept; more than merely accept, accept and find illuminating; it will not, of course, be a substitute for faith, for it is of a different logical type, being a series of statements about faith. Such a philosophy was unnecessary, maybe impossible, until awareness of other ways of being religious developed; but with that awareness it became a necessity (much as theology had for long been a necessary part of religious faith?) A philosophy of religion that violates a religious community's self-understanding is, for that very reason, unacceptable. Such a philosophy is necessary for religious persons who have become aware of different ways of being religious, in order to understand how there can be other genuine ways of being religious, and to understand what this means for the way one is religious oneself.

V. Views and Reality

The fourth challenge suggests that we can never get outside of our world view - and that therefore we cannot encounter reality itself. This question arises because as we become aware of different world views we want to compare them with our own world view; indeed we do not come to recognize that we have a world view until we recognize others' world views; without that recognition we simply see the world; we see what there is and our framework for seeing is not distinguished from seeing. Only through comparing seeings or views do we come to distinguish between our views of the world and the world itself. Now we are pushed to the opposite extreme, from having naively assumed the identity of our view with the world, we now begin to wonder how we can ever get beyond our view to the world itself. Perhaps all we ever have is our world view, never the world; and each culture or person has their own world view, a kind of personal or cultural solipsism. But something is wrong here; note that it is only through the process of comparing that we come to recognize that we have a world view and that our world view differs from another's world view. To compare, of course, we must be able to hold in view both our own world view and the world view of the other. And yet, this comparison is thought to yield the truth that we can never get outside of our own world view! We need to recognize that information (knowledge) is primarily of differences; the recognition of differences constitutes our information; but this recognition requires a basis, a basis in sameness or sharedness. Difference and sameness are themselves different, but differences within a larger sameness which allows for their recognition and comparison. If we couldn't compare them we couldn't recognize their difference; but we couldn't compare them unless we could bring them both within the same view. But this is no reason to equate our view of the world and the world - and then to claim a plurality of world's corresponding to our plurality of views. Once the worlds are different there seems no way to unite them or even to genuinely encounter them; each of us locked in our own world - a personal or cultural solipsism. This stems from the mistake of taking the individual as the primary locus of being. Once the isolated individual is taken as the primary being and the source of all knowledge, then everything else, including the individual's own body, becomes an object, which as something in itself (*ding an sich*) is forever beyond reach. We can now see this as a mistake; we now know that personal existence is inherently social; that our being is intrinsically relational. It is interesting that the more closely we focus on "local" histories the more clearly we see that not only are they histories of interrelationships (rather than of independent, separate identities), but also that they are histories of relationships with "other" histories in an ever-expanding circle that, at its extreme is global.

The recognition of our shared history across both times and cultures supports Radhakrishnan's call for a new religious attitude that will overcome the provincialisms and rivalries of the past as it seeks "a fellowship of religions, based on the foundational character of man's religious experience."

References

1. Paul Schilpp (ed., *The Philosophy of Sarvepalli Radhakrishnan* (New York : Tudor, 1952), p. 13.
2. *Ibid*, p. 26.
3. *Ibid*, p. 17.
4. *Ibid*, p. 19.
5. *Ibid*, p. 14.
6. *Ibid*, p. 31.
7. S. Radhakrishnan, *Eastern Religions and Western Thought* (London : Oxford University Press, 1939), p. 32.
8. Ben-Ami Scharfstein, "The Contextual Fallacy," *Interpreting Across Boundaris* ed. by Gerald Larson and Eliot Deutsch (Princeton : Princeton University Press, 1988), p. 94.

9. *The Philosophy of Sarvepalli Radhakrishnan*, p. 109.

PART III

RADHAKRISHNAN'S METAPHYSICAL QUEST

21
"Saving the Appearances" in Plato's Academy

PURUSOTTAMA BILIMORIA
Deakin University and
Melbourne University

I. Preamble

The basic thrust of my paper is that Radhakrishnan, clearly one of the doyens of modern Indian Philosophy, was much preoccupied with Western thought - of which he took the classical tradition as his model - and he spent a good part of his speculative life trying to tailor Indian thought to fit the vesture, or maybe the *toga*, of his Greek heroes, namely Plato and Plotinus. I intend to demonstrate this by focusing on some examples from his prolific writing, particularly as these relate to the issue of 'appearances' vis-à-vis *avidyā*. *En passant*, I might say that not a few of us who straddle the two worlds of Eastern and Western thoughts are altogether immune from such a tendency as haunted Radhakrishnan: it is just that we may have shifted our models and changed our audience somewhat.

This presentation carries an autobiographical note on the margin, for it is all too easy for one, after some years of training in Western philosophy and encountering Indian philosophy through the pen of Radhakrishnan, to be impressed, intrigued and even taken in by the familiarity of what seemed to be the problems and issues tackled by the erstwhile Indian minds. One finds oneself led into all kinds of vistas and exciting promises in the vast terrain of Indian *thought* (wherein, we are persuaded, the distinction between philosophy and religion is totally obliterated). In retrospect, and only after one begins to read the original and that too in some depth, the realization occurs that many of the comparisons simply do not hold and there has been a blurring of boundaries beyond the more specialized interests or the treatment accorded to 'the problems' in each of the two or three traditions in question. It nags one that something of the uniqueness of each is lost in the unselfcritical quest for overarching 'truths' and universals in human reflections, past and present, hither and thither.

II.

My basic thesis is that Radhakrishnan found the notions of *māyā* and, in particular, *avidyā*, to be rather embarrassing for they tended to reduce the world to a mere shadow of "appearances" with no basis to their reality. *Māyā* he could handle and deal with, by interpreting it as a creatively-willed "power" of God, but *avidyā*, since it has epistemological overtones, proved a little more formidable. He remained dissatisfied with classical approaches to give a world-redeeming account of *avidyā*, and so ventured to proffer his own, but he travelled far, so to say, to do this.

Now, struggling to explain the nature of reality according to the Upaniṣads, and struck by the text's inscrutability that defy in their account a firm description or commitment either way, hedged also by all sorts of heuristic and negative devices, such as *na iti na iti*, Radhakrishnan stumbles upon certain self-contradictory passages in the *Bhaagavad Gītā* which he thence takes to be supporting a certain metaphysical view of the Upaniṣads, though in a rather curious way. The passage in question states the Supreme to be "unmanifest, unthinkable, and unchanging," "neither existent nor non-existent" (*Bhg* II. 25, XIII.12; his trans.). He swiftly moves to adduce that these predicates bring out the two-fold nature of the Supreme as *being* and *becoming*, only to be qualified by the terms 'transcendent' (*parā*) and immanent (*aparā*).[1] Note that the pairs of equivalents in parenthesis are not isomorphic, but never mind that. Radhakrishnan believes that he has found evidence that takes us away from the preponderant *apersonality*, or in his own words, "the impersonality of the Absolute," for the Upaniṣads, he claims, "support Divine activity and participation in nature and give us a God who exceeds the mere infinite and finite." In the very next sentence Radhakrishnan moves to draw attention to an amazing parallel between the Upaniṣadic teachings and Plato's doctrines, in the following words : "The interest which inspired Plato's instruction to the astronomers of the Academy "to save the appearances," made the seers of the *Upaniṣads* look upon the world as meaningful."[2] Indeed, there was to be more than a mere meaningful glee in the astronomical eyes of the seers!

Just as it was to be the agenda of the astronomers and philosophers in Plato's Academy to "save the appearances" - which culminated in Aristotle's disavowal of "appearances" altogether - the Upaniṣadic seers had also, some centuries earlier, pursued this noble inspiration. Radhakrishnan then goes on to invoke various passages from Śvetāśvatara and similar Upaniṣads which tend to lend credence to the view that the Supreme, which is immutable and unthinkable, is also the source of origin, the active power in and the Lord of the Universe. There is on the one hand the transcendental supracosmic Brahman, eternal and outside time and space, and there is on the other hand the dynamic, cosmic aspect, the immanent will, the uncaused cause, the unmoved mover, that ensouls the evolutionary spirit lording over the matrix of temporal moments, and himself embodies the ideals of truth, beauty, love and value or *the good.* This is Radhakrishnan's way of making the scriptures do the "appearance saving" job.[3]

The parallelism that Radhakrishnan traces between the ideas of the Upaniṣadic seers and those worked over in Plato's Academy goes beyond mere interesting or coincidental phases in the Brahmanical life in the Gangetic planes and that in the aristocratic circles of Athens; rather, Radhakrishnan has a deeper inkling that the two traditions are related or relatable, if not in blood, than possibly via mutual fecundation and the flow of ideas from East to West and West to East.

Let me make another brief divergence before I return to the actual moves that Radhakrishnan gives us for the view he evolves. This divergence relates to his comments on the history of philosophy.

III.

Radhakrishnan saw parallels not just for the sake of the kind of intellectual comparativism he was engaged in, but because, I think, he really believed that the Greeks and Indians were, in some historical sense, *"bhai bhai,"* or in brotherly relation. This comes out clearly in his *East and West Some Reflections* (Beatty Lectures, McGill). In itself, this text makes for a worthy supplement to the rather one-sided view of the history of philosophy (albeit Western philosophy) that has prevailed since the 19th century. Radhakrishnan believed that just as traders, merchants, kings, princes and their ambassadors travelled and exchanged goods, gifts and gems since the 3rd millennium contact between India and Asia-minor that gradually extended to Greece, so philosophers and priests also exchanged ideas or gifts of the mind across the ancient civilizations. Or just as the gods and goods of different lands met at the market place, different streams of human thought also met and mingled.[4] This contact continued into the later days, with Alexander (c. 335 BCE) who, counselled by Aristotle (384-322 BCE), invaded India only to find that its philosophy rivalled that of his master's. Though Seleucus denied a sophist to Bindusārā, there was no dearth of Greek wine, raisins, and Sophist ideas flowing to the Mauryan courts, especially during Candragupta's reign (321-296 BCE).[5] The Mauryan kingdom was visited upon by Megasthenes, Deimachus, Dionysius from Ptolemy, then King Menander (175-150 BCE). Some, like Heliodorus, were converted to local faiths or Bhāgavata sects; and with King Aśoka's conversion to Buddhism, Buddhist emissaries were despatched to Greek regal houses on the frontier, such as at Takshila.

There was, then, considerable fusion of Orient in the Greece of Hellenistic days, and there were innumerable similarities between the ancient Greeks and Vedic Indians.[6]

But there was a profounder and rather more sublime influence of the Orient, possibly Indian in origin, that had found its way into the pre-Homeric and pre-Hellenic cultures of Greece, namely, in the Orphic beliefs and Dionysian cult practises. Euripides is invoked as having indicated the source of the latter to the "Asian lands" (*Bacchae*).[7] The Orphic myths harboured such beliefs as rebirth of the soul, deferring of mortality (cf. Aristotle's *Nichomachean Ethics*), the need of perfection and spiritual striving by men (possibly a Zarathustran impact), purification by ascetic practises, *theoria* or contemplation, and the quest for order in reality that supersede the seen reality. At the same time there was for the Greeks "a yearning aspiration for the Unseen Reality," and "turning away from the forms of the world." This tradition, which is unlike the standard (Homeric) Greek thought, and so like the philosophy of the Upaniṣads, remarks the author, is to be found in the Orphic and the Eluesinian mysteries, via Empedocles, Pythagoras, Pindar, and Plato.[8] These "mysteries" survived Aristotle's scientific ravages and passed over to the Neo-Platonists and from them to the medieval mystics. Afterall, did not Pythagoras travel to the East? and was not the digit "zero" in Western mathematics a gift from India, and wasn't this the subtle message at the entrance of Plato's Academy? Speculations go on. The rhetorical question is raised : "If Indian philosophy is older than Greek, could we rule out possible influence and establish relations, whether direct or indirect, between India and Greece?"[9] A case is made out for foreign influence, possibly Indian, on the Orphic "mystery" religion.[10]

But the influence that Radhakrishnan is interested in went both ways, for Greek astronomy apparently was to have an impact on Indian astronomy in the 4th century CE. India had become familiar with Greek knowledge and its influence was felt among the learned circles. Alas, either the influence was not powerful enough or it was overridden by the Buddhists who in turn were succeeded in the same tasks by the so-called *māyāvādins,* or better still, *avidyāvādins,* from Gauḍapāda through Śaṁkara to Śrīharṣa, *et al.*[11]

IV.

Radhakrishnan poses the metaphysical problem and gives us the moves : "if the fundamental form of the Supreme is *nirguṇa,* qualityless and *acintya,* inconceivable, the world is an appearance which cannot be logically related to the Absolute. In the unalterable eternity of Brahman, all that moves and evolves is founded . . . . While the world is dependent on Brahman, the latter is not dependent on the world. This one-sided dependence and the logical inconceivability of the relation between the Ultimate Reality and the world are brought out by the term "*māyā.*" The world is not essential being like Brahman; nor is it mere non-being. It cannot be defined as either being or non-being. The sudden discovery, he goes on, through the religious experience of the ultimate reality of spirit inclines us sometimes to look upon the world as an illusion rather than as a misapprehension or a misconstruction. *Māyā* does not imply that the world is an illusion or is non-existent absolutely. It is a delimitation distinct from the unmeasured and the immeasurable.[12]

As Charles A Moore rightly notes but wrongly adjudges, it was one of Radhakrishnan's "major objectives to explain the seemingly extreme doctrine of Śaṁkara and to show that even the doctrine of *māyā* does not entail the illusory character of the empirical world, human history, and human endeavour."[13] Says Moore, "Radhakrishnan is expressing the essence of the great traditions of all idealism - from Plato on - when he espouses the belief that the empirical world is between being and non-being, that it is not ultimate but neither is it nothing or illusion.[14] But why confound 'non-being' with 'illusion'? To say, as some traditionalist might want to, that the world is non-being is not necessarily to say that it is an illusion : this is a cliché that has stuck in Western reading ever since Gough. But if we consider for a moment that Śaṁkara's metaphysics makes a case for radical non-being, then Radhakrishnan's attempt to place Śaṁkara's "idealism" between being and non-being seems indelibly strained and untenable. I have no qualms with Radhakrishnan developing his own strain of spiritual idealism, but when he goes on to suggest that such a view is consistent with the 'spirit' of Vedic thinkers and Upaniṣads, even in a reading of Śaṁkara's *māyā*, this calls for criticism.

Equally disconcerting is the evolutionary, indeed neo-Hegelian strain in Radhakrishnan's reading of traditional Indian thought in the following account : Although we do not know the exact "how" of the creation of the universe, we can recognize an intelligible evolutionary process by which the ultimate spiritual reality is ever more progressively expressed in advancing forms - such that in point of fact, the world we know is essentially the world of such evolution, for "... beginning and the end are merely ideal ...."[15]

V. The Status of Non-being in Radhakrishnan's Scheme

To be sure, Radhakrishnan does not dispense with the notion of non-being, but non-being for him is identified with *prakṛti* or matter which is moulded by Divine form, the *puruṣa*, and the cosmic process that results is the world. The eternal "I" confronts the "not-I" (*prakṛti*). "When the element of non-being is introduced in the Absolute, its inwardness is unfolded in the process of becoming. The original unity becomes pregnant with the whole course of the world."[16]

Our attention is drawn to Proclus who regarded matter as a 'child of God' which is bound to be transformed. Matter, the substance of which the world is made of, is patently a minus in the universe, it is evil for it presents resistance to form, the principles of being. "Only in God," claims Radhakrishnan, "*prakṛti* is completely penetrated and overcome. The world as it is, then, far from being an illusion, or a total obscurity, is a necessary moment in reality for the unfolding of the Supreme and non-being is the material web in which the ideas of God are actualized." Becoming is the process, being is the end or the perfection to be reached. The language here is heavily Platonic, and the term "pregnant" in the earlier quote is chosen deliberately, for the allusion is to be Cosmic-Egg, comparable to the *Hiraṇyagarbha*, which to Radhakrishnan answers to the *Logos*, the Word of Western thought, the archetypical Idea of Plato and the principle of Reason in the Stoics,[17] or the world-soul which survives the apocalypse of the manifest world. This world-soul, in another manifestation, is *Īśvara*, the personal God and architectonic producer of the world. There is here more than a faint echo of Plato's *Timaeus*.

Plato is accredited with having made the same distinction as in the Upaniṣads between Absolute Principle (Brahman) which is the Idea of the good in the *Republic* and the Demiurgus, the personal God and creator (*Īśvara*) or the soul of the universe (*Hiraṇyagarbha*) in the *Timaeus*. "In his Academy the three original principles the One, the first cause, the reason or the *logos* and the Soul or the Spirit of the Universe were represented as three gods bound to each other by an ineffable generation . . . ."[18] It was imperative for Radhakrishnan to find the three or comparable principles in Indian thought if the world were not to be relegated to the realm of the illusions. And as the parenthetical terms indicate, he had no difficulty in finding the correlates. To be sure, Īśvara does not create the world out of nothing any more than Plato's artificer does more than give form to a pre-existing primitive substance.

VI. The World as Appearance

The world is indeed one large bag of appearances, but these appearances or the world-as-appearance is not for Radhakrishnan a result of ignorance or *avidyā*, as Śaṁkara's reading of the Upaniṣads, following closely on the footsteps of Gauḍapāda, would have it; *avidyā* is rather explained as the power of self-manifestation possessed by the Supreme, now identified with *ātmamāyā*, a kind of yogic creative potency.[19] And there is "no suggestion that the forms, events, the objects produced by *māyā* or the form-building power of God, the *māyin*, are only illusory." Indeed, how could Plato's Demiurge produce an illusory world when the forms at his behest are real and the receptacle contains a primitive substance relatable to the forms? What is delusive about the world are the forms, the ideas, the real that remain hidden behind the manifest world and that too by virtue of divine *māyā*.

Now scattered throughout the subsequent translations and notes to the passages in the *Bhagavad Gītā*, and to the *Principal Upaniṣads*, there occur numerous references to Plato, Plotinus, Aristotle, always with a view to finding parallel motifs or support for the view being championed. Certainly, more arguments are adduced in his other works, but the intent remains the same.

Consider the following remark : "The *puruṣa* of Sāṁkhya is not unlike the God of Aristotle. Though Aristotle affirms a transcendent God as the origin of the motion of the world, he denies to him any activity within the world."[20] But this comparison is fallacious, for *puruṣa* in Sāṁkhya does continue to be active in the world, via its evolutes of *mahat* and *buddhi*, or intelligence, if not in a causal relation then certainly by its proximate relation, something denied in Aristotle's deism. But these are minor quibbles. Let us look at something more substantive for a quibble.

VII. Avidyā

Most illustrative in this regard is Radhakrishnan's treatment of Śaṁkara's notion of *avidyā*, and its relation to the world. Throughout there is concern that if *avidyā*, in the sense of an illusory-making disposition in the individual, is accepted then it may never be possible to affirm the reality of the world in human experience. For Radhakrishnan *avidyā* in Śaṁkara's scheme is just the lower limits of knowledge, and not its negation or improbability. But the argument never really turns upon the deeper epistemological issues that Śaṁkara raises. Radhakrishnan invariably resorts to metaphysical speculations to account for the fact of appearances. Appearances only become a problem if we proceed to divorce Brahman from bearing any logical relation to the world of appearances *qua appearances*. This is the root of the problem as Radhakrishnan sees it, and he does his utmost to dissuade the reader from gaining the impression that Śaṁkara, in his alleged Vijñānavāda moment, just might have thought that the world is a cinematic projection of *avidyā* that is rooted in the individual's consciousness. And here is how he does it.

Radhakrishnan is contend to say that Śaṁkara incorporated certain Buddhistic elements, such as the doctrine of *māyā* and monasticism into the Vedānta philosophy. But the rest of Śaṁkara's dialectics, he patiently argues, is a systematic refutation of key Buddhistic tenets prevalent in his time.[21] And if the Buddha is said to have developed certain views of the Upaniṣads, then why should Śaṁkara not have recourse to Buddhist thought, other than the apparently nihilistic elements among the Buddhist dialecticians.[22]

Much of this is redherring. The issue as I see it is not whether Śaṁkara saw behind the experienced world, or the *vyāvahāra*, that transcendental absolute, *paramārtha* - which do also correspond to the Buddhist distinction between *paramārtha* and *samvṛti* - but whether Śaṁkara was prepared to forego altogether the reality of the world. Further that he would deny to the world any logical cohesion, ultimate purpose or teleology, such as the historical or evolutionary attainment of perfection or the uncovering of a hidden treasure that would make life in all its ramifications meaningful and worth living to the full. Or, alternatively, was Śaṁkara a realist and so denied the idealist preoccupation with appearances. The latter certainly not, although Radhakrishnan at one point tries to make Śaṁkara out to be a 'radical realist.' To this I shall return.

I have no problem with Radhakrishnan's representation of Śaṁkara's argument from the existence of self to the affirmation of Brahman; but the same does not necessarily follow from arguments to the existence of the world, or any such ontological moves (as Kant indeed pointed out). Metaphysically, both moves are marred by enormous difficulties, but the latter more than the former, and Śamkara, I believe, recognized this fact - that is why he never considered the self to be an entity or a category one with things in the world. The truth of one (i.e. self) is based on the intuition of self-consciousness, while of the other is derived from our apprehension of the world, which itself is of doubtful character. Hence immediate self-certainty is denied to our awareness of things of the world; and herein lay the roots of the doctrine of *avidyā*.

VIII. Avidya Revisited

Radhakrishnan takes Śamkara to have refuted subjectivism, for apparently Śamkara had no difficulty with the reality of the chair or the table or the tree that we perceive in ordinary life, even though we might generally mistake a post for a tree and *vice versa*. Even for the fully enlightened consciousness, we are told, there are objects to be posited, and "the world seen," felt, tasted and touched is as real as the being of man who sees, feels, tastes and touches."[23] This is Śamkara's "radical realism!" But Radhakrishnan retracts this attribution, as otherwise that would imply a compromise to the kind of idealism Radhakrishnan himself feels happy about - albeit a non-subjectivist idealism, because Śamkara also distinguished between waking state and dream states, which a subjectivist perhaps does not.[24]

The world of appearances, however, are not phantoms of our creation but, as objects of knowledge, they are verily "phases of the spirit" (*viṣayacaitanya*) - a term borrowed from the *Vedāntaparibhāṣā*. "The world is in God who is all-aware and all creative : everything is spiritual in character, for everything reflects the ideal embodied by God's being." God also is the *apauruṣeyatva* ("superhuman") origin of the Vedas, which bespeak "a rational order of the universe," or God's mind itself.[25] The world is an appearance for

Radhakrishnan also, as one can see, but for a different set of reasons. It is not absolutely different from Brahman, for "if the Ātman were absolutely different from the states of waking, dreaming and sleeping, then the repudiation of the reality of the world or the three states cannot lead us to the attainment of truth. We shall then have to embrace nihilism and treat all teaching as purposeless."[26] While Śaṁkara's most powerful philosophical contribution was the deconstruction of the notion of *difference* altogether, so that in the final analysis not a vestige of difference, not even, if we anticipate, of difference would survive. Hence it makes no sense to speak of Ātman or Brahman being non-different or different from the world : this binary is/has no position in the Absolute, and it is only by the displacement (*déplacement*) of the Absolute that difference is made possible, and it is this difference that is read as the text of the world. One does not attain liberation by hotly pursuing the signs of the world, but by overcoming them, by, in fact, repudiating or negating them. And contrary to what Radhakrishnan might think, in Śaṁkara's scheme the things of the world as signs do not legitimate themselves as the signifiers of that great signified, the One or the Absolute, for this itself is a binary that is marred by the same problematics of difference and thus has to be rejected *tout court*. To get this sort of a sense one has to turn to Śaṁkara's treatment of *adhyāsa,* a radical device used in the context.

Adhyāsa

But here too Radhakrishnan equivocates as he moves to consider the impact of *adhyāsa* on Śāṁkaran metaphysics. No one can escape the logical contours that Śaṁkara draws with this device, for with the notion of *adhyāsa* Śaṁkara systematically destroys the identification of the world of appearances with what he takes to be the ultimately real. All our delusions arise from identifying X with what it is not, Y. And this leads to *avidyā* or the negation of knowledge (not its mere delimitation, as Radhakrishnan had earlier told us). Radhakrishnan acknowledges at this point that "*avidyā*, or the natural tendency to *adhyāsa* is involved in the very roots of our being," but candidly adds, "and is another name for our finitude."[27] The qualification says nothing of significance. And hereon Radhakrishnan gets distracted as he begins to make moves to reassociate the world with some supernal, logical order that defies our empirical experiences. Just as language, whose grammar exudes an enormously intricate order and law-abidingness, appears to point via its significations to a world of matching order (a supposition that took a Wittgenstein in the West to demolish), for Radhakrishnan, "the whole world reality in its fulness and complexity postulates a universal and perfect mind, Īśvara, who sustains parts of the universe which are unperceived by us. Our phenomenal knowledge suggests the noumenal as a necessity of thought; but not as something known through the empirical pramāṇas . . . The universal reality is viewed as a central personality or subject with the whole world as subject."[28]

One can see that Radhakrishnan slides from the more challenging epistemological considerations to giving non-sequitor metaphysical arguments, totally overlooking the several objections that have over the centuries been raised against such speculative attempts, more forcefully in the West.

IX.

It is not, however, in argument that one comes to be convinced of the truth of this 'postulate,' but, in the last analysis, it is revealed in 'intuition,' for this truth has nothing to do with logic. Here I take Radhakrishnan to be saying that intuition has the capacity to disclose a higher reality than the objects of the world involved in perceptual flux. Immediately, we are directed to compare this with

Plato's realism, "where reason discloses the world of reality colourless, formless, intangible . . . visible to the mind alone who is lord of the soul."[29] But Śaṁkara recognizes only one "essence," that is why we get Brahman as the object of intuition, and not "the many things-in-themselves of Kant, or the self of Fichte, or the continuum of Schelling, but the Ātman or the universal consciousness." It is compared to Plotinus' The One, "not presented as an object, but is in immediate contact above knowledge."[30] We end with a kind of mysticism, where the metaphysics of Plato is finely blended with the spicing of Orphic mysteries which is suggestive of some esoteric praxis, possibly traced back to India, or Asia at least anyway, but which never became the main current of Western thought, a fact for which Radhakrishnan made a generation of Indian intellectuals lament. But then India erred too, not on the side of mysticism, of which it had a plentiful share, but in foresaking the realism that due to Plato and more to Aristotle's credit was a turning point in Western metaphysics, that eventually gave rise to empiricism and science, which forever guaranteed the redemption of the appearances. And Western thought has been better for that; while Indian thought, especially with Śaṁkara and the Buddhist dialecticians, has given the overwhelming impression of being an unedifying brand of subjective idealism.

X.

Radhakrishnan wants to provide a corrective to this impoverished state of affairs. For this we would have to suppose that, by *avidyā* Śaṁkara did *not* intend that all knowledge is delusory in character and therefore the objects of knowledge are illusory, but that because the phenomenal world is affected with traces of unreality, knowledge obtained are empirical and therefore of a lower rung (*aparāvidyā*).[31] "Lower knowledge is not illusory or derivative, but is only relative: if not, Śaṁkara's elaborate and even passionate discussion of the lower knowledge will border on the grotesque."[32] So be it, I think I hear Śaṁkara saying.

I do also think the following paragraph brings home the point I have been labouring to make in this discussion. It wants to champion, in the interest of metaphysics, the distinction between the *existent* and the *real*. "It is there in the "matter" of the Milesians, the "elements" of Empedocles and Anaxagoras, the "numbers" of Pythagoras, the "atom" of Leucippus and Democritus, the "ideas" of Plato, and the "Antelechies" of Aristotle - all these represent the results of the search for the real behind the appearances."

References

1. *The Bhagavad Gītā, with an Introductory Essay, Sanskrit Text, English Translation and Notes*, by S. Radhakrishnan, George Allen & Unwin, 1970, Introductory Essay, p. 22.

2. *Ibid.*, p. 22.

3. We have scarcely gone past p. 25 of this Introductory Essay (*ibid.*) and already there are scattered references, though mostly in the notes, to Lao Tze, Plotinus, Jesus, St. John of Damascus, Areopagite, Eckhart, Rūmī, Augustine, Jacob Boehme *et al*, all with a view to bolstering a kind of mysticism that crudely relates to the Upaniṣadic idealism.

4. See S. Radhakrishnan, *East and West Some Reflections*, (Beatty Memorial Lectures, McGill University, Ontario), George Allen & Unwin, London, 1955, pp. 18-19, esp note 3, 4, and pp. 56-61; much of the ideas here seem to bounce off from a short Introduction by Maulana Abdul Kalam Azad (but I wonder who really authored it), to Radhakrishnan edited *History of Philosophy Eastern and Western*, George Allen & Unwin, London, 1952, esp. p. 21ff.

5. *East and West*, p. 60. Alexander had carried the Hellenic culture to the banks of the Indus, and this culture was kept alive for three centuries in Afghanistan and the Punjab.
6. *Ibid.*, p. 46, p. 60. Such similarities extended to the names as well of their respective gods, e.g. Jupiter, Zeus vs. pitā, devas, Varuṇa vs Ouranos, Eos vs Uṣās ... these "similarities suggest that the two peoples ... must have been in communication with each other ..." p. 46.
7. *Ibid.*, pp. 53-54.
8. *Ibid.*, p. 51.
9. Although these are the words of Maulana Azad (Introduction, p. 25), they do reflect similar sentiments in Radhakrishnan's Preface to the same *History of Philosophy East and West* and in his *East and West*.
10. *East and West*, p. 53.
11. *Ibid.*, p. 25.
12. *The Bhagavad Gītā*, Introduction, p. 38.
13. Charles A. Moore, "Radhakrishnan's Metaphysics and Ethics," in *The Philosophy of Sarvepalli Radhakrishnan*, edited by Paul Arthur Schilpp, Tudor Publishing Co., New York, 1952, p. 303.
14. *Ibid.*
15. *Ibid.*, p. 299.
16. *Ibid.*
17. *The Principal Upaniṣads*, edited with Introduction, Text, Trans. and Notes by S. Radhakrishnan, George Allen & Unwin, London, 1968, pp. 61-62. "The androgynous other half of *ātman* splitting himself into two." *Bṛh Up* I 4 6, *cf* Plato's *Symposium* 189; in *Prin Up*, p. 164.
18. *East and West*, p. 57.
19. *The Bhagavad Gītā*, comment on p. 40.
20. Radhakrishnan : *Indian Philosophy* (Volume II), George Allen & Unwin, London/MacMillan New York, 1962; pp 289ff.
21. *Ibid.*, p. 47; and taken over apparently by Śrīharṣa, Madhusūdana Sarasvatī, *et al.*

22. Radhakrishnan is quite frightened at the prospect of nihilism having a greater say in Indian thought than it did in the West. This would be even more embarrassing for him. Thus he would have both the material and the mental to be equally objective, against the grain of, say, the Vijñānavādins.
23. *Indian Philosophy*, pp. 497-499.
24. *Ibid.*, p. 498.
25. This is a misleading use of the term *apauruṣeya* and its superhumanness is not what, nor necessarily just that, is implied by this Mīmāṁsā term.
26. *Ibid.*, p. 582, *Śaṅkarabhāṣya* on *Māṇḍ. Up.* II. 7 is quoted, but this in itself is probably a Gauḍapādian tact.
27. *Ibid.*, p. 508.
28. *Ibid.*, p. 509.
29. The reference is to *Phaedrus* (exact location not given), *ibid.*, p. 512 fn. 2.
30. *Ibid.*, p. 513.
31. *Ibid.*, p. 515.
32. *Ibid.*

22

Radhakrishnan's Pantheism : Internal Relations of God's Modes of Being

RICHARD W. STADELMANN
Texas A & M University

> This world has its roots above and branches below, says the *Bhagavad Gītā*. "I am from above; ye are of this world." These passages suggest that the perception of the truth is derived from the nature in us which is above the earthly. Spiritual power from beyond the dimensions of space-time breaks in. Man is the point of interaction between time and eternity..... This to my mind is the teaching of Christianity (Radhakrishnan, *Recovery of Faith*, p. 159).

Charles Hartshorne in his 1953 book, co-authored with William L. Reese, *Philosophers Speak of God*, classifies Radhakrishnan as a "modern pantheist."[1] A "panentheist" is a philosopher of religion who affirms that the world is internal to God and that God's being, while immanent in the world, also transcends the world.

Hartshorne presents an extensive selection, exclusively from Radhakrishnan's *An Idealist View of Life*, in which Radhakrishnan writes, "God, though immanent, is not identical with the world until the very end. Throughout the process there is an unrealized residuum in God, but it vanishes when we reach the end; when the reign is absolute the kingdom comes. God who is organic with it recedes into the background of the Absolute."[2]

It appears that Radhakrishnan has a panentheism of the present creatively advancing toward a pantheism when there is not unrealized residuum in God, and God itself is "in the background."

In *Philosophers Speak of God*, Hartshorne mildly reflects "We fear only that in certain phrases the door is half-open to monopolar misinterpretation."[3] I find the outside storm doors wide open with God in three modes, luring humans to open the inner door.

Hartshorne does present the following criticisms : "To speak of 'limiting down the Absolute to its relation with the actual' suggests that the absolute as such is *more* than the supreme as relative to the world. But the logical construction is rather that the absolute as such is an empty abstraction, a mere ingredient in the richness of actuality, world or divine. And we think it somewhat objectionable to use 'the Absolute' as expression for the supreme in its totality of aspects, or to speak of the Absolute 'selecting' among possibilities for actualization. The subject which really owns such an act of selection is relative if anything is."[4]

Hartshorne also notes parenthetically, " 'Precosmic' indeed is open to the objection that it may seem to imply a beginning in the temporal process."[5] Indeed, had Hartshorne quoted from Radhakrishnan's many commentaries on Hindu religious literature, such as the quotation noted in the beginning of this article, he would have used stronger words than "seem to imply."

Hartshorne continues his objections by stressing that God as actual includes the Absolute, though not exhausting it because "the relative, according to surrelativism, includes the absolute, as the concrete the abstract, so that to say that the absolute is in any sense more than the relative is to say that X is more than XY. . . . so we conclude that God as relative to the world, though not exhausting the possibilities inherent in the Absolute as his own abstract essence, is in no sense less than this essence but in every sense in which it is distinguished at all from it simply more than its deficient reality."[6]

Hartshorne had raised similar criticism in his 1952 article "Radhakrishnan on Mind, Matter and God" in *The Philosophy of Sarvepalli Radhakrishnan.*[7] However, in this work Radhakrishnan had replied, "Professor Hartshorne . . . raise[s] the question of the relation of God and the Absolute. These are not to be regarded as exclusive of each other. The Supreme in its non-relational aspect is the Absolute; in its active aspect it is God. The Supreme, limited to its relation to the possibility which is actually accomplishing itself in the world, is the World Spirit. Professor Hartshorne says that the concrete and relative is more than the abstract and the absolute. This view assumes that the distinction of God and the Absolute is one of separation, which is not the case. The actual is more than the possible. The abstract possibility and the concrete realization are both contained in one reality, which is Absolute-God. The two aspects represents the absolute silence of the Spirit and its boundless movement. The silence is the basis of the movement, the condition of power. The distinction is only logical. The Supreme has three simultaneous poises of being : the transcendent Absolute, *Brahman*; the creative freedom, *Īśvara*; and the wisdom, power, and love manifest in this world, *Hiranya-garbha*. These do not succeed each other in time. It is an order of arrangement and logical priority not of temporal succession."[8]

For Radhakrishnan there are at least five terms applied to modes of deity : (1) The Supreme, which is all-encompassing, (2) God that is the Absolute, "the pure and passionate being which transcends the restless turmoil of the cosmic life" (Brahman) (Radhakrishnan, *An Idealist View of Life*, p. 271); and God who is (3) Creator (Brahman), (4) Sustainer (Viṣṇu), and (5) Judge of this world (Siva).[9]

Radhakrishnan writes, "God who is creator, sustainer and judge of this world, is not totally unrelated to the Absolute. God is the Absolute from the human end. When we limit down the Absolute to its relation with actual possibility, the Absolute appears as Wisdom, Love and Goodness. The abiding 'I am,' the changeless centre and the cause of all change is envisaged as the first term and the last in the sequence of nature."[10]

It is difficult and perhaps impossible to understand how there can be a sequencing of nature in the internal relations of God's modes of being, including the relationships with the Absolute; or in the three poises of the Supreme, the Absolute, the creative freedom and wisdom, power and love manifest in this world without there being a succession in time. Hartshorne's criticism does, indeed, depend on a succession in time among the modes of God's being.

Rama Shanker Srivastava notes Hartshorne's criticisms of Radhakrishnan and contends that Radhakrishnan has successfully responded to Hartshorne because the Absolute and God are not exclusive. "The Reality is Absolute - God. The former is its primordial aspect and the latter is its projected aspect."[11] Srivastava contends that "the main contribution of Radhakrishnan consists in the reconciliation of the Absolute with God."[12]

However, defining "The Reality" in such a way that it has the Absolute and God as two aspects does not respond to Hartshorne's criticism, for the sequencing still remains between the two, or three or four aspects, depending on one's classifications. And if time is real, as Radhakrishnan maintains, then Hartshorne's critique holds.

First we shall look at the corresponding problem that occurs in the conceptualization of the logical and temporal relationships of God's modes of being as found in Alfred North Whitehead and in Charles Hartshorne. Then we shall suggest a root metaphor derived from the mystic experience, or "intuition" as Radhakrishnan would call it, that my offer a way to experientially respond to problems in both Eastern and Western panentheism.

Charles Hartshorne believes that for Whitehead "the Godhead is a linear sequence which implies that he is a perfectly ordered society of occasions."[13]

Hartshorne argues :

(1) Whitehead indicated that in a conversation with A.H. Johnson.

(2) A person is conscious and individual. God is conscious and individual.

Therefore, God is a person or community of actual occasions.[14]

Hartshorne's first argument is weak because A.H. Johnson did not himself believe that Whitehead considered God to be a person.

His second argument contains an undistributed middle. An actual occasion could also be conscious and individual. Hartshorne's views of the consciousness of God is based on his interpretation of Whitehead that God is conscious of all the actual. If God is conscious of all the actual his personality is implied.

However, to assert the personality of God as a society from the fact that the consequent nature of God prehends all the actual is to assume that societies only have personalities, a step required for Hartshorne because he eliminates eternal objects, which include for Whitehead moral or personal characteristics as well as mathematical.

To argue that God is a person because God is a linear sequence is also question-begging. To say God is a linear sequence is to maintain that God has external relations between actual occasions in the primordial or the consequent nature of his being.

Robert Whittemore adequately maintains that Whitehead's God is not temporal. His argument is as follows :

(1) God as primordial is by definition non-temporal. Therefore, God as primordial is not an actual entity.

(2) God as consequent is not temporal. The consequent nature is the character of becoming, but becoming is not itself extensive. The consequent nature is not an entity.

(3) God as a whole is not temporal because if we consider the epoch of time to be God's eternal continuum, it creates a new question : How does quantum differ from eternity? This would lead to pantheism, which Whitehead opposes.[15]

Hartshorne considers Radhakrishnan's concept of the Supreme as temporal in the same way that he considers Whitehead's God temporal.

This leads Hartshorne to his basic criticisms of Radhakrishnan's descriptions of the relationship of the Absolute and the creator, the sustainer and the judge.

However, if we interpret Whitehead's God to be an actual entity that is not a society of actual occasions, as stated by Whitehead.[16] a problem of interpreting sequencing remains, though it is no longer to be posed with God in time as a society of actual occasons. In the same sense,

Radhakrishnan's Supreme is not in time as a series of asymmetrical temporal events moving from abstract possibility in the Absolute through creation in God Brahma, sustenance in God Visnu, and judgment in God Siva, with each pulsation through the series basically altering and causing growth and change in the Supreme, while the Absolute remains abstract and unaltered.

The new challenge to Radhakrishnan's viewpoint parallels a challenge to Whitehead's viewpoint. If Whitehead's God and Radhakrishnan's Supreme are both viewed as single entities and not societies, both have time within their being in the sense that sequences take place within their interior modes, and not between momentary modalities of their total beings.

If, for Whitehead, God as a whole is an organic absolute, how is it possible for the actual entity God to unite its conceptual (primordial) pole and its physical (consequent) pole? Whitehead intends for the order of relevance of the abstract eternal objects in the primordial pole to be derived from interaction between concepts and prehensions, or the consecrences of the superjective nature into the consequent. "The consequent nature is the weaving of God's physical feelings upon his primordial concepts."[17]

In Whitehead's concept of God, the primordial nature of God with its eternal objects provides the framework of abstract possibility and personality serving as the lure for the concrescence of actual occasions in the superjective phase. At the point of concrescence, the consequent nature aiming for the actualization of all eternal objects saves all that can be saved of the world.

On the much-debated issue of what can be saved, I would agree with A.H. Johnson and William A. Christian that God's consequent nature, as the physical prehension of God, cannot share the subjective immediacy of the actual occasion. What is prehended is the objectification of the occasion. Hartshorne argues that all immediacy is prehended, but his argument is dependent upon his view of the interrelationship of God's nature as a society of actual occasions. However, if God is not a society and actual occasions are immanent in each other only because they are immanent in God, as Whitehead maintains, a major problem presents itself. God is immanent in actual occasions because all actual occasions are immanent in each other because they are immanent in God.

We are now involved in the classical infinite regress of the problem of similarity, with two says out.

(1) We can appeal to God as a mystery or an exception to the rules for entities. [This is similar to the classical solution to the problem of how a person can love someone beneath him without becoming corrupted, and the answer, following Augustine, is that we redirect our love through God, who can love those beneath him without loss because the identification and sacrifice involved in God does not necessitate loss for God.] But process theologians reject this type of solution to basic ontological problems.

(2) We can collapse the panentheism into a pantheism. This appears to be the way taken by Radhakrishnan in the sense that both before God's appearance, when the Absolute selects from among the possibilities creating the world, and at the end, when the world lured by the Absolute returns to unity with the Supreme, all actual entities could, indeed, mutually prehend the full subjective immediacy of their collective experiences. However, in this pantheistic state of being, all subject-object distinctions are eliminated, so the prehension would be one total intuition in the sense in which Radhakrishnan uses this word. Radhakrishnan thus has an option not available to Hartshorne in which to argue for the awareness of the Supreme, through the natures of God, to save all prehensions, including the subjective immediacy of the prehension.

For Whitehead and Hartshorne, actual occasions can not prehend their temporal contemporaries. This restriction would also seem to me to apply to any ability of the Viṣṇu or Siva mode of God for Radhakrishnan. Certainly the Absolute as abstract is not involved in perception. However, the Radhakrishnan Supreme uniting all modes of God would have no contemporaries, or would be contemporary with all reality, depending on how we wish to use the word "contemporary" because of the state of identity and timelessness in which all events are the Supreme.

Hartshorne's criticism of Radhakrishnan depends upon thinking of Radhakrishnan's Supreme as equivalent to the Society of Actual Occasions that he conceives Whitehead's God to be. Conceptually, they are not equivalent. Moreover, if we compare Whitehead's God as an actual entity with Radhakrishnan's Supreme, Radhakrishnan has a pantheistic solution to the way in which actual occasions may be prehended by the Supreme without loss of subjective immediacy of prehensions. However, the type of experience posited by Radhakrishnan would be an intuition that is both cognitive and without subject-object distinction, in other words, precisely the type of experience emphatically denied from the realm of possibility by most Western epistemologists.

We turn now from Radhakrishnan's Supreme and Whitehead's God, where preconceptions differ, to the "phenomenal" world of Radhakrishnan's God in three poises (Brahma the Absolute, Viṣṇu the Preserver, and Siva the Judge); and to Whitehead's God's two modes (conceptual and physical), and three poises (Primordial, Superjective, and Consequent). Radhakrishnan, in responding to Edgar Sheffield Brightman, objects to the use of "phenomenal" for Iśvara, or God, while viewing Brahman, or the Absolute, as real.[18] I am using the term "phenomenal" to include the Absolute, but distinguishing the triune God logically only from the Supreme. In this domain, a problem appears, and I will propose a lure toward an experiential root metaphor that offers a way to frame the experiences of human (and perhaps non-human) actual occasions or societies thereof.

Both Radhakrishnan and Whitehead interpret space and time in terms of the experiences of actual occasions, not the other way around. Christian presents a significant analysis of Whitehead at this point, with relevant comparisons to Hartshorne.[19]

Radhakrishnan writes, "Space-time is the natural condition of finiteness, limitation, change which characterizes all events. It is not a real homogeneous structure, but an integral aspect of reality. It is not a sort of stage on which different kinds of material exhibit their dance, but refers only to certain rules and modes of expressing the broadest features and relationships within a universe of mobile events. A space-time relatedness applies to the whole of nature and confers unity on it. Since relatedness is not by itself a fact, the ultimate fact of nature is conceived as a process, a passage, single and not multiple. The name 'event' is applied to parts or aspects of this process. Nature is an essentially unanalysable and individual process of change in which certain formal attributes called space-time and certain material characteristics called objects, as matter, life, etc., exhibit themselves as standing in many relations to each other and the whole."[20]

Within the realm of Radhakrishnan's "nature" or Whitehead's actual occasions, time and space appear.

Looking first at Whitehead, we find that actual occasions with their conceptual pole and physical pole manifesting themselves as objects to their successors reach concrescence and pass into the consequent nature of God. Subjective immediacy is lost in the process. Is anything else lost? There has been much debate on this subject. Johnson argues for the elimination of data such as destructive evil.[21] However, Whitehead writes, ". . . antithesis is solved by rating types of order in relative importance according to their success in magnifying the individual actualities, that is to say in promoting strength of experience."[22] In this discussion of tragedy, Whitehead seems to believe that all elements are arranged in the consequent nature insofar as they fulfil the subjective aim of God, which is the promotion of intensity of feelings. Love is proper respect and maintenance of all feelings.

I believe that in Whitehead's view, destructive evil receives objective immortality, but as mere fact. It is not saved as a high enough order-type to enable it, except in a gross physical way which maintains the continuity of nature, to influence future ordering of relevance in the primordial nature.

Now what is the process of transmutation that enables God to arrange his data in order-types in the consequent nature that solves the problem of contradiction and destructive evil, and that allows God to guide or lure the historical process?

Just as the ever-changing order of relevance of eternal objects in the primordial nature of God is determined by the consequent nature of God, the order of items in the consequent nature is determined by "transmutation." Whitehead does not define "transmutation." But the physical feeling of actual occasions in the consequent nature of God have a particular pattern which explains how creative novelty is to arrange the concresced occasions. The physical nexus and a nexus that objectifies the intensity of the prior occasion, the feeling and the feeling of an objectively existing feeling, conditions the order-types of the consequent nature so that creativity cannot run amok. The subjective form of the physical feeling of God conforms to the objectified feeling of the dead actual occasion. The objectified feeling which is conformed to is the subjective form of the dead actual occasion. Only the qualitative elements of an actuality become part of the subjective form. If one subjective form is derived from another, there must be a qualitative identity which makes this transaction possible. Such an identity would be an eternal object. The ordering of the eternal objects for the actual world is determined by the objective ordering of the facts of objective immortality in the consequent nature of God. Whitehead writes, "The primordial nature of God is the concrescence of a unity of conceptual feelings including among their data all eternal objects. The concrescence is directed by the subjective aim, that the subjective form of the feeling shall be such as to constitute the eternal objects into relevant lures of feelings severally appropriate for all realizable basic conditions."[23] This is a circular process.

But what is the eternal object that can mitigate the wild drive of creativity? Can the satisfaction of God itself be a factor in arranging objective immortal order-types in the consequent nature which weave the arrangement of the eternal forms in the primordial nature which serve as structure and lure for nature?

It could be if God is a society of actual occasions, as Hartshorne maintains; but if God is (as I have maintained) non-temporal, how can it itself reach the final phase of concrescences which leads to satisfaction or consciousness? Must we open Pandora's Box and let Hartshorne out? No, for it is precisely because God is non-temporal and because an actual entity is non-temporal that it is possible for God to have satisfaction and all other phases of concrescence at the same time. Satisfaction is a result of the internal relationships of God, the unification of prehensions, physical and conceptual, with the subjective aim. The principle which determines transmutation is God's subjective aim. The aim is the attainment of value in the temporal-physical world, God's inner being. It is the "lure for feelings, the eternal urge for desire." It is the superject of creativity which had the primordial nature of God as its primordial place, but as pure creativity it is the ultimate metaphysical ground. God's internal relationships are non-temporal, so his satisfactions are continuous. Satisfaction is genetically last, not temporally last, for God.

Hopefully, the similarity between Whitehead and Radhakrishnan is now clearer. For Whitehead within God's three modes time and space appear. The primordial nature offers the abstract eternal objects, including God's character. In the realm of the present, these modes set the limits of human action and action of all entities. Actual occasions lured by novelty seek satisfaction and concresce into the consequent nature. The point of concrescence is the superjective nature. In the consequent nature, the immediacy of feeling is lost except as objectified, but evil is not lost. Prior feelings in the consequent nature along with God's drive for satisfaction transmute the given into order-types in the consequent nature, thus both utilizing and controlling creativity. These order-types then cause the arrangement of relevance of the eternal forms in God's primordial nature, and the circle is complete. But for the unitary God, satisfaction is constant and non-temporal.

In the writings of Radhakrishnan, we are not given such details concerning the process. A major problem is that in Radhakrishnan's many magnificent commentaries on Indian literature and philosophers, we are left unsure of Radhakrishnan's own viewpoint. But *An Idealist View of Life* gives the basic outline. "The one God creates as Brahma, redeems as Viṣṇu and judges as Siva. These represent the three stages in his plan, the process and the perfection."[24] The Absolute, which is termed by Radhakrishnan, quoting the *Rig Veda*, "the breathing breathless,' the pure alone and unmanifest, nothing and all things, transcends any definite form of expression and yet is the basis of all expression, the one in whom is found and yet all is lost."[25] In an act of free creation creates one universe from an infinite number of possibilities. "As to why there is realization of this possibility, we can only say that it is much too difficult for us in the pit to know what is happening beyond the screens. It is *māyā*, or a mystery which we have to accept reverently."[26]

Radhakrishnan suggests the concept of the Absolute overflowing or the frequent Indian suggestion of the God at play, but concludes only "Though the creation of the world is an incident in the never-ending activity of the Absolute, it satisfies a deep want in God."[27] This want in God (which I take to be the Absolute plus Brahma, Viṣṇu and Siva, as with Hartshorne I find it impossible to understand a want in the Absolute conceived separately) is very similar to the description of God's drive for satisfaction in Whitehead. Once this universe out of many possibilities is created, then Viṣṇu acts to save and Siva to judge, or to use Radhakrishnan's other triune description, the Absolute, creative freedom, Īśvara, and wisdom, power and love manifested in this world create, save, and judge.

For Radhakrishnan the goal of existent trinity is to return their creation to unity in not the Absolute, but the Supreme. With such a goal it is natural for the human to ask why was nature created in the first place? Radhakrishnan's answer, a want in God, is not satisfactory because it is a want in the Supreme that is the issue. The ultimate answer offered is māyā, or mystery (not illusion) as Radhakrishnan uses the word. Whiteheadian possible answers could involve an appeal to the raw force of creativity, which is a logical answer, though one with many religious perils. Hartshorne sees in God perfection, and perfection requires continual growth. Creation is God's nature and a necessity for the perfect being.

Radhakrishnan criticizes Whitehead by saying, "What happens to God when the plan is achieved, when the primordial nature becomes the consequent, when there is an identity between *natura naturans* and *naturata*, to use Spinoza's expression, is not clearly brought out."[28]

For Whitehead the primordial nature could never become the consequent. Eternal objects can not become concresced events. Forms can become appropriated in the order of relevance of the objective immortal order-types in the consequent nature, which in turn would affect the order of relevance of the eternal objects, but the process would continue. Creativity would also have to be conquered or cease to function, and God's need to seek satisfaction cease before the primordial could become the consequent. This would be equivalent to the non-existence of God. The possibility exists for an aeon where there are vastly different forms relevant.

Hartshorne raises the questions of why Radhakrishnan should speak of God's plan as reaching an end. Why could not the divine purpose be inexhaustible.[29] Radhakrishnan replies by giving the pragmatic argument, "If we are not certain that the divine purpose with regard to this world will be realised, the cosmic process will turn out to be an unending pursuit of a goal which will forever remain unaccomplished. There must be the assurance of the eventual triumph of this possibility, the realization of the ideal. Apart from this, life and effort would be meaningless."[30] However, for Hartshorne, God's nature which is perfect requires growth. Does a person have to have assurance of final victory in order to have meaning? Can not participation in an ongoing process bestow meaning on an activity or a life? I think it can. Or life *could be* meaningless. It is significant that just as Whitehead's God might actualize vastly different eternal objects creating a different nature, so too could Brahma breathe out again even after the realization of the one ideal for one nature.

A similar problem remains for both Whitehead and Radhakrishnan. If we admit God's purposeful form of seeking satisfaction in Whitehead and the Radhakrishnan Absolute actualizing one possible world and then seeking through the poises of God union with the Supreme, both of these enterprises are processes that create time and space. Time is real for the interior of God or of the Supreme's nature. Yet in Whitehead the non-temporal God-Actual occasion must act without time lag in transferring the ordering of dead fact in its consequent nature to the ordering of relevance in the primordial nature of the actual world. But if this is without time lag, the new actual occasion occurs instantaneously with the death of the old actual occasion. The new past is instant with the old present. For Radhakrishnan, the temporal process of nature moves within, from and to a non-temporal being, not in process, that contains the temporal within. In both, the problem is: How can a non-temporal God interact with a temporal world?

Both Radhakrishnan and Whitehead are concerned with integration in process. The former expects ultimate integration, the latter does not. They reach this problem not from conceptual deductions, but from a root metaphor of experience that expresses for Whitehead purposeful process that aims at maximum intensity, and for Radhakrishnan purposeful process that aims at unity. For both, the root metaphor is to be found in their experience of God.

Whitehead writes, "Religion is founded on the concurrence of three allied concepts in one moment of self-consciousness, concepts whose separate relationship to fact and whose mutual relationship to each other are only to be settled jointly by some direct intuition into the ultimate character of the universe. These concepts are:

1. That of value of an individual itself.
2. That of the value of the diverse individuals of the world for each other.

3. That of the value of the objective world which is a community derivated from the interrelationship of its component individuals, and also necessary for the existence of these individuals."[31]

These concepts are prehended in one moment of religious intuition. I will call it a cognitive mystic experience.

Whitehead writes that "on the broadest basis of religious experience, a universe is disclosed that is :

1. Interdependent. The body pollutes the mind, the mind pollutes the body.

2. The individual is formative of the society, the society is formative of the individual.

3. The world is at once a passing shadow and a final past.

4. There is a kingdom of heaven prior to the actual passage of actual things, and there is the same kingdom findings its completion in the end.

5. The world is a scene of solitariness in community."[32]

How strikingly similar this description is to the descriptions of religious experience and of creative intuition for Radhakrishnan.

Radhakrishnan, in arguing for religious experience as the root principle of all thought, says "The root principles of all thought and life are not derived from perceptual experience or logical knowledge."[33] "The order of nature is a unity because the self is itself a unity." "Thought is guided by the spirit in man, the divine in us."[34] ". . . that the realms of nature and spirit, existence and value are not alien to one another . . . for intuition it is a fact."[35] "The ethical soundness, the logical consistency and the aesthetic beauty of the universe are assumptions for science and logic, art and morality, but not irrational assumptions. They are the apprehensions of the soul, intuitions of the self . . ."[36] "Even the sun and moon would go out if they began to doubt. We are not ourselves alone, we are God-men."[37] "The world is in the making and is being created constantly and the reality of the world means a plastic world."[38] "The control of the whole is present in the growth of the parts . . . the process of the world is creative synthesis."[39]

The mystic experience suggested by both Whitehead and Radhakrishnan suggests to me the Quaker word "concern." The word is technical. It implies a mystic union of the individual in his solitude with the community of worshippers and with God leading to a new drive, or concern, for any goal, a new subjective aim, a creativity emerging from unity with the ground of being, a process ensuing from reality.

Whitehead writes, "Reason mocks at majorities, the rational satisfaction or dissatisfaction in respect of any particular happening depends upon an intuition which is capable of being universalized. This intuition is not the discernment of a form of words, but a type of character. It is the characteristic of the learned mind to exalt words. Yet mothers can ponder many things in their hearts which they cannot express. The many things which are thus known constitute the ultimate religious evidence beyond which there is no appeal."[40]

Within the framework of this suggestion of a root metaphor of experience, one can find, I believe, common ground to justify the experience of unity that transcends problems involved in the internal relationships of the trinity of both Radhakrishnan and Whitehead.

On the day following a devastating killer earthquake at Yellowstone National Park that had rolled me down a hillside uninjured protected in my mummy sleeping bag, I was surprised by a double rainbow appearing out of nowhere, framed in the Grand Canyon of the Yellowstone. For a moment time collapsed, subject and object disappeared and "concern" for life appeared. In moments like this, there is no difficulty in encountering a root metaphor that is then expressed in one's philosophical and religious tradition, uniting the organic with the creative, and a Whitehead with a Radhakrishnan. The clouds internal and external quickly hide the perception and distort the conception, but the intuition lasts forever.

References

1. Charles Hartshorne and William L. Reese, *Philosophers Speak of God* (Chicago : University of Chicago Press, 1953), pp. 306-310.
2. S. Radhakrishnan, *An Idealist View of Life* (London : Allen and Unwin, 1932), p. 269, quoted in Hartshorne and Reese, *Philosophers Speak of God,* p. 308.
3. Hartshorne and Reese, *Philosophers Speak of God,* p. 310.
4. *Ibid., p.* 310.
5. *Ibid.*
6. *Ibid.*
7. Paul A. Schilpp, *The Philosophy of Sarvepalli Radhakrishnan* (New York : Tudor Publishing Co., 1952), pp. 315-322.
8. *Ibid.,* p. 797.
9. S. Radhakrishnan, *An Idealist View of Life,* p. 268.
10. Paul A. Schilpp, *The Philosophy of Sarvepalli Radhakrishnan,* p. 273. Radhakrishnan consistently treats the Hebrew expression *"ehyeh 'asher 'ehyeh"* (Exodus : 3 : 14) as the classical Aristotelian "unmoved mover." Most modern Biblical scholars prefer a more active translation. James King West notes Albright's "I cause to be what I cause to be," saying "This rendering captures the dynamic element in the Hebrew description of Yahweh, who is in no case a god of static being but ever the Lord of historical process, who acts creatively and providentially in the whole realm of human experience. The response becomes an assertion of

his creative lordship" (James King West, *Introduction to the Old Testament* (New York : MacMillan, 1981, 2nd ed.), p. 157. I prefer Will Herberg's translations, "I aming what I aming," or "I am doing what I am doing" (Conversations with Will Herberg, c. 1957).

11. Rama Shanker Srivastava, *Contemporary Indian Philosophy* (Delhi : Munshiram Manohar Lal, 1965), p. 333.
12. *Ibid.*, p. 335.
13. Hartshorne and Reese, *Philosophers Speak of God*, p. 274.
14. Paul A. Schilpp, *The Philosophy of Alfred North Whitehead* (Evanston : Northwestern University Press, 1941), p. 549.
15. Robert C. Whittemore, "Time and Whitehead's God," *Tulane Studies in Philosophy*, IV (New Orleans : Tulane University Press, 1955), P. 85, 87.
16. A.N. Whitehead, *Process and Reality* (New York : Harper Torch Books, 1960), p. 168.
17. *Ibid.*, p. 524.
18. Paul A. Schilpp, *The Philosophy of Sarvepalli Radhakrishnan*, p. 797.
19. William A. Christian, *An Interpretation of Whitehead's Metaphysics* (New Haven : Yale University Press, 1959), p. 331.
20. S. Radhakrishnan, *An Idealist View of Life*, p. 182.
21. A.H. Johnson, *Whitehead's Theory of Reality* (Boston : Beacon Press, 1952), p. 217.
22. A.N. Whitehead, *Adventures of Ideas* (New York : The New American, 1959), p. 291.
23. A.N. Whitehead, *Process and Reality*, p. 134.
24. S. Radhakrishnan, *An Idealist View of Life*, p. 268.
25. *Ibid.*, p. 271.
26. *Ibid.*, p. 272.
27. *Ibid.*, p. 273.
28. *Ibid.*, p. 262.
29. Paul A. Schilpp, *The Philosophy of Sarvepalli Radhakrishnan*, p. 320 ff.

30. *Ibid.*, p. 797.
31. A.N. Whitehead, *Religion in the Making* (New York : MacMillan, 1926), p. 59.
32. *Ibid.*, p. 87f.
33. S. Radhakrishnan, *An Idealist View of Life*, p. 121.
34. *Ibid.*
35. *Ibid.*, p. 122.
36. *Ibid.*, p. 123.
37. *Ibid.*, p. 124.
38. *Ibid.*, p. 269.
39. *Ibid.*, p. 269.
40. A.N. Whitehead, *Religion in the Making*, p. 66f.

23
Radhakrishnan's Understanding of the Human Body

CARL OLSON
Allegheny College

According to the metaphysical position of Radhakrishnan, if the world in which human beings find themselves originated, is sustained and limited by Brahman, a transcendent and immanent reality, this implies that the world is not independent nor self-sufficient.[1] The world, even though it possesses no explanation of itself, does manifest a unity and meaning regardless of its ever changing character.[2] Within the world, every existent possesses an organization with its own specific mode of relatedness. These worldly organisms tend towards an interactive unity with their environment. Moreover, they always drive towards a higher level.[3] As an organism within the world, human beings suggest an unwholeness or something yet to be achieved. To gain wholeness is difficult due to the basic human situation.

According to Radhakrishnan, the human situation is precarious because humans are immersed in unsteady and contradictory surroundings. Human beings are oppressed by doubts and inspired by new horizons. Plagued by the constant fear of death, knowledge of isolation, tormented by doubt, fear and suffering, one's worldly existence is fragmentary.[4] The worldly surroundings of human beings are not the only aspect of human existence that is foreboding. There is an inner conflict within humans that must be resolved before one can achieve wholeness. Since human existence is essentially temporal one is involved in non-being. "It is non-being that derives Being from its immovable self-identity and enables it to express itself."[5] Since non-being is included within Being itself, non-being is dependent on the Being that it negates. Thus life is a constant overcoming of non-being by Being and a perpetual becoming of non-being to Being. Human beings also inhabit a contradictory position within the natural world because humans are also spiritual. Human beings form the bridge between the natural and spiritual worlds. To belong exclusively to only one of these worlds - natural or spiritual - involves ceasing to be human. "Life is a perpetual drama between the visible and the invisible."[6] This drama is played within one's body, which assumes an important role in Radhakrishnan's philosophy.

The role of the human body in Radhakrishnan's philosophy has tended to be neglected by scholars. A possible reason for this lack of attention by scholars to his understanding of the human body is due to Radhakrishnan's failure to fully develop this aspect of his philosophy. This paper will attempt to elucidate some of the things that he does say about the body and indicate areas that he failed to discuss or fully develop. The areas of his philosophy where Radhakrishnan does have much to say about the body are : (1) the relationship between self and body; (2) body and rebirth; (3) the body and the path to liberation. This essay will discuss each of these areas and also indicate other aspects of Radhakrishnan's philosophy that could be more fully developed with respect to the human body. In following this procedure, I will review Radhakrishnan's philosophical works and his commentaries on important Indian classical texts because he recognized these various classic works to be not only significant for Indians but to be also universally valid.[7]

Self and Body

An individual is composed of body, mind and spirit. The individual is thus a unity : "The whole man, body, mind and spirit, is one; Spirit is not to be delivered out of the entanglement with the body."[8] This assertion suggests some important implications : (1) the body is not a lower evil aspect of human nature; (2) one must not despise the body nor abuse it; (3) the body is a necessity for the soul; (4) the individual embodied person is not an inanimate object; (5) it is with our body that we attain liberation. Radhakrishnan's philosophical position suggests that the body is a personal possession of the individual; it is thus mine. However, even though the body is mine, it must not be understood as our true identity.[9] The impermanent nature of the body makes it impossible for one to find true identity with it. Thus the body, a mixture of being and non-being, is subject to change.

The changing nature of the body cannot be affirmed of the self. Radhakrishnan asks a non-rhetorical question :

> What is our true self? While our bodily organization undergoes changes, while our thoughts gather like clouds in the sky and disperse again, the self is never lost. It is present in all, yet distinct from all. Its nature is not affected by ordinary happenings. It is the source of the sense of identity through numerous transformations. It remains itself though it *sees* all things." It is the one thing that remains constant and unchanged in the incessant and multiform activity of the universe, in the slow changes of the organism, in the flux of sensations, in the dissipation of ideas, the fading of memories.[10]

If the body is a combination of being and non-being, the self is to be comprehended as "the core of being, the inner thread by being strung on which the world with all its variety exists. It is the real of the real, *satyasya satyam*."[11] When the physical body dies the existence of the self is unaffected, even though an injury to the body affects the self.[12]

The limited character of the body is manifested by its spatio-temporal nature : "Space-time is the natural condition of finiteness, limitation, change which characterises all events."[13] Since the body inhabits time, its temporality is indistinguishable from it. With regards to its spatial nature, the human body does not occupy a position in the world; it rather is located in a situation of existence, although precarious and contradictory, that includes space and time as its basic relation to the world. This world, a self-manifestation of the creative energy of Brahman, is not illusory, even though it is dependent upon Brahman, which alone is the absolute, independent reality. This implies that in comparison to Brahman the world is relative and dependent, just as the body is in relation to the immortal self. "The world is not a phantom, though it is not ultimately real."[14] Although the world is not an illusion, it exists between being and non-being, a situation analogous to the body. The relative, dependent and non-illusory characteristics shared by the body and the world suggests that for a self to be embodied implies its location and interaction within a world. The body is an organized system much like the world, even though they are both subject to change.[15] This is made clearer by Radhakrishnan's commentary on the *Bhagavad Gītā* when he refers to the body as a field in which events happen.[16] Radhakrishnan suggests that the body - the field - includes space and time. Since the world is also a field of sorts, the body and world are correlations that are internally related, and they together constitute a system. To be embodied is the medium by which human beings interact with the world. Thus Radhakrishnan implies that the body and world are an inseparable, internal relation just as the self is internally related to the body.

To comprehend more fully the relationship between the body and self, it is useful to look briefly at the nature of consciousness (*caitanya*), a nonobservable external phenomenon. Consciousness does appear when it assumes corporeal form.[17] In other words, consciousness manifests itself to our sight when it is embodied, and is not experienced by us apart from the body. We must not, however, construe consciousness as a quality of the body because it is rather a quality of the self, which is by nature pure consciousness.[18] Thus consciousness occurs when there is a body, the basis for consciousness and memory.[19] Even though the self and body form a unity and the body is the basis of consciousness, Radhakrishnan does not affirm that, unlike Merleau-Ponty,[20] the individual is one's body.

Body and Rebirth

Just as previous Indian thinkers have done before him, Radhakrishnan makes a distinction between the subtle body and the gross body. This distinction helps to explain the organic relationship between the self and its body. The gross body (*sthūla-śarīra*) consists of the gross elements like flesh, whereas the subtle body (*liṅga-śarīra*) is composed of life, senses, mind and subtle elements.[21] The subtle body, an image of our total personality, is transparent and invisible, forms the basis of consciousness and memory; possesses form and subtle material and is different from the gross body, although the subtle body is not discontinuous with the gross body. Carrying the impressions of past tendencies, the subtle body is the bearer of an individual's *karma*.[22] The gross body is modelled on the subtle body. And upon death it is the gross body that perishes, whereas the subtle body plays a role in rebirth by attracting the physical elements necessary for a new existence.[23] Thus it is the subtle body that serves as a vehicle for the immortal self.

By making the distinction between the gross body and subtle body, Radhakrishnan wants to maintain that life is not a mere product of the body, even though human life is manifested in a body. The self, which animates the entire physical organism, rules over the body and requires the body for its worldly activity. At the same time, Radhakrishnan wants to suggest that embodiment is very significant for this world and forms the starting point for spiritual development. By means of its inner dynamic and structure, the body seeks to bring to full actualization the complete development of a coherent self-conscious existence. "Though based on the body, the characteristic unity of the self is spiritual, more complete and permanent than any achieved by any individual being."[24] Thus we must not misconstrue the concept of rebirth to be a meaningless, eternal recurrence destined for nowhere.

Although rebirth is indicative of physical and mental change, it is not a circuitous route of a hopeless cycle of suffering from one bodily form to another. Radhakrishnan re-interprets rebirth as "a movement from man the animal to man the divine, a unique beginning to a unique end, from wild life in the jungle to a future Kingdom of God."[25] Thus the continual embodiment of the eternal self is conceived by Radhakrishnan to be a process of self-renewal and a development toward total self-enlightenment. Therefore, rebirth and embodiment of the self are essential for an individual's spiritual development. It is also a misconception to assume that the body must be treated with contempt, or that we should fear bodily desires and biological drives and come to hate our bodies. The human body is rather an instrument in an ethical sense for righteous living (*dharma-sādhanam*) and a vehicle for achieving liberation.[26] For the body to become such an instrument, it must, of course, become disciplined and thus a vehicle of liberation and not of bondage.

Path to Release

If one is ever to attain spiritual release (*mukti*), it is absolutely essential to have a body. Radhakrishnan makes this absolutely clear :

> A disembodied soul cannot undergo the discipline for attaining knowledge, which only an embodied being can do according to its liking. So if the works of a knower persist after the fall of the body, it will not be possible for him to get rid of them seeing that there is no possibility for acquiring further knowledge.[27]

Thus release does not consist of ridding oneself of one's body, a negative attitude that can only lead to continued bondage. This also does not suggest that one should become identified with one's body, but rather become aware of the spiritual importance of the body.

In order to gain release, one must take some form of action because to be embodied implies activity. If an individual's actions are not to result in further bondage, actions must be performed without attachment and avoiding actions pervaded by desire.[28] Unless one can renounce personal desire by surrendering all to God, one cannot perform actions correctly and attain detachment from the world. The renunciation of personal desire and performance of right action are complementary and form a unity in respect to the way one should act. Actions are to be renounced inwardly and not outwardly because one should offer works as an offering to the Supreme in which alone is immortality.[29] There are two types of renunciation : one accompanying true spiritual knowledge and the other without such knowledge. The correct kind of renunciation consists in the accomplishment of the necessary action without an inward striving for reward. When one acts not for self-possession or gain but to achieve an anchorage in God-consciousness, the preliminary step to liberation, is attained.

Since the seeker for liberation quests for freedom in an embodied condition, one must organize the body, mind and self into a unity. Radhakrishnan's position contains important implications : (1) worldly activity is not renounced; (2) the individual's body and social relationships are maintained;[30] (3) release is not some disembodied state.[31] After attaining release or salvific knowledge, embodiment continues to persist, even though the self is free.[32] Thus knowledge of Brahman co-exists with embodiment and continued participation in the world. Full release does not involve the necessity of bodily death. "Release relates to the frame of mind. It does not depend on embodiment or non-embodiment."[33] A further explanation is offered when Radhakrishnan comments on a passage from the Śvetāśvatara Upaniṣad (2:12) :

> The Yogin does not become disembodied. The elements composing his body are elevated to the level of their subtleness, sūkṣmatva. He leaves his gross body and attains an indefectible one. It is a consciousness-body akin to that of the Supreme with whom the contemplator has identified through meditation.[34]

It is a grave mistake to assume that embodiment is a sign of continued ignorance and bondage to the law of karma. The attainment of release is not simply an individual accomplishment because it involves working for the liberation of all (sarva-mukti).

Since the individual quests for liberation with one's body and gains enlightenment while embodied, the body possesses religious and metaphysical significance and thus is not to be neglected nor discarded either before or after attaining one's spiritual quest. With relation to the bodily and spiritual aspects of human life, Radhakrishnan wants to emphasize a moderate philosophical position because one should not over emphasize one aspect of a human being over the other. Radhakrishnan makes this perfectly clear :

Spirit without mind or spirit without body is not the aim of human perfection. Body and mind are the conditions or instruments of the life of spirit in man, valuable not for their own sake but because of the spirit in them.[35]

Even though one can find some negative statements about the body in his philosophical works and commentaries of classical Indian texts,[36] Radhakrishnan certainly tries to maintain a balanced and moderate philosophical position with respect to the body and is not overly concerned with stressing the need to leave the body behind in the quest for liberation (*mokṣa*).[37]

Ethical Implications

Radhakrishnan's comprehension of the human body possesses important implications for some aspects of his ethics. If our goal is to attain full selfhood, and if we accomplish this task within our body, the path to our goal is not to be done suddenly and/or immediately : "It has to be reached through a progressive training, a gradual enlarging of the natural life accompanied by an uplifting of all its motives."[38] This is exemplified by the four ends of life (*puruṣārthas*) : end of worldly possessions, wealth (*artha*); end of enjoyment or ordinary pleasures of life (*kāma*); religious and moral duties (*dharma*); and release or liberation (*mokṣa*). These goals can only be reached by a person from an embodied condition. Since we have discussed the final end of life already, we can illustrate the implications of Radhakrishnan's understanding of the body for the ends of life by concentrating on the second third ends.

Because the second end of life refers to love, desire, and pleasure, it is obvious that one needs a body in order to reach this goal and be able to enjoy its fruits. It also suggests that one can attain spiritual freedom without having to surrender ordinary life or one's body. Moreover, the end of *kāma* suggests that one is not denied the emotional aspect of one's life because "kāma refers to the emotional being of man, his feelings and desires."[39] Rather than the excesses of life, *kāma* represents normal or harmonious pleasures of life and does not deny the emotional aspect of life. Otherwise, without reaching the goal of *kāma*, there is a danger that a person could become a victim of repressive introspection and continually live under the strain of self-inflicted moral torture, which could prove ruinous to one's sanity and physical well-being.

With relation to the third end of life (*dharma*), Radhakrishnan interprets it to mean a total way of life and a set of guidelines that gives coherence and direction to the different activities of life : "It is the complete rule of life, the harmony of the whole man who finds a right and just law of his living."[40] Rather than conforming one's life, for instance, to one's desires and becoming dominated by them, it is much wiser for one to adhere to the rule of right practise (*dharma*), a law of one's inner being. "Dharma tells us that while our life is in the first instance for our own satisfaction, it is more essentially for the community and most of all for that universal self which is in each of us and all beings."[41] This implies an ethical life conforming to the guidelines of *dharma*. Ethical life is not an end in itself : "Ethical life is the means to spiritual freedom, as well as its expression on earth."[42] Thus, *dharma* is not the beginning nor the end of human life, but it is rather a preliminary step to liberation (*mokṣa*). Within the context of his understanding of *dharma*, Radhakrishnan calls the human body the *dharma sādhanam* by which he means that the body is the instrument available to a person that enables him/her to perform his/her duties.[43]

If one needs a body to achieve release, and if an ethical life is a necessary propaedeutic to a more spiritual form of existence, it is obvious that one also needs a body in order to perform good deeds. If one looks within oneself, one can discover the moral law and know how to act in order to cultivate the moral discipline necessary for spiritual insight. "Ethics is the basis of spiritual life and its substance."[44] Because of free will and being a prisoner of evil actions, not all individuals adhere to the moral law within themselves. Even though one can freely choose for or against the moral law while embodied, it is only choices in conformity with the moral law that leads to spiritual perfection.

Although Radhakrishnan may emphasize some different ethical features, the choices of correct actions are, for the most part, essentially in conformity with the ancient tradition of Indian philosophy. A person striving for spiritual development and attainment must act without attachment and avoid actions pervaded with desire. To act in such a way is to be free from the karmic results of one's actions.[45] It is also important to surrender everything to God, renounce personal desire, and do one's moral and ethical duty, depending on one's *dharma*, without any personal attachment or hope of reward.

Two essential features of Radhakrishnan's ethical theory are *satya* (truth) and *ahiṁsā* (non-violence). The former term means truthfulness, honesty, and sincerity, although Radhakrishnan also uses *satya* to mean inward awareness.[46] By maintaining an identity between thought, word and deed, *ahiṁsā*, an active reverence for all life, is the renunciation of intent to injure other beings by either thought, word or deed. To follow the path of *ahiṁsā* is to lead a life of compassion for other existing entities, to be devoted to all that lives, and to share a sense of union with all that exists. Moreover, it is not to be construed as a negative abstention from doing injury to living things, but to have sympathy, compassion and positive love for all. This single ideal is the supreme moral law for Radhakrishnan.[47] He relates it directly to love : "Love is non-resistance. Conflicts are to be overcome not by force but by love."[48] Radhakrishnan finds justification for universal love in the Upaniṣad doctrine of *tat tvam asi* located in the Cāndogya Upaniṣad (6.8.7), where it is one's duty to love one's neighbour because one is one's neighbour. From another perspective, the moral law of *ahimsā* can be construed as the non-violent interaction between bodies in space and time.

If we combine Radhakrishnan's conviction about the reality of the world and human body with his ethical philosophy and its emphasis on non-violence, it is apparent that a person's goals should be this-worldly and humanistic. It is everyone's responsibility to make themselves useful to society by striving to eliminate poverty and disease, spread education, and end war and strife. We can empathize with the plight of those less fortunate and try to assist them because we and they are also embodied. It is our bodies that relate us to others and the world and enable us to help the needy.

Concluding Remarks

In the *Puruṣasūkta* (10.90) of the *Ṛg Veda*, the story of the creation of the universe and society by means of the dismemberment of the body of a primal, cosmic being is offered by this religiously and philosophically influential hymn. The upper strata of ancient Indian society is created from the higher parts of the cosmic body and the lower levels of society are derived from the lower extremities of its body. Since the head of this cosmic being is significantly higher and more meaningful than its feet or lower part, the body of the cosmic *Puruṣa* is hierarchically ordered. This hierarchical type of conception of the body is also present in Radhakrishnan's understanding of the human body and self. Radhakrishnan's philosophical thinking is hierarchical in the sense, for instance, that the mind, associated with the higher part of a person, is superior to the body.[49] The life of the human self is also not centred in the body because the self, an immortal and unchanging aspect of the person, is superior to the body.[50] The personal identity of a person, regardless of the intimate relationship between the self and body, is never stated in terms of one's body by Radhakrishnan. The individual possesses a body, but it cannot be affirmed that one is a body. Moreover, the gross body is modelled on the subtle body forming another type of hierarchy. This type of hierarchical thinking is a reflection of Radhakrishnan's conviction that the spiritual, which is associated with the higher part of a human being, is of greater value and significance than the gross matter that constitutes the body. This observation is an acknowledgment of the Indian cultural influence that shaped the philosophical reflections of Radhakrishnan and is generally characteristic of Indo-European thought.

If one quests for liberation with one's body, gains liberating knowledge with one's body, and is liberated while embodied, the human body represents a potential metaphysical significance. It is merely potential because Radhakrishnan does not fully develop the philosophical implications for his conception of the human body. Radhakrishnan's discussion, for instance, of the relationship between the body and consciousness is not fully developed. Radhakrishnan seems to suggest that the body limits consciousness. Moreover, the relationship between the body and world could be more fully developed in order to demonstrate the implications of their interrelationship. It is possible that the body and world represent a system of intentional relations. If the world and body are correlations, this might imply that to experience the body is to perceive the world and vice versa. These are just a couple of areas of Radhakrishnan's conception of the body that could be more fully developed, even though he made a positive contribution to a contemporary comprehension of the body for his culture.

References

1. S. Radhakrishnan, *The Brahma Sūtra : The Philosophy of Spiritual Life* (London : George Allen & Unwin Ltd., 1960), p. 120.
2. Idem, *Eastern Religions and Western Thought.* Second Edition (Oxford : Oxford University Press, 1940), p. 89.
3. Idem, *An Idealist View of Life.* Second Edition (London : George Allen & Unwin, 1957), p. 312.
4. Idem, *Eastern Religions and Western Thought*, p. 43.
5. Idem, *Recovery of Faith* (New York : Harper and Brothers Publishers, 1955), p. 83.
6. Idem, *Fellowship of the Spirit* (Cambridge : Harvard University Press, 1961), p. 3.
7. Robert M. Minor, *Radhakrishnan : A Religious Biography* (Albany : State University of New York Press, 1987), p. 97.
8. S. Radhakrishnan, "The Religion of the Spirit and the World's Need : Fragments of a Confession," in *The Philosophy of Sarvepalli Radhakrishnan*, ed. Paul Arthur Schilpp (New York : Tudor Publishing Company, 1952), p. 30. See also *East and West in Religion* (London : George Allen & Unwin Ltd, 1933), p. 81 and *The Bhagavad Gītā.* Second Edition (London : George Allen & Unwin Ltd., 1970), p. 46.
9. Idem, *The Principal Upaniṣads.* Third Impression (London : George Allen & Unwin Ltd., 1969), p. 458.
10. Idem, *Eastern Religions and Western Thought*, p. 26.
11. *Ibid.*, p. 30.
12. Idem, *An Idealist View of Life*, p. 291.
13. *Ibid.*, p. 230.
14. Idem, *Eastern Religions and Western Thought*, p. 86.

15. Idem, *An Idealist View of Life*, p. 266.
16. Idem, *Bhagavad Gītā*, p. 300.
17. Idem, *Brahma Sūtra*, p. 498.
18. *Ibid.*, p. 499.
19. *Ibid.*, p. 124.
20. Maurice Merleau-Ponty, *Phenomenology of Perception*, trans. Colin Smith (London : Routledge and Kegan Paul, 1962), p. 150.
21. Radhakrishnan, *Upaniṣads*, p. 806.
22. Idem, *Brahma Sūtra*, p. 205.
23. Idem, *An Idealist View of Life*, p. 295; *Bhagavad Gītā*, p. 108.
24. Idem, *Brahma Sūtra*, p. 190.
25. *Ibid.*, p. 193.
26. *Ibid.*, p. 159.
27. *Ibid.*, p. 483.
28. Idem, *Bhagavad Gītā*, p. 163.
29. *Ibid.*, p. 178.
30. Idem, *Brahma Sūtra*, p. 218.
31. *Ibid.*, pp. 215-16.
32. *Ibid.*, p. 222.
33. *Ibid.*, p. 216.
34. Idem, *Upaniṣads*, p. 723.
35. Idem, *Eastern Religions and Western Thought*, p. 98.
36. Idem, *Bhagavad Gītā*, p. 125.
37. In contrast to this position is S.J. Samartha's criticism of Radhakrishnan's understanding of the body : "A close examination of Radhakrishnan's conception of *mokṣa* gives the impression that in spite of his emphasis on man as a unity of body and spirit, in the last analysis body is something to be left behind," in *Introduction to Radhakrishnan : The Man and His Thought* (New York : Association Press, 1964), p. 82. See a confirmation of my interpretation in *Bhagavad Gītā*, p. 111.

38. Radhakrishnan, *Eastern Religions and Western Thought*, p. 351.
39. *Ibid.*, p. 352.
40. *Ibid.*, p. 353.
41. *Ibid.*, p. 353.
42. *Ibid.*, p. 353.
43. Idem, "Fragments of a Confession," p. 7.
44. Idem, *Brahma Sūtra*, p. 154.
45. Idem, *Bhagavad Gītā*, p. 163.
46. Idem, *Brahma Sūtra*, p. 158.
47. *Ibid.*, p. 160.
48. Idem, *An Idealist View of Life*, p. 118.
49. *Ibid.*, p. 291.
50. *Ibid.*, pp. 139, 291.

24

The Perceptual, the Conceptual and the Spiritual : Radhakrishnan's Metaphysical Quest

K. SUNDARAM
Lake Michigan College

In his essay on "The Metaphysical Quest," Radhakrishnan argues for a faith that 'has to be a rational one.' He starts out by asserting, "Metaphysical ideas are founded on a basic awareness of what is implied in experience and cannot be altogether justified by scientific measurement or rational logic."[1] The positivism of August Comte (1798-1857) was not a theory but a method that sought scientific explanations in every field of experience and rejected theological dogmas or speculative metaphysics. But an analysis of positivism leads Radhakrishnan to conclude that 'positivists themselves had expressed metaphysical convictions like the doctrine of physicalism.' In a similar vein he argues that existentialism is a way of thinking which takes self-conscious existence as the proper subject and point of departure for philosophy and to study the meaning and values of existence, 'we have to pass beyond science.' Such a study, for Radhakrishnan, has to be based on spiritual experience as opposed to perceptual or conceptual.[2] Further, such a metaphysical quest should attempt to 'assess the reasons for and the limitations implicit in the presuppositions and of science and logic.'[3]

The questions in metaphysics are the most general and have to be answered - or, at least, presupposed - before we seek answers to specific questions about matter, life, and society, the subject matter of the physical, the biological, and the social sciences. Doubts about the solutions to the metaphysical problems result in doubts about the solutions to problems in these sciences, very much like any residue of uncertainty regarding the nature of knowledge in general in epistemology functions as uncertainty regarding the nature of particular kinds of knowledge in the various studies. Metaphysics, or the study of it, as an inquiry into the universal characteristics of existence, share many features with a study of epistemology. That is why it is possible to 'assess the reasons and limitations implicit in the presuppositions of science and logic,' by studying the differences between the experiences which are spiritual, perceptual, or conceptual.

Plato, in books 6 and 7 of the *Republic*, contrasts perceptual knowledge as "opinion" with real knowledge, to the latter's glory. From the time of Aristotle, philosophers have admitted the indispensability of both the sensory and the intellectual contributions. Greek philosophers formed the notion that a knowledge of so-called 'universals,' consisting of concepts of abstract forms, qualities, numbers, and relations was the only knowledge worthy of the truly philosophic mind. For the rationalists conceptual knowledge was the more noble and it originated independently of all perceptual particulars. According to them concepts such as God, perfection, eternity, infinity, immutability, identity, absolute beauty, truth, justice, necessity, freedom, duty, worth, etc. and the part they play in our mind, are impossible to explain as results of practical experience. The various conceptual universes can be considered in complete abstraction from perceptual reality, and when so considered, we can discover all sorts of fixed relations among their parts. Conceptual knowledge can develop its own *a priori* sciences such as logic and mathematics.

As opposed to this the empiricists have argued that the significance of concepts consists in their relation to perceptual particulars. Thus David Hume makes a distinction between 'Relations of Ideas' and 'Matters of Fact,' and, in his *Enquiry Concerning Human Understanding* (1748) finds it to "be a subject worthy of curiosity, to inquire what is the nature of that evidence which assures us of any real existence and matter of fact, beyond the present testimony of our senses, or the records of our memory." Matters-of-fact statements are judged to be true or false based on sensory perception. Matter-of-analysis statements are judged to be true or false based on logical consistency. Thus the matter-of-fact statements refer to the perceptual and the matter-of-analysis statements refer to the conceptual. Despite the problem of induction, for Hume, both the perceptual and the conceptual originate in sensory experience. But for Radhakrishnan experience is not limited to sense experience. "We cannot deny the experience of purpose, of choice, of vision, of beauty, of apprehension, of truth, though they may not be capable of scientific measurement."[4]

Woken from his dogmatic slumbers by Hume, Kant attempted a distinction between the percept and two kinds of concepts - empirical and *a priori*. For Kant, a concept is a rule of combination or synthesis. And he claims that "combination does not lie in objects but is an affair of the understanding alone."[5] In his *Logic,* he distinguishes between *intuition* that is a singular presentation, and *concept* that is a general or reflected presentation. Of the two types of concepts, empirical concept springs from the senses through comparison of the objects of experience and receives, through the understanding, merely the form of generality. But the pure or *a priori* concept is one that is not abstracted [*abgezogen*] from experience but 'springs from the understanding even as to content.' Both types of concepts are forms of unity and reflect the spontaneous and synthetic function of the understanding. The difference between them appears to be that empirical concepts refer directly to intuitively given data while *a priori* concepts refer to data only by way of empirical concepts. Thus greenness may be taken as typical of empirical concepts. The class of categories may serve as *a priori* concepts. In the *Critique* the main distinction between the two turns out to be while the empirical concept is contingent, the *a priori* concept is necessary. Metaphysics for Kant deals with *a priori* concepts.[6] Apart from possible experience we have no justification for claiming that the categories have an application or even a meaning, since their meaning consists in their function as principles for the unification of experience.

As a logical construction, a concept signifies a possibility. The value of many concepts seems to be functional. The most important part of a concept's significance may be held to be consequences to which it leads. It is this idea about concepts that lead William James to formulate his Pragmatic Rule. "The Pragmatic Rule is that the meaning of a concept may always be found, if not in some sensible particular which it directly designates, then in some particular difference in the course of human experience which its being true will make."[7] Thus Western epistemology has clearly recognized the distinction between perception and conception. The former is solely of the here and now; the latter is of the like and unlike, of the future, of the past, and of the far far away.

In what way, then, the spiritual different from the perceptual and the conceptual? Radhakrishnan acknowledges that we have no other sources of knowledge than experience. But the spiritual is based on experience other than sense experience. He refers to the spiritual as the "expressions of the spirit in us." But we cannot clearly understand what this spiritual is if we stay within the confines of epistemology. No amount of epistemological study would point out the difference between the conceptual and the spiritual. For this we have to integrate our ontological commitments with our epistemic theories. We can find examples of this in the history of science.

At this juncture, I wish to discuss two examples, rather briefly. The first one refers to Einstein's commitment to Machist sensationism and empiricism in his earlier years and to a rational realism in his later years. The earliest of Einstein's known letters is dated March 19, 1901, and was written to the chemist Wilhelm Ostwald, whose book *Allgemeine chemie* is the first book mentioned by Einstein in all of his published works. In this and other letters, Einstein talks about the influence of Ostwald on him. Now, Ostwald - and Mach, Stallo, and Helm - opposed a mechanical interpretation of physical phenomena. Those scientists did not want to accept ideas like ether, which cannot be directly observed, but wanted to "consider anew the ultimate principles of all physical reasoning, notably the scope and validity of the Newtonian laws of motion and the conception of force and action, of absolute and relative motion."[8] And this precisely was what Einstein set out to do in the next few years. His insistence upon an epistemological analysis of the conceptions of space and time and on the identification of reality with what is given by sensations in his famous 1905 paper, reflect this commitment. There were few social or economic or even cultural conditions that demanded any change in the attitudes toward physical explanation. Even Max Planck, who was enthusiastic about the special theory of relativity, but could not accept the general theory or Einstein's attempted revision of Maxwell's theory to accommodate the probabilistic character of the emission of photons, felt that a basic aim of science "is the finding of a fixed world picture independent of the variation of time and people," or, "the complete liberation of the physical picture from the individuality of the separate intellects."[9] In fact in a letter to Mach written in December of 1911, Einstein laments that the only thing which he could bring forward in favour of his theory against Planck was Mach's epistemological argument that Einstein has accepted.

In a similar manner, we can explain Einstein's later thought experiments about his field theories and his disagreement with Niels Bohr on the complementary principle in terms of his new commitments to what he calls the rational realism.

Now on to our second example, this one from economics. Paul A. Samuelson concluded an eulogy he wrote on the occasion of Keynes' death in 1946 with the following words:

"The classical philosophy always had its ups and downs along with the great swings of business activity. Each time it had come back. But, now for the first time, it was confronted by a competing system - a well reasoned body of thought containing among other things as many equations as unknowns. In short, like itself, a synthesis; and one which could swallow the classical system as a special case.

A new *system*, that is what required emphasis. Classical economics could withstand isolated criticism. Theorists can always resist facts; for facts are hard to establish and are always changing anyway, and *Ceteris Paribus* can be made to absorb a good deal of punishment. Inevitably, at the earliest opportunity, the mind slips back into the old grooves of thought since analysis is utterly impossible without a frame of reference, a way of thinking about things, or in short a theory."[10]

Samuelson's initial belief that "truth is not in the eye of the beholder, and that certain regularities of economic life are as valid for a Marxist as for a classicist, for a post-Keynesian as for a monetarist," seems to have guided his work all along. His fondness for the lectures of Aaron Director, a strong libertarian of the Frank Knight - Fred Hayek school, at the University of Chicago, did not detract from his later descriptions of corporations as the "price-administering oligopolists."[11] He did not seem to have any difficulty going from the classic formulation of the marginal utility theory by Alfred Marshall (in his *Principles of Economics*) to the economics that, as Samuelson calls it, was 'waiting for the invigorating kiss of Maynard Keynes.' He could do that because of his acceptance of the independent nature of the economic life. What was needed was a new theory, a mathematical theory, to enable us to understand the economic life. What is involved here is not just difference in methodology, but rather the metaphysical assignment of independent status to economic life. As opposed to Keynes and Samuelson, we find F.A. Hayek and L. Von Mises, two prominent exponents of marginal utility analysis, to be dedicated to methodological individualism with its often found confusion between the ontological thesis that the ultimate constituents of the social world are individual people, and the reductive thesis that statements about social phenomena are deducible from psychological statements about human individuals.[12]

These and other examples would show that individual scientists are committed to certain methodological and metaphysical positions which prescribes for them what is rational and what is not. The driving force in one's life, especially in one's intellectual life, is one's philosophical, in the sense of the ontological and epistemological, commitments. It is this combination that should be referred to as the spiritual for its appeal is to a judgment more basic than either sense-experience or rational logic. Questions regarding the ontological commitments that enable one to formulate the conceptual provide us with an opportunity to "assess the reasons for and the limitations implicit in the presuppositions of science and logic." And, perhaps, this is one way in which we can come face to face with the 'spirit in us.'

For Radhakrishnan the question is not whether we should have a metaphysics or not for we all have one. The question is whether it is to be an unexamined and even unconscious metaphysics or a system of ordered thought which is deliberately achieved. His answer is that we ought to examine the metaphysical systems because no culture can last unless it supports the metaphysical effort and encourages the confidence that 'man is capable of insight into the nature of the process in which he participates' (p. 108). But any defense of such metaphysical underpinnings have to be in the context of and by using the concepts and percepts of our epistemology. The appeal of metaphysics may be to the insights and intuitions of humans but such appeals can be assessed only in terms of our epistemic concepts and percepts. There truthfulness and validity would be, at best, at the same level as that of the axioms that constitute the fundamental theories in the various sciences. From this perspective looking for a rational, or empirical, or realistic (as Radhakrishnan says) basis for our metaphysical commitments destroys any distinction between the conceptual and the spiritual.

References

1. S. Radhakrishnan, "The Metaphysical Quest" in *Religion and Culture* (Delhi : Hind Pocket Books, 1968), p. 90.
2. *Ibid.*, p. 95.

3. *Ibid.*, p. 109.
4. *Ibid.*, p. 94.
5. I. Kant, *Critique of Pure Reason*, B. 135.
6. *Ibid.*, A : 90-95; B : 123-129.
7. William James, *Pragmatism*, Ch. ii.
8. J.T. Merz, *A History of European Thought in the Nineteenth Century* (New York : Dover, 1965), p. 199.
9. M. Planck, *A Survey of Physical Theory* (New York, 1960), p. 24.
10. Paul A. Samuelson, *Collected Scientific Papers*, II (Cambridge: M.I.T. Press, 1966), p. 1533.
11. Paul A. Samuelson, quoted in *Newsweek*, September 8, 1975, p. 62.
12. F.A. Hayek, *The Counter Revolution of Science* (Glencoe, Ill.: 1952), especially chapter 4.

The Nature and Significance of Intuition**
(A View based on a Core Idea held by Sarvepalli Radhakrishnan)

Hope K. Fitz
Eastern Connecticut State University

Prefatory Remarks

Before presenting my account of the nature and significance of intuition, I want to state that in this short paper, I will simply highlight some of the major ideas which are discussed at length in the book on intuition which I am writing.

I am indebted to Sarvepalli Radhakrishnan for the core idea of intuition that I culled from his writings, and which inspired the line of thought that I follow in my book. However, sometimes Radhakrishnan speaks as if intuition were a kind of knowledge, or an independent way of gaining knowledge, while, as I will explain, I hold that intuition is simply *one* means of knowledge. Furthermore, I argue that any view according to which intuition is taken to be a form or independent way of gaining knowledge, will be rejected by those critical thinkers who take knowledge to be a discursive process of the mind or the result thereof.

Unless intuition is recognized as one means to knowledge, much of human experience is inexplicable and/

or meaningless. The problem is that many modern critical thinkers do not recognize intuition as a means to knowledge. Furthermore, since intuition is not so recognized, it is not generally accepted as a criterion for justification of a belief. The problem with not accepting intuition as *one* criterion for justification of a belief is that those beliefs which draw from evidence of an intuitive nature are either ignored or rejected because they are judged to the unjustified.

The result of this rejection is that many beliefs which make sense of human existence, including both metaphysical and religious beliefs, are regarded as meaningless.

The reason that many rigorous thinkers have been reluctant to recognize intuition as a means to knowledge, and thus accept it as one criterion for the justification of a belief, is that the commonly held view as to the nature of intuition is inconsistent with what these thinkers take knowledge to be.

The commonly held view as to the nature of intuition, is that it is immediate apprehension.[1] In general, "apprehension" means a mental grasping, and "immediate" means not mediated by the reasoning process. Thus, immediate apprehension is taken to be a nondiscursive form or independent way of gaining knowledge. The problem with this view is that as far as modern rigorous thinkers are concerned, knowledge, whatever else it may be, is taken to be the process and/or result of reasoning about experience. Also, since humans can make errors with regard to perception and reasoning, claims to knowledge require justification. Thus, knowledge, by its very nature, is taken to be discursive, i.e., mediated by the reasoning process. Yet, via immediate apprehension, one can make claims to knowledge. Thus, if you and I were engaged in a logical argument, and you asked me to state the reasons for a claim that I had made, I could say, "Oh, I have no reasons, I simply know" ("know" by intuition). I think that the acceptance of any view which could lead to this kind of statement is ludicrous.

In light of the foregoing problems which I have elicited, concerning the view that intuition is immediate apprehension, I propose that this view be rejected in favour of the view which I will offer. Given my view, intuition and reason are complementary processes of the mind which can, together with sense perception, lead to knowledge.

My view as to the nature of intuition is based on a core idea of that nature which I culled from the writings of Sarvepalli Radhakrishnan. In a loose sense, Radhakrishnan spoke of intuition as any cognitive process of awareness which is direct or immediate in contrast to what is inferential, i.e., mediated by the reasoning process.[2] He included both perceptual knowledge and what he called "integral insight" in the foregoing sense of intuition.[3] In a strict sense, he confined "intuition" to integral insight.[4] It is this latter sense with which I am concerned.

Although Radhakrishnan neither defined nor clearly explained what he meant by "intuition,"[5] he did describe it.[6] Based on his descriptions, I take intuition to be an integral process of awareness which culminates in an act of insight. The process itself involves both perception and conceptual activities, including the formulation of concepts and memory. Also, although he sometimes spoke as if inherence formed a part of the process,[7] as I indicated earlier, he characterized intuition as noninferential.[8] Thus, I surmise that he thought that inference forms a part of the memories which are involved in the process, but not the act of insight in which the process culminates.

Finally, based on Radhakrishnan's statements that the whole mind is involved in integral insight,[9] and his observation that one is not an idle spectator in this process,[10] I conclude that the process is intentional or directed.

Based upon what Radhakrishnan said about intuition, Martin Heidegger's notion of a focus of concern,[11] and some of my views about the nature of the intuitive process,[12] I take intuition to be an intentional or directed process of awareness in which present impressions and relevant memories are brought to bear on a certain focus of concern. This process culminates in a mental act of insight. Also, whereas the process is grounded in reason, i.e., reason was used to form many of the thoughts which are now memories, the mental act in which the process culminates includes neither inference nor mental structuring, e.g, the comparison of ideas.

Intuition, as I have described it, is *not* a nondiscursive form of knowledge. Neither is it an independent way of gaining knowledge, because I take it to be only one of three interrelated means to knowledge, namely, sense perception, intuition, and reason. Via sense perception, one becomes aware of the physical or material aspects of experience. Via intuition, one becomes aware of those aspects of experience which transcend that which is merely physical or material. Via reason, one structures what is sensibly perceived or intuited. Also, it is reason which enables one to construct and also to analyze logical arguments, i.e., to determine if an inference from premises to a conclusion, i.e., a belief, is warranted. Thus, given my view, intuition and reason are complementary processes which, together with sensible perception, can lead to knowledge.

Accepting the view that intuition is an integral process of the mind, I want to briefly consider what I take to be two kinds of intuition, namely, penetrative and creative. I am not aware that Radhakrishnan or any other philosopher has identified these two kinds of intuition, yet, it appears to me that these distinctions are implicit in their accounts of the subject.[13]

I take penetrative insight to be the insight into the structure of : (1) a situation; or (2) a problem when the pertinent facts are available. I think that the structures which one recognizes vary from the simple to the complex.

Penetrative insights into simple structures include those in which one suddenly sees a better way to : organize some material; perform a task; learn some subject; etc.

Penetrative insights into more complex structures involve problems or situations in which one does not have all the pertinent information available. Several examples are :

(1) a physician who is able to cure a rare disease because of a hunch as to its nature, and a hunch as to the required treatment;

(2) a biologist who is able to discover the full nature and cure of a new disease;

(3) a detective who is able to intuit missing pieces of evidence at the site of a crime; and

(4) a person who can very quickly discern the nature of a situation, be it social, professional, etc.

Penetrative insights into even more complex structures are sometimes referred to as metaphysical and spiritual insights. These are the insights into the nature of reality, and/or the source of that reality. Such insights are rare. This is so not only because of the complexity of the structure involved, but because such insights seem to require considerable life experience, maturity, and a high degree of intellectual and/or intuitive development. Furthermore, spiritual insight also seems to require a high level of moral development.[14]

Having stated what I take penetrative insight to be, let me turn now to a brief consideration of creative insight. Via creative insight, one can gain some intimations as to:

(1) the chain of events which may lead to an eventuality; or

(2) the logical transitions which may lead to a solution of a problem.

With regard to the first kind of creative insight, the chain of events may lead to a scientific discovery, a possible scientific explanation, an invention, a musical composition, or an artistic creation, etc.

With regard to the second kind of creative insight, a series of logical transitions may be steps in a logical or mathematical proof, or simply the steps involved in balancing one's check book.

In general, creative insights are not as common as penetrative insights. The exceptions would be the penetrative insights which I have referred to as metaphysical and spiritual. Part of the reason that creative intuition is not so common, in my view, is that persons need to develop their creative abilities, and to be encouraged to do so.[15]

One final point about creative and penetrative insights is that they often occur together, e.g., the creative person is often one who has profound insights into the nature or structure of life, and then that person is able to express those insights in some work of art, etc.

Given my view as to the nature of intuition, and that it is one means to knowledge, it should be so recognized, and thus, accepted as one criterion for justification of a belief. If intuition is so recognized and accepted, then those experiences which are difficult, if not impossible, to explain without an appeal to intuition, are understandable and/or meaningful. Also, many beliefs, especially those having to do with ontological or spiritual matters, can be justified.

I believe that the few examples which I have given of penetrative and creative insights make clear that unless intuition is recognized as a means to knowledge, and thus accepted as one criterion for a belief, many of the experiences which I have described, and the beliefs based upon these experiences, make little sense.

Of course, the person who does not recognize or accept intuition is apt to explain the simple intuitions as simply educated guesses, and to dismiss the more complex intuitions, especially those concerned with metaphysical or spiritual dimensions, as flights of imagination or fanciful thinking.

One thing to note about persons who ignore or reject intuition, and accept only sense perception and reason as means to knowledge, is that they usually want to reduce human experience to one particular dimension, be it physical, e.g., biological, or mental, i.e., psychological, or cultural, e.g., anthropological or sociological, etc.

The problem with any form of reductionism is that it flattens the human experience. Also, those holding such views are unable to account for much of our human experience, and many of our beliefs.

Because of the stricture of time, I will consider only one human experience, some forms of which are difficult to explain without an appeal to intuition, and others which are impossible. Most of us are familiar with this experience, even if we have not had it.

The experience which I want to consider is often referred to as a "calling" or being "called." This experience can be described as a felt need to pursue some life-plan or goal. The need in question is not simply a desire or psychological drive, nor an attraction to something. Rather, it is an urge to respond to some calling or beckoning. This urge impels the person to pursue whatever the calling may be.

The more mundane callings are those with which most of us are familiar, in that we have either had some such experience, or known someone who has. Included in these callings are : the felt need to pursue a vocation, and humanitarian pursuits of either a social or a political nature.

Other more rare callings are concerned with metaphysical and/or spiritual dimensions of experience. I will mention three such callings, and persons who I believe had them :

(1) a person has a call to pursue and understand the nature of truth of Being. Martin Heidegger expressed what I take to be such a calling, when he described his felt need to pursue Being qua Being.[16]

(2) A person has a call to live her or his life in pursuit of truth. Mahatma Gandhi comes to mind here. As most of you know, *Sat* or truth was more fundamental to Gandhi's system of beliefs than *Ahimsa*.

(3) A person has a calling to study and understand comparative views of truth or reality, and to offer syncretic, or at least harmonious, explanations of these views. Sarvepalli Radhakrishnan seems to have had such a calling.

The mundane experiences of being called, which I have mentioned, are difficult to explain without an appeal to intuition. For sense experience and reason alone cannot adequately account for a response to a call that becomes the very focus of one's life, and often the centre of one's being.

The experiences of being called which have to do with ontological and/or spiritual matters are, in my view, impossible to explain without an appeal to intuition. Such is the case because all sense experience and reason can give us is some understanding of the physical world. Given these means, alone, the ontological dimension of existence, and/or the source of this dimension, remain unknowable. Of course, the acceptance of a Heideggerian view of reality, as revealed Being,[17] which I accept, enables one to consider reality as accessible to the human mind (unlike all subjectivist views of knowing, which start with Aristotle and culminate with Kant).[18] However, even Heidegger realized that intuition is needed for the revelation of that aspect of Being which is hidden or unrevealed.[19]

Having explained what I take intuition to be, and the significance of it, I want to conclude this paper by again expressing my indebtedness to Sarvepalli Radhakrishnan, for it was his core idea of intuition which enabled me to develop a view of it which is not at odds with reason. Finally, in tribute to him, I want to say that, in my view, he fits the Greek ideal of the philosopher-king, in that as President of India, from 1962-1967, he, as a philosopher, not only knew what was good for his people, but he acted on that knowledge.

References

** Since published in the *Journal of the Indian Council of Philosophical Research*, Vol. VI, 1989. Reprinted with the permission of the publisher and the author.

1. For a history and analysis of the term, see : Hope Fitz, *Intuition as an Integral Process of the Mind,* a dissertation submitted to the Faculty of Claremont Graduate School in partial fulfilment of the requirements for the degree of Doctor of Philosophy in the Graduate Faculty of Individual Degrees (Asian and Comparative Philosophy), 1981.
2. Sarvepalli Radhakrishnan, "Reply to Critics," in *The Philosophy of Sarvepalli Radhakrishnan,* ed. by Paul Arthur Schilpp (New York, Tudor Publishing Company, c. 1952), p. 791.
3. *Ibid.*
4. *Ibid.*

5. I think that part of the confusion was because Radhakrishnan did not distinguish the kinds from the uses of intuition. See : Sarvepalli Radhakrishnan, *An Idealist View of Life* (London, George Allen & Unwin Ltd., c. 1932); *Radhakrishnan : Selected Writings on Philosophy, Religion, and Culture*, ed. by Robert A. McDermott (New York, E.P. Dutton and Company, Inc., c. 1970), pp. 153-160; Radhakrishnan, "Reply to Critics," pp. 790-804.

6. Radhakrishnan, "Reply to Critics," pp. 790-794; *Radhakrishnan : Selected Writings on Philosophy, Religion and Culture*, p. 160; *Contemporary Indian Philosophy*, ed. by Sarvepalli Radhakrishnan and J.H. Muirhead (London, George Allen & Unwin Ltd., 1936), pp. 486-487.

7. Radhakrishnan, "Reply to Critics," p. 792.

8. *Ibid.*, p. 791.

9. *Ibid.*, pp. 790-791.

10. *Ibid.*

11. Heidegger's notion of "focus of concern" can be grasped, in part, by studying what he had to say about a region, i.e., the area of one's focus of attention, in which beings come to have meaning for him. Martin Heidegger, *Being and Time* (New York, Harper & Row, Publishers, c. 1962), pp. 95-107, 114-122, 138-148. Also, with regard to things, one can gain an understanding of the "focus of concern" by reading what Heidegger said about circumspection. Heidegger, *Being and Time*, pp. 98-99, 107, 111-112, 146.

12. From my experience, research, and reflection on the intuitive process, I realized that present impressions, and relevant past experiences, were being brought to bear on a focus of concern. As one example of this process, consider a philosopher who, while working on a subject, has been struggling with a philosophical problem. Her mental processes have included reason, as well as observation, reflection, etc. She leaves the subject for a while (The length of the time will vary with the person and the problem.) When she returns to the subject, the present impressions plus the relevant memories of her work, on the subject, are brought to bear on the problem. Suddenly, she has an insight, she sees a solution to her problem. The act of

insight does not involve reason, although it is grounded in it.

13. Radhakrishnan writes about creative insight or intuition. See : *An Idealist View of Life*, Chapter V. Also, he sometimes speaks of intuition as a kind of direct seeing into. In the "Reply to Critics," p. 791, he says that *pratyaksa*, direct knowledge, in its original form *intuitus*, implies a sense of sight. Henry Bergson, whose views of intuition were familiar to Radhakrishnan, thought of intuition as a kind of "entering into." See : Henry Bergson, *An Introduction to Metaphysics* (New York, G.P. Putnam's Sons, c. 1912). Also, Heidegger made clear that the creative expressions, which found and originate truth, are the result of penetration into the hidden or unrevealed Being. See : footnote number 1, pp. 90-93.

14. In general, Hindu scholars, hold that intuition is a higher process of the mind. As such, it requires both a high level of moral development and reasoning. Radhakrishnan's thought is in accord with this Hindu view. See : Radhakrishnan, *An Idealist View of Life*, pp. 196-199.

15. Hope Fitz, "The Role of Intuition in Creativity," Chapter IV of a book in progress, *Intuition : Its Nature and Uses in Human Experience.*

16. William J. Richardson, S.J., *Heidegger : Through Phenomenology to Thought* (The Hague, Netherlands, Martinus Nyhoff, c. 1963), pp. 4-7.

17. Heidegger held that that which is given in experience, i.e., Being, is real, and man can come to understand the revealed aspects of what is real or true, because he is the being to whom Being is revealed.

18. Given Kant's view, what is known of experience is mind-constructed. Thus, all man can know is what appears to him. Locked into a world of appearance, he can only speculate as to the nature of things in themselves.

19. This is clear from Heidegger's account of poetry, i.e., the creative expression of an insight into unrevealed Being; his view that poetry founds truth; and that truth is a revelation of Being. See endnote number 1, pp. 87-96.

26
The Individual and the Avatāra in the Thought of Radhakrishnan : An Application to Modern American Life

JUDY D. SALTZMAN
California Polytechnic State University

The ideas of the individual (*jīva-ātman*), civilization in the sense of world welfare (*lokasangraha*) and the Supreme Spirit (*Ātman-Brahman*), are the epitome of Radhakrishnan's thought. Following the *Upaniṣads*, Radhakrishnan holds that, the distinction of this individual ego, although relevant, does not mean it is spearate from other egos and capable of acting entirely independently of them :

> The individuals, in a sense, created by God after His own image and His own likeness, but has his creaturely form. We do not know our own possibilities. The individual ego is subject to avidyā or ignorance when it believes itself to be separate and different from all other egos. The result of this separatist ego sense, *ahaṁkara*, is failure to enter into the harmony and unity of the universe. This failure expresses itself in physical suffering and mental discord. Selfish desire is the bad result of subjection or bondage. When the individual shakes off this avidyā he becomes free from all selfishness, possesses all and enjoys all.[1]

Radhakrishnan affirms, just as the individual never will be complete until the unity with the Supreme is a reality for it, civilization will never be a reality until it is a world wide concern for the welfare of all (*sarvodaya*). Although an ego may appear to be a mere flux, it is not. As *jīva* it is a unity of our life, mind and intellect. "The ego is a changing formation on the background of Eternal Being, the centre around which our mental and vital capacities are organized."[2] Whereas this ego can fall into extremely limited, selfish, hedonistic and diabolical delusions, as *jīva-ātman*, it is potentially capable of unlimited transcendence. However, to achieve this, the ego must identify itself with the Supreme Brahman, not with external delusions. From an Advaita Vedānta viewpoint, Radhakrishnan accepts the idea that there is no reality but the Supreme. From an empirical standpoint, however, each man and woman is a complex of elements and *kośas* which he or she has created and which must be worked out on the plane of human action. Paradoxically, a person is both separate and one with the Supreme. Another seeming contradiction is that, although the very notion of the individual is an illusion or a misnomer, it is only the individual who, in realizing its identity with the Supreme, can create the foundation of civilization. For Radhakrishnan, civilization is an act of spirit, not of body and mind. Since what we are depends on what we have been, the development of a real civilization depends on the elevation of each individual to a true sense of humanity and community. Otherwise, forgetting our inner nature, will lead to the suffering we have all experienced:

> Alienation from our true nature is hell, and union with it is heaven. There is a perpetual strain in human life, an effort to reach from the arbitrary into an ideal state of existence. When we divinise our nature, our body, mind and spirit work flawlessly together and attain a rhythm which is rare in life.[3]

In spite of this hope, the world's great religions and philosophies agree that the pall of karma and the veil of māyā are so powerful that, without help, no possibility of deliverance (*Jīvan-mukti*) exists for the average soul. Ironically, if Brahman creates Māyā, and we are Brahman, we must raise ourselves by our "bootstraps" - an act which cannot be done without sacrifice. Here the mystery of the Avatāra is fundamental and paramount. In Radhakrishnan's view, it is a mystery which can never totally be comprehended. However, there is a sense in which every truth seeking individual either consciously or unconsciously feels the presence of the Avatāra. The descent of the *Avatāra*[4] (*Avatarana*), can be viewed from different philosophical and religious perspectives, but it is an expression of the universal sacrifice :

> The theory of the *Avvtāra* is an eloquent expression of the law of the spiritual world. If God is looked upon as the saviour of man, He must manifest Himself, whenever the forces of evil threaten to destroy human values. An *Avatāra* is a descent of God into man and not an ascent of man into God, which is the case with the liberated soul.[5]

Radhakrishnan affirms the idea that the *Avatāra*, as eternal soul, will somehow always be present with us :

> Though the *Gītā* accepts the belief in Avatāra as the divine limiting Himself for some purpose on earth, possessing in His limited form the fullness of knowledge, it also lays stress on the eternal Avatāra, the God in man, the Divine consciousness always present in the human being. The two reflect the transcendent and immanent aspects of the Divine and are not represented as incompatible with each other.[6]

In the *Gītā*, this divine sacrifice comes into manifestation under cyclic law :

> Time am I, world-destroying, grown mature, engaged here in subduing the world. Even without thee [they action], all the warriors standing arrayed in the opposing armies shall cease to be.[7]

The presence of Kṛṣṇa as *Avatāra*, which is only partially comprehended by Arjuna, is *Adhiyajna*, the Great Sacrifice. Arjuna is awed, grateful, and successful in battle, but he forgets and must be reminded later, as recorded in the *Uttara Gītā*. Kṛṣṇa, as Avatāra, is present throughout Kali Yuga, the Iron Age of violence. He can be described as the Higher Self, the Universal Spirit, a Divine Child, and a perfect human being. As *Avatāra*, he is not a personality. He has been Rama, Kṛṣṇa, Buddha, and will be Kalki. Yet he is often envisioned as a personal god and friend of humanity:

> The religious devotee envisages the Supreme Reality in the form of a personal God who is the source, guide and destiny of the world. The difference between the Supreme as absolute Spirit and the Supreme as personal God is one of standpoint and not of essence. It is a difference between God as He is and God as He seems to us. Personality is a symbol, and if we ignore its symbolic character it shuts us out from the truth.[8]

God is a fact, for Radhakrishnan, not of science, history or law, but an ultimate "truth" upon which all being and all consciousness depend. Truth can be very terrifying as the eleventh chapter of the Gītā reveals. At the midnight hour, it brings the individual back to himself and heals the division in the soul. If the division in each of our souls were healed, can we conclude that each of us is an *Avatara*? Yes and no. In our deeper nature, we may share the consciousness of the *Avatāra*, but no fluctuating personality, however noble, is THAT. Even a *Jivanmukta*, a liberated ego, is not in the same exalted state of an *Avatāra*.

The skeptical, hard headed Amerian may ask, now did Radhakrishnan know all this to be true? The answer is probably as dissatisfying as it is enlightening. For Radhakrishan knowledge is not separated into academic departments, nor is it accumulated facts. In Radhakrishan's view, human knowledge, in its true essence, is unified. Integral knowledge, as it is called, consists of (1) the experience of the world; (2) Intuition by the purified use of emotion and Intellect, and (3) mysticism—a direct cognizance of supersenuous reality. We are all capable of the first two acts of knowledge, although only a few are capable of mystical consciousness in any given incarnation. Real knowledge then is *vidya* like Plato's noesis, it does not separate the subject from the object. It does not deny logic, but goes through and beyond logic to experience *para vidyā* or higher wisdom. Integral knowledge, of course, cannot be understood by those who do not attempt to lift themselves out of limited and crudely empirical traps. Just as the world religions all contain fundamental truths because they come from one source, so are the different branches of knowledge unified as *vidyā* and *para vidyā*.

Part II. Radhakrishnan's Philosophy and Modern Life

After being inspired by Radhakrishnan's integral view of knowledge and the divine potential of the individual, one might ask what application such sublime doctrines might have in everyday frantic Western existence? Especially in the United States in which the idea of individual liberty has always been dominant, how acceptable would be the Upaniṣadic view of Ātman=Brahman? What does liberty mean to a people, few of whom can articulate the difference between liberty and license?

In the distinguished study of 1985, *Habits of the Heart Individualism and Commitment in American Life,* Robert Bellah points out that Alexis de Toqueyille warned us over 100 years ago that individualism could be undermining as well as liberating. Bellah's study struggles with this warning by tracing the lives of four American "individualists." Each of these Individuals had become entangled in and damaged by the overwhelming value placed on external success in America. However, all of these "ordinary people," instead of falling into the extremes of selfishness, stupidity and sensuality, found meaningful ways in dealing with the tension between the individual and the community, and the magnetism between the Individual and the universal.

Bellah outlines two distinct types of individualism. One is utilitarian individualism. This type of individualism is common to political philosophers such as Hobbes and Locke. It entails the idea that a person enters into a society to advance his or her own self-interest. Any other reason is secondary and trivial. The other kind is expressive individualism which Bellah relates to American transcendentalism : a person enters into social relations to find a greater identity with humanity, the universe, and God.

The four Americans in search of their own identity and something beyond it, traced in Bellah's book are Brian, Margaret, Joe and Wayne. The first two find renewal in family and in interpersonal relations, and the second two in community and civic responsibility. After years of frantically seeking success, Brian found new life in a second marriage and family. Margaret found it as a psychotherapist, Joe as a New England civic leader, and Wayne, after going AWOL from the marines, as a tenant organizer in the Campaign for Economic Democracy. All of these people were influenced by utilitarian individualism, but later in their lives, by expressive Individualism. It could not be said of any of these people that they have entirely given up their selfishness. However, it could be said that each seems to have found a larger, and less limited conception of "self."

To explain the theory of the text, Bellah and his associates cite Benjamin Franklin as the epitome of the American utilitarian individualist, whereas Walt Whitman is the crowning glory of the expressive individualist in *The Leaves of Grass*, "The Song of Myself" is a celebration of the self both as immament body and transcendental ego. In "Passage to India," the poet hails the Motherland of wisdom, intuition, the most sublime notion of the self :

> O soul, repressless, I with thee and thou with me,
> Thy circumnavigation of the world begin,
> Of man, the voyage of his mind's return,
> To reason's early paradise.
> Back, back to wisdom's birth, to innocent intuitions,
> Again with fair creation.[9]

As Whitman articulates, the American search for something primordial in the self leads one to far vistas and to imagining higher stages of consciousness. Whitman envisions a state of consciousness circumnavigating the globe from one culture and continuing in another.

Just as one American poet can imagine a state of consciousness shifting from one culture to another, so can the sense of American individualism shift from utilitarian to expressive. Bellah also tell us that there has been another shift the shift in the image of the "teacher" or *guru* from Lord and Pastor to manager and therapist. In fact, since 1976, Bellah reports that American has been a largely therapeutic culture. However, in spite of the dominance of this culture, and of utilitarian individualism, he concludes :

> But on the basis of what we have seen in our observation of middle class American life, it would seem that this quest for purely private fulfilment is illusory. It often ends in emptiness instead. On the other hand, we found many people, some of whom we introduced earlier in this chapter, for whom private fulfilment and public involvement

are not antithetical. These people evince an individualism which is not empty, but full of content, drawn from active identification with communities and traditions.[10]

In spite of the ghoulish image of Wallstreet and narcissism, the American people may be turning away from simply maximizing "what is good for you."

Nevertheless, the notion of individualism will not soon leave American life. It has a mythic tone to it around the stories of Washington and Lincoln and Emerson's "nonconformist.' However, the noble ideas of these men hardly articulates what certain so called American individualists have in common : self-orientation, consumerisn, cash, convenience, charge accounts and competition . . . . Futhermore, liberal Protestantism which once offered a sense of community to and perhaps softened the materialism of 70 per cent of the American population is on the decline. Will it simply be replaced by mass media and television evangelism? Probably not, in spite of all the publicity. In the section on religion, Bellah writes :

> The church reminds us that in our independence we count on others and helps us see that a healthy, grown-up independence is one that admits to healthy grown-up dependence on others. Absolute independence is a false ideal. It delivers not the autonomy it promises but loneliness and vulnerability instead.[11]

In spite of the fact that only about 40 per cent of the American population attend any church, synagogue or religious group, American spirituality remains a powerful influence on the population. About 80 per cent of the population believe in God in some way. As one of Bellah's subjects put it, "I am not very religious, but I am very spiritual."[12] This innate spirituality has led many Americans to realize their "interdependence" with each other, not in the mass society but in the smaller nuclear community. However, this new American spirituality, which can be born only out of the ashes of "success," in the present does little to dispel the image other nations have of us. The idea that we are all selfish and deluded like the "J.R.'s" of "Dallas" is as false as the notion that all Soviet citizens are cruel and mechanical like the Soviet boxer in "Rocky IV." If living to benefit humanity and not themselves only is the first step toward a universal conception of civilization, Bellah concludes that many Americans at least want to take it.

Part III. Moral Ecology and Universality

In *Habits of the Heart* Bellah also speaks of moral or social ecology. This phrase, coined by Stephen Toulmin, refers to the science of living beings existing in relation to one another in a common habitat. The shocking revelation of the four people in Bellah's book that they could not be fulfilled as isolated or even "ordinarily selfish" individuals can be analogized to a larger context. Just as the human individual does not survive or prosper alone, so finally the nations of the world must come to realize that the future existence of their populations depends on economic morality. After repeated warnings, the DuPont Company has finally stopped manufacturing Clouroflourocarbons, an elementary, but significant first step.[13] However, the decent act of a major American company after so many indecencies, can hardly mean that their has been a shift of wealth and power as means to social solidarity and not ends in themselves. Nevertheless, Robert Bellah's message in *Habits of the Heart* and in *Religion and Technology in Japan and the United States* is optimistic toward this end :

> We find ourselves only in giving to each other and in concern for the whole world. That of course is simply what the Gospel says, but perhaps it is the essential message that will help us avoid one more frenzied round of competition that could be our last.[14]

In affirming the essential religiosity of the American and Japanese spirit, Bellah also affirms the universality of their quest. To speak specifically of America, this universalty which was once so evident in Emerson, Thoreau, Bellamy and all the transcendentalists of the American renaissance, can re-emerge out of the pluralist and often limited religious viewpoints. A point of convergence can be found here. Radhakrishnan is also absolutely universal in his "religion of the spirit." All individual religions are reflections of this spiritual fountain. A commentator on Radhakrishnan, Ishwar C. Harris writes of this spirituality:

> From this perspective, the unity of mankind becomes essential, as in and through the Spirit all things and all people are seen as parts of the whole. By the virtue of the spirit, being within them they stand in relation to each other and to the Absolute Spirit. Thus, Radhakrishnan's religion of the spirit can be viewed as a reminder of the fact of *unity*. His religious universalism is a description of the nature of reality as it is. What is required on the part of man is this *gnosis* which comes through a religious experience.[15]

A critical observer could accuse Radhakrishnan of imposing a spiritual religious umbrella over all religions which is really in itself empty of content. In other words, can we say that there is a world universal religion where none appears to be? Can we speak of religion itself, or religion of the spirit? Certainly we can speak of both. Even in the ancient context it can be understood that an individual must be concerned not only with his own *dharma,* but also with *Sanatana dharma* : the eternal religion or highest duty. If Bellah's research is an indication of where we are headed, there is hope. However, it may take Americans as a people well into the next century to comprehend this idea. However, a little imaginative exploration of Radhakrishnan's and Bellah's

The Nature and Significance of Intuition 415

writings may show us that in some sense to be an American is to be like a Hindu. The term "Hindu" loosely amalgamates a wide variety of religious viewpoints. To individuals such as Thoreau to be American is to be as one who once lived on the "other side of the Indus River" - universal, not defined by a limited tradition of creed, ethnicity, race or politics. Of course, most Americans have not learned to give up distinctions nor to reach to the level of Thomas Paine, whose ideas helped frame the American Republic and the Constitution, and whose mantra was "My mind is my church." Paine wrote in *The Age of Reason* a universal message :

> It is only in the CREATION that all our ideas and conceptions of a *word of God* can unite. The Creation speaketh an universal language, independently of human speech or human language, multiplied and various as they may be. It is an everexisting original which every man can read. It cannot be forged; it cannot be counterfeited; it cannot be lost; it cannot be altered; it cannot be suppressed. It does not depend upon the will of man whether it shall be published or not; it publishes itself from one end of the earth to the other. It preaches to all nations and to all worlds; and this *word of God* reveals to man all that is necessary for man to know God.[16]

As Tom Paine says, just as the teaching of nature is universal, so is the teaching of the *Avatāra*. For Radhakrishnan, the *Avatāra* is a universal religious symbol. Kṛṣṇa, Buddha and Christ all share in its essence and glory. Kalki : the Tenth and Future *Avatāra* of Viṣṇu is symbolized by a white horse or man riding on a white horse. In philosophical writings, Kalki is also identified with the future Saviour of the world's great religions : Maitreya, Sosiosh, the Messiah and the Second Advent. In the teaching of the *Avatāra*, all the stages of evolution from fish to dwarf to man to perfected man to divinity are depicted. The Kalki Avātara is He who destroys evil and makes humans at last "the sons of God."[17] This Great Sacrifice happens as often as virtue declines in the world under cyclic law.

In the spirit of the teaching of the *Avatāra* in the *Gītā* and in Hindu thought in general, like the sociologist Bellah, the philosopher Radhakrishnan remains a perpetual optimist. Radhakrishnan thinks that we will survive and somehow even arrive in the world. However this "survival" and "arrival" entails the willingness to give up narrow and nationalistic tendencies :

> Gandhi once said : "I want my country to be free. I do not want a fallen and prostrate India. I want an India which is free and enlightened. Such an India, if necessary, should be prepared to die so that humanity may live."[18]

How many Americans are ready to make the same commitment about their nation?

> Nationalism is not the highest concept. The highest concept is world community. It is that kind of world community to which we have to attach ourselves. It is unfortunate that we are still the victims of the concepts which are outmoded, which are outdated, so to say. We are living in a new world, and in a new world a new type of man is necessary, and unless we are to change our minds, to change our hearts, it will not be possible for us to survive in this world.[19]

If no nation, including the United States, is willing to die so that the world may live, at least the U.S. should be willing to live in a manner so that the world will not die. As Radhakrishnan affirms, civilization cannot exist without an idea of universal welfare and international unity. This sublime notion is also elucidated by Prof. Raghavan Iyer in *Parapolitics : Toward the City of Man :*

> The embryonic world community exists already - all nations share a common political fate - but it provides no practical hope of becoming, in the near future, an actual world polity sharing a common and integrated political structure. Regardless of the inherited dissimilarities of traditional religious and secular beliefs and values, or of socio-economic status, nationality, and national power, we may discern the silent member of the invisible world political community. There is an increasing awareness among individuals (among scientists and artists, civil servants, busnessmen, and even some politicians, and especially among disinherited youth) that an invisible but tangible parapolitical community is coming into being. This awarness may well be heightened under the growing pressure of influences for transformation working upon the system of interdependent nation-states. At the least, we have more cosmopolitans in the negative sense in which some of the Cynics and Stoics spoke of the cosmopolis, men and women with weaker roots in national tradition, more fragile loyalties to national ideologies, alienate from their own impersonal societies, with less hostility if not greater empathy for people abroad.[20]

The cosmopolitan community which Iyer is discussing comes originally from the Stoic ideal *ex chaos cosmopolis* - from all this disorder will perhaps come a world order, a true *novus ordo seclorum*.

However, for Radhakrishnan, a world community and civilization, although a most noble idea, is more than just that. It will be a community which would aggrandize and maximize the potential of every individual (*jīva-ātman*) in it. For, according to Radhakrishnan's interpretation of the classical teaching of the *Upaniṣads,* each of each of us is destined for liberation in Brahman, if we do our duty. Regarding this hope and the process of time, Radhakrishnan wrote in his brilliant Hibbert Lectures. An idealist view of life :

> To evade this difficulty, it is sometimes argued that the historical process will never terminate. It is possible for individuals here and there to be released but the world as a whole will never be redeemed. The world exists from everlasting to everlasting. It follows that no individual can attain a perfect hamony both within and without. Perfection is unthinkable. It is given to us to strive after perfection and actualize it at best in fragments. We have to rest in the idea of perpetual effort. But this view ignores the solidarity between man and nature, values and reality. It cannot be a question for perpetual travelling. We should also arrive. It cannot be interminable singing; there should be such a thing as completion in a song. There must come a time when all individuals will become sons of God and be received into the glory of immortality. When the world is redeemed the end of the plot is reached. Earth and heaven will be no more; the timeless and transcendent remain.[21]

In summation, it is clear that we owe to Radhakrishnan much thanks for his integral knowledge method and redemptive vision of humanity. The seekers in *Habits of the Heart* all share in this redemptive vision because they are redeeming themselves. If America, as a leader of nations, could follow Radhakrishnan's and the example of Gandhi's vision of India, and lift itself beyond the dark spectre of nationalism, a new age of universal brotherhood would dawn. Indeed, the teaching of the Avatāra is that the individual must redeem the world, just as the *Avatāra* redeems the Individual in the *Gītā* Radhakrishnan boldly affirms that humans themselves have a cosmic purpose :

> It cannot be that certain individuals will remain for all time unredeemed. If they are all redeemed, it cannot be that they sit down in heaven, praising God and doing nothing. So long as some individuals are unredeemed, the other freed souls have work to do and so retain their individualities. But when the world, as such, is saved, when all are freed and nothing remains to be done, the time process comes to an end. The threats of science that the world will be wound up one day need not depress us. The universe, although "unbounded" "Is" "finite." The end of time may mean the perfection of humanity, where the earth will be full of knowledge of the spirit. The cosmic purpose is consummated so far as the conditions of space and time allow.[22]

Radhakrishnan and modern science teach that ours is a finite universe with infinite possibilities. This optimistic view of human destiny is characteristic of his life and thought. We must be eternally grateful to Radhakrishnan for helping us to articulate the meaning of the Individual and the vision of the *Avatāra*. In a world of ideas that sometimes appears empty and chaotic, his philosophy is a beacon light for human fulfilment and purpose in the future.

References

1. S. Radhakrishnan, *Radhakrishan : Selected Writings on Philosophy, Religion and Culture,* Edited with an Introduction by Robert A. McDermott, New York : E.P. Dutton and Company, Inc.-1970., p. 151.

2. *Ibid.*, p. 149.
3. *Ibid.*, p. 152.
4. I use the word *Avatāra* with the final "a" as it is in Radhakrishnan's texts, instead of the usual English transliteration from the Hindi, Avatar.
5. S. Radhakrishnan, *The Bhagavad Gītā*. With an Introductory Essay, Sanskrit text and English Translation and Notes, New York : Harper Torchbooks, 1973, p. 34.
6. *Ibid.*, p. 35.
7. *Gītā* XI, 32, p. 279.
8. S. Radhakrishnan, *Indian Religions*, New Delhi : Orient Paperbacks, 1985, p. 104.
9. Wait Whitman, "Passage to India" cited by Robert Bellah, et al, *Habits of the Heart Individualism and Commitment in American Life*, Berkeley : University of California Press, 1985, p. 34.
10. *Ibid.*, p. 163.
11. *Ibid.*, p. 247.
12. Robert Bellah, *Habits of the Heart*, p. 246.
13. *Los Angeles Times*, March 25, 1988.
14. Robert Bellah, *Religion and the Technological Revolution in Japan and the United States*. The University Lecture in Religion, Arizona State University, February 19, 1987.
15. Ishwar C. Harris, *Radhakrishnan : the Profile of a Universalist*, Columbia, Missouri : South Asia Books, 1982, p. 265.
16. Thomas Paine, *Age of Reason*, New York : Peter Eckler, 1794, p. 30.
17. H.P. Blavatsky, *Isis Unveiled : A Master Key to the Mysteries of Ancient and Modern Science and Theology*, Los Angeles : The Theosophy Company, 1931, Vol. II, p. 274.
18. S. Radhakrishnan, *A World Community*, Washington, D.C., Embassy of India, 1963, p. 53.
19. S. Radhakrishnan, A World Community, Washington, D.C., Embassy of India, 1963, p. 54.
20. Raghavan Iyer, *Parapolitics : Toward the City of Man*, New York : Oxford University Press, 1979, p. 338.

21. Radhakrishnan, *An Idealist View of Life*, New York : Barnes and Noble, 1957, p. 308.
22. *Ibid.*, p. 310.

Bibliography

Arapura, J.G. *Radhakrishnan and Integral Experience*, London : Asia Publishing House, 1966.

Bellah, Robert N.; Madsen, Richard; Sullivan, William; Swindler, Ann, and Tipton, Steven M., *Habits of the Heart Individualism and Commitment in American Life*. Berkeley : University of California Press, 1985.

Bellah, Robert N. *Religion and the Technological Revolution in Japan and the United States*. Tempe : Arizona State University, 1987.

Blavatsky, H.P. *Isis Unveiled : A Master Key To the Mysteries of Ancient and Modern Science and Theology*. Los Angeles : The Theosophy Company, 1969.

Cremer, Wilhelm. *Die Universales des Geistes, Religion und Religionen Sarvepalli Radhakrishnan*. Inaugural Dissertation Muenchen, 1966.

Harris, Ishwar C. *Radhakrishnan : The Profile of a Universalist*. Columbia, Missouri : South Asia Books, 1982.

Iyer, Raghavan. *Parapolitics : Toward the City of Man*. New York : Oxford University Press, 1979.

Iyer, Raghavan Editor, *The Mystery of the Avatar*. Santa Barbara : Concord Grove Press, 1987.

Paine, Thomas. *Age of Reason*, New York : Peter Eckler, Publisher, 1794.

Radhakrishnan, S. *A World Community*. Washinton D.C. : Embassy of India, 1963.

Radhakrishnan, S. TR. *The Bhagavad Gītā with an Introductory Essay, Sanskrit Text*, English Translation and Notes. New York : Harper Torchbooks, 1973.

Radhakrishnan, S. *Indian Religions*. New Delhi : Orient Paperbacks, 1979.

Radhakrishnan, S. *An Idealist View of Life.* New York : Barnes and Noble, 1957.

Radhakrishnan, S. and Moore, Charles A. *Indian Philosophy.* Princeton, N.J. : Princeton University Press, 1973.

Radhakrishnan, S. *Radhakrishnan : Selected Writings on Philosophy, Religion and Culture,* Edited by Robert A. McDermolt. New York : E. P. Dutton and Company, 1970.

27

The Third Sense of Idealism

ARINDAM CHAKRABARTY
University of Washington

That which is really inside awareness as its object aspect appears as if it is outside....
— Diṅnāga (*Ālambanaparikṣa*)

Seeing the world as contained within oneself like a city appearing on a mirror....
— Śaṁkara (*Dakṣiṇāmūrtistotra*)

... those who would penetrate into the real and true causes will speak of the world as contained by the soul and not the soul by the world.
— Berkeley (*Siris*, # 25)

Space itself, with all its appearances, as representations, is indeed, only in me.
— Kant (*Critique of Pure Reason* A-375)

... reality in itself, ... the primary ontological fact, is consciousness (*caitanya*).
— Radhakrishnan (*Indian Philosophy*, Vol. II, p. 138)

Section Zero

Common English parlance makes a distinction between *idealism* (being an idealist) and *realism* (being a realist, a practical hard-headed person) which we tend to unlearn when we pick up the philosophical use (or uses) of those terms. An idealist, colloquially, is one who relentlessly pursues a certain perfect state of things - a global moral end, and evaluates every actual state in the light of that envisaged goal. A realist, in this sense, is someone who refuses to dream about any such ideal and tries to call a spade a spade. When Radhakrishnan embraces idealism of the third kind he seems to come back to this pre-philosophical sense of "idealism" by, as it were, un-unlearing it. In this paper I try to trace out the somewhat Hegelian triadic pattern among the three senses of "idealism" that Radhakrishnan distinguishes and see how far he has good reasons to accept the third sense as a synthesis of the two other senses one of which refutes the other.

Radhakrishnan, who has been uncontroversially understood as a modern Indian idealist in the tradition of the Upaniṣads and Advaita Vedānta, himself distinguishes at least three different senses of the term - "idea" upon which the meaning of the term "idealism" would depend. It could mean a subjective mental representation or the universal Absolute spirit, or, somewhat broadly and thinly, the underlying meaning, purpose, or unifying principle of some apparently chaotic process. Centering round these senses we get, respectively, *Subjective Idealism* (of a Diṅnāga or a Berkeley), *Absolute Idealism* (of a Śaṁkara or a Hegel) and Radhakrishnan's own version of idealism.

Radhakrishnan rejects the doctrine "*esse est percipii*" and yet maintains that all reality is based upon, essentially related with and is progressively moving to be fully synthesised in some higher unifying consciousness. He is neither a straight-forward Advaitin, still less a follower of Kant; but with both Śaṁkara and Kant he shares this interesting, and to some extent puzzling combination of flouting subjectivism and adopting a profoundly idealist view of life.

A re-examination of Śaṁkara's and Kant's refutations of mentalistic idealism should, therefore, help us understand and assess Radhakrishnan's own double insistence that the external world is real yet consciousness is the sole reality.

In the first part of what follows we shall go through some of the details of Śaṁkara's arguments against the Buddhist Vijñānavāda, trying to clearly state the points at which Śaṁkara's own idealism really contrasts with that of his target of attack.

In the second part I shall briefly recount the steps of Kant's *Refutation of Idealism* critically noting the cash-value of the so-called empirical realism.

Finally, in the third part, I shall try to evaluate Radhakrishnan's own preferred variety of so-called 'objective idealism' - which Hartshorne suspected was only a mere phrase.

Section One

Commenting upon Brahma-Sūtras 2.2.28 - through - 30, Śaṁkara picks up his dispute with the idealist Buddhist. In the classical Indian style, he starts by building up a case for a pan-internalist metaphysics and epistemology.

The Vasubandhu-Diṅnāga-Dharmakīrti line of elimination of a material external world bases itself on broadly four major arguments:

First, no consistent theory of the material world is seen to be possible. The manifest middle-sized objects of our ordinary wakeful experience can neither be admitted to be indivisible nor explained as collections of atoms. The partlessness of atoms make their size-increasing partial contact impossible. Admission of a collection as a single entity over and above the elements goes against the grain of the reductionist-nominalist Buddhist. These whole-part problems do not arise with immaterial sensation particles to which, therefore, we must confine ourselves.

Secondly, the variety of cognitions in terms of objects, e.g. "sensation of a pillar" "Sensation of a wall" etc. is to be explained from within the cognitions themselves. The dual conditions of objecthood, viz. being a form-lending intended topic and being a causal support are not satisfied by any physical object. The atoms may *cause* my perception but they do not show up as *topics,* while the immediately floated *topics* - tables and chairs are not real enough to *cause* my perception. If we confine ourselves to the inner world of the flow of successive self-luminous perceptual states simultaneously caused and coloured by their own objective aspects, we can manage to construct a more parsimonious and coherent picture of the world.

Thirdly, awareness and its object are constantly co-cognised. We do not find in ordinary experience an objectless cognition or an uncognised object. If it is impossible to isolate them, they must be the same.

Fourthly, our wakeful awareness is phenomenologically indistinguishable from dream-awareness or other such illusory or hallucinatory awareness. Hence they must be equally devoid of any outer support.

Śaṁkara represents more or less all these arguments, in his preliminary mock-defense of subjectivism. All these lead to the conclusion that no objects outside the mind exist. This conclusion is first attacked head on as simply counter-intuitive. The aphorism of Vādarāya says sententiously:

Not absence (of outer objects) because (they are) apprehended *(NA) (Abhavaḥ) (Upalabdheḥ)*

A pillar, a wall, a glass, a table-cloth - this or that external object is lit up by every piece of awareness. To deny them would be as dishonest as disowning that one has eaten after enoying a full meal. The thrust of the argument is basically like Moore raising his hands or Dr. Johnson kicking a stone.

If the subjectivist responds that he is not after all denying the existence of objects but only denying that such objects are anything beyond the awareness itself, Śaṁkara's reply is a refinement of the initial objection. The same awareness which testifies to the existence of the object also testifies to the distinction between the object and the awareness. No one has ever perceived or felt the pillar seen to be pillarish seeing, a sensation of blue as a blue sensation.

At this point, an elegant supporting argument is given to refute the idealist diagnosis that what is within us looks *as if* it is outside, due to our inherent ignorance or - as they say - "beginningless addiction to two" [anādidvaya-vāsanā].

If, really being a physical object in space is as spurious or impossible as being a barren woman's son, how can things even look *as if* they are out there in space? We cannot even misperceive Viṣṇumitra as appearing *like* a barren woman's son. Things can look *like x* only if they can really be *x*. Coins could be counterfeited only if coins could be genuine.

Thus, establishing the initial implausibility of the "only - awareness" - view of the world, Śaṁkara tries to meet all the major refutations of physical objects mentioned above.

As against the dilemmatic destruction of the possibility of divisible physical objects, Śaṁkara observes that the possibility or otherwise of a certain entity should be judged by the evidence of our knowledge of it, rather than evaluating our knowledge by abstract alternative possibilities. If our atomistic analysis cannot account for such undeniably and immediately perceived physical objects, so much the worse for our *analysis*! If all our alternatives are equally spurious it is no wonder that they will fail to capture the physical objects. Śaṁkara, of course, cannot *defend* the atomistic realist. He is no Vaiśeṣika. He only urges that if "likeness of form with some external object" is indelibly etched in our consciousness, that by itself should compel us to admit external objects, and adjust our ontology accordingly.

He next disposes of the argument from constant co-cognition by pointing out that such constancy of togetherness only proves that awareness of a thing our only way to reach that thing, not that awareness is the same as the thing. In Bhāmatī, Vācaspati strengthens this rebuttal by mustering other standard realist counterpoints like the following! That the two are necessarily cognised *together* proves *distinction* rather than sameness. Or else, if we stretch the meaning of "co-cognisability" as "cognisability qua one and the same." (*Sahopalambha* construed as *ekopalambha*) the inferential mark will not be counterprobative but it will be itself unestablished (*āsrayāsiddha*) because awareness and object are not, in fact, cognisable as one and the same. Even if they were inseparably available in some sense like light and colour, that would not prove their identity. It would only show that light and colour, one is a unique means to get at the other.

Then Śaṁkara gives his major positive argument to show that although awareness and object are so inextricably presented together - they can be conceptually separated. The proof here anticipates Moore's central point in the *Refutation of Idealism*. When we compare experience of a pencil with experience of a flower, we can isolate experience as the constant factor while the objects vary. Conversely, when we compare perception of a table, with memory of a table, the table which is the object can be isolated as the invariant element while the cognitive states vary in quality.

Against such an argument from agreement and difference, recently A.J. Ayer has tried to hold that it might have shown that we cannot *identify* consciousness simpliciter with consciousness of blue because there is also consciousness of green, but it does not show that blue can exist without consciousness of blue. A dance of Waltz shares the *dance* factor with a dance of Tango, but that does not show that there can be an undanced Waltz or a Tango isolated from a dance of Tango.

Finally, the comparison with dreams is challenged by Śamkara on the basis of some essential disparity or qualitative distinction between dreams and waking experiences.

Subsequent cancellation and inner incoherence characterise dreams as detectably illusory - whereas the coherence and uncancelled nature of waking experiences testifies to their truth. When we are ushered into the dream, there is no such jerky or clear subversion of the previous waking life as we feel at our exit from dreams.

Going to emphasise this disanalogy, Śamkara not only goes back upon his own and Gauḍapāda's favoured comparison of our ordinary experience with dream - recall the *Māṇḍukyakārikā*

"Svapna māye Yathā dṛṣṭe
Gandharva-nagaraṃ Yathā.
Tathā Viśvamidam dṛṣṭam
Vedānteṣu Vicakṣaṇaih." - but seems also to overdo it by claiming that.

"The pillars etc. which are apprehended in waking experience are *never* in any state of consciousness sublated or rejected as unreal.

Was he forgetting the Advaitic waking up of the realised soul who starts to see *one* where we see *many*? Does not the waking world dissolve to him like a broken dream?

Radhakrishnan emphasises over and over again that Śamkara is no illusionist. "The world is not so much negated as reinterpreted." "Unreal the world is, illusory it is not." Or "That kind of dream which God creates and of which God is the substance is no dream at all." Such statements abound in his apologetic account of Śaṁkara's Advaita Vadanta. But he too must have been irked by some difficulty. While he records in a footnote (p. 583, Indian Philosophy Volume II) that later Advaita compares the socalled real world to a protracted dream, he could not have forgotten that many passages of Śaṁkara himself yield very easily to a "dṛṣtrisṛṣti" (creation by perception something like : *awareness maketh nature*) line of interpretation which is hardly distinguishable from the much-maligned Vijñānavāda.

Not only does Śaṁkara's realistic zeal strike us as strange, even his insistence on the knowledge independence of objects in the context of refuting the argument from constant co-cognition looks a it disingenuous. Radhakrishnan draws our attention to a pregnant passage in Śaṁkara's commentary on Praśna-Upaniṣad (VI, 2).

"The suggestion that there exists in reality something which is not known does not stand to reason. It is like saying that a visible form is seen but there is no eye to see its. This or that object apprehended may be absent but apprehension itself is never absent. Where there is no awareness there is no object of awareness either." (*Vastutattvam bhavati kincid na jñāyate iti ca anupapannam*).

Is not that a clear admission of the essential knowledge dependence of objects?

How can we reconcile these two aspects of Śaṁkara's philosophy which led Radhakrishnan to assert first that Śaṁkara upholds a "metaphysical idealism" in regarding even objects as phases of spirit (*viṣaya-caitanya*) and then, in the very next paragraph that Śaṁkara's theory of truth is strictly speaking a "radical realism?" Are metaphysical idealism and radical realism so obviously compatible?

Cichés like : "It God's dream, not mine" have their own problems because the whole distinction between God and myself is a dreamt distinction. We can better locate the real contrast between subjectism and Śaṁkarite idealism in the latter's relegation of both inner and outer experience to mere *māyā*. In the technical sense of falsity (which consists, upon analysis, in a refusal to tolerate either the title of reality or that of total unreality) both our mental world and our physical world are *equally* false. The psychological is not realler than the material, because they are equally *objects*, equally rent with *plurality*, and equally temporally and spatially *limited*. The *Caitanya* or Pure Consciousness has no bias towards the mental. It is not an accusative of any awareness. Insofar as even fleeting cognitive states - the Vrttijñānas are objects of the witness-consciousness - Śaṁkara jettisons the Buddhist hypothesis of their self humaniousity by a mockery regarding fire burning itself - they too are objects hence false. The witness consciousness is itself Self-luminous, not in the sense of being an *object* of itself but in the sense of being an imperishable ever-subjective light which illuminates everything including itself like Sun.

So, Śaṁkara can, in a phenomenal, practical, empirical sense, regard the physical world to be as much (which is to say, transcendentally, as little) real as the mental world. Both are objective because both consist of objects of sensation or introspection. It remains true, however, that Śaṁkara regards only the Supreme Subjectivity that is Ātman-Brahman as reality in its full sense.

Unlike the Vijñānavādin who gives the inner cognitive states an ontological priority, Śaṁkara regards them as equally removed from reality, because they are not subjective enough. A mentalistic idealism is refuted because it accepts one half of the immediately experienced world - the grasping aspect, while rejecting the other - the grasped.

But a metaphysical idealism is upheld because nothing but the never-negated. One consciousness is ultimately real. One is tempted to call this the public or universal mind. But it is better to resist that temptation because neither the public/private distinction nor the matter/mind distinction have any value from such an ultimate stand point.

When we try, in the above manner, to discriminate between these two sorts of idealism we are, as it were, extending the Lockean distinction between primary and secondary qualities even to the mental realm. Like colour, taste, smell, even wish, doubt, pain, memory and perception are also only apparent qualities of the same *substance*. Not only does Brahman falsely appear to be inert, spatial, and many, it also equally falsely appears to be enjoying happiness, suffering pain, perceing objects. I am not sure whether this is radical realism or radical idealism; perhaps it is too radical to be called either.

Radhakrishnan tries to clarify Śaṁkara's exact conceptual coordinates in this apparent ambivalence between the world being my projection and this limited myself with its inner and outer being wholly a projection of some universal consciousness by clarifying the relationship between Māyā and Avidyā, between the big I and the Small I. But while contrasting Śaṁkara's Idealism with the refuted idealism, Radhakrishnan brackets Kant with the Yogācāra Buddhist. "The latter view" - he remarks "is represented by the Yogācāra Buddhist who, *like Kant*, regards the empirical world as a subjective appearance." This remark comes to us as a shock when we notice how Kant too refuted Idealism with no less vigour than Śaṁkara.

Section Two

Though Kant calls himself a transcendental idealist or sometimes when he is tried of being misunderstood - a *critical idealist,* he claims to have supplied, for the first time in the history of Philosophy, a definite refutation of idealism, and a "strict" and "only possible" proof of the reality of the external world.

Branding Descartes and Berkeley, respectively, as a *problematic* and *dogmatic* idealist, he argues against any position which takes only our inner experience as immediate and certain, while outer things are taken as either purely imagined or at best unreliably inferred. Let us rehearse the steps of this well-known argument (to be found in C.P.R. B275-279).

   A. I perceive myself (persisting and) changing through time.

   B. This experience of a continually altering myself presupposes something permanent as a backdrop.

   C. This permanent background is not to be found within myself in the introspected world which is wholly in time therefore only changeful.

   D. Therefore, the presupposed permanent must lie *outside* me in space.

   E. So, objects in space, far from being inferred, invented or imagined on the basis of the data of inner reflection must be logically and epistemologically prior to even our awareness of ourselves and our mental states.

If, therefore, inner experiences are indubitable, outer experiences, in general, must be equally, if not more, indubitable.

It is quite staggering to hear this from a philosopher who not only regards space as transcendentally ideal, and gives the *inner sense* a priority, but also claims to have brought about a revolution in philosophy by showing us that "we can know *a priori* of things only what we have ourselves put into them."

As it stands, the argument seems weak at the crucial point, viz. step C. Why can't we make the self or the transcendental unity of apperception itself the required permanent background of our inner experience of changing states? Why must it be something outside me? It may be technically replied that the synthetic unity of apperception cannot itself be empirically *known* or *perceived,* it remains only a transcendental presupposition of all other perceptual knowledge. But then the argument does not make it clear in what way outer world can offer us anything more permanent, which is not merely *represented* but is also really a *thing* outside me. The outer world is equally perceived through time and should, therefore, be equally changeful. It is difficult to imagine how I can place my stream of consciousness against tables and chairs to feel its passing character!

A modern attempt by J. Bennett, to salvage Kant by reformulating the argument runs, roughly, as follows (It borrows its idiom from Wittgenstein).

(A) I can distinguish between "I seem to remember having been in State M" and "I *was* in state M" only if I have a notion of an objective past.

(B) We cannot have any useful notion of an objective checkable past unless we have a notion of a real external world given to *our* immediate experience.

(C) Without such a notion of past, the very notion of a *correct* and *consistent* use of a *concept* is impossible.

(D) To have any experience even of my own inner states (e.g. to identify a certain sensation as *pain,* or as the same uneasiness once again) we must have the notion of a correct application of a concept and hence the notion of an objective past and hence must admit an immediately experienced external world.

Now, people *have* questioned the validity and intelligibility of Wittgenstein's *Private Language Argument*. And whether the above adaptation of it which Bennett calls the realism-argument *is* what Kant had in mind when he was refuting idealism is highly questionable.

Whether Kant succeeds to refute Idealism or not he surely goes *too* far in trying to exhibit that his philosophy is the farthest from Berkeley's. The inner inconsistency becomes glaring when he plays on the word "Idealism." He claims on the one hand that though he makes reality in itself unknowable,

"The *existence* of the thing that appears is not thereby destroyed, as in *genuine Idealism.*" (Prolegomena p. 37) - yet, in the Critique, on the other hand, he clearly enunciates : "The term *'idealism'* is not to be understood as applying to those who deny the existence of external objects of the senses, but only to those who do not admit that their existence is known through immediate experience."

The two definitions of idealism seem to be opposed to each other. As Barry Stroud has recently observed (Kant & Scepticism, p. 420) "The desired refutation of idealism can succeed only if idealism is true, the things we directly perceive can be shown to be spatial things and independent of us only it they are appearances dependent on us."

Still, Kant insisted, somewhat like Śaṁkara, that he has shown the immediately perceived material objects in space to be empirically real, not in spite of but *because* of their transcendental unreality.

Such a rehabilitation of the external world hardly satisfies commonsense or a serious realist. It also fails to distinguish substantially Kant's position from that of Berkeley who, after all, did not treat all experience as illusory but provided for the possibility of my experience being checked as true or false against the objective world of God's experience.

Their idealism look less alien to each other when we notice that both Kant and Berkeley give coherence-criteria for truth. Berkeley gives - like Śaṁkara - *consistency* or *mutual connectedness* and the lack of it as the distinguishing marks of wakeful as against dream experience. The laws of connection of our ideas give the scientists better insight into real nature of things because the real nature is nothing but the mind of the *Author of Nature*.

Berkeley describes his own move as a revolt from metaphysics to plain common sense restoring rather than destroying the immediacy of our contact with material bodies. Kant too questions the possibility of transcendent metaphysics and shows that outer experience is really immediate.

There is a coherentist interpretation of Kant's notion of "Synthesis" as endowing objectivity to our experience. In the postulates of emperical thought, the actual is defined as that which is bound up with the material conditions of experience. If we can synthesise the loose data of different senses and moments according to the "analogies" which are rules of putting experience together - then we can have the best and only available certainty concerning the actuality of the objects perceived.

Thus Kant seems to pay only lip-service to realism. Both the temporal self which is empirically experienced and the Spatial world perception of which is allegedly presupposed by all inner experience—are only phenomenal, mere appearances. Here again, perhaps subjective idealism is avoided by occupying a position neutral between the psychological and the physical, for the thing-in-itself or *noumenal* reality seems to lie equally far from both.

Kant's rehabilitation of the outer world is no more serious or full-blooded than Śaṁkara's insistence that the walls and pillars are really distinct from our awareness of them. The "really" here is quite evidently tongue-in-cheek.

Section Three

It is extremely difficult to distill out from Radhakrishnan's writings his *own* view from mere restatements or interpretations of others. History of contemporary and classical thought constitute almost the whole of even his "FRAGMENTS OF A CONFESSION" where, at least, one would expect him to come out with his original ideas. Of course, we can detect sympathies and disapprovals, and through them make a guess at his philosophical temperament. This temperament, all interpreters agree, - was generally more concerned with life, practice and some sort of a vision of a universal religion - "a church of Spirit," than with offering a theory about the nature of the world and our knowledge of it. He even compares himself with Marx, as being more on the side of changing than of interpreting. Hence, it is common to take his "idealism" in the popular sense of setting an *ideal* for human life, rather than belief in some kind of a primacy of *ideas*. Attractive and committed as that may sound, this characterisation does injustice to the theoretical content of his philosophy; indeed, it makes him out as *evasive* rather than *committed* about central epistemological and metaphysical issues.

Radhakrishnan started to philosophies in a broadly Hegelian milieu, and had a heavy dose of Advaita already in him. But, by the time his final testaments and philosophical autobiographies were written, the ascendency of Logical Positivism, Existentialism and Marxism had rendered metaphysics something to be ashamed of.

Luckily we are now breathing freer philosophical air. Metaphysical issues like the Realism/Idealism debate have come back with a new rigour to the forefront of analytic philosophy. So, now is the time to open up Radhakrishnan the theoretical philosopher who was, amidst all his religions cultural and grander practical missions, I believe, still a metaphysician.

When, in his *An Idealist View of Life*, Radhakrishnan discusses matter and what modern physics (of his times) said about it, he starts by granting that in the beginning of the cosmic evolution inert matter must have existed without any life or mind to enjoy or perceive it. This sounds like *realism*. But then he goes on to use scientific and philosophical evidence to establish that matter is not inert but moving, concluding that "it is as truly creative as living organism or mind." (*IVL* p. 185). Here is already a substantial slant towards *idealism*.

The Advaitic attitude of ending analysis in wonderment, of treating materiality as a magical recalcitrance to the two-valued framework of *Sat* and *Asat*, makes him very often wind up with remarks like

"Existence is a continuous miracle."

With this goes his rejection of both materialism and mentalism. His Absolute is neutral between individual sentience and the physical spatial world, consciousness and extension *cit* and *acit* being merely two attributes of that Substance sometimes construed in a Rāmānujite fashion, sometimes in a more Spinozistic fashion. While he shares with Śaṁkara this picture of a spirit which is avowedly unpsychological he also shares the ambivalence which we have detected in Śaṁkara and Kant, for he writes:

> "We may feel that we know all about matter, that its existence is undoubted ... but all that we know about is the effect it produces on us. When we come to think of it, it reduces itself to certain feelings and relation among them .... It is experience and possible experience" (*IVL* p. 191).

This is a frank and unabashed movement from what Kant called *problematic idealism* to a *dogmatic one*. Yet, Radhakrishnan does not approve of Eddington's overhasty reduction of indeterminacy to freedom, relativity to mind-dependence, of all the world to "mind-stuff." He is critical of the sweeping Whiteheadian extension of terms like 'feeling,' 'experience' and 'value' to cover even the behaviour of sub atomic particles. (cf. IVL pp. 194 - 196).

But, if in the way indicated above Radhakrishnan wants to both refute and reject idealism at the same time, he also gives it a new meaning by drawing our attention to what we mentioned at the outset as the *third sense* of the term '*idea.*'

> "When we ask with reference to any thing or action :
>
> "What is the idea?" We mean, what is the principle involved in it, what is the meaning or purpose of its being, what is the aim or value of the action? What is it driving at? . . . . An idealist view finds that the universe has meaning, has value." (IVL p. 10).

Radhakrishnan is not only a *practical* idealist but also a *metaphysical* idealist, for he asserts that *all* existents are *intrinsically connected* with some kind of a *final cause*.

His recommended *task* for mankind follows from his theoretical *view* about reality, his *project* is based on his *ontology*.

An idealist in *this* sense is not logically obliged to embrace either a subjective or an objective idealism, either a dogmatic or a problematic idealism, he need not be even a transcendental or critical idealist in Kant's sense. Radhakrishnan's idealism can steer clear of both Vasubandhu and Śaṁkara, both Berkeley and Kant. It only urges us, more prophetically - I'm afraid - than philosophically, to ask teleological "why" questions about every level of existence, to search for continuity, holistic pattern, purpose and progress everywhere.

But, can something have a *purpose* without being conscious in some minimal sense? In the Sāṁkhya Kārikās (57-59) we get such a model of unconscious matter being motivated to move, like the flow of the milk from the udder for nourishment of the calf ("*acetanamapi prayojanam prati pravartamānam*" - Vācaspati)

But Radhakrishnan cannot adopt the Sāṁkhya schism between inactive consciousness and active corporeality without giving up his integral picture of complete continuity. Unless we take this teleological idealism to be just a heuristic device for better understanding of nature, it is hard for Radhakrishnan to shirk the ontological responsibility of ascribing some sort of psyche to *all* nature.

Śaṁkara in his Dakṣiṇāmūrti Stotram tells us that we are all living in a looking glass world. In one looking glass world, a couple of erratic philosophers Tweedledum and Tweedledee told the little girl Alice that she and they themselves were all mere characters in the dream of the sleeping red king. If the king wakes up they will all go out bang! - like an extinguished candle. Yet they did not know how from inside his dream one could awaken the king. If any one is scandalised by this flippant analogy, let us recall Yājñavalkya's reference to such a view in his famous dialogue at Janaka's court

"ārāmam asya paśyanti, na taṁ paśyanti ke cana taṁ nāyatam bodhyet ityāhuh."

(Vṛhadāraṇyaka, 4.3.14).

Even there one is warned not to wake up the Absolute suddenly because his dreams are our wakeful life.

When Śaṁkara or a Kant tells us that our own inner cognitive life too is as merely "apparent" as the physical world, we are not sure how to non-esoterically encash that idealism. Can Radhakrishnan deliver us out of this confusion as regards who dreamt it after all and in what sense is the Absolute's experience *experience* at all? If he can, then the third sense of idealism will really be a substantial alternative. That Radhakrishnan's idealism is through and through teleological should not by itself count against it. Concern with the meaning of life and building a teleological ontology around that notion had once, in the hey-day of linguistic philosophy, looked like a rather old-fashioned and even muddle-headed thing. But towards its end, twentieth century philosophy has come around to admitting once again the importance of such deep questions. It seems that after Thomas Nagel has talked about life being *absurd* or meaningless (see his *Mortal Questions*), and Robert Nozick has reopened the issue of the value of life as a whole - the question of meaningfulness need not be confined to sentences and words alone!

28

The Advaita of Śaṁkara and Radhakrishnan An Appraisal

SAKUNTHALA GANGADHARAM PATTISAPU

Among the six systems (Ṣaddarśanas) of Indian philosophy (Nyāya, Vaiseṣika, Sāṁkhya, Yoga, Mīmāṁsa and Vedānta), only Yoga and Vedānta are prominent in that they are capable of influencing the contemporary Indian mind. Among these, Yoga received universal acclaim as a path for spiritual sadhana and has thus become popular both in the East and West. However, as a system which can afffect social change and which can give us a social philosophy, it is not the eminent. On the other hand, Vedānta is entirely different. Its presuppositions make it a system of universal political and social significance and has attracted the attention of many leading minds. It is correct to say that nineteenth and twentieth century renaissance in India is largely due to the Vedānta doctrine.

In the modern period beginning from Raja Ram Mohan Roy, a galaxy of leaders adhered to this system. For example, besides him, Svami Rama Tīrtha, Svami Vivekananda in the Nineteenth Century, and Rabindranath Tagore, Mahatma Gandhi, Sri Aurobindo and Sarvepalli Radhakrishnan in the twentieth century, drew much of their inspirations from Vedānta, for their reform movements and nation building activities.

Among the first group, Svami Vivekananda pioneered the Vedānta movement in a big way both in the East and West. For him Vedānta was not only a doctrine of universal significance, but also a harbinger of social revolution and political freedom. Similarly, among the philosophers of the 20th Century, Radhakrishnan is unique, in bridging Eastern and Western Philosophical thinking.

The Indian mind perhaps found in Vedānta a solace and an ideology which can stand on equal grounds to ideologies like humanism, liberalism, secularism etc. In it the modern Indian philosopher felt that India too has an ideology of its own, and can give a message of universal religion, devoid of cultural ethnocentrism and religious bigotry.

Radhakrishnan's Exposure to Indian Philosophy

Born in a religious pilgrimage place, Tiruttani, South India, and of parents with deep religious convictions, it is but natural for Radhakrishnan to have strong adherence to basic values of Hinduism. In his autobiographical note he states that his "approach to the problems of philosophy from the angle of religion, as distinct from that of science, was determined by his early training."[1] This religious outlook was strengthened during his student days at Christian institutions in South India like the Lutheran Mission High School, Tirupati, Voorhees College, Vellore, and the Madras Christian College, Madras. Living faith in God was inculcated into his mind for a period of twelve years in his childhood. Apart from its positive influence, this Christian environment also determined his thoughts negatively. Criticism of Indian religion and thoughts which he continuously heard from his teachers disturbed his strong faith in Hinduism. Thus a "critical study of Hindu ideas was forced"[2] in him and the challenge of Christian critics impelled him to make a study of Hinduism and find out what is living and what is dead in it.[3] The need for philosophy arises when the faith in tradition is shaken.[4]

His thesis on the "Ethics of Vedānta" submitted in 1908 for his M.A. examination, showed that even as a student he was dissatisfied with the prevailing conception of Advaita philosophy. The thesis was a reply to the criticism that "Advaita Vedānta has no firm basis in practical conduct."[5] Starting from this, he continued his philosophical career, defending Vedānta against the charge that it had no room for ethics. In this process, he became more and more involved in showing Vedānta as the means for establishing a universal philosophy, and worked consistently and explicitly towards a synthesis of Indian and Eastern philosophies.

Influence of Indian Philosophies on Radhakrishnan

Many of the modern and ancient Indian philosophers and thinkers influenced Radhakrishnan to a great extent. Among these, three, Vivekananda, Tagore and Śaṁkara are unique.

In his laborious analysis of several philosophical positions like naturalism, materialism, positivism etc., Radhakrishnan found them to be utterly inadequate and felt that only idealism can give a consistent philosophy and world view. His philosophical reflection has five decades of continuity, with minor shifts, but all through he remained an idealist. At no stage did he leave this philosophical position.

Radhakrishnan's concept of idealism is very wide and does not insist on acceptance of any epistemological position as a necessary condition for acceptance of idealism. He says "An idealistic view of life only contends that the universe has meaning, has value. Ideal values are dynamic forces; they are the driving power of the universe. The world is intelligible only as a system of ends. Such a view has nothing to do with the problem whether a thing is only a particular image or a general relation.[6]

There may be different idealisms but he considers that they are in matter of style and language. "If we are not carried away by the noise of the controversies among philosophical sects, but watch the deeper currents that are shaping them, we seem to find a strong tendency to insist on the insights of idealism, though of course the language and style may differ."[7] He insists that idealism makes life significant and purposeful, and that the notion that it makes reality as irrational or blind is erroneous.[8]

Radhakrishnan applied his idealism to educational, political and social fields. From philosophy, and metaphysics and epistemology he shifts his interest to ethics, religion and society. He always felt that philosophical speculation must be related to society and its problems. Philosophy must be always practical and have social concern. It is bound up with life.

According to Charles A. Moore, "Radhakrishnan's basic approach to philosophy is the recognition of, and demand for, the organic unity of the universe, of the different sides of human nature, of man and the universe, of the finite and the infinite, the human and the divine."[9] If spiritualism can be used for philosophy, we can describe Radhakrishnan's philosophy as spiritualism. According to him, the "Real is spiritual, the ultimate principle of reality is not matter - solid, stubborn, unconscious. It is the very essence of spirit."[10] But Radhakrishnan prefers the term Idealism to spiritualism. He says : "In my opinion, systems which play the game of philosophy fairly and squarely, with freedom from presuppositions and with religious neutrality, all end in Absolute Idealism."[11] He feels that many Western Philosophers are not in a position to accept absolute idealism because of their religious affiliations.

Among all the forms of idealism of both East and West, Radhakrishnan felt that Śaṁkara's philosophy, which he calls absolute idealism as more rational, consistent and dear to his heart than the other idealistic systems. He accepts Śaṁkara's concept of Brahman and feels that at the higher philosophical level, the concepts of Īśvara cannot satisfy us. He feels that "while the character of God as personal, meets certain religious needs, there are other needs that are not fulfilled by it. In the highest spiritual experience we have a sense of rest and eternity and completeness. These needs have provoked from the beginning, of human reflective concepts of Absolute as pure and passionless, which transcends the restless turmoil of cosmic life."[12]

Radhakrishnan also describes Śaṁkara as a social idealist. He says : "The greatness of Śaṁkara's achievement rests on the peculiar intensity and splendour of thought with which the search for reality is conducted, on the high idealism of spirit, grappling with difficult problems of life, regardless of theological consequences, and on the vision, of a consummation which places a divine glory of human life.

Supreme as a philosopher and a dialectician, great as a man of calm judgment and wide toleration, Śaṁkara taught us to love truth, respect reason and realize the purpose of life. Twelve centuries have passed, and yet his influence is visible. He destroyed many an old dogma, not by violently attacking it, but by quietly suggesting something more reasonable, which was at the same time more spiritual too. He put into general circulation a vast body of important knowledge and formative ideas which, though contained in the Upaniṣads, were forgotten by the people, and thus recreated for us the distant past. He was not a dreaming idealist but a practical visionary, a philosopher, and at the same time a man of action, what we may call a social idealist on the grand scale. Even those who do not agree with his general attitude to life will not be reluctant to allow him a place among the immortals."[13]

Parallelism Between the Missions and Achievements of Radhakrishnan and Śaṁkara

There are many parallelisms between Śaṁkara and Radhakrishnan in their approaches and achievements in Advaitic Vedānta Philosophy. Both were instrumental in consolidation and interpretations of the important divergent aspects of Indian philosophy and thoughts existing in their respective times. Both also achieved monumental success in their endeavours.

Śaṁkara had to sort out the confusion existing in his time and establish an order of philosophy, which he called Advaita or Non-dualism. It is generally contended that the Advaita doctrine is transcendental in nature and has nothing to do with the empirical world. We find Indian Renaissance owes much to this Advaita doctrine. In this process, Śaṁkara had to define the concept of Brahman and evolve the concept of "Māyā" or Illusion. Māyā is the hindering for masking force covering the reality of Brahman. Śaṁkara acted as a strong proponent and systematizer of the Advaita doctrine, based on the knowledge already available in the Upaniṣads, Brahma Sūtras and Bhagavad Gītā. He wrote monumental commentaries on these three works, known as "Prasthana Traya."

Radhakrishnan had a similar task. He also wrote extensive commentaries on "Prasthāna Traya." He had to expound the greatness of Vedāntic philosophy, since at that time, serious doubts were created in the minds of people mostly due to influence of Western philosophy. As discussed earlier, from his student years, he was drawn to Vedāntic philosophy and thought, and in his thesis on the "Ethics of Vedānta" he showed his dissatisfaction with the then prevalent criticism that "Advaita Vedānta has no firm basis in practical conducts."[14] Naturally he had the highest admiration for Śaṁkara and has drawn heavily from his works.

Brahman and Īśvara of Śaṁkara and Absolute and God of Radhakrishnan

For both Radhakrishnan and Śaṁkara, spirit and the concept of the self are symbols of unity of all existence. This spirit is the supreme reality and supreme value and has thus become the central theme of philosophy as well as of religion. It is the Atman. Both Śaṁkara and Radhakrishnan acknowledge the reality of the spiritual intuition of the ultimate fact of spirit, as an intuited certainty. "The monistic, non-dual vision of the supreme," when associated with the adjuncts called *Upadhis,* make possible all relational operations and attitudes on the part of the individual. It also creates possibilites of strong association between the worshipper and the worshipped, the ruler and the ruled, the creator and the created order, and the omniscient mind and the intelligible order. This monistic vision is the highest truth and the highest experience.[15] On the other hand, "the relational vision of the supreme, because it is not a vision of reality by itself, and comes to us only through the molds of associated adjuncts, is incomplete and inadequate, and full of ignorance."[16] The problem of reconciliation of spirit to the objective order, is therefore still unresolved.

"This ignorance presents the real as something other but not the very self. That means the supreme appearance as qualified by associated adjuncts, which ultimately becomes a pragmatic and practical attitude and not one of pure awareness of superior Brahman."[17] The concepts of Brahman and Īśvara, according to Śaṁkara, are the attitudes of *Jñāna* and *Upāsana.* The supreme in its original, non-relational and non-dual aspects is called the *Jneya-Brahman,* and in its relational, cosmic aspect is called the *Upāsya-Brahman,* the Brahman meditated or worshipped.[18] The supreme, in its transcendent and non-relational aspect is called the absolute by Radhakrishnan, and, in its cosmic aspect, is called as God.[19] Both agree that these two are not exclusive of each other and are one reality.

Radhakrishnan accepts Śaṁkara's concept of ultimate reality as impersonal Brahman and feels that philosophy at its highest level, has to transcend the notion of personal Īśvara or God. He says "while the character of God as personal, meets certain religious needs, there are other needs that are not fulfilled by it. In the highest spiritual experience, we have a sense of rest and eternity and completeness. These needs have provoked, from the beginning of human reflection, conceptions of the absolute as pure and passionless being, which transcends the restless turmoil of the cosmic life."[20]

The Concept of Maya of Śaṁkara and the Concept of Cosmic Evolution of Radhakrishnan

Śaṁkara created the concept of Māyā, in order to bring out the supremacy of Brahman. According to him, the supreme Brahman, while remaining in its transcendent, absolute, pure and non-dual being, takes upon itself its cosmic aspect by virtue of its own power, which is called Māyā.[21] The dominant note of Śaṁkara, is renunciation, and through it, emancipation from cycle of worldly existence. Worldly existence itself is a vicious one and one who wishes to reach Brahman, should turn his back to it.[22] Māyā wears two forms : one consisting of eternal and unlimited knowledge,[23] which is the very essence of the creative power,[24] and the other consisting of "Name and Form" which is also called "Avidya" the basis of limitation.[25] Avidya exists in the supreme as the essence (Ātmabhūtam), exists by virtue of the supreme as a creative reality and fulfils a divine purpose.[26]

Radhakrishnan accepts the viewpoint of Śaṁkara and gives his own interpretation. He accepts that reality can be described as "not this, no this (neti, neti)," and feels that there is nothing wrong in applying this method to know the nature of Supreme Brahman. He thinks that the negative description of the Absolute serves a definite purpose, and that Śaṁkara employed this concept to denote the distance between time and eternity, and between appearance and reality. He says that "Māyā does not mean that the empirical world, with the selves in it, is an illusion, for the whole efforts of the cosmos is directed to one sustained by the one supreme self."[27]

Analyzing further his concepts of Māyā, Radhakrishnan stressed that "When the Hindu thinkers ask us to free ourselves from Māyā, they are asking us to shake off our bondage to the universal values that the dominating us. They do not ask us to treat like an illusion or be indifferent to the world's welfare."[28]

We find in the philosophy of Radhakrishnan, another aspect of the doctrine of Māyā. It is more poetic and imaginative. He feels that the entire history of philosophy has been "one long illustration of inability of the human mind to solve the problem of creation."[29] Questioning "how the primal reality in which the divine light shines everlastingly can yet be the source and find of all empirical beings," he says that "we can only say that it is a mystery, Maya."[30] This mystery also arouses our sense of wonder and makes our universe more interesting than it would otherwise have been. However, he is not in agreement with the Advaita position of asceticism. His view is nearer to the "*Anasaktiyoga*" of Śaṁkara. He says that "detachment of the mind, and not renunciation, is what is demanded of us."[31]

Naravane tried to interpret the concept of Māyā and analyze the viewpoints of Radhakrishnan and Śaṁkara. He rightly pointed out that "the theory of Māyā is only a continuation of the effort to distinguish the highest reality from lower grades of reality, to imprint upon the human mind the difference between the absolute truth and the conditioned truth. The aim is practical to transfer attention from that which is transitory to that which is the ground of all value. He also feels that Radhakrishnan's interpretation of Māyā may not be acceptable to the follow of Śaṁkara. He says that "scholars may disagree regarding the extent to which Radhakrishnan's interpretation of the Advaita text is justified. It is an interpretation which certainly tones down the rigor of Śaṁkara's absolution and present it in softer hues."[32]

Concept of Jagat or the World

Both Śaṁkara and Radhakrishnan agreed that the world or "Jagat" is real and not illusionary. However, Śaṁkara sometimes tended to compare the world to illusion and mirage, and sometimes to foam and dream, in order to emphasize certain truths about the world and the supreme.[33] Radhakrishnan always stressed the realities of the greatness of the world. In fact, he stated that the world should progress, since only then, man will progress. According to Śaṁkara, the experience of the world is one aspect of the supreme existence, merely supporting the cosmic play. This is a divine element.[34] It will be like a great sleep[35] in which the worldly souls are caught in the nets of transimigratory existence and therefore unaware of their real nature. The empirical world of Śaṁkara is one made up of objects and subjects, forming an inextricable network of existence which is nourished by nescience and it's accompaniments. That is desire and action.[36]

First, according to Śaṁkara, "just as the self is not reducible to the non-self, similarly non-self, the empirical world, is not to be reduced to the self. Śaṁkara rises above one-sided subjective idealism and one-sided materialism, both of which are beliefs in reductionism of some sort. For him it is all spirit."[37] The universe is essentially spirit. Second, the empirical world as moment of external realization, being the basic nature of the supreme, is external. It has no beginning and no end. Third, the conflict between "nescience and the world is externally resolved in reality, by virtue of its nature as supreme consciousness, which is external awareness of the form, "I, Brahman, am all this." There is no creator confronting and confronted by a created order."[38] Finally, it is correct to state that every line written by Śamkara reveals his anxiety "to save the supreme Brahman" from disintegration and loss of its authentic being. When unity and plurality were viewed as equally real and equally significant, then Brahman and the world were assigned equality of status.[39] The task which Śamkara assigned himself was the task of saving Brahman's integral unity of existence, while recognizing the factual character of the many-sidedness of the cosmic order. This was the mission of his Mayavada.[40]

For Radhakrishnan, "Śamkara's concepts of illusionary character of the world, seemed to be a mockery of the oneness and absoluteness of Brahman. Radhakrishnan's principal problem became the formulation of a concept of cosmic evlution so as to "save the world and give it a real meaning."[41] His reaction to the dominant note of the illusionary character of the world of ordinary experience assumes the form of a concerted repudiation of the view that the world is an illusion and affirmation of a thorough going evolutionary advance.[42] In this aspect, he fundamentally differs from Śamkara who never subscribed to the concept of evolution, and who strongly believed in the completeness of the world. For Radhakrishnan, the world is not a complete act; it is still in the process of completion.

According to Radhakrishnan, the reality of the world is grounded, in its being willed by God, though it has a dependent created reality.[43] He is so anxious to "save the world and give it a real meaning" that his account of the world "has in it the promise," not of a spiritual idealism,[44] but of a spiritual realism. He also upholds the cosmic evolution to be capable of revealing the spirit which lives in the world.[45] But, unlike Śaṁkara, he holds that the cosmic process progressively reveals the richness of life of the supreme, and the passage to the supreme is not a flight to it but an ascent, for which "life, personality and history become important."[46] Reality gives value to empirical objects and earthly desires.[47] The world is a passage from existence to reality.[48] Therefore, we are not to neglect worldly welfare or despise body and mind. Radhakrishnan unlike Śaṁkara, is interested not only in the ascending movement, but in the descending movement of the divine,[49] as well, in which alone Śaṁkara discovers the significance of the world process. This descending movement also constitutes the "central drive of the universe," and its position in the scheme of reality.[50]

The View Point of Jiva or the Individual as Seen by Śaṁkara and Radhakrishnan

Inspired by absolute thinkers like Bradley and Bosanquet, people questioned whether Śaṁkara's philosophy considers Jiva or the individual as real, and whether Jiva possesses a substantial or adjectival existence. In essence, these authorities raise the basic question on the concept of non-duality of the soul and the separation of body and soul which Śaṁkara expounds.

According to Śaṁkara, the individual existence and its present status is the status of Atman associated with and limited by the adjuncts of body, the gross, the subtle and the seed body.[51] The last one is constituted by nescience, which is the original limiting adjunct. The present existence is individualized or particularized existence of the Atman. But its true life and nature are completely non-embodied. It exists as pure consciousness, as pure "I." The embodied existence is the self, is the twilight existence between being and non-being. The embodied existence is terminable and its termination is liberation. Annihilation of the embodied existence does not cease termination of the individual

"Atman." Atman may give up the particular dwelling, the embodied existence, but it's real nature will remain.[52] It cannot thus be destroyed by any means, but appears in the Absolute.

The question of adjectival existence of the individual self does not have a direct bearing of Śaṁkara's thinking. He is interested only in the question whether the true life (*Jiva*) is eternal or does it have an individual existence. Individuality according to Śaṁkara, is determined by individual adjuncts but not native to Atman. Annihilation of the limiting adjuncts mark the end of the individual self, but not the self itself, whose very nature is universal.[53]

In this context, there is a subtle difference between the concepts of Śaṁkara and Radhakrishnan. Śaṁkara says that the liberated invidual ultimately reaches Brahman, with no further necessity or opportunity to pass through the birth-death cycle of the body. Radhakrishnan holds the view, that the liberated soul stays with Brahman, in a sort of independent existence and will do so as long as the world exists. Only when the world terminates will he merge with Brahman.

Radhakrishnan's View on Śaṁkara

Radhakrishnan developed his philosophy into a world culture, based essentially on Śaṁkara's Advaita Vedānta concepts. It should be stressed however, that in Śaṁkara, Vedānta was more a tool with a strong ascetic note, to achieve personal salvation. With Radhakrishnan, on the other hand, it emerged as a universal culture for an international community and fellowship of man.

There were occasions when Radhakrishnan appeared to criticize Śaṁkara. This might be due to the influence of Rabindranath Tagore, but soon he corrected his notion about Śaṁkara, whom be continuously adored thereafter.

He states that "whether we agree or differ, the penetrating light of his (Śaṁkara's) mind never leaves us where we were."⁵⁴ In another context, he says that "it is impossible to read Śaṁkara's writings, packed as they are, with serious and subtle thinking, without being conscious that one is in contact with a mind of very fine penetration and profound spirituality.... Śaṁkara stands out as a heroic figure of the first rank in the somewhat motley crowd of the religious thinkers of medieval India. His philosophy stands forth complete, needing neither a before nor an after."⁵⁵ Advaita Vedānta thus comes nearest to his convictions.⁵⁶

Radhakrishnan's View on Ramanuja

Śaṁkara always upheld spiritual wisdom (*Jñāna*) to know and understand Brahman and Īśvara. In this process, he does not deny devotional approach (*Bhakti*), a path strongly advocated by Ramanuja. Radhakrishnan accepts the position of Śaṁkara on most fundamental points, but he accepts certain views of Ramanuja also. He feels that Absolute and God are not mutually exclusive concepts. God as creator, sustained and judge of the world, does not denote a principle which is separate from the ultimate reality. He says that in the metaphysical sense, Śaṁkara represents the truth which is the truth of the Absolute. But Ramanuja's view is the highest expression of that truth.⁵⁷

Conclusion

Radhakrishnan firmly believed and endorsed the Advaita philosophy of Śaṁkara. In some cases he clarified some doubts about Śaṁkara's concepts. For instance, when people questioned whether Śaṁkara absorbed the Buddhistic principles, Radhakrishnan answered that it is not so, stating that the similarities are due to the fact that both Buddha and Śaṁkara drew their knowledge from the same source, the Upaniṣads and the Vedas. Also Radhakrishnan mentioned that the world is real and dynamic, and it should progress, if man has to survive and progress.

In Śaṁkara's opinion, there can be no question of the world being "in the process of completion." It is a completed act of Īśvara. Śaṁkara is not aware of that aspect of the universe which has been disclosed to moderns by the emergence of the scientific theory of evolution; and, even when he is aware of it as a process he is not aware of it as an evolutionary process with its emergent levels.[58] "The universe is essentially dynamic and the human individual is the growing point of the future, the agent as well as the offspring of the creative process."[59] The cosmic life according to Śaṁkara is a dialectical antinomy which is finally and fully resolved in the total integration of the transcendent aspect of the supreme life.[60] Both Śaṁkara and Radhakrishnan utilized the concept of Maya in different ways, with relevance to their attempts to save the Brahman and the world. Finally one can say that Radhakrishnan endeavoured to save the world while Śaṁkara struggled to save Brahman.

References

1. Paul A. Schilpp (Ed.), *The Philosophy of Sarvepalli Radhakrishnan* (N.Y.: Tudor Publishing Co., 1952).
2. V.S. Naravane, *Modern Indian Thought* (Asia Publishing Co.), p. 232.
3. S. Radhakrishnan, *My Search for Truth* (Agra : S.L. Agarwala, 1937), p. 9.
4. *Ibid.*, p. 5.
5. V.S. Naravane, *Modern Indian Thought*, p. 234.
6. S. Radhakrishnan, *An Idealistic View of Life*, (London : George Allen & Unwin Ltd., 1947), p. 15.
7. *Ibid.*, p. 17.

8. *Ibid.*, p. 15.
9. Charles A. Moore, "Radhakrishnan's Metaphysics and Ethics," in *The Philosophy of Sarvepalli Radhakrishnan*, Paul A. Schilpp (ed.), p. 282.
10. S. Radhakrishnan, *Religion and Society* (London : George Allen and Unwin, Ltd., 1948), p. 29.
11. D.M. Dutta, "Radhakrishnan and Contemporary Philosophy," in *The Philosophy of Sarvepalli Radhakrishnan*, Paul A. Schilpp (ed.), p. 671.
12. S. Radhakrishnan, *An Idealistc View of Life*, p. 342.
13. S. Radhakrishnan, "Śaṁkara : A Social Idealist," *Bhavan's Journal*, 1988, Vol. 34, No. 18, p. 23.
14. V.S. Naravane, *Modern Indian Thought*, p. 234.
15. *Bṛhadaranyakopaniṣad (Śaṁkara-bhasya)*, (Gorakhpur : Gita Press), 1:14, p. 201.
16. Ram Partap Singh, "Radhakrishnan's Substantial Reconstruction of the *Vedānta* of Śaṁkara," *Philosophy East and West*, XVI (January - April, 1966), p. 13.
17. *Ibid.*
18. *Ibid.*
19. *Ibid.*
20. S. Radhakrishnan, *An Idealistic View of Life*, p. 342.
21. Ram Pratap Singh, "Radhakrishnan's Substantial Reconstruction of the Vedānta of Śaṁkara," p. 14.
22. *Ibid.*
23. *Bṛhadaranyakopaniṣad (Śaṁkara-bhasya)*, (Gorakhpur : Gita Press), III, vii, 12. p. 199.
24. *Ibid.*, II.i.5, p. 27.
25. *Ibid.*, II.i. 14, p. 201.
26. *Aitaaareya Upaniṣad (Śaṁkara-bhasya)*, (Gorakhpur : Gita Press, 1937), pp. 25f, 149, 157.
27. Radhakrishnan, S. *Eastern Religions and Western Thought* (Oxford : Oxford University Press, 1940), p. 28.
28. *Ibid.*, p. 47.

29. Radhakrishnan, S. *The Bhagavad Gītā* (London : Allen Unwin, 1948), p. 38.
30. Radhakrishnan, S., *Eastern Religions and Western Thought*, p. 90.
31. *Ibid.,* p. 101.
32. V.S. Naravane, *Modern Indian Thought*, p. 238.
33. Ram Pratap Singh, *op. cit.,* p. 18.
34. *Brahma Sūtra (Śaṁkara-bhasya)*, Narayana Ram Acarya, ed., (Bombay : Nirnaya Sagar Press, 1948), p. 188.
35. *Ibid.,* p. 149.
36. Ram Pratap Singh, *op. cit.,* p. 20.
37. *Ibid.,* pp. 20-21.
38. *Bṛhadaranyakopaniṣad (Śaṁkara-bhasya)*, (Gorakhpur : Gita Press), III, viii, 12, p.21.
39. *Ibid.*, III, viii, 1, 11, 12, 14.
40. *Ibid.,* Also see *Bhamati*, 11, 1, 28.
41. *The Philosophy of Sarvepalli Radhakrishnan*, p. 800.
42. S. Radhakrishnan, *An Idealistic View of Life*, p. 338.
43. *The Philosophy of Sarvepalli Radhakrishnan*, p. 41.
44. S. Radhakrishnan, *An Idealistic View of Life*, p. 87.
45. *The Philosophy of Sarvepalli Radhakrishnan*, p. 44.
46. S. Radhakrishnan, *East and West in Religion*, p. 137.
47. S. Radhakrishnan, *The Brahma Sūtra* (New York : Harper Brothers, 1960, p. 142.
48. *Ibid.,* p. 143.
49. *Ibid.,* p. 157.
50. Ram Pratap Singh, *op. cit.,* p. 23.
51. *Ibid.,* p. 25.
52. *Ibid.,* p. 26.
53. *Ibid.,* p. 26.
54. S. Radhakrishnan, *Indian Philosophy*, p. 447.
55. *Ibid.,* p. 447.

56. V.S. Naravane, *Modern Indian Thought*, p. 233.
57. S. Radhakrishnan, *An Idealistic View of Life*, p. 338.
58. Ram Pratap Singh, *op. cit.*, pp. 23-24.
59. S. Radhakrishnan, *The Brahma Sūtra*, p. 157.
60. Ram Pratap Singh, *op. cit.*, p. 24.

29

The Idealist Tradition : Sarvepalli Radhakrishnan and George Berkeley

B. David Burke
Eastern Connecticut State University

This investigation into the philosophical idealism of George Berkeley and Sarvepalli Radhakrishnan will seek to : (1) place their works in historical perspective, (2) establish that Berkeley and Radhakrishnan (the one conversant only with the Western theological and philosophical traditions, the other conversant with the philosophies and religions of both India and West) employ the term 'Idealism' in very different senses, and (3) compare the efforts of these two philosophers in the areas of ontology, metaphysics, and ethics.

George Berkeley was born near Kilkenny, Ireland, in 1685. His parents were established comfortably; and, at the age of 15, he entered Trinity College, Dublin. He graduated in 1704 with a B.A., and in 1707 was admitted as a Fellow of Trinity College. As all Fellows were required to be clerics, Berkeley received ordination at this time. In 1709, he published an *Essay Towards a New Theory of Vision*, in 1710, the *Principles of Human Knowledge;* and, in 1713, *Three*

Dialogues Between Hylas and Philonous. These were the major publications of his life - all completed between the ages of 25 and 28; the *Principles* clearly and succinctly setting forth the tenets of Idealism.

A notable lack in these works in any sustained discussion of *These*. There are several passing remarks in the *Principles* which make it clear that Berkeley wanted to secure a firm footing for morality and that the rejection of materialism was essential to this. One can only regret that he did not explicity set forth his ethical theory. However, it is safe to venture that had he done so, it, in the main, would have conformed to Christian ethical values.

As an explanation of this seeming lack of detailed concern for ethical theory, Colin M. Turbayne has this to stay:

> "Berkeley holds that the end of speculation is practise. Accordingly, these books are to prepare men's minds for the study and practise of virtue. The *Principles* was the first part of a plan which included at least a second part on psychology and ethics, a third on physics, and probably a fourth on mathematics. None of the later parts was published, although the bulk of the second was written and then lost during Berkeley's travels."[1]

Being a theologian, Berkeley was very disturbed about what he felt to be the rising tide of materialism. Scientific thought was coming into prominence, and philosophical speculation was ripe. In the scientific community Galileo, Harvey and Boyle had recently died and Isaac Newton was still alive. In the philosophical community Bacon, Hobbes and Descartes had all come into prominence as had Spinoza; and Locke and Leibnitz were contemporaries.

Berkeley was most influenced by Locke's philosophical writings. The *Principles* was written as a refutation of the concept of matter put forth by Locke who had come to accept the notion of his scientific contemporaries that the universe was essentially mechanistic in its construction. For Locke, one comes to have ideas in one's mind about the qualities of a particular substance and all that can be known for certain are these ideas. All that we can say about "matter" is it is that in which ideas "inhere." We have no direct experience of matter and are merely forced to postulate it so that there is something to "bundle" the related qualities together.

Berkeley disliked this view of the universe. If the world consists of substances which are in causal relationships with each other and whose movements are purely mechanical, then the position of God is precarious. Other than being the Prime Mover, God would have no ongoing role in the maintenance and preservation of an orderly universe. Applying Occam's razor, Berkeley found no need for the concept of matter; and so he denied what had come to be the basis of materialism.

> "Let us examine a little the description that is here given us of *Matter*. It neither acts, nor percives, nor is perceived; for this is all that is meant by saying it is an inert, senseless, unknown substance; which is a definition made up of negatives, except in only the relative notion of its standing under or supporting. But then it must be observed that it supports nothing at all, and how nearly this comes to the description of a *nonentity* I desire may be considered. Now, I would fain know how anything can be present to us, which is neither perceivable by sense nor reflection, nor capable of producing any idea in our minds, nor is it all extended, nor bath any form, nor exists in any place."[2]

Instead of matter being the substratum of qualities, Berkeley pronounced his famous dictum *esse est percipe* or *esse est percipere*.

"Their being is to be perceived or known so long as they are not actually perceived by me, or do not exist in my mind or that of any other created spirit, they must either have no existence at all, or else subsist in the mind of some Eternal Spirit. From what has been said it is evident that there is not any other Substance than Spirit, or that which perceives."[3]

In contemporary Western philosophy, it is not enough to claim that the universe is somehow or other spiritual for the claim to hold that that view is what is properly termed Idealism. Although most Idealists do hold that the universe is spiritual in nature, Berkeley's dictum must also come into play. As G.E. Moore has stated :

"Indeed I take it that modern Idealists are chiefly distinguished by certain arguments which they have in common. That reality is spiritual has, I believe, been the tenet of many theologians, and yet, for believing that alone, they should hardly be called Idealists. There are besides, I believe, many persons, not improperly called Idealists, who hold certain characteristic propositions, without venturing to think them quite sufficient to prove so grand a conclusion . . . . That whatever you can truly predicate *esse* you can truly predicate *percipe*, in some sense or other, is, I take it, a necessary step in all arguments, properly to be called Idealistic, and, what is more, in all arguments hitherto offered for the Idealistic conclusion."[4]

For Berkeley, God plays a pivotal and ongoing role in the universe. With God's constant perception, all our common-sense notions about objects - such as that objects are continuous in existence and have a reality independent of any particular observer - apply, except the notion that the objects really exist "out there." While Berkeley felt himself to be a champion of common-sense, the fact that on his

The Idealist Tradition: Sarvepalli Radhakrishnan and George Berkeley

system objects exist only as ideas in the mind (God's or a human's) and not "out there" is far from what one can regard as a common-sense position. By not admitting matter, all mechanistic explanations of the universe were challenged and, for Berkeley, God resumed His proper role of Creator and Sustainer of the universe.

In India, along with the development of the Vedic and Upaniṣadic literature came the development of the *sūtra* literature of the six philosophical schools. These schools have traditionally been grouped together into the three sister schools of Nyāya - Vaiśeṣika, Sāṁkhya-Yoga, and Pūrva Mīmāṁsā-Uttara Mīmāṁsā (Vedānta). Nyāya-Vaiśeṣika was, in the main, concerned with the development of epistemological, logical, and atomistic theory. Theism was a later development of the school Sāṁkhya-Yoga presented a dualistic conception of the universe with *puruṣa* and *prakṛti* as equal ontological principles. Enlightenment is seen as the result of certain physical and mental disciplines (yoga) which enable the *puruṣa* to be recognized as being in a state of freedom from *prakṛti*. The Purva Mīmāṁsā-Uttara Mīmāṁsā (Vedānta) school investigated the earlier and later Vedic texts with a view towards understanding *dharma,* duty. One's principal aim in life is seen as fulfilling one's *dharma* and by so doing obtaining release from the cycle of rebirths. This school of thought was later to be emphasized, particularly in its non-dualistic (*advaita*) aspect, by the Hindu reform movement of which Radhakrishnan was such an articulate spokesperson.

With British rule came the introduction of Christian missionary schools, colleges, and universities whose primary mission was to teach English literature and culture to those Hindus who were to comprise the civil service class, replacing Hindu religious practices with Christian belief. As a result of this educational/indoctrinational process, there arose a class of Indians who were very knowledgeable about the Western intellectual tradition.

Spearheaded by this small, but influential, group of British—educated Indians, various Hindu social and religious reform movements were undertaken The Brāhmo Samāj was the first of these. Its founder, Rammohan Roy, was a strong supporter of Western scientific education and "advocated a rational theism based on the Vedas and Upanisads.[5] He denounced image worship and the caste system, and emphasized the fundamental unity of the focus of worship of Hinduism, Islām, and Christianity.

Two of the Brāhmo Samāj's important leaders after Roy were Devendranath Tagore and Keshub Chunder Sen Devendranath Tagore was most influenced by Hinduism and "responded to the rationalist attitudes of younger members of the society by moving away from the early doctrine of Vedic infallibility to a principle of natural and universal theism."[6] Under his guidance, the Brāhmo Samāj began actively seeking social reforms Keshub Chunder Sen was strongly influenced by Christianity while yet considering himself a devotee of the goddess Kālī, the Bengali mother goddess who is propitiated by blood—sacrifice. He rejected idol worship, but introduced the Hindu practice of devotional singing (saṃkīrtana) into the religious practices of the Brāhmo Samāj.

Towards the end of Rammohan Roy's life, Dayananda Saraswati was born. He was to found the Ārya Samāj, the second great reform movement. While the Brāhmo Samāj was strongly influenced by Western scientific ideals, the Ārya Samāj was to emphasize the teachings of the Vedas. A distinction was drawn between Hindu religious/philosophical teachings and Hindu social practices. The principle aims of the Ārya Samāj are to unify all segments of Hindu society, rectify the social evils of caste restrictions and child marriage, and emphasize the monotheistic aspects of the Veda. A new sense of Hindu pride has been instilled in its followers; and the Ārya Samāj, more readily than the Brāhmo Samāj, appeals directly to the Hindu masses among

The Idealist Tradition : Sarvepalli Radhakrishnan and George Berkeley

whom the various gods and goddesses have never ceased to be worshiped. While neither of these reform movements gained large numbers of adherents, they have been very influential in bringing about social reforms due to the educational level and social importance of their leaders.

About the same time as these two reform movements were gaining strength, (mid-1800's), Rāmakrishna was born. He was named Gadadhar by his parents and lived in a small village near Calcutta for the first sixteen years of his life. At sixteen, he went to live with his brother in Calcutta. When he was nineteen, his brother was made priest of a Kālī temple just north of Calcutta on the Ganges; and he was made priest of a small Kṛṣṇa temple in the same area. His brother died a year later, and Rāmakrishna took over his duties at the Kālī temple. He often went into deep meditative states (*samādhi*), and some of the devotees considered him insane. Relieved of his position, he was sent back to his home village, but he later returned. For the last 25 years of his life, he remained at the Kālī temple. He was initiated into Tantric practises and yoga. He studied certain aspects of Advaita Vedānta, Islām, and Christianity and was in contact with the leaders of the Brāhmo Samāj. Before his death, he had come to be considered a saint by his devotees.

Upon his death, his disciples remained together. Chief among these was Vivekānanda who in 1893 attended the Parliament of Religions in Chicago. Vivekānanda remained in America for three years lecturing and touring, and by the time he returned to India he had established the Vedānta Society of New York. Returning to India, he founded the Rāmakrishna Mission in Calcutta. This mission had a permanent order of monks who placed emphasis on Rāmakrishna's religious ideals and worked for social reform. From Calcutta, centres were set up throughout India; and Vivekānanda himself set up centres in London and San Francisco on a return trip to America.

Coming on the heels of this modern Hindu reform movement spearheaded by the Brāhmo Samāj, Ārya Samāj, Rāmakrishna, and Vivekānanda were four men who were to have great influence on both this reform movement and on the West. Rabindranath Tagore as a poet, playwright, educator, and visionary; Mohandas Gandhi as a social reformer, politician, and popularizer of the Bhagavad Gītā's ideal of selfless action (*karmayoga*); Sarvepalli Radhakrishnan as a philosopher-theologian and statesman; and Aurobindo as a mystic-saint.

While Aurobindo's influence on the social reform movement was minor, his influence on the religious aspect of this reform movement must be recognized. After an early career as an Indian nationalist which saw him jailed several times, Aurobindo withdrew to live the life of a Tantric yogin. He established his *āśram* at Pondicherry and taught the religious ideal of internal purification through meditation and Tantric practise emphasizing the total integration of all life through the Tantric union of Siva and Sakti and designating this philosophy by the term 'integral yoga.' Whereas Gandhi captured the hearts and souls of his countrymen through his emphasis on the religious ideal of selfless action directed outward, Aurobindo gathered a following both in India and the West through his ideal of selflessness through inner purification.

Thus, the modern-day Hindu social and religious reform movement has occurred through a combination of religious saints (Rāmakrishna and Aurobindo), intellect social idealists (Ram Mohan Roy, Devendranath Tagore, Keshub Chunder Sen, Dayānanda Saraswati, and Rabindranath Tagore), social-religious activists (Vivekānanda and the Ramakrishna Missions), and political-religious activism (Mohandas Gandhi). It was for Sarvepalli Radhakrishnan to throw the doors of India's magnificently rich philosophical/ religious heritage open to the West.

Sarvepalli Radhakrishnan was born in 1888, some 203 years later than George Berkeley. His birthplace was at Tiruttani, about 40 miles north of Madras. Until the age of twelve, he lived at Tiruttani and Tirupati which were both famous as pilgrimage centres. He was educated as a child and as a young man in Christian missionary schools. During this time he was taught Christianity but adhered to his Hindu beliefs.[7]

At the age of twenty, to partially answer the criticisms levelled by the Christian missionaries, Radhakrishnan "prepared a thesis on the *Ethics of the Vedānta* which was intended to be a reply to the charge that the Vedānta system had no room for ethics." The Principal of Madras Christian College, A.C. Hogg, praised Radhakrishnan's treatment of the philosophical problems involved, accepted the thesis for the M.A. degree, and saw his work through to publication.

From 1908-1918, Radhakrishnan served first as an Assistant Professor and then as a Professor of Philosophy at Presidency College, Madras. In 1918, he was appointed Professor of Philosophy at the University of Mysore. In that same year, he published the first of his major works, *The Philosophy of Rabindranath Tagore*. He had met Mahatma Gandhi in 1915, and he now met Tagore in 1918.

In 1920, he published *The Reign of Religion in Contemporary Philosophy*. This book was a major challenge to the Western philosophical thought of Leibniz, James Ward, M. Bergson, William James, Rudolf Eucken, and Bertrand Russell. The purpose of the book has been ably stated by Radhakrishnan in his Preface.

> "This book attempts to show that of the two live philosophies of the present day, pluralistic theism and monistic idealism, the latter is the more reasonable as affording to the spiritual being of man full satisfaction, moral as well as intellectual. It is my opinion that

systems which play the game of philosophy squarely and fairly, with freedom from presuppositions and religious neutrality, naturally end in absolute idealism...."[8]

At the time Radhakrishnan was a student, and even today, Indian universities have placed emphasis on Western philosophy while relegating Indian philosophy to the status of a poor cousin. As is evident from his writings, there is no doubt that Radhakrishnan was thoroughly conversant with the history of Western philosophy through the time of Russell and Whitehead. His language skills in Sanskrit, English, Bengali and Hindi were prodigious; and Western and Indian audiences alike were enthralled with his eloquent lecture style. One of Radhakrishnan's primary accomplishments was to reappraise Indian philosophy both for his countrymen and for Western students of philosophy. Since he also served as President of India, Radhakrishnan has been favourably compared with Plato's ideal of the philosopher-king.

In *An Idealist View of Life,* Radhakrishnan's primary concern was to examine the scientific analysis of the objects of the universe to show that the scientific method, while pragmatically useful, leaves one unfulfilled. There is a point beyond which science cannot reach. And, for Radhakrishnan, this is the interesting domain. By limiting human knowledge to a verification principle as scientists do, one must remain eternally bound to one's body. The things of the soul - which is a very real entity for Radhakrishnan - can never then be known.

On the first page of *An Idealist View of Life,* Radhakrishnan takes cognizance of Berkeley's philosophy.

"Idealism is an ambiguous word and has been used to signify a variety of views. An 'idea' is taken as a particular mental image peculiar to each individual and attempts are made in the Buddhist Vijñānavāda (mentalism) and English empiricism to reduce all knowledge to ideas in this sense. Whatever is real in the universe is such stuff as ideas are made of. Ideas or images are regarded as self-contained existence and not as avenues of the apprehension of a world which is at once more ideal and more real than themselves. The term 'idea' has also been used to signify the universal notion, which is not an existent here and now, but a quality of the existent which is shareable by other existents and knowable by other minds. While Berkeley's first statement is more of a mentalism holding that existence consists either in perceiving or being perceived, his modified view with its emphasis on 'notions' brings it under the second type."[9]

It is Berkeley's second usage of the term in which Radhakrishnan is interested. For the rest of the book, he ignores Berkeley's primary dictum of *esse est percipi* or *perciperi* and takes the term 'idealism' as designating the primacy of ideals and belief in the ultimate spiritual reality of the world.

The concept of "notions" that Berkeley introduced was postulated because he wanted to account for our knowledge of other minds or spirits and relations between things and ideas and felt that the term 'idea' would be improperly extended, since it would include the perceiver as well as the perceived, if it were to cover this aspect of knowledge as well as what is typically called "sense data." Berkeley himself was vague about this concept of notions and did not develop it very satisfactorily.

For Western philosophers, Berkeley's dictum of *esse est percipi* or *perciperi* is concerned with the first definition of the term 'idea' and this has been considered the interesting point of his philosophical system. It must not be forgotten, however, that Berkeley considered himself primarily a theologian and secondarily a philosopher. Radhakrishnan, on the other hand, took the approach of a philosopher first although he saw no ultimate difference - beyond the mundane level - between philosophy and religion.

The Sanskrit term for philosophy - *darśana* - includes far more than striving for an intellectual comprehension of the universe. The term literally means "viewpoint." And a viewpoint includes not only an intellectual understanding but also a transformation of one's very being in an effort to attain enlightenment, *mokṣa*. Philosophy is to take charge of one's life. One must strive to more than an intellectual realization of the truth of that highest dictum of the Upaniṣads *tat tvam asi*, thou art that. Philosophy that does not lead to a spiritual change in one's life - that is not mixed with theology - is not a complete *darśana*.

Radhakrishnan examined Western philosophical systems primarily with an eye to establishing their theological consequences. He did not consider the search for Truth to be an end in and of itself. Truth must transform one's life or its pursuit is fruitless. Since Berkeley's dictum sets up a division between God and man, it was not acceptable to Radhakrishnan. Rather, he taught that one must break through his seeming barrier and realize God within oneself.

> God does not create the world but becomes it. Creation is expression. It is not a making of something out of nothing. It is not making so much as becoming. It is the self-projection of the Supreme.[10]

Radhakrishnan's point is that the true realization of God is to be found only in mysticism which seeks the ultimate nature underlying the world of predication. The Absolute (*Brahman*) is beyond space and time, is beyond any possible manner of conceptualization. It is the underlying essence of Reality in everything and is alone the truly real.

One particular problem here is that the term 'Absolute Idealism' does not seem to adequately characterize Radhakrishnan's position. It certainly does not meet G.E.

Moore's criteria. Radhakrishnan does not make the claim that *Brahman* is the Ideal this, that, and the other thing, neither is *nirguṇa Brahman* seen as the All-Knower. *Brahman* at the highest level is not the nexus of a set of Ideal Universals; but, in fact, is held to be beyond all attributions. Simultaneously, Radhakrishnan held that *Brahman* is the spiritual essence of the Universe, the essence shared by all creatures and manifested in myriad ways. Is this attempting to have your cake and eat it too?

A few remarks about the term 'Idealism' may be *apropos* here. The term, as Radhakrishnan recognized, is an ambiguous one. This stems from its being etymologically associated with both the terms 'idea' and 'ideal.'[11] Subjective Idealists such as Berkeley emphasize the term 'idea,' while Absolute Idealists emphasize the term 'ideal.' Because of the two etymological associations of the term, both Berkeley and Radhakrishnan are often referred to as Idealists. But one must keep in mind that, since Berkeley, Idealism in Western philosophy primarily hinges on the importance of the term 'idea.' Of course, in the Western tradition also, there has been a history of the blending of both. As Srivastava has stated :

> "Plato's philosophy, for example, is an idealism of ideals. Though he used the term 'ideas,' his "ideas" are nothing but the standards or ideals for the objects of the senses. The idea of horse is the ideal horse, the idea of man is the ideal man, and these ideals alone are the realities, in terms of which the actual horse or man is to be understood.[12]

One of Radhakrishnan's major contributions of East-West dialogue has been his exposition of the doctrine of *māyā* which term Westerners have generally taken to be synonymous with 'unreality.' Radhakrishnan does not want us to consider the world to be an illusion. *Māyā* is not unreality, but neither is it Reality. It is real but its reality is not ultimate.

"Śaṁkara who is rightly credited with the systematic formulation of the doctrine of māyā, tells us that the highest reality is unchangeable, and therefore that changing existence such as human history has not ultimate reality (pāramārthika sattā). He warns us, however, against the temptation to regard what is not completely real as utterly illusory. The world has empirical being (vyāvahārika sattā) which is quite different from illusory existence (prātibhāsika sattā). Human experience is neither ultimately real nor completely illusory. Simply because the world of experience is not the perfect form of reality, it does not follow that it is a delusion, without any significance. The world is not a phantom, though it is real. *Brahman* is said to be the real of the real, *satyasyasatyam*.[13]

The problem of *māyā* has important implications for ethical theory. If the world is truly illusory, then ethics loses its importance. If *māyā* means illusion or unreality, then one's self and one's actions *both* are illusory. One's behaviour in an illusory world simply would not matter. Radhakrishnan will have none of this.

[G.E.] Moore asks, whether it is not true that morality, on my scheme, has but a relative status and is not of absolute validity. It is true that the moral situation refers to the world of individuals and has validity in regard to it. As the world is rooted in the absolute reality, morality has also an ultimate significance.[14]

In *Eastern Religions and Western Thought*, Radhakrishnan has been more explicit.

While this doctrine [of *māyā*] suggests that the world may not be worthy of being lived in, it holds that life in it is worth living if it is directed by spiritual ideals.

Enthusiastic service of humanity is possible only if we have faith in a transcendent goal. Mere morality without spiritual conviction or *jñāna* is incapable of giving us satisfaction.

Jñāna, or seeing through the veil of *māya,* is the spiritual destiny of man. It is something more than ethical goodness, though it cannot be achieved without it. The difference is that between perfection and progress, between eternal life and temporal development, between time suspended and time extended. One is an improvement of human nature, while the other is a reorientation of it.[15]

Ethical actions, then, have importance in the temporal realm. They are a cleansing process, ridding one of self-centeredness. In order for one to rise above egoism, ethical acts are essential. As the Absolute (*Brahman*) generates the world, ethical acts have an ultimate importance. For humankind to realize its identity with *Brahman,* for the Upaniṣadic formula of *tat tvam asi* to finally become complete in all aspects, morality cannot be ignored but is integral to the religious quest. Ethical acts fall within the realm of *māyā,* but for one to see one's identity with *Brahman,* there is no other way than a moral life diligently undertaken. Morality is a necessary ingredient, though not sufficient.

While many Western scholars of Radhakrishnan's thought - scholars such as Charles A Moore, A.N. Marlow, Lawrence Hyde, P.T. Raju and Edgar L. Hinman - offer no direct criticism of Radhakrishnan's interpretation of the doctrine of *māyā,* but are content to merely state his position in this regard, certain exceptions have been taken. A glaring example is by M.N. Roy in his article "Radhakrishnan in the Perspective of Indian Philosophy":

Radhakrishnan's idealism is not subjective; therefore, he is not confronted with the problem of solipsism. But the fallacy of Absolute Idealism is more formidable : the Absolute Being is Absolute Nothing. How could the phenemenal world of experience come out of nothing? Radhakrishnan evades the question by postulating an anthropomorphic God, and falling back upon Śaṁkarāchārya's subterfuge of the *Māyāvāda* - the world is an illusion, and as such a reality.[16]

Roy, like many other interpreters of Radhakrishnan, has no trouble in seeing him as a faithful interpreter of Śaṁkara and the Advaita Vedānta school; but he does not accept the doctrine of *māyā* as anything other than an attempt by a theologian to circumvent the dictates of logic.

> How do we discover this fundamental fact of metaphysics?, this conclusive notion about the unfoldment of the Absolute into the actual . . . . So the absolute reality is known, and its nature comprehended intuitively . . . . Nowhere except in the Hibbert Lectures has Radhakrishnan expounded a philosophy of his own. Even therein he is mainly preoccupied with finding fault with the modern naturalist and rationalist trends of thought. As a matter of fact, if he expounds any philosophy, it is admittedly the philosophy of religion; that is to say, theology, which tries to rationalize the belief in God . . . . Any doubt or dogma about the endlessness of the cognitive faculty of the human mind results only from the blind faith that reality, being spiritual, is inaccessible to it. If it is unknowable to the human mind, the philosopher, being also a human being, cannot have any idea about it. If philosophy is defined as the love of knowledge, then speculation about the *unknowable* evidently is not philosophy.[17]

Roy's charges against Radhakrishnan are that : (a) he is principally a theologian and not a philosopher, and (b) he has expounded no philosophy of his own, other than the philosophy of religion. These charges deserve to be commented upon. In *The Reign of Religion in Contemporary Philosophy*, Radhakrishnan states :

> Both religion and philosophy ask the why and wherefore of things. Both try to grasp the sum total of things and understand the good of it all. Yet, the end in view is different. While the salvation of the soul is the end of religion, the discovery of truth is the object of philosophy. Also the method of approval is different .... While philosophy is a product of thought and inquiry, religion turns to be a product of thought and fancy. Philosophy answers the problem of the whole by logic, while religion answers it by faith. Philosophy tries to interpret the meaning of things by the concepts of understanding while symbols which satisfy the heart are the field of religion. Religion happens to insist on mere authority .... The religious attitude suppresses the logical. It warms the heart but silences the mind. Philosophy arises out of the logical demands and aims at theoretical satisfaction. While the philosopher reasons and argues, the religious man believes and acts, lives and loves .... Religion, as it appeals to the emotions, has a large following which philosophy cannot hope to have.[18]

Thus, Radhakrishnan has clearly demarcated the respective boundaries of philosophy and religion. Throughout his writings his approach to the ultimate nature of the universe is the approach of the philosopher first and theologian second. Radhakrishnan has even charged Western philosophers with not being rigorous enough logicians. His recurring theme is that if we are consistently logical, then no matter what philosophical system we begin with we will end is absolute idealism. If this seems to be a theological conclusion as well as a philosophical one, it is because, Radhakrishnan continues,

> True philosophy will result in true religion, as ultimately there cannot be any conflict between faith and reason.... When we say that true religion and true philosophy will agree, we do not mean that the religious experience of the primitive savage and the totem worshipper will be acknowledged to be valid by the philosopher. We mean that the specialist in religion, the mystic with his experience, wisdom and insight will agree with the rational thinker. A religious system, though the terminus of philosophic study, should not be its governing influence. It does not augur well for the future of either religion or philosophy if religion becomes the starting-point and dominating motive of philosophy.[19]

For M.N. Roy to sustain his charge against Radhakrishnan, it must be demonstrated that Radhakrishnan himself has violated the rules of logical analysis in his enthusiasm to establish absolute idealism. And I believe that no serious interpreter of Radhakrishnan would so impugn him. If any mistakes of logical procedure have occurred - and what philosopher has been immune from this charge? - it was not through want of integrity or enthusiasm for logical rigor.

As for the charge that Radhakrishnan has expounded no philosophy of his own, other than the philosophy of religion, this charge is off-the-mark. Radhakrishnan was first and foremost a teacher of philosophy. As such, his universally acknowledged grasp of the principles of Indian and Western philosophical systems served him well. Radhakrishnan was a bridge-builder, an interpreter of India's philosophical heritage to the West and vice versa. His philosophical writings were largely concerned with trying to reconcile the seeming disparities among the world's philosophies and religions. He saw God as being One no matter what aspect of Him a particular religion empnasized. Radhakrishnan's strength lies in his compassion for people and his teaching that, on an ultimate level, no one is different from another but all are God's children. His constant theme was for understanding and cooperation among the world's diverse cultures and nations and an end to religious bigotry and persecution. He was primarily a philosopher of religion, it is perverse to fault him for not pursuing other areas of philosophy with the same vigour. His humanitarianism was consistent and deep-seated, and one can see that the shift to politics from academia was a natural transition for him. In the political arena, he could attempt to implement the humanitarian ideals he stood for as a philosopher/theologian.

While his social ideals were undoubtedly his strength as a man, they, unfortunately, were his weakness as a philosopher. His constant effort to show parallels among the world's philosophies and religions led him to force all religions into a similar mold even if a particular religion would not quite fit. The differences he ignored as minor were often major. For instance, his great desire to seek harmony between the Hindus and Muslims of India led him to construe the Hindu's *Brahman* as containing within itself (as Īśvara) the God of Islām, Judaism, and Christianity. This, of course, totally overlooked the fact that in these latter three religions there is seen a basic gulf between God and oneself that cannot be transcended. A human being may draw nearer and nearer to God, but one cannot be construed as God. *Tat tvam asi* is heretical to these relgions.

In Radhakrishnan's defense, an answer to this charge that would be consistent with his exposition is that the seeming heresy is confined to the world of *māyā*. If we but take a broader perspective, he might say, we will be forced to the conclusion that God as known by the mystics of Hinduism, Islām, Judaism, and Christianity is the same God. For Radhakrishnan, it is *māyā* and *avidyā* that lead us to posit a difference. Our religious quarrels are limited to the earthly realm, not the transcendental realm where all dualities are resolved. Of course, while this answer might be acceptable to those subscribing to Hindu religious/philosophical principles, it has not been acceptable to the followers of the Judeo, Christian, or Islāmic traditions.

There is, then, a basic difference in the Idealism of George Berkeley and Sarvepalli Radhakrishnan. Berkeley's Idealism preserves the distinction between God and man. The world is spiritual for Berkeley, but God's Spirit and human spirits are not the same entity. God is needed as the basic support of the universe to keep things from popping into and out of existence. He gives stability to the universe due to His omniscience and man's lack of it. Berkeley's form of Idealism - with its emphasis on the role of observer versus observed - has been termed Subjective Idealism, and also Theistic Idealism. Radhakrishnan's Idealism is not this. It all but ignores Berkeley's dictum of *esse est percipi* or *perciperi*. Rather, Radhakrishnan's Idealism has been said (by himself and others) to be that of Absolute Idealism. *Brahman* comprises all and is all. A person (Ātman) is not different from *Brahman* - not just not different, but identical to *Brahman*. Radhakrishnan sees no ultimate distinction between observer and observed but points to a realm in which all dualities are resolved - *Brahman*. For him, *māyā*, while not ultimately real, must be granted a degree of existence as it emanates from *Brahman*. While some Western philosophers may get up in arms over the concept of degrees of reality, Radhakrishnan had no such qualms.

And this is entirely with his goal as a writer. While all his writings are thoroughly researched and some of his writings are fairly formal - *An Idealist View of Life* being one of the more formal works - Radhakrishnan's main concern as a writer was to reach out to the educated public and instill a basic humanitarian respect for the views of others. As a result, his works often fail to satisfy the professional philosopher. But, given his overall Vedāntic viewpoint, his writings constitute an amazing effort to find the Unity underlying seemingly divergent positions.

For one who does not accept his basic premise that there is a Unity underlying the universe, he ultimately fails to establish it. But this is because the concept "Unity" is a primitive of his system. His efforts were directed towards exemplifying this presupposition and leasing out the absolutist implications of the major works of Western philosophy, not in constructing a rigorous proof. This, of course, is not entirely satisfactory. Sheer numbers of examples are irrelevant if the presupposition of Unity is itself, in its very nature, incapable of being known (i.e., verified) due to its metaphysical nature. Radhakrishnan's recourse to intuition, on this point, fails to satisfy the demands of contemporary Western philosophy. However, he did yeoman service in bringing the world's attention to Indian philosophy; and it has been for later philosophers (East and West) to continue the argument and establish that there is philosophical enterprise (in the Western sense) within the Indian *darśanas*.

Berkeley is important primarily as a philosopher. He clearly set forth the position known as Subjective Idealism, and all subsequent Idealist philosophers (of whatever school in the Western tradition) have subscribed in one form or another to his dictum *esse est percipi* or *perciperi*. However, as a theologian, his views were quite conventional. He apparently had no interest in religions other than Christianity, and his philosophical writings were designed for the ultimate purpose of defeating atheistic materialism and securely establishing God as the pivot of the universe. This being done, he felt that religion, i.e, Christianity, would be secure from its detractors.

Radhakrishnan is important primarily as a philosopher of religion. His humanitarian ideals and his quest to bridge the gap between the world's diverse religions place him in the ranks of the great teachers of religion. He carried the intellectual aspects of the Hindu reform movement beyond the geographical boundaries of India and helped to open the doors of the West to the Indian philosophical systems. As these systems combine both philosophical and religious thought within themselves, so did the works of Radhakrishnan their expounder.

Bibliography

Arapura, J.G. *Radhakrishnan and Integral Experience.* Bombay : 1966.

Berkeley, George. *Three Dialogues Between Hylas and Philonous.* Colin M. Turbayne, Editor. New York : The Liberal Arts Press, Inc., 1954.
The Principles of Human Knoweldge. G.J. Warnock, Edictor. Glasgow : William Collins Sons & Co., Ltd., 1981.

Diwakar, Dr. R.R. and Munshi, Dr. K.M. General Editors. *Radhakrishnan Reader : An Anthology.* Bombay : Bharatiya Vidya Bhavan, 1969.

Dutt, K. Iswara. General Editor, *Sarvepalli Radhakrishnan.* New Delhi : Popular Book Services, 1966.

Ewing, A.C. *The Idealist Tradition : From Berkeley to Blanshard.* Glance, Illinois : The Free Press, 1957.

Hopkins, Thomas, J. *The Hindu Religious Tradition.* Encino, Calif : Dickenson Publishing Company, Inc., 1971.

Inge, W.R. ; Jacks, L.P.; Hiriyanna, M.; Burtt, E.A. and Raju, P.T. Editors. *Radhakrishnan : Comparative Studies in Philosophy Presented in Honour of His Sixtieth Birthday.* London : George Allen and Unwin, Ltd., 1951.

Locke, John. *An Essay Concerning Human Understanding.* Woozley, A.D. Editor. Glasgow : Wm. Collins Sons & Co. Ltd., 1980.

McDermott, Robert A. Editor. *Basic Writings of S. Radhakrishnan.* Bombay : Jaico Publishing House, 1981. *Radhakrishnan : Selected Writings on Philosopy, Religion, and Culture.* New York : E.P. Dutton, 1970.

Moore, Charles A. and Radhakrishnan, Sarvepalli. Editors. *A Source Book in Indian Philosophy.* New Jersey : Princeton University Press, 1967.

Moore, G.E. *Philosophical Studies.* London : Routledge & Kegan Paul Ltd., 1965.

Radhakrishnan, Sir Sarvepalli. *An Idealist View of Life.* Bombay : George Allen & Unwin (India) Private Ltd., 1976. *Eastern Religions and Western Thought.* New Delhi : Oxford University Press, 1982. *Faith Renewed.* Delhi : Hind Pocket Books (Pvt.) Ltd., 1979. *Philosophy Eastern and Western, Volumes I and II.* London : George Allen & Unwin Ltd., 1953. *Our Heritage.* Delhi : Orient Paperbacks, 1976. *Religion and Culture.* Delhi : Orient Paperbacks, 1968. *The Hindu View of Life.* London : Unwin Paperbacks, 1980. *The Reign of Religion in Contemporary Philosophy.* London : MacMillan and Co. Ltd., 1920. *Towards a New World.* Delhi : Orient Paperbacks, 1980.

Schilpp, Paul Arthur. *The Philosophy of Sarvepalli Radhakrishnan.* New York : Tudor Publishing Company, 1952.

Singh, Dr. Har Nagendra. *Contribution of Sarvepalli Radhakrishnan.* New York : Tudor Publishing Company, 1952.

Srivastava, Ripusudan Prasad. *Contemporary Indian Idealism.* Delhi : Motilal Banarsidass, 1973.

References

1. Berkeley, *Three Dialogues Between Hylas and Philonous,* p. ix.
2. Berkeley, *The Principles of Human Knowledge,* p. 99.
3. *Ibid.,* p. 68.

4. Moore, *Philosophical Studies* ("The Refutation of Idealism"), pp. 3-6.
5. Diwakar and Munshi, *Radhakrishnan Reader*, p. 460.
6. Hopkins, *The Hindu Religious Tradition*, p. 134.
7. Diwakar and Munshi, Radhakrishnan Reader p. 5.
8. Radhakrishnan, *The Reign of Religion in Contemporary Philosophy*, p. vii.
9. Radhakrishnan, *An Idealist View of Life*, p. 9.
10. McDermott, *Radhakrishnan : Selected Writings on Philosophy, Religion and Culture*, p. 141.
11. Radhakrishnan, *The Reign of Religion in Contemporary Philosophy*, pp. 4-6.
12. Srivastava, *Contemporary Indian Idealism*, p. 5.
13. McDermott, *Basic Writings of S. Radhakrishnan*, p. 19.
14. Schilpp, *The Philosophy of Sarvepalli Radhakrishnan*, p. 803.
15. Radhakrishnan, *Eastern Religions and Western Thought*, pp. 86-87.
16. Schilpp, p. 545.
17. *Ibid.*, pp. 546-547.
18. Radhakrishnan, *The Reign of Religion in Contemporary Philosophy*, pp. 4-6.
19. *Ibid.*, pp. 22-23.

30
The Mystery of Creation in the Thought of Radhakrishnan and Sri Aurobindo

ROBERT M. KLEINMAN
Pensacola Junior College

1. Introduction

A serious consideration of the mystery of creation presupposes a realistic attitude toward the world. For it is only when we take the world to be real that the problem of creation acquires its compelling significance. Today, scientific cosmology has led many scientists to re-open the question of a beginning of the universe. A pressing need has surfaced to find some way of accurately determining the initial conditions of the present world-order.[1] But the idea of a cosmic beginning is not identical with "creation" in a deeper metaphysical sense. The concept of creation has been the perennial concern of theists, who wish to account for the existence of the universe in terms of a primordial creative act of a personal God. The Indian tradition, however, has been decidedly ambivalent about this question. On the one hand, it recognizes the transcendent character of ultimate reality, while on the other, there has been a persistent tendency to regard the world as less than fully real, if not an outright illusion. Although modern interpreters down-play the idea of the unreality of the world, it is undeniable that emphasis on the pure transcendence of the Absolute has encouraged a negative attitude toward the future prospects of life in this world. Hence, since the time of the Upaniṣads, the major preoccupation has been with ways of liberating the soul from the tribulations of worldly existence, rather than with the primal mystery of creation. There is a certain justification for this neglect, if creation is considered to be an event which lies in the remote past, without any continuation throughout the course of time. But, if this world is viewed as the result of the activity of an eternal reality which transcends time altogether, the situation becomes quite different. In this case, there is not only the possibility of a constant recurrence of worlds in a never-ending succession of cosmic cycles, but it is even possible that the universe itself is, or could become, an eternal expression of the nature of the Absolute.

The thoughts of Radhakrishnan and Sri Aurobindo bear directly on this topic. Since both of them clearly affirm the reality of the world in relation to a transcendent Absolute, the mystery of creation takes on special significance for them. Both men incorporate the concept of evolution into their ideas about creation. Creation is not viewed as a completed act, but as an on-going process through which the Absolute is progressively realizing itself under the conditions of space and time. Radhakrishnan is close to Advaita Vedānta in maintaining that the origin of the world is ultimately an insoluble mystery which is locked away in the inscrutable depths of *māyā*. In working out the details of his position, he contributes a number of fresh insights into the nature of creation and the relation between God and the Absolute. But the mystery is only darkly illumined by the philosophic mind, and seems to require the more intuitive perception of a master poet. Sri Aurobindo, who was both poet and yogin, sought to enter more deeply into the heart of creation in order to discover the secret he believed to be concealed within it. While recognizing the limitations of the mind in pursuing such an inquiry, he developed the wealth of his spiritual experience to offer an original picture of cosmic existence. But, even though there are significant differences in the ways that Radhakrishnan and Sri Aurobindo elucidate the problem of creation, both conceive creation as the release (*sṛṣṭi*) of pre-existent potencies in the Absolute, rather than an evocation of the world from absolute nothingness. In addition, they agree that the world is real and that evolution is proceeding toward higher levels of spirituality.

II. Radhakrishnan's Idealistic Philosophy of the Spirit

Radhakrishnan's philosophy can be characterized as a version of absolute idealism in which the universe is considered to have an ultimate purpose and meaning.[2] Brahman, the supreme spiritual reality, is the logical ground of the universe, but transcends everything finite. At the same time, Brahman reveals itself in the world and represents the inner unity of all things. The multiplicity of the universe does not affect the essential oneness of Brahman, which remains unsullied by the fluctuations of the world-process. Brahman is the Absolute, and is conceived by Radhakrishnan as "pure consciousness and pure freedom and infinite possibility."[3] Creation is the act of manifesting this universe out of the infinite number of possible worlds available to the Absolute. Thus it is a free act of the supreme consciousness, and the existence of the world is in no way essential to the Absolute. Radhakrishnan is at great pains to maintain the freedom of the creative act, in order to avoid any suggestion of pantheistic emanationism. The universe is a limited manifestation of the Spirit, which is eternally perfect and beyond all of its finite expressions. Because of its wholly transcendent character, the Absolute cannot be fully comprehended by the human mind. Although the universe is a phenomenal reality, its relationship to the Absolute is incomprehensible. But, in order to bridge the gap between them, Radhakrishnan introduces the concept of God as the creator.

God is identified as the Absolute engaged in the act of creation. Since the Absolute itself is beyond all ontological relationships, the idea of God must be employed. The orderliness of the world requires an explanation in terms of a supreme creative principle. Thus, from the standpoint of creation, the Absolute is conceived as God. Radhakrishnan's God has relations with the universe, but the latter falls short of the unchangeable perfection of absolute being.[4] God is viewed as possessing the usual attributes of wisdom, love and goodness, and these, in turn, give direction to the world-process. Evolution is the means by which higher grades of reality emerge in the course of time. There is a progressive march of the world through various phases from matter upward to life and mind. A future culmination of this process is anticipated, when the entire world becomes spiritualized. Radhakrishnan suggests that this will represent the complete identification of God and the universe; then God fades into the Absolute, and time ceases to be.[5] But the crucial question concerns how this cosmic process can be reconciled with the original conception of a transcendent and totally free Absolute. Can a rational account be given of the act of creation itself?

The Indian tradition supplies certain hints on how to deal with this question, and Radhakrishnan exploits them fully. He grants that there is no answer for the "why" of creation. The Absolute is so utterly transcendent that no reason can be offered for the existence of this particular universe. Creation is conceived as the *līlā* (joyful play) of the Absolute. For there is an *ānanda*, or pure joy, in the play of the possibilities out of which the world emerges. The Absolute grows into a world because it is its nature to do so; there is no conscious purpose involved in the process. But its freedom is not denied, since there are an infinite number of possible worlds which could have been chosen. Why our universe was the one selected by God for manifestation remains an eternal mystery. The power by which the universe is brought out of the Absolute is identified as *māyā*.[6] Drawing on an earlier meaning of the term, traceable to the Vedas, Radhakrishnan associates *māyā* with the power of God to focus the infinite realm of possibilities on the creation of this unique world. The operation of *māyā* remains an impenetrable secret of the Absolute, but in no way suggests that the world is an illusion. The world as *māyā* is unreal only in the sense that it lacks the full reality of the Absolute.[7] It will be seen later that this marks a fundamental difference between Radhakrishnan and Sri Aurobindo. But, in a manner which is reminiscent of Advaita Vedānta, we are left with an inexplicable mystery concerning the wherewithal of creation.

III. Sri Aurobindo's Integral Vision of Reality

Like Radhakrishnan, Sri Aurobindo recognizes the utter transcendence of the Absolute, but he makes a more sustained attempt to penetrate the obscurity surrounding the creative process. He also maintains that the existence of the Absolute is fully consistent with the reality of the world. There is some difference, however, in the way that he conceives the relation between them. The eternal nature of the Absolute is identified as Saccidananda; it is an integral union of Existence, Consciousness and Bliss, each of which possesses a distinct truth of its own as well as being an aspect of a single Absolute.[8] The Consciousness of this supreme trinity is a creative Force (*śakti*) through which worlds can be manifested. Together, *sat* and *cit-śakti* account for being and becoming as two inseparable aspects of the one Reality, and *ānanda* is the essential self-delight of the Absolute expressed in the multifarious display of its teeming possibilities.

Sri Aurobindo argues that the order and lawfulness of the universe suggests, even to our partial and limited mental view, that the material world possesses profound value and significance. This is because the work of the Absolute is guided by a supreme power of Knowledge, the Supermind, or divine Truth-Consciousness.[9] Supermind has complete Knowledge of the unity of Saccidananda, and constitutes the necessary link between this world and the Absolute. It is always conscious of the integral reality of the spirit, but also has the capacity to make differentiations within the primal unity. These differentiations eventuate in the creation of the universe through the agency of the Overmind, a transitional power by which Supermind acts indirectly on the evolving world. First *sat* emerges as matter, then *cit* as life, *ānanda* as psyche, and Supermind (*vijñāna*) as mind. The direct manifestation of Supermind itself will depend on the world's receptivity to supramental transformation.

The process of creation is described by Sri Aurobindo as a "plunge into Ignorance" in which the Absolute veils from itself its true nature.[10] Ignorance is not identified with the absence of knowledge, but is a form of incomplete knowledge. It represents the power of divine consciousness to partially withhold itself, and is not to be construed as a deficiency within the Absolute. There is no primal ignorance in the Absolute, but what is called ignorance can be a means of cosmic manifestation. Creation is viewed as an initial concealment of Saccidananda in an apparently inert consciousness followed by a long evolutionary progress of self-discovery.[11] The stages of this movement are marked by the successive emergence of matter, life, mind, and eventually even Supermind, on this earth. Evolution of the spirit can proceed beyond Supermind, and no cessation of the process of creation need be envisioned. Like Radhakrishnan, however, Sri Aurobindo must deal with the question of the "why" of creation, and he also employs the traditional Indian concepts of *līlā* and *māyā*.

We are faced here with the question of why the Absolute should choose to create a world out of ignorance. Since the creative process is characterized as *līlā*, there is no compulsion to do so. But there are various kinds of *līlā*, and even though there is no external law governing the creative process, this in itself does not preclude the utilization of a purpose in creation. Play is intrinsically an expression of delight, and the greatest delight lies in an orderly and purposive display of latent possibilities.[12] The Absolute could not be denied the capacity for the realization of all of its powers in an evolutionary world based on matter. The process presupposes a graded involution of Saccidananda into nescience, after which its powers reveal themselves in sequential order. Ignorance is the condition which prevails between the original state of nescience and the full manifestation of divine consciousness. Throughout the entire process, Saccidananda is present in the world, but is partially hidden behind the scenes. For Sri Aurobindo, the world is not a mixture of the real and the unreal; its evolutionary movement is not from lower to higher grades of reality, but from self-concealment to self-revelation of the one ever-present Reality. The term *māyā* refers to the Absolute's power to conceal itself, and does not imply partial unreality or illusion. If used in a negative way, it simply designates the fact that the world is not the essential truth of the Absolute.[13]

IV. Concluding Remarks : Different Interpretations of the Ṛg Veda

In conclusion, we may briefly consider how the divergence between Radhakrishnan and Sri Aurobindo, concerning the nature of creation is rooted in their understanding of the Indian tradition. I think that this can be discerned in the different interpretations they give to the significance of the Ṛg Veda. Radhakrishnan sees in the Vedic hymns a succession of stages from primitive nature worship to the first stirrings of philosophic speculation.[14] A transitional phase between these two stages is monotheism, which, from the Indian standpoint, is not antithetical to polytheism. Both forms of theism are taken up and reconciled in the later development of monism. Radhakrishnan applies this view, for example, to the famous "Hymn of Creation" (*R.V.* 10.129), which he considers to represent a late phase of the transition from Vedic theism to Upaniṣadic monism. The key term in this hymn is *tapas*, which conveys the image of a cosmic creative fire by which That One emerges from the dark primordial ocean. Radhakrishnan considers this to be a quasi-mythic precursor of the later, more abstract, approach of Vedānta philosophy.[15]

Sri Aurobindo, however, interprets the Vedas differently, For him, the Vedic hymns embody a secret meaning known only to the poet-seers (*kavis*) who composed them. The more external aspect of the hymns as descriptions of natural phenomena was meant only for those who had not undergone the spiritual discipline necessary to understand their esoteric significance.[16] A composition like the "Hymn of Creation" does not indicate a late development in the progress of primitive thought, but expresses a view of reality which is fully consistent with the Vedic vision as a whole. He defines *tapas* as "concentration of power of consciousness,"[17] and explains it as the turning of consciousness inward upon itself in order to generate the energy necessary for the creation of the universe. The Absolute, through *tapas*, initially constricts itself, and then unfolds as the world. Sri Aurobindo's understanding of *tapas* is consonant with the practise of certain forms of yoga, and suggests that the Vedic ṛṣis employed some kind of spiritual discipline in composing their hymns.[18] By analogy, they viewed cosmic creation as a process involving intense concentration which releases the hidden potencies of That One. Since That One brings everything out of itself in the absence of any other reality on which it could draw, the cosmic creative process is not a mimetic one, but an original expression of the essential power (*śakti*) of the Absolute.

This interpretation of *tapas* has an uncanny resemblance to the contemporary scientific picture of the universe emerging from a stupendous primeval fireball. Of course, there are a number of intermediate stages between spirit and matter, but, whatever the validity of scientific cosmology may turn out to be, it has certainly demonstrated the unimaginable might of the forces that have shaped the universe. It is extremely unlikely that such an immense display of energy is the insignificant by-product of an unconscious force, let alone an illusory appearance of an uninvolved Absolute. Moreover, a careful scrutiny of the principle of an evolutionary Will at work in the cosmos might prove to be sufficient for the explanation of its known physical properties.[19] As we have seen, Radhakrishnan and Sri Aurobindo both reject interpretations which portray the universe as a meaningless process. But, whereas Radhakrishnan sees the evolving world as both real and unreal, and creation as ultimately inexplicable, Sri Aurobindo finds that, in a higher supramental sense, there is no unreality as such and creation is fully comprehensible. Its purpose is to manifest all of the powers of the Absolute by an evolution of spirit in matter, and the way in which this is carried out is by *tapas*, an action of the Consciousness-Force (*cit-śakti*) of Saccidananda.

References

1. A variety of approaches to this problem are exhibited in contemporary scientific cosmology : see S.W. Hawking, *A Brief History of Time : From the Big Bang to Black Holes* (New York : Bantam Books, 1988); H. Pagels, *Perfect Symmetry : The*

Search for the Beginning of Time (Simon & Schuster, 1985); J. Silk, *The Big Bang* (San Francisco : W.H. Freeman, 1980); J.S. Trefil, *The Moment of Creation* (New York : MacMillan, 1983); S. Weinberg, *The First Three Minutes : A Modern View of the Origin of the Universe* (New York : Basic Books, 1977).

2. S. Radhakrishnan, *An Idealist View of Life* (London : George Allen & Unwin, 1937), p.10.

3. *Ibid.*, p. 272.

4. S. Radhakrishnan, "The Spirit of Man" in *Contemporary Indian Philosophy*, ed. S. Radhakrishnan and J.H. Muirhead, 3rd ed. (London : Allen & Unwin, 1966), pp. 498-499; P.A. Schilpp (ed.), *The Philosophy of Sarvepalli Radhakrishnan* (New York : Tudor, 1952), pp. 39-42, 44.

5. Radhakrishnan, "The Spirit of Man," p. 500.

6. References to Radhakrishnan's view of *māyā* are scattered throughout his works. See especially : *Indian Philosophy* (New York : MacMillan, 1923); *The Hindu View of Life* (New York : MacMillan, 1969); *Eastern Religions and Western Thought* (Oxford : Oxford University Press, 1939). An important summing up of his position is given by Radhakrishnan himself in P.A. Schilpp (ed.), *The Philosophy of Sarvepalli Radhakrishnan*, pp. 800-802. A concise summary of the main points can be found in V.S. Naravane, *Modern Indian Thought* (Bombay : Asia Publishing House, 1964), pp. 247-249.

7. S. Radhakrishnan, "The Spirit of Man," p. 499.

8. *In the Life Divine*, the Sanskrit term *Saccidānanda* is transliterated as "Sachchidananda," and characterized as the original "self-form" (*svarūpa*) of the Absolute. See Sri Aurobindo, *The Life Divine* (New York : E.P. Dutton & Co., 1949), pp. 142, 290-91. Also in the *Sri Aurobindo Birth Centenary Library* (Pondicherry : Sri Aurobindo Ashram Trust, 1973), Vol. 18, pp. 152, 320-321. Hereafter referred to as SABCL.

9. The Supermind plays a central role in Sri Aurobindo's conception of creation. See particularly *The Life Divine*, BK, I, chs. XIV-XVI; Also in SABCL, Vol. 18.

10. *Ibid.*, p. 147; SABCL, Vol. 18, p. 158.
11. *Ibid.*, pp. 526-527; SABCL, Vol. 18, pp. 591-592.
12. *Ibid.*, pp. 369-370, SABCL, Vol. 18, pp. 410-411.
13. *Ibid.*, pp. 95-96; SABCL, Vol. 18, pp. 101-102.
14. S. Radhakrishnan, *Indian Philosophy*, Vol. 1, pp. 68-72.
15. *Ibid.*, pp. 100-102.
16. Sri Aurobindo, *The Secret of the Veda*, SABCL, Vol. 10, pp. 5-6.
17. Sri Aurobindo, *The Life Divine*, p. 511; SABCL, Vol. 18, p. 573.
18. It is interesting to observe that some corroboration of this approach to the Vedas has appeared recently in the writings of the Vedic scholar Jeanine Miller. See J. Miller, *The Vision of Cosmic Order in the Vedas* (London : Routledge & Kegan Paul, 1985). See also an earlier work by G. Feuerstein and J. Miller, *A Reappraisal of Yoga* (London : Rider & Company, 1971), especially chs. 2, 3 and 6.
19. Debate in recent scientific cosmology has focused on the question concerning the properties that the universe must have in order to support life as we know it. A number of remarkable concidences have been discovered between the values of the fundamental physical constants which make life on earth possible. These constants link human existence to the universe in rigorous network of interdependencies. If we ask why just the right values for sustaining life exist in our universe, science cannot as yet provide a definitive answer. The presumption is that the laws of physics will eventually explain things, but why does a specific set of laws prevail? The probiem seems to demand a metaphysical solution. See, e.g., P.C.W. Davies, *The Accidental Universe* (Cambridge : Cambridge University Press, 1982); J.D. Barrow and F.J. Tipler, *The Anthropic Cosmological Principle* (Oxford : Oxford University Press, 1986). For a good critical estimate of the present situation in cosmology, see M.K. Munitz, *Cosmic Understanding : Philosophy and Science of the Universe* (Princeton : Princeton University Press, 1986), especially ch. 7.

31
The Problem of Evil in Radhakrishnan and Aurobindo

Kevin Sullivan
University of Ottawa

The problem of evil in the form of human pain and suffering has confounded numerous thinkers, East and West. It has been particularly acute for those who have accepted an ultimate ground of being and value. In Western thought the problem has been why an all-powerful, all-knowing and completely benevolent God allows evil and suffering to exist? The traditional answers given have attempted to circumvent the issue by either denying the reality of evil altogether or refuting the omnipotence, omniscience or goodness of God. For Radhakrishnan and Aurobindo this specific problem of evil arises because of a false notion of a personal extra-cosmic deity who is responsible for creating a universe filled with suffering and pain. If however one holds to the idea of an integral Absolute, where the universe is seen to be a concrete manifestation of God rather than a creation *ex nihilo*, then the question significantly alters : it is not why God allows evil to exist in the world but why he allows evil to exist in himself? This paper, then, aims to show how Radhakrishnan's and Aurobindo's conception of an integral

Absolute underpins their views concerning the instrumentality and transcendence of evil, and how each of their positions conforms to what has been called a "harmony theodicy."[1]

Instrumentality of Evil

Since Radhakrishnan and Aurobindo believe there is nothing but Brahman who is the supreme reality, the phenomenon of evil must ultimately be traced to Brahman's integral nature. Brahman, according to each thinker, is both transcendent and immanent, and is said to have two aspects: the *Nirguna* Brahman or Brahman without qualities, and the *Saguna* Brahman or Brahman with qualities. The *Nirguna* Brahman, or what Aurobindo calls the *Paratpara* Brahman (the Brahman beyond the beyond), is the Absolute-in-itself whose transcendence defies all human characterizations, whereas the *Saguna* Brahman represents the free, creative power of the Absolute which partially express itself in and through the finite world of space and time, and acts as the foundation for the whole cosmic process.

This *Nirguna-Saguna* distinction casts a double perspective on the problem of evil. From the standpoint of *Nirguna* Brahman there is no problem since it is beyond all dualities including good and evil. It is thus only from the perspective of *Saguna* Brahman, or the Brahman-in-relation-to-the-world, that the problem of evil arises. This is because Brahman manifests itself as a world only for the sheer joy of it and so there appears to be a contradiction between *Saguna* Brahman's pure joy or bliss on the one hand, and the existence of human pain and suffering on the other. The specific problem facing Radhakrishnan and Aurobindo then is to explain how suffering and bliss can be made compatible.

Each thinker attempts to reconcile these two concepts by relating the idea of bliss (*ananda*) to that of *līlā* or play.

From the perspective of *Nirguna* Brahman, self-manifestation occurs out of playful joy or self-delight and for no other reason. In this sense creation remains a mystery. But from the standpoint of *Saguna* Brahman this playful joy is not entirely meaningless. Indeed, Radhakrishnan insists "the analogy (*līlā*) is not intended to suggest that the universe is a meaningless show made in jest,"[2] while Aurobindo believes there must be some "ultimate significance of the divine play, the *līlā*."[3] What this suggests is that *Saguna* Brahman's play is teleological for it works towards a particular goal.

But what is this goal? Simply, to freely fall into limitation and disharmony and return again to blissful unity. In other words, *Saguna* Brahman deliberately conceals itself in the form of multiplicity for the sole purpose of delightfully rediscovering its true, divine nature. Thus by manifesting itself as a finite world *Saguna* Brahman initially experiences bliss in its limited forms of pleasure, pain and indifference, but eventually regathers and reaffirms its own completeness. All this is clear when Radhakrishnan says : "The highest product of cosmic evolution, ānanda or spiritual freedom, must also be the hidden principle at work, slowly disclosing itself. Spirit creates the world and controls its history by a process of perpetual incarnation. Spirit is working in matter that matter may serve the Spirit."[4] It is also evident in Aurobindo's remark that "the possibility worked out here in the universe of which we are a part, begins from the concealment of Saccidananda in that which seems to be its opposite and its self-finding even amid the terms of that opposite."[5]

What this suggests is that for both Radhakrishnan and Aurobindo evil has a positive role to play in *Saguna* Brahman's journey of self-rediscovery. "Suffering," in Radhakrishnan's words, "is not punishment but the prize of fellowship. It is an essential accompaniment of all creative endeavour."[6] Similarly for Aurobindo, "the appearance of these contrary phenomena (of evil)" must have "some significance, some function .... in the economy of the universe."[7] In my opinion this bears resemblance to a harmony theodicy whereby evil is shown to be instrumental to the emergence of a greater good or harmony. More specifically, it is similar to a "vale of soul-making" theodicy where evil is deemed necessary for the achievement of a perfected existence that is God's ultimate goal for humanity.[8] The important difference is that for Radhakrishnan and Aurobindo it is not just the individual soul that is struggling towards divine life but the entire cosmos. It would thus be more accurate to say that their's is a "vale of divine world-making" theodicy.

But what are the details of this kind of theodicy? How do Radhakrishnan and Aurobindo explain and justify the existence of evil in reference to the greater harmony to be achieved?

They do this, in short, by showing how human pain and suffering are simply a phase in the evolutionary ascent towards divine life. For Radhakrishnan evolution begins with matter and then proceeds to life and mind. At the level of mind self-consciousness develops in human beings and with it the perception of dualities. By distinguishing itself form other things the individual ego falls subject to ignorance (*avidya*) and believes itself to be separate and independent. This in turn gives rise to selfish desire whereby the ego becomes obsessively attached to things in the world. Ignorance and selfish desire then, in Radhakrishnan's words, are "two phases of one phenomenon" which lead to "evil and suffering."[9] Evil, however, has a positive use for Radhakrishnan because it helps the individual to grow and to develop spiritual values. He in fact refers approvingly to Keat's letter on "soul-making" and states : "If the purpose of human life is the shaping of human souls through conflict with evil and pain and conquest over uncertainty and scepticism, this world is not ill adapted for that purpose."[10]

Like Radhakrishnan, Aurobindo sees evil as arising from the evolutionary process but documents this in much greater and profounder detail. The end point of *Saguna* Bahman's involution is what Aurobindo terms the "inconscience.' The inconscience is a totally indeterminate and self-absorbed state where *Saguna* Brahman almost loses all consciousness of itself. The divine Śakti however is still at work seeking to push the movement upwards towards the light of the Supermind.[11] This movement first appears on the level of matter as a subconscient material force or energy, and then at the level of life as the desire soul or will-to-life. Eventually at the level of mind the striving takes the form of the ego which consists of physical, vital and mental elements. The ego takes an aggressive stance, as Aurobindo explains, because "It has a difficult task in pulling itself out of . . . . the inconscience."[12] And it is precisely this conflictual struggle between the downward movement of the inconscience and the upward movement of the ego that causes human pain and suffering to occur. The instrumentality of evil then lies in facilitating the pull out of the inconscience towards the higher levels of being. That is why "all evil," in Aurobindo's view, "is in travail of the eternal good."[13]

We are now in a position to see how Radhakrishnan and Aurobindo answer the question posed at the beginning of the paper, namely, why does *Saguna* Brahman allow evil and suffering to exist in itself? The reason is that by experiencing those things that are seemingly opposite to itself (i.e. discord, pain), *Saguna* Brahman is able to rediscover and reaffirm its own divine completeness and the ultimate value of its possibilities. Bliss and suffering wherefore are reconciled because *Saguna* Brahman's delightful play of self-manifestation has the purpose of achieving a greater good or harmony (at least from its own perspective and that of individual souls) which evil helps in establishing.

A serious problem, however, emerges at this point. If bliss and suffering are made compatible because there is a purpose to *Saguna* Brahman's self-manifestation, how do they reconcile the idea of purpose with playful joy? Does not the idea of *līlā* suggest an action that is wholly spontaneous and without purpose, something done for the sheer joy of it and nothing else? How can Radhakrishnan and Aurobindo bring these two seemingly incompatible concepts together?

They accomplish this by positing various levels of being or like principles within the integral Absolute. As mentioned earlier, both Radhakrishnan and Aurobindo believe the Absolute to be transcendent and immanent. From its completely transcendent side, the *Nirguna* Brahman, there is only free play, no purpose. But from the immanent side, called *Saguna* Brahman, there is both play and purpose. This is because the *Saguna* is linked to the transcendence of the *Nirguna* on the one hand, and to the meaningful cosmic process on the other. This does not mean there are two ontological principles, the *Nirguna* and the *Saguna*; there is just one integral Absolute which has a transcendent and immanent side. Since the highest conception we can have of this Absolute is as *Saguna* Brahman, we see its play as being inherently meaningful. It is analogous to a game of chess where there is both the sheer thrill of the game itself along with the prescribed goal of checkmating your opponent's king.[14]

There is a further connecting link between the *Saguna* Brahman and the world which is the World Spirit or Supermind. From its perspective there is only purpose since it is responsible for guiding the specific manifestation. Finally, there is the soul or psyche which goes through the evolutionary process by a series of rebirths and so acts as a link between the cosmic purpose and the individual.

Transcendence of Evil

But not only does the idea of levels or link principles help reconcile the notions of cosmic purpose and play; it also explains how evil can be overcome. Unlike some dualistic systems, such as Zoroastrianism, Radhakrishnan and Aurobindo do not see evil as a permanent feature of the world. It can, in short, be transcended. Both believe evil can be transcended by a combination of self-effort and God's grace. Through different yogic and meditative practises the disciple prepares the way to receive the divine grace and love. *Saguna* Brahman is thus pushing and pulling the aspirant towards higher grades of being. This is possible because of the integral nature of the Absolute which is both transcendent and immanent. What happens is that the Absolute, in containing an infinite number of possibilities, possesses an active power - what Radhakrishnan calls *Īśvara* or God, Aurobindo the divine *Śakti* or Mother - which freely selects one of these possibilities and actualizes it as a world. The specific manifestation, however, is carried out by what Radhakrishnan terms the "World Spirit" (*Hiranyagarbha*) and Aurobindo the "Supermind." These, as previously noted, act as link principles connecting the Infinite One to the finite many. They guide and control the expression of one possibility in *Saguna* Brahman (God) and for this reason must possess the transcendent unity of *Saguna* Brahman as well as the capacity to manifest its potential multiplicity. They must, in other words, contain the two inseparable elements of knowledge and power, *Śiva* and *Śakti*.

This process of involution forms the basis for the evolutionary ascent towards divine life. As a result, both Radhakrishnan and Aurobindo posit principles which explain how the lower levels are taken up and integrated into the higher levels. For Radhakrishnan this takes the form of a Hegelian type dialectic where "evil, error and ugliness . . . are transmuted into their opposites through a gradual process."[15] This process is not predetermined but expresses real novelty. Opposites are raised up into an integral unity of identity-in-difference.

Aurobindo makes this even more explicit with his idea of the "logic of the Infinite." Here matter, life, and mind are not so much superseded as they are transformed or divinized. What thus seems contradictory at a lower level is no longer contradictory at a higher-level due to a dialectical process of widening, heightening, and integration. But complete transformation, according to each thinker, can only take place when *Īśvara* or the Mother descends into the lower spheres to raise them to higher levels. Thus the presence of pain and suffering do not contradict the divine bliss because it is simply God's way of experiencing a world of ignorance and limitation. In this way evil actually points to bliss and will be transcended when ignorance is transformed into integral knowledge and the world divinized.

The transcendence of evil, so Radhakrishnan and Aurobindo claim, results in individual and cosmic liberation (*mokṣa*). The divinization of individual life produces what Radhakrishnan terms "*jivanmuktas*" and Aurobindo "gnostic beings" who are "beyond good and evil." This means they are no longer subject to moral conventions because their will is united with the divine goodness.

The whole cosmos too becomes divinized, a state Radhakrishnan refers to as the "*Brahmaloka*" or the "Kingdom of God," and Aurobindo the "gnostic supernature." Radhakrishnan, however, sometimes writes as if the *Brahmaloka* simply consists of a community of liberated souls rather than a terrestrial transformation. But he also insists that the *Brahmaloka* involves the "transfiguration of the cosmos" where "cosmic existence lapses into Absolute Being."[16] It is this idea of a divinized cosmos, I think, that sets Radhakrishnan and Aurobindo apart from other thinkers, East and West, (with the possible exception of Teilhard de

Chardin), and reveals their unique contribution to soteriology.

Thus Radhakrishnan and Aurobindo attempt to solve the problem of evil by putting in the context of Brahman's integral and dynamic nature. Brahman allows evil to exist in himself because he is engaged in a meaningful play of self-concealment and self-disclosure with evil facilitating the movement from the one to the other.

References

1. For a good description of harmony theodicy see *Exploring the Philosophy of Religion*, D. Stewart, Engelwood Cliffs : Prentice-Hall, 1980, p. 250.
2. *Eastern Religions and Western Thought.* Oxford : Oxford University Press, 1940, p. 93.
3. *The Life Divine.* New York : Indian Library Society, 1965, p. 349.
4. "Fragments of a Confession," in *The Philosophy of Sarvepalli Radhakrishnan*, P.A. Schilpp (ed.), New York : Tudor Publ., 1952, p. 31.
5. *The Life Divine*, p. 103.
6. *East and West in Religion.* London : George Allen and Unwin Ltd., 1933, p. 121.
7. *The Life Divine*, p. 6.
8. In his article "The Central Argument of Aurobindo's *The Life Divine*," Stephen Phillips claims "Aurobindo's view of the instrumentality of evil is in many respects close to various Romantic or 'soul-making' theodicies." See *Philosophy East and West*, 35, No. 3, (July 1985), p. 283.
9. *Eastern Religions and Western Thought*, p. 95.
10. *Recovery of Faith.* London : George Allen and Unwin Ltd., 1956, p. 87.

11. For a description of the Supermind see chapter XIV of *The Life Divine*, pp. 114-22.
12. *The Life Divine*, p. 767.
13. *Ibid.*, p. 366.
14. I am indebted to Professor Robert M. Kleinman of Pensacola Junior College for suggesting this analogy.
15. *An Idealist View of Life*. London : Unwin Books, 1961, p. 264.
16. "Fragments of a Confession," pp. 45-46.

32

Radhakrishnan and Whitehead : Their Philosophical Methods from West-East Perspectives

ANIL K. SARKAR
Calfornia State University, Hayward & California
Institute of Integral Studies, S.F.

This paper considers the philosophic methods of Radhakrishnan (1888-1975) of India, and Whitehead (1861-1947) of Great Britain and America - to indicate how these two master-minds from their respective cultural backgrounds - ventilate their approaches and pursuits from the confronted perceptual order of experiential processes, within a continuously changing cosmic-psychic milieu.

Their sense of reality as confronted is not pinned to the waking consciousness alone, in terms of a fixed concept or intuition, as prevalent in the early stages of Western and Indian thought, in general, but each approaches to an interpretation of focal presented consciousness, by way of a contrast, involving a dynamic inner urge - of a pervasive non-sensuous past (Whitehead), or illuminating transcendent Spirit (Radhakrishnan) as basis and proceeding towards a prospective emergent experiential possibility of different dimensions of a living human personality, within a many-dimensional cosmic-psychic milieu, not restricted in a categorical way, but as symbolically oriented, with a 'may-be' process, as the confronted universe emerges or vanishes, not categorically, but with an ever-fresh novelty.

Hence the presented situation, as confronted by a human organism, has a symbolical relation between the perceiving organism and the confronted changing universe.

Whitehead contends that the emergent awareness as placed within Nature, has a deep 'feeling basis,' confronting a changing and perishing universe of alternative, many-dimensional hypothetical characters of perceptual elements from 'spatio-temporality,' followed by some abiding characters, or 'possibles,' variously discerned as 'eternal objects,' providing a ground for further orders of 'suppositional processes' or processes in connection (nexus) called 'propositions' (by Whitehead, in a special sense). These 'propositional processes' rise to prospective 'cognitive situations,' of a conscious individual, in a special qualitative direction, called by Whitehead, 'intellectual processes.' These have further possibilities in higher dimensions of 'insightful orders' of Whitehead's 'wisdom processes' - 'God' and 'Creativity' - in a special sense of Whitehead. They do not have any past theological or philosophical implication from Aristotle to Hegel, bringing in abstract mode of 'ultimate reality.' Whitehead's philosophy is naturalistically based from the beginning to end, and entertains a continuous possibility with 'novelty' in varied qualitative directions.

This mode of novel deliberation from 'spatio-temporality' to 'creativity' - constitutes Whitehead's varied many-dimensional concrete principles. These principles transcend all past abstract conceptual' and 'empirical' modes. They are dealt with, in details in his two books - 'Process and Reality'[1] and 'Adventures of Ideas.'[2] Here he flouts all absolutist modes from Plato to Spinoza, Kant and Hegel, stretching this process further to the advanced realist and pragmatist modes of Europe and America of the present century.[3]

In 'Adventures of Ideas' - Whitehead does not pursue any specific logic, psychology or philosophy, in any restricted sense of the past philosophical tradition, he abandons all 'simplicist modes, by fostering a process of complexity in experiential contexts, in terms of 'general ideas,' not of Socrates, but in the advanced aspects of philosophical and scientific deliberations, outmoding Aristotle's 'formal logic,' and even threatening Einstein, if he interprets his 'general theory of relativity,' in any 'restricted positivist sense.'[4]

His is also a going beyond Russell's 'symbolic logic,' where, the 'propositions' of the perceptual situation, cherished by the human mind, have a dual-character, with some 'constant' symbolical forms, having a reference to changing and varied situations (variables).[5]

According to Whitehead, Russell's 'propositions - are not really - emergent, in the sense of novelty in accord with Whitehead's emerging and perishing, of Nature, in many-dimensional ways. They are just granted in some specific senses, according to Russell.

To Whitehead, a human organism is placed within a milieu of a possible panoramic universe, of contrasting orders of appearances, from 'spatio-temporality' to 'creativity' - having relative significance. One has to pursue these processes, with a hypothetical-symbolical attitude, not knowing fully, what exactly will be the 'emergent appearances,' in different dimensions, with a prospective 'meditative attitude' and 'concern', detaching oneself totally from the 'abstract discursive analysis' or assuming them, in some specific abstract senses.[6]

One has to study Whitehead's other books along with the earlier works, as 'The Religion in the Making,'[7] 'Science and the Modern World'[8] and 'Modes of Thoughts,'[9] continuing in general his main trends, where all emergent occasions and principles are construed empirically, as possible processes of Nature.[10]

If one chooses, one may as well read this writer's 'Whitehead's Four Principles From West-East Perspectives'[11] - in the background of Western thought from Plato and Aristotle to Kant and Hegel, stretching to American realists and evolutionists, post-Hegelian Neo-Hegelians like Bradley, and French evolutionist Bergson to American Pragmatists and Instrumentalists - from Pierce to James and Dewey.[12]

In this context, one may also cross the Western boundaries to Indian thought, to touch the Buddha's non-discursive meditative modes leading to "Peace" - to determine how one can be completely free from 'abstract thinking' and understanding of concrete possible experiential situations.[13]

Whitehead does not often develop Western thought, in clear-cut historical order, but one can understand the development in general of his historical sequence. Similarly his reference to the Buddha's thought, in Indian thought, is from a non-discursive meditative perspective, without pursuing the details of Indian thought, but his mode of deliberation is certainly by a detachment from all traditional abstract thinking of the major past Western thinkers, and also of the thinkers of his time, if there were any tinge of 'abstract mode.' To be completely free from any abstract mode, in his insightful pursuits from Truth to Beauty, and from both to Art - and therefrom to Adventure, in general - he develops a progressive rise to transcendent non-discursive thinking, similar to, or not exactly similar to the meditative processes in development of the Indian thought, in general - in his 'Adventures of Ideas.'[14]

The speciality of Whitehead, in contrast to Western thinkers in general, from the ancient to the modern times, lies in his detachment from any specific ideological mode. He entertains, the emergent 'ideas' of a conscious human organism within Nature - as 'contrasts' both in cosmic and in psychic and cultural bases - in general, taking note of other possible non-Western cultural processes.[15]

In this context, he has an eye towards the cultural processes of humanity in general insofar as he could be aware of or interested in. He is critical of the intellectual categories, in general, for, they give prominence only to a particular aspect of thought, in the following elemental ways, by 'emphasis,' 'selection,' 'transmutation,' 'distortion,' 'simplification,' 'clarification,' 'discrimination,' and even, 'attenuation.'[16]

The abstract intellectual pursuits subsequently end up with 'bloodless abstractions,' shunting the concrete universe to a ghostly region, reminding one of a Neo-Hegelian Bradley, author of 'Appearance and Reality.' Whitehead admits of his criticism of the 'intellectual categories,' sharing with him the continuous presence of a pervasive 'feeling-process' as an 'integral experience governing the human mind, and even transcending the restricted intellectual level.[17]

Whitehead's criticism of the intellectual ways, has a closeness, with the advanced Indian thought, of an acceptance of a profound silence as the sustaining background of all experiential process. This inner experience, is very similar to the transcendent experience of the depth of one's 'silence' of the Upaniṣadic thinkers, as providing the basis of a double-consciousness, or a 'transcending consciousness' as an elevating process, in any reflective activity.[18]

Hence Whitehead's philosophic position is not as exclusive and restrictive perspective of Philosophy, Religion, Psychology, Sciences or Cultures - his was a cultivation of 'interrelated processes,' closing up gulfs between subjects and cultures. He, therefore, admits without any difficulty the advanced thought-processes of the different cultures, in togetherness, and in symbolical ways, through a development of the symbolic suggestions of Zero in Indian Mathematical thought, in relation to the transcendent process of profound silence or solitude, or complete vacuity of all intellectual forms, as suggested by the Buddha, transcending all possible intellectual forms, in progressive ascents to his 'non-discursive' experience of 'Peace.'[19]

In a way through his symbolic Logic, and Symbolic Mathematical ways, and through Algebraic ways and differential calculus - Whitehead could speed up the process of Sciences from Einstein's 'special theory' of relativity, to 'general theory' of relativity, developing a scheme of 'detachment from all specific theories, to progressive insightful processes and possibilities.'[20]

Almost, in a similar way, from a retrospective - prospective attitude, on advanced Indian and Western thought - in togetherness - Radhakrishnan - thinks by a critical study of both Western and Indian thought - that one's sensible or conceptual experience, can be transcended by a cultivation of a detached non-discursive attitude. Here he refers to India's cultivation of a transcendent consciousness, which is independent of sensible and conceptual thinking - but taking note of them as just basic processes of emerging consciousness.[21]

Since the days of the Upaniṣads[22] - symbolically reresenting the insightful understanding of the experiential processes, by way of direct communication between the teacher and the student - any confronted experience - was understood as a dual-consciousness - in which there is a continuous subject seeing or an understanding a presented sensible or reflective situation.[23] Again this presented psychic consciousness - belongs to Waking consciousness, in contrast to two other lapsed consciousness of dream and deep-sleep.[24]

So that the tentative possible waking consciousness is an oscillating emergence, and a continuously perishing process. It needs a constant control of the supervising-experiencing subject.[25]

Radhakrishnan - a great insightful thinker of the present century - has a credit of mastering not only the advanced thought to the stage of Whitehead along with his contemporaries - he is also aware of the developments of the entire Indian thought from the Vedas to the present-day neo-Vedāntic processes of Indian thought like Hiriyanna, K.C. Bhattacharyya and others, leading to contemporary alternative 'Movements' becoming totally detached from all 'abstract' or 'restricted' modes, in a similar and yet not similar ways of Whitehead, understanding the full understanding of the 'ideas' as emergent in human consciousness, as 'tentative contrasts.'[26]

Indian thought, is a resultant process of a series of Western European thinking from the Greeks onwards since Alexander's invasion. Thereafter with the invading Western, Central Asian people through the centuries, culminating with the Mogul rule of India for ten centuries - till the European impact, with the final British rule of India - and education - through English of the advanced scientific thinking - India can always be proud of its intensely mixed cultural heritage of the world, now touching the New Hemisphere, with the American cultural processes - in contrast to the Western and also someway related to the ancient civilized processes of the original inhabitants of America called American Indians.[27]

The speciality of Indian cultural process lies in its universalist liberal attitude. The details of these and other operational modes of the Indian cultural processes, with progressive novel insights, in terms of the concrete and changing situations - are well depicted, with the masterly English language of Radhakrishnan's inspiring philosophical works - both big and small - as in the case of Whitehead. Both these master minds end up with a religious - philosophic consciousness as a resultant process of the insightful experiences, through one's 'solitude' or 'detached non-discursive attitude.' These are all deliberations in the line of 'Peace.'[28]

Radhakrishnan's writings, and extempore lectures, in India and in foreign countries - England, Europe and America - through his varied positions as an educationist, and as occupying various official positions after Indian Independence - as Ambassador in Russia, during the time of Stalin,[29] and as Vice-President and President - of the Indian Republic - were not only a creditable achievement for Radhakrishnan himself, but they also added to the prestige of India, as Radhakrishnan was an outstanding personality as Rabindranath Tagore, Gandhi, Sri Aurobindo, and Nehru, the great Prime Minister of India - and propagator of non-alignment, as an insightful political ideal or policy for Universal Peace.[30]

Radhakrishnan's main works from 'Indian Philosophy'[31] to 'An Idealist View of Life,'[32] interspersed with other big or small volumes - express his insights for detailed understanding of both Indian and Western thought with a togetherness and a prospect - interpreting the future of religious, philosophic, psychological and scientific experiences in their broadness.

The volume entitled, 'Radhakrishnan (Comparative Studies in Philosophy, Presented in Honour of his Sixtieth Birthday[33] - edited by The Very Rev. W.R. Inge and others - is the record of a broad philosophic attitude and method, where Radhakrishnan courageously says - 'We are not so much in need of a keen analysis of particular problems, as those of essence and existence, sense and perspectives, or a pragmatic insistence on methodology, and the futility of metaphysics, interesting as they are, but philosophy in the larger sense of the terms, is a spiritual view of the universe, broad based on the results of sciences and aspirations of humanity' (Introduction).[34]

These insightful philosophical glimpses expressed in a nut-shell represent the conflicting trends of the Western thought of the major trends of the pre-Hegelian and the post-Hegelian philosophy, with the over-all reactionary processes of post-Hegelian transcendental modes in European thought, in terms of Husserl's transcendental Phenomenology and Kierkegaard's transcendental Existentialism - were subsequently challenged by the New Evolutionist philosophy and religion of French Bergson, who responded and helped develop further the path of scientific modes of deliberation of Peirce, with further touches of new interpretation of 'ideas.' This led William James to interpret 'ideas' as having a currency value, and Dewey and Mead to construct a view of the Self, as not an apriori or a basic notion, but wholly an emergent process resulting out of the communication with language, as the symbolic basis substituting for animal genstures as an efficient instrument of communication.[35]

Radhakrishnan is aware of these conflicts of Western thought as a whole, and deals with Indian thought, developing its non-discursive transcendent modes in continuity from the Vedas to the Upaniṣads, and from both to the transcendent theistic ideas of the Bhagavad Gītā without deviating from the Upaniṣads.[36] Then he develops the post-Upaniṣadic thought - beyond the Buddhist processes - of the three types - Theravāda, Mahāyāna-Mādhyamika, and Vijñānavāda - reviving some general idea of Mādhyamika-Yogācāra process - in an aspect to develop two types of logic - of Gauḍapāda and Śaṁkara - preparing the background for Śaṁkara and his followers, and in contrast - Rāmānuja's new Vedānta, and also of other Vedāntins - Nimarka, Madhva and Vallabha to the stage of

Jīva Goswāmī of Bengal Vaiṣnavism, beyond Caitanya. To Jīva Goswāmī, the manifest universe is real, as a consequent integral process, as in Vallabha or Caitanya, and not merely a confronted process of appearance only, in the pathway of Māyā-Avīdya of Śaṁkara.[37] Here the interpreted 'Knowledge,' not as ultimately real, but as an expression of a transcendent background of 'power' as a concrete elevating power, in association with other transforming powers of the human nature as love, devotion and surrender.[38]

Radhakrishnan, in his two Volumes of 'Indian Philosophy',[39] - performs this novel scheme with the scholarly vision of comparative West-East thought in development. He with Charles Moore of America, in a shortened form, with a new skill - writes his 'A Source-Book in Indian Philosophy'[40] - with a wonderful brevity and insight - the entire Indian philosophy from the Vedas to contemporary Indian thought - dealing with the philosophy of Śri Aurobindo, and his own Philosophy.

His general Introduction to the History of Indian Philosophy, clarifying its dominant inner spirit, and Introductions to each important period and system of Indian thought - are helpful guides, with detailed 'references to source materials' to scholars of comparative philosophy.

In determining Radhakrishnan's final choice for a liberate condition, or for ecstatic experience of profound solitude - one may refer to his varied intuitional experiences as represented in his, 'My Search For Truth',[41] and in 'An Idealist View of Life.'

Radhakrishnan's 'An Idealist view of Life' like 'Whitehead's Adventures of Ideas' - brings out the novel philosophic methods, from a comparative perspective - with the specialized idea of common visions of these master minds.[42]

Speciality of Radhakrishnan lies in his not totally abandoning any Absolute as in Whitehead, except as progressive contrasting ideas - but interpreting the final philosophic mode, as constituting a vast realm or Habitat of Possibilities - operative as if sheltering all confronted possibilities to be confronted, and then providing a final shelter to the termination of their respective functions.[43]

His interpretation of the confronted universe - with God and the World - as a dual consciousness - in relation and togetherness - resembles God and the World of Whitehead's 'Process and Reality' - as 'contrasts' - one is incomplete without the other - none of these aspects of Creativity, are without the other.[44] They serve their respective purposes with the help of the other. God is needed for 'order' - the World for 'fluency' - and 'Creativity' for continuous possibility of passage and novelty.

In this connection, Whitehead, is very critical of Western philosophic or theistic religions - for, they either insist on an 'abstract philosophic principle' or an abstract ultimate reality. But concrete reality lies in the tender elements in the world, which may be symbolically represented as Love.

Whitehead, in his, 'Process and Reality' - 44 in his Chapter on 'God and the World' - develops these contrasting ideas - in connection with his 'Creativity,' not as an ultimate, but as an infinite possibility - touching the depths of Buddhist non-discursive process, with a frankness - flouting Aristotle's 'Abstract Metaphysics' - of an 'Unmoved Mover' or the Scholastic God of a transcendent Creator of Christianity and of Islam (or Mahomedanism).[45]

Whitehead's interpretation of a superject possibility - is not a mere consciousness of 'permanence' and 'fluency' - but fluency (or actuality) with permanence (World) - and permanence with fluency (God).[46] In Bixler's words - this experience is 'twoness-is-one'[47] - projected to many-dimensional possibilities.

Radhakrishnan's Indian philosophy, with his idealist attitude as developed in his 'An Idealist View of Life' - is an exalted view of life - which is symbolically a Hindu mode of life - emphasizing the importance of all stages of life of continuous transformation in progressive disciplined modes with liberal allowances for insightful enjoyment - from the stage of a student learning from an insightful teacher - to householder's life of marriage enjoying family and social life and preparing oneself progressively for a detached way of life, by making oneself free from family attachments as to live a pure life of contemplation by a total separation from others. This sounds as ascetic ideal to follow - specially towards one's final stages of life. It might appear as a relentless prescription. But it was admitted as an ancient Indian ideal mode of life, at least for those who were so capable.

Radhakrishnan entertains a Psychology that is a continuous process from an unfathomable past to an infinite possibility - in an aspect - expressing a Whiteheadian spirit - of a continuous detachment, and lift of oneself to transcendent heights, as if giving a new turn to the Hindu law of Karma - as man's inner propensity to hold on to the confronted, and not becoming detached from that basic disposition, preparing the grounds for repetitive process, with no effort to be free from that process.

Radhakrishnan's interpretation of Karma, is all very general, as he was aware of the different interpretations of 'Karma' according to various Vedic systems - and also the interpretation of 'Karma' according to non-Vedic Jaina system, and no such beliefs of the Carvaka and other forms of materialists.

My evaluation of Radhakrishnan veers round his autobiographical expressions and the general ideas pervasively present in his, 'An Idealist View of Life.'

My researches on Indian thought, from West-East Perspectives - are found in 'Dynamic Facets of Indian Thought - in Four Volumes,'[48] and Changing Phases of Buddhist Thought[49] - three editions, mainly following Radhakrishnan's suggestions, but also taking note of other great Indian contemporaries - as my seniors, research directors, colleagues, teachers, examiners or well-wishers : S.N. Dasgupta, R.D. Ranade, M. Hiriyanna, K.C. Bhattacharyya, A.R. Wadia, N.A. Nikam, G.R. Malkani, D.M. Datta (my teacher), Humayan Kabir, S.C. Chatterjee, Rasvihary Das, T.R.V. Murti, S.S. Suryanarayan Sastri, B.L. Atreya, P.T. Raju, T.M.P. Mahadevan and others too many to mention - I have made the best use of their thoughts in relevant places.

My books on Whitehead : 'An Outline of Whitehead's Philosophy,' (Arthur H. Stockwell Ltd., London, 1940),[50] is a short monograph. But my book after my researches on Whitehead at the London University and at Patna University - reflects my researches on comparative West-East thought - with detailed references to Western and Indian thought as shaped by both Whitehead and Radhakrishnan.

In my researches - I have tried to give a new perspective to the advanced aspects and trends of both Western and Indian Philosophy - acknowledging the contributions of the two master minds of the world of this century, bearing in mind also the transforming ideas of Rabindranath Tagore, in his poetical mood, 'Where the mind is without fear and the head high, where the knowledge is free, and where the world has not been broken up into fragments of narrow domestic walls.'

References

1. *Process and Reality,* first published, 1929, The MacMillan Company, first Free Press Paperback Edition, 1969, New York, vide specially Ch. I, Sec. I.
2. *Adventures of Ideas,* The Free Press, New York, 1967, first published, 1933, The MacMillan Company, Ch. XV, Philosophic Method.
3. *Readings On Logic,* second edition, by Irving M. Copi & James A. Gould, The MacMillan Company, New York, 1972, vide, *Artistotle's Logic,* by B. Russell, Part Two, also B. Russell, *Logic As the Essence of Philosophy,* Part One, and A.N. Whitehead : *The Importance of Good Notation,* Part Five.
4. *Adventures of Ideas,* Parts III & IV.
5. Russell's Papers in *Readings on Logic,* by Copi & Gould.
6. Whitehead's *Adventures of Ideas,* Part IV.
7. *Religion in the Making,* The World Publishing Company, New York, seventh Edition, 1967, first published, 1926, by the MacMillan Company, vide specially, pp. 127-154, for reenforcing, the experience of one's 'solitude' in religious experience.
8. *Science and the Modern World,* The Free Press, New York, 1967, first Published, 1925, The MacMillan Company.
9. *Modes of Thought,* Cambridge University Press, 1936.
10. Whitehead's *Adventures of Ideas,* Parts III & IV.
11. A.K. Sarkar's *Whitehead's Four Principles From West-East Perspectives,* Bharati Bhawan, Patna, India, 1974, for a general understanding of Whitehead's principles, in the context of different periods of Western thought, and in relation to India's Buddhist thought, from West-East perspectives.
12. *Ibid.,* & Whitehead's *Adventures of Ideas,* Parts III & IV.
13-16. *Ibid.*
17. *Ibid,* and also, Bradley's, *Appearance and Reality* (Oxford Paperbacks), with Introduction by Richard Wollheim, Oxford University Press, London, Oxford, New York, second edition, 1969, first edition, 1893.

18. A.K. Sarkar's *Dynamic Facets of Indian Thought,* Vol. I, Ch. IV.
19. Whitehead's *Adventures of Ideas,* Part IV.
20. *Ibid.*
21. Radhakrishnan's *An Idealist View of Life,* George Allen & Unwin Ltd., first edition, 1932, fifth Impression, 1957, with special reference to advanced Indian and Western thought.
22-25. Vide Sarkar's *Dynamic Facets of Indian Thought,* in Four Vols.
26. D.M. Datta : *The Chief Currents of Contemporary Philosophy,* The University of Calcutta, Calcutta, India, First edition, 1950, Second edition, 1961, vide, Ch. III, K.C. Bhattacharyya, S. Radhakrishnan and Sri Aurobindo, in contrast to Western and Asian contemporaries.
27. Sarkar, A.K., *Dynamic Facets of Indian Thought,* in four Vols., and Riepe, Dale : *The Philosophy of India and Its Impact on American Thought,* Charles C. Thomas, Publisher, Springfield, Illinois, 1970, for a comparative perspective.
28. Whitehead's *Adventures of Ideas,* Part IV.
29. Balasubramanian : *Indian Philosophical Annual : Special Number on Radhakrishnan,* Volume Twelve 1977-78, The Dr. Radhakrishnan Institute for Advanced Study in Philosophy, University of Madras, 1979, specially paper: 1, by Raghavachar : A Philosopher with a difference, and Paper 5, Rangaraja Rao : Radhakrishnan's Contributions to Indian Philosophy and Comparative Religion.
30. McDermott, Robert, ed., by : *Radhakrishnan : Selected Writings on Philosophy, Religion, and Culture,* New York : E.P. Dutton and Company, 1970, for a general survey on Radhakrishnan's life-history and activity.
31. Radhakrishnan, S., *Indian Philosophy,* Vols. I & II, London : George Allen & Unwin Ltd. first Published, 1923, eighth impression, 1966.
32. Radhakrishnan : *Being the Hibbert Lectures for 1929,* London : George Allen & Unwin Ltd., fifth impression 1957, Ch. VIII, for his general view of reality from a comparative perspective.
33. W.R. Inge & others, as editors : *Radhakrishnan : Comparative Studies in Philosophy in Honour of His*

Sixtieth Birthday : London : George Allen & Unwin Ltd., 1951, second Impression, 1968.
34. *Ibid.*, Introduction.
35. Sarkar, A.K. *Dynamic Facets of Indian Thought*, Vol. I. Chs. I & II.
36. Radhakrishnan & Moore, Charles A., ed by, *A Source Book in Indian Philosophy*, Princeton : Princeton University Press, 1957, Ch. III, The Bhagavad Gītā, chiefly, pp. 101-102.
37-38. Radhakrishnan : *Indian Philosophy*, Two Vols., in development.
39. *Ibid.*
40. Radhakrishnan & Moore : *A Source-Book in Indian Philosophy.*
41. McDermott, Robert A. Ed. by, *Radhakrishnan : Selected Writings*, Part I : Autobiographical : My Search For Truth.
42. Reference is here to both Radhakrishnan and Whitehead - in their advanced interpretations of "ideas," of an idealistic choice, or attitude of living life, in the case of Radhakrishnan, and an interpretation of 'ideas' as progressive contrasts, in philosophic-socio-natural universe of mankind in general, in the case of Whitehead. In both there is a reference to their boos, as mentioned, and also very specially with Radhakrishnan, who always refers to Whitehead.
43. Radhakrishnan's critical and comparative visions in the context of contemporary Western thought of Whitehead and Alexander, and his reflections, by way of contrast, as in his, *An Idealist View of Life*, Specially Ch. VIII.
44-45. Whitehead's *Process and Reality*, Part V.
46-47. Sarkar A.K., *Whitehead's Four Principles from West-East Perspectives*, specially Chs., IV & V, for Bixler's 'two-ness-in-one' in the context of God, vide
48.
49.
50.

PART IV

RADHAKRISHNAN, SOCIETY AND ART

33
Radhakrishnan on Man, God and the State

ANAND MOHAN
City University of New York

Had Radhakrishnan been alive today, he would, very likely, have deplored the reign of religion in contemporary politics, just as he had, early in his life, protested against "the interference of religious prejudice with the genuine spirit of speculation,"[1] and warned : "A religious system, though the terminus of philosophical study, should not be its governing influence. It does not augur well for the future of either religion or philosophy, if religion becomes the starting point and dominating motive of philosophy."[2] It is in the conviction that a combustible mix of conventional religion and agitational politics would prove disastrous to mankind that Radhakrishnan has offered us his conception of a democratic, secular society, which had no room in it for "any metaphysical theory of the State,"[3] nor for any mode of arriving at consensus on social issues other than through rational, commonsensical discourse, rooted in our common humanity.

However, Radhakrishnan's idea of secularism is fundamentally different from that which prevails in the West in general, and the United States in particular. We must examine at some length this Western conception of secularism in order to understand the implications of Radhakrishnan's views on the relationship between religion and politics. The insistence upon erecting a wall of separation between Church and State and the adoption of the Establishment Clause of the First Amendment to the American constitution are both traceable to the once dominant role which organized religion has historically played in the evolution of Western political institutions. The rise of the Christian Church, as a distinct institution entitled to govern the spiritual concerns of mankind independently of the State, was quite a revolutionary event in the history of Europe, in respect both of the exercise of political power and the formulation of political philosophy. Where the Roman constitutional lawyers had stressed that the ruler's authority was derived from the people, the New Testament writers stressed the view that political obedience was a moral obligation imposed by God. The King of the Jews was habitually spoken of as the Lord's anointed at the hands of the prophet, and once the Jewish scriptures were accepted, the Christian conception of rulership also implied a theory of divine right, since the ruler was a minister of God. For St. Augustine, the Church became quite literally "the march of God in the world" - to borrow the expression which Hegel applied to the State - and a true and just commonwealth therefore had to be, of necessity, Christian. Churchmen began to chain that "In a Christian kingdom even the laws of State ought to be Christian, that is, in accord with and suitable to Christianity."[4] The Jewish notion of kingship found its culmination in Islamic jurisprudence, where sovereignty rests with God, and the ruler becomes the sole defender of the faith. The faith itself was considered *dini-wa-dunvawi*, that is to say, both religious and secular, and God placed on earth a *khalifa* to "judge between the people with truth."[5] "Classical Islamic political theory had seen the faith as ideally the regulator of life and society, assigning each his with the temporal ruler's function that of carrying out religious decrees."[6]

The characteristic position developed by Christian thinkers in the age of the Fathers, often spoken of as the doctrine of the two swords, implied a dual organization and control of human society in the interest of the two great classes of values. Spiritual interests and eternal salvation were in the keeping of the Church and formed the special province of the clergy; temporal or secular interests and the maintenance of peace, order, and justice were in the keeping of the civil government. But despite the principle that the two jurisdictions ought to remain inviolate, each respecting the rights which God had ordained for the other, the doctrine of mutual helpfulness left almost no line that might not rightfully be crossed when society was threatened by anarchy in temporals or corruption in spirituals. Even so, the doctrine of the two swords became the accepted tradition of the early Middle Ages and formed the point of departure for both sides when the rivalry between the Pope and the Emperor made the relation of spirituals and temporals a matter of controversy.

Marsilio of Padua, the medieval Averroist Aristotelian, was the first to define and limit in the most dramatic manner the pretensions of the spiritual authorities to control the action of secular governments, and to say that secular questions have to be decided on their own rational merits without reference to faith. Following the Aristotelian principle of the self-suffering community capable of supplying both its physical and its moral needs, and basing his theory of secular government directly upon the practise and conceptions of the Italian city-states, Marsilio concludes that whatever reverence faith may deserve as a means of eternal salvation, it has become from a secular point of view simply irrelevant, and that religion cannot be brought into a political consideration of rational means and ends. As a historian of political theory comments : "Such a separation of reason and faith is the direct ancestor of religious skepticism, and in its consequences amounts to a secularism which is both anti-Christian and anti-religious."[7]

It is this principle which, through the twists and turns of history, has come to be articulated as the Jeffersonian conception of a wall of separation between Church and State, and has found juridical expression in a leading case decided by the Supreme Court of the United States :"[8]

> 'It is an unfortunate fact of history that when some of the very groups which had most strenuously opposed the established Church of England found themselves sufficiently in control of colonial governments in this country to write their own prayers into law, they passed laws making their own religion the official religion of their respective colonies. . . .

'By the time of the adoption of the Constitution, our history shows that there was a widespread awareness among many Americans of the dangers of a union of Church and State. . . .

'When the power, prestige and financial support of government is placed behind a particular religious belief, the indirect coercive pressure upon religious minorities to conform to the prevailing officially approved religion is plain. But the purposes underlying the Establishment Clause go much further than that. Its first and most immediate purpose restored on the belief that a union of government and religion tends to destroy government and to degrade religion . . . . The Establishment Clause thus stands as an expression of principle on the part of the Founders of our Constitution that religion is too personal, too sacred, too holy, to permit its "unhallowed perversion" by a civil magistrate. Another purpose of the Establishment Clause rested upon an awareness of the historical fact that governmentally established religions and religious persecutions go hand in hand....

'... it may be appropriate to say in the words of James Madison, the author of the First Amendment:
> "Who does not see that the same authority which can establish Christianity, in exclusion of all other Religions, may establish with the same ease any particular sect of Christians, in exclusion of all other Sects?"'

However, as often as this wall of separation between Church and State was sought to be erected, so often have attempts also been made to have it demolished. The current crew of demolitionists in the United States is a motley crowd of adherents of several Protestant denominations as well as of the Catholic church. Elsewhere in the world, too, we have been witnessing the catastrophic consequences of the murderous mix of politics and religion. Islamic fundamentalism and militancy in West and South Asia, a Sikh terrorism that totally borders on the irrational and pathological, and a Hindu and Buddhist revivalist nationalism run rampant have all brought death and destruction in their trail. But the advocates of "historical religions" insist that the social disorders of our time are the result, not of the intrusion of religion into the political realm, but of the resistance of the latter to conform to the imperatives of the former. Aside from the men of the cloth, there are academics and publicists who, bemoaning the rise of secularism, have argued that the experiential growth of modern States without the simultaneous articulation of appropriate religious norms to undergird political conduct has resulted in the triple tragedy of modern times - the loss of a sense of community as the chief moralizing agency of the citizen that Rousseau was the first to detect; the disappearance of domestic tranquillity from the State which, in Weber's typology, possesses a monopoly of coercive power and yet has failed to secure the lives and limbs of its citizens; and the elusiveness of peace in the anarchical society which constitutes the Hobbesian world of sovereign states.

Radhakrishnan would have looked upon the forays of such religious men into the political realm with suspicion and dismay. Warning us that when religion gets mixed up with politics, it becomes degraded into a species of materialism, he observed : "Religions, by propagating illusions such as the fear of hell, damnation, and arrogant assumptions of inviolable authority and exclusive monopolies of the divine word, and politics, by intoxicating whole peoples with dreams of their messianic missions, by engendering in them false memories, by keeping the old wounds open, by developing in them megalomania or persecution complex, destroy the sense of oneness with the world and divide humanity into narrow groups which are vain and ambitious, bitter and intolerant."[9]

Robert Minor points out that Radhakrishnan, in his recurring criticism of the "historical religions," faults them specifically on three grounds." The first is that religions are unscientific. Their beliefs do not agree with the discoveries of science, and they surrender to dogma and unchallenged human authority. Modern man, relying on the empirical method for ascertaining fact, is opposed to "the fervent irrationality implicit in revealed religions."[10] The certainty and complete assurance which the adherents of revealed religions expect and demand have been pretty thoroughly discredited by scientific naturalism. Radhakrishnan's second criticism of "historical religions" is that they have been ethically indifferent and ineffective. They have condoned, if not actively justified, social iniquities, economic exploitation, political oppression, and imperialistic aggrandizement, all on the assumption that religion was divorced from politics. The man of the cloth would seem impervious to the social agony of his fellow human beings because he is commanded only to save their souls. Finally, Radhakrishnan criticised the "historical religions" for being divisive. They cause divisiveness by their exclusivism and their dogmatism which, in turn, are caused by their ignorance, distortion, and misperception of the true nature of religious experience. While naturalism categorically denies the existence of God, the dogmatism of closed religions, with their ritualistic and creedal narrowness, affirms that it knows all about God. Both agree in abolishing all mystery in the world.

When Radhakrishnan says that "Religion is not mere eccentricity, not a historical accident, not a psychological device, not an escape mechanism, not an economic lubricant induced by an indifferent world," he means that religion, in most cases, unfortunately, is all of these things which it should not be. And when he maintains that religion "is an integral element of human nature, an intimation of destiny, a perception of the value of the individual, an awareness of the importance of human choice for the future of the world,"[11] he is actually suggesting that religions fail this promise more often than not, when in fact they should not. Each missionary religion believes in its own superiority. Each professes that it is in possession of the highest truth. One's own religion is contrasted with other religions as truth against falsehood. The absolutist claims made by these faiths are in their very nature incompatible with the existence of several such faiths."[12] Radhakrishnan concludes : "The illogical idea of a single religion for all mankind, one set of dogmas, one cult, one system of ceremonies which all individuals must accept on pain of persecution by the people and punishment by God, is the product of unreason and the parent of intolerance."[13]

So far, then, Radhakrishnan's views on secularism do not appear to be very different from those prevalent in the Western world which argue for a separation of Church and state. In many countries of the world today, the citizen body does not constitute a homogeneous religious community. There is a multiplicity of religions to which various segments of society give their adherence. These religions hold a diversity of opinions on several social issues. The State cannot enforce, except at the peril of inducing communal disharmony and social disorder, conformity with a social conduct demanded by the dictates of any one particular religion. The experience of history indicates that "The world has bled and suffered from the disease of dogmatism, of conformity, of intolerance. People conscious of a mission of bringing humanity to their own way of life, whether in religion or politics, have been aggressive towards other ways of life."[14] Radhakrishnan therefore opts for a polity in which the State refrains from following any religious dogma in reaching decisions on social issues.

However, Radhakrishnan does not stop there. He goes on to distinguish between the "historical religions" and the "religion of the Spirit." The essence of religion, he tells us, "is not in the dogmas and creeds, in the rites and ceremonies which repel many of us, but in the deepest wisdom of the ages, the *philosophia perennis*, sanatana dharma."[15] Nor is religion a mere social phenomenon, "an apologetic for the existing social order;" possessing an autonomous character, it is "something inward and personal which unifies all values and organises all experiences." As a spiritual experience and an integral intuition, it displays an instinct for the real and "an incurable dissatisfaction with the finiteness of the finite, the transiency of the transient."[16] Radhakrishnan argues that "When rational thought is applied to the empirical data of the world and of the human self, the conclusion of a Supreme who is Pure Being and Free Activity is reached;" that "There is a tradition of direct apprehension of the Supreme in all lands, in all ages and all creeds;" and that "The experience of a pure and unitary consciousness in a world divided gives rise to the two fold conception of the Absolute as Pure Transcendent Being lifted above all relativities, and the Free Active God functioning in the world."[17] Conventional religion may call for a particular way of life, but the religion of the Spirit is the way of all life. Where the former posits truth in belief, the latter compels belief in Truth.

Radhakrishnan offers us here two aspects of the Supreme Being - first, the supracosmic transcendence of the Absolute which is an inexpressible, relationless mystery, and second, the cosmic universality of God whose mystery is directed towards the world and who reveals himself to man. "The fundamental truths of a spiritual religion" therefore "are that our real self is the supreme being, which it is our business to discover and consciously become, and this being is one in all."[18] The unitive knowledge of God here and now becomes the final end of man. Viewed in such a light, "Human history is not a series of secular happenings without any shape or pattern; it is a meaningful process, a significant development." When we look at history from the outside, we are impressed by the pomp, the circumstances and catastrophe of its political vicissitudes, "but below in the depths is to be found the truly majestic drama, the tension between the limited effort of man and the sovereign purpose of the universe."[19]

It is in this context that Radhakrishnan firmly maintains that the State, far from distancing itself from the religion of the Spirit, must actively encourage it and reinforce its foundations. It is the duty of the State "to create and maintain forms of social organisation which offer the fewest possible impediments to the development of the truly human life." The religion of the Spirit "is the way in which the individual organises his inward being and responds to what is envisaged by him as the Ultimate Reality." The function of the state is to promote the religion of the Spirit and inculcate in the citizens its discipline, so as "to further the evolution of man into his divine stature," develop "increased awareness and intensity of understanding" and bring about a better, deeper and more enduring adjustment in life."[20] Modern civilization has failed to the extent to which these ideals are denied or betrayed. Radhakrishnan calls for a recovery of faith in the religion of Spirit. Pointing out that "History is continuity and advance," he nevertheless cautions that continuity of tradition is "not mere mechanical reproduction" but "creative transformation" and that "We must preserve the precious substance of religious reality by translating it out of the modes and thoughts of other times into terms and needs of our own day and generation."[21]

Radhakrishnan's democratic theory is a logical extension of the principles underlying his religion of the Spirit. For "religion includes faith in human brotherhood, and politics is the most effective means of rendering it into visible form. Politics is but applied religion."[22] Radhakrishnan subscribes to the modern notion that government should rest on the consent of the governed, that individuals must enjoy freedom of expressions and protection against the abuse of power, and that, in this imperfect world, democratic government is the most satisfactory.[23] The individual in Radhakrishnan's thought, however, is not the egoistic, self-centered member of an atomistic society, either of the Hobbesian or Lockean variety. Rather, "The human individual is the highest, the most concrete embodiment of the Spirit on earth and anything which hurts his individuality or damages his dignity is undemocratic and irreligious."[24] If democracy respects the dignity of man and recognizes his fundamental right to develop his possibilities, it is because "the common man is not common" but "precious" and "has in him the power to assert his nature against the iron web of necessity."[25] The human being is treated by living religions as a sacred entity because God is in man, and "The real unit of life is the individual with the beating human heart, the baffled human will, the sense of vast dignities and strange sorrows."[26] Rejecting alike Marx's characterization of the individual as merely "the ensemble of social relations" and Hegel's characterization of the State as nothing short of "the actualization of freedom," Radhakrishnan asserts : "There is nothing final or eternal about States and nations, which wax and wane. But the humblest individual has the spark of spirit in him which the mightiest empire cannot crush. Rooted in one life, we are all fragments of the divine, sons of immortality, amrtasya putrah."[27]

Radhakrishnan suggests that "the progress of the consciousness of freedom is the essence of human history" and sees evidence of it in that "serfs are becoming free men, heretics are no longer burned, nobles are surrendering their privileges, slaves are being freed from a life of shame, rich men are apologizing for their wealth . . . ."[28] However, the freedom that Radhakrishnan talks about is not to be confused with the liberty of liberal democratic social theory which, between Locke and Mill, "depended less on logic than on its agreement with the interests of the class that mainly produced it."[29] Indeed, Radhakrishnan would have no compunctions in making common cause with the English Idealists and arguing that liberty was not merely the absence of restraint from government interference any more than beauty was the absence of mere ugliness, and that the good life of the individual depended on the creation by the State of those conditions in which alone the human personality could flourish. Sarvepalli Gopal reports that Radhakrishnan himself once summed up his political philosophy as 'civilized individualism' and goes on to explain that "The civilizing process he had in mind was economic betterment and equality in social status."[30] This is a theme on which Radhakrishnan spoke frequently, passionately, and through many a forum. He insisted that "the poorest have a right to sufficient food, to light, air and sunshine in their homes, to hope, dignity and beauty in their lives."[31] He lamented that although the Indian conception of individuality was rooted in the religious tradition, and it was recognized that "in man alone does the Universal come to consciousness," and that "faith in the one Supreme means that we, His offspring, are of one body, of one flesh," India failed to understand the social implications of this seminal principle of spiritual equality.[32] As one interpreter puts it : "On the one hand, he has been keenly sensitive to human misery, and on the other, as a rationalist, he has felt that this misery is unnecessary.... Both freedom and justice are, according to him, expressions of man's innate rationality...."[33]

Consistent with his view that history is purposive and that its goal is freedom, Radhakrishnan advances a teleological theory of democracy when he says "Democracy is the political expression of the ethical principle that the true end of man is responsible freedom."[34] The individual man, however, possesses two selves - the outer, which is social, and the inner, which is spiritual. While the inner Self can claim to be absolutely free, the social self cannot lay claim to a similar status. Kant's celebrated moral principle holds that all men are centres of absolute value. As such, all are capable of gaining absolute freedom. This freedom is none other than the last of the *puruṣārthas* - *Mokṣa*. Along with Vivekananda, Aurobindo, Tagore and Gandhi, Radhakrishnan thinks that this alone is true freedom. For each of them, we saw the individual as a fragment of the Absolute, "it followed .... that the highest aim of man should always remain the discovery of his own nature; the attainment of this goal they called self-realisation or spiritual freedom."[35]

If ancient Greek thinkers made no such distinction between State and society as moderns do, with Aristotle suggesting that the State is even anterior to society, classical Indian thought envisioned society as being sustained by the cosmic principle of *Ṛta*, and in which both individuals and social groups conducted themselves in accordance with the dictates of *Dharma*. Among ancient Indian thinkers, there was "general agreement that government is an unfortunate necessity in the age of universal decay."[36] Whereas in the West, the State came to imply a corporate entity which maintained its identity through all changes of government, and was sometimes romanticized as a living entity, greater than the sum of its parts, "In India such political mysticism was discouraged by the doctrine of *Dharma*, which concerned society and not the State, and by the fundamental individualism of all the metaphysical systems."[37]

In keeping with the tradition of the ancients, Radhakrishnan writes that "The aim of *dharma* is to take the natural life of man and subject it to control without unduly interfering with its largeness, freedom, and variety." The *dharma* has two aspects to it — "*varna dharma* which deals with the duties assigned to men's position in society as determined by their character (*guna*) and function (*karma*); the *asrama dharma* which deals with the duties relevant to the stage of life, youth, manhood, or old age."[38] Emphasizing the deep, mysterious, and primordial relationship between man and society and their concrete interdependence, he says : "Man is not only himself, but is in solidarity with all of his kind. The stress of the universal in its movement towards the goal of the world is the source of man's sociality. Society is not something alien, imposed on man, crushing him, against which he rebels in knowledge and action. There is a profound integration of the social destiny with that of the individual."[39] If Radhakrishnan does not deify the State, he does not demonize it either. He would not share the view of an idealist like Bosanquet that "the State has no determinate function in a larger community, but is itself the supreme community," nor would he agree with a philosophical anarchist like Gandhi that "The State represents violence in a concentrated and organized form." He accepts the emergence of the democratic State neither as "a law of nature" nor as the inevitable outcome of "an evolutionary process destined to establish itself" but as "a precious possession won by enlightened people after ages of struggle."[40] Radhakrishnan desires that "The State must become the instrument of true civilization, and educate its members to an entirely new conception of social responsibility."[41] On the other hand, he is insistent that "The inviolable sanctity of the human soul, the freedom of the human spirit, is the sole justification for the State."[42]

In Radhakrishnan's ideal scheme, the State and the social order partake more of the nature of an organism than of an organization. As a member of society and a social being, man must do his duty by society and, at the same time, as an individual fulfil his own nature. There is thus a strong correlation between *svadharma,* one's duty, and *svabhava,* one's nature. Our *svabhava* confers upon us certain propensities and predispositions, the cultivation of which, in the light of *lokasamgraha,* the principle of social action which is designed to hold the human race together in its evolution, becomes our *svadharma.* Nature and nurture combine to produce the special vocation of the individual, the way in which, in a particular set of circumstances, he can best realize his possibilities. The twin prescriptions for this neat social scheme are regulation of the social self and freedom for the inner self. The basis of society is individual self-limitation. A balance of liberties and an organized harmony of individual freedoms is held to be the ideal, since unrestricted freedom, whether of the individual or of a class is a danger for other individuals and for other classes, and hence for the whole community. Here as elsewhere, says Radhakrishnan, the truth lies in the union of opposites, in a reconciling synthesis.[43]

Radhakrishnan's social scheme has drawn fire for its hierarchical structure which is seen to be directly in conflict with modern democratic principles,[44] and also for its unattractiveness in competing with other traditional models such as the Buddhist organization of society.[45] Radhakrishnan admits that so long as caste is treated as hereditary, there is no way by which one can pass from one caste to another, and hence there is no justification for caste rigidity.[46] He declares in unmistakable terms that any scheme based on heredity is both undemocratic and unspiritual. But once heredity and endogamy are eliminated, we are left with the division of society into classes on the basis of specialization of skills and the virtues of competence and excellence. Such a scheme, in Radhakrishnan's view, should be unexceptionable. He calls to his aid Plato's definition of justice in the *Republic* as "doing one's work according to nature," for in these conditions "more will be done and better done and more easily than in any other way." However, he does not believe that there is a fundamental difference between the Brahmanical and Buddhist views of social organization and maintains that "Individualist egalitarianism is a modern motive." He argues that "Both systems are opposed to a conception of society which makes it an inorganic multiplicity where all are proletarians with no vocations but jobs. The principle of society is not uniformity but unity in variety.[47]

Radhakrishnan looks upon the twentieth century as marking a period of intense cultural change and the end of one period of civilization and the beginning of another. For him the historical process is not a mere chain of events but a succession of spiritual opportunities. Man must not lose himself in the historical process but attain mastery over it for the realization of the super-historical goal. Radhakrishnan suggests that there is an historical fulfilment and destiny for the cosmic process. Empirical observation, rational inference, and intuitive understanding all point to the evolution of the historical process toward the emergence of the community of all mankind as a potent political ideal. "Truth will be victorious on earth," proclaims

Radhakrishnan, and suggests that "it is the nature of the cosmic process that the finite individual is called upon to work through the exercise of his freedom for that goal through ages of struggle and effort.

The religion of the Spirit is essential for the realization of the super-historical goal of creating a community of mankind in all its concreteness in order to bring forth the world's unborn soul. The States of the world must be secular not only in the sense that they will not favour and particular creed or sect, or identify themselves with or be controlled by any particular religion in their internal affairs, but also non-ideological in their external relations. Political ideologies are nothing more than secular religions, and Radhakrishnan criticizes them for the same reason that he does the "historical religions" - that they are unscientific, ethically indifferent, and divisive. Alluding to the secular religion of capitalist democracy, he observes : "A society which is acquisitive in its nature, unhealthy in its pleasures, disillusioned in its ideals, is a murderous machine without a conscience." And referring to the political theology of the Communists, he remarks : "Those who are anxious to regulate our lives and make us 'happy' even against our wills have to remember that man does not live by bread alone."[48]

The Cold War is the result of an attitude of mind in which the distinction between Church and State is obliterated, and the State itself simply becomes an armed Church. Imperium and Sacerdotium are combined in the same hands, and a kind of Caesaro-Papism is exercised in both camps. Ideological variations within each armed camp are comparable to the old denominational differences and sectarian rivalries, while the hostility between the two armed camps is comparable to the fever of ancient crusades. Philosophical justification is invented to rationalize these religious passions. Professor F.S.C. Northrop argues that the oriental doctrine of toleration is inappropriate to the

Western mode of knowing in which "moral man is not merely determinate man but also propositionalized man," and therefore "when propositionalised conceptions turn out to be self-contradictory, then ideological conflict is the result."[49] Retorts Radhakrishnan : "The believer in a dogma must burn the heretic!"[50]

The *Raja-Dharma* or the moral obligation of the modern state in a shrunken world of warring sovereignties is not so opaque as to require the special vision of a philosopher-king to illumine its recesses or delineate its dimensions. The ordinary operations of human consciousness - the perceptional, the logical, and the intuitive - are adequate to discern and distil the *Raja-Dharma*. Radhakrishnan identifies the real enemy as "the anonymous machine which brings about great concentration of power and subjects the majority of people to a state of montonous automatism, encouraging the use of power for unworthy ends." To put it bluntly, the problem of our times, in the democracies as much as in the dictatorships, is that a majority of people, with their fears and insecurities rooted in ignorance, are manipulated to give their acquiescence to policies formulated by a leadership that thrives on intellectual dishonesty and moral insensitivity.

But there is no need to despair. The religion of the Spirit informs us of the dawn of a new *Yuga-Dharma* - the *dharma* of a New Age. It is the business, especially of us, intellectuals, to usher this *dharma* in. As Radhakrishnan reminded his colleagues in UNESCO : "We are a priesthood of the spirit. We cannot compromise, though politicians may."[51] And with uncompromising zeal, we must cultivate attachments that are "not local, racial or national but human" so that "we will fight not for our country but for civilisation."[52] This is not to say that nations or national loyalties are to be adjured. Radhakrishnan grants that "The moral validity of national societies is justified. Nations are natural and necessary forms, constituting an intermediate stage between the individual and mankind."[53] There are differences of national tradition and temperament, and since this variety enriches the beauty of the whole, "We do not advocate an undifferentiated universalism ... We must develop the right temper of mind, a world loyalty through a spirit of fellowship among mankind."[54] And, in Platonic fashion, Radhakrishnan argues that this is the task and the end of education. "The State must become the instrument of true civilisation, and educate its members to an entirely new conception of social responsibility ... We must educate man into the reality, the nature and the responsibility of human brotherhood. It is a new psychology that we have to develop."[55] Political wisdom and social progress are not questions of appearance or cosmetics. They are determined by "man's intimate transcendent experiences. We must work for the renewal of the heart, the transformation of values, the surrender of the spirit to the claims of the eternal."[56] We must reaffirm the religion of the Spirit, for "when we raise the question about the unifying agency in selfhood, we are rasing the more general question of the principle of unity in all existents."[57]

References

1. S. Radhakrishnan, *The Reign of Religion in Contemporary Philosophy*, London : Macmillan and Company, 1920, p. vii.
2. *Ibid.*, p. 23.
3. S. Radhakrishnan, "Reply to Critics" in Paul Arthur Schilpp, ed., *The Philosophy of Sarvepalli Radhakrishnan,* New York : Tudor Publishing Company, 1952, p. 840.
4. Archbishop Hincmar of Rheims, quoted in *A History of Mediaeval Political Theory of the West*, R.W. Carlyle and A.J. Carlyle, New York : 1903, Volume I, p. 277.

5. For a study of Prophet Muhammad as head of state, and the evolution of the office of *Khalifa*, see W. Montgomery Watt, *Islamic Political Thought*, Edinburgh University, Press, 1968. pp. 20-45.
6. Wilfred Cantwell Smith, *Islam in Modern History*, Princeton University Press, 1957, p. 36.
7. George H. Sabine, *A History of Political Theory*, New York : Henry Holt and Company, 1947, p. 294.
8. Mr. Justice Black, writing the majority opinion for the Court in *Engel v. Vitale* 370 U.S. 421 (1962).
9. S. Radhakrishnan, *Eastern Religions and Western Thought*, Oxford University Press, 1940.
10. Robert N. Minor, *Radhakrishnan — A Religious Biography*, State University of New York Press, 1987, p.40.
11. S. Radhakrishnan, *Education, Politics, and War*, Poona : International Book Service, 1944, p. 31.
12. S. Radhakrishnan, *Recovery of Faith*, London : George Allen and Unwin Ltd., 1956, p. 36.
13. S. Radhakrishnan, *The Religion We Need*, 1928, Reprinted in P. Nagaraja Rao et al., eds., *Radhakrishnan Reader — an Anthology*, Bombay : Bharatiya Vidya Bhavan, 1969, pp. 81-82.
14. S. Radhakrishnan, "Indian Religious Thought and Modern Civilization," Address delivered at Annamalai University, December 26, 1955. Quoted in S.K. Ray, *The Political Thought of President Radhakrishnan*, Calcutta : Firma K.L. Mukhopadhyay, 1966, p. 43.
15. S. Radhakrishnan, *Religion and Society*, London : George Allen & Unwin Ltd., 1948, p. 43.
16. S. Radhakrishnan, *An Idealist View of Life*, London : George Allen & Unwin Ltd., pp. 88-89.
17. S. Radhakrishnan, "The Religion of the Spirit and the World's Need," in Paul Arthur Schilpp, ed., *The Philosophy of Sarvepalli Radhakrishnan*, pp. 60-63.
18. *Eastern Religions and Western Thought*, p. 32.
19. *Ibid.*, p. 1.

20. "The Religion of the Spirit and the World's Need," pp. 66-68.
21. *Recovery of Faith*, p. 8.
22. *Education, Politics, and War*, p. 2.
23. *Ibid.*, p. 40.
24. *Ibid.*, p. 8.
25. *Ibid.*, p. 38.
26. *Religion and Society*, p. 55.
27. *Ibid.*, p. 66.
28. S. Radhakrishnan, ed., *Mahatma Gandhi*, London : George Allen & Unwin Ltd., 1939, p. 20.
29. Sabine, *A History of Political Theory*, p. 531.
30. Sarvepalli Gopal, *Radhakrishnan - A Biography*, Delhi : Oxford University Press. 1989, p. 372.
31. *Mahatma Gandhi*, p. 19.
32. *Education, Politics, and War*, pp. 30-32.
33. Humayun Kabir, "Radhakrishnan's Political Philosophy" in Schilpp, *The Philosophy of Sarvepalli Radhakrishnan*, p. 704.
34. *Religion and Society*, p. 90.
35. Dennis Delton, *Indian Idea of Freedom*, Gurgaon : The Academic Press, 1982, p. 3.
36. A.L. Basham, "Some Fundamental Ideas of Ancient India" in C.H. Philips ed., *Politics Society in India*, London : George Allen and Unwin Ltd., 1963, p. 13.
37. *Ibid.*, p. 21.
38. *Eastern Religions and Western Thought*, p. 355.
39. *Ibid.*
40. *Religion and Society*, p. 98.
41. *Ibid.*, p. 97.
42. *Ibid.*, p. 61.
43. *Education, Politics, and War*, p. 97.
44. A.R. Wadia, "The Social Philosophy of Radhakrishnan" in Schilpp, *The Philosophy of Sarvepalli Radhakrishnan*, p. 775.

45. B.K. Mallick, "Radhakrishnan and Philosophy of the State and Community" in Schilpp, p. 749.
46. "Reply to Critics" in Schilpp, p. 841.
47. *"The Religion of the Spirit and the World's Need"* in Schilpp, p.80.
48. "Reply to Critics" in Schilpp, p. 942.
49. F.S.C. Northrop, "Radhakrishnan's Conception of the Relation Between Eastern and Western Cultural Values" in Schilpp, p. 654.
50. "Reply to Critics" in Schilpp, p. 826.
51. Quoted in Minor, *Radhakrishnan*, p. 85.
52. *Religion and Society*, p. 17.
53. *Ibid.*, p. 81.
54. S. Radhakrishnan, Newton Baker Lecture delivered at the Council on World Affairs, Cleveland, Ohio on March 27, 1958. Quoted in Ray, *The Political Thought of Radhakrishnan*, pp. 55-56.
55. *Religion and Society*, pp. 97-100.
56. *Ibid.*, p. 227.
57. *An Idealist View of Life*, p. 272.

34
Radhakrishnan and Humanism

YEAGER HUDSON
Colby College

It is a doubly ironic paradox that Radhakrishnan should have offered such a resounding criticism of the domination of Western philosophy by religion, in his 1918 book, *The (reign of) Religion in Contemporary Philosophy*,[1] when we remember, first, the extent to which he also criticized Western thought for its spiritual shallowness and blindness to religious values, and second, the extent to which his own philosophy is saturated with religion. It is not to religiousness as such, and certainly not spirituality, that he is objecting. Openminded, non-dogmatic religion, is not what he thinks has been dominant in the West. What he is criticizing, of course, is the domination of Western philosophy by a particular religious orthodoxy, a specific creed, that of Christianity. It is the fact that Christianity is creedal and is highly intolerant of other approaches to religion which Radhakrishnan finds particularly objectionable. It is also the fact that Christianity co-exists so comfortably with the materialism of the scientific West and with the oppressive colonialism which Western Christian nations have perpetrated against much of the rest of the world. But it is not this superficial paradox but a much more interesting one that I want to discuss here, one in which we find Radhakrishnan rigorously criticizing and rejecting a philosophical position to which upon close examination, I shall argue, his own thought actually turns out to be remarkably similar, namely, naturalistic humanism.

Radhakrishnan has usually been identified with an Absolute monistic Idealism of the sort somewhat like that of Josiah Royce or F.H. Bradley, and firmly rooted in the Advaita Vedānta tradition and the teachings of Śaṁkara. Without doubt he was. And yet, there are aspects of his philosophy which are distinctly theistic and as such tend strongly in the direction of dualism. Indeed, it is this feature of his philosophy with which he often seems most preoccupied. He appears less greatly concerned to expound, develop, or defend Absolute Idealism as a technical philosophical system, than to explain and advocate it is in the more popular sense which he referred to as "an idealist view of life."[2] It is because a theistic philosophy, despite its propensity toward dualism, serves this practical purpose that he concentrates much of his philosophical writing on such theistic thought even though he also sometimes suggests that in the strict sense and in the final analysis Absolute Idealism is the true view.

He is talking about an idealist view of life which is distinctly a religious or spiritual view of life. He uses the terms "idealism" and "religion" almost interchangeably as he examines the arguments of the materialists, the behaviourists, the agnostics, and the naturalists.[3] And he tells us that by "idealism" and "religion" he means the view of life which assumes that the universe has a meaning, that life is significant and purposeful, that man's moral and spiritual intuitions answer to a reality which is objective, that despite suffering and evil our existence is worthwhile and our efforts to make it better are not destined to ultimate frustration. It is not that his assumptions on these points are dogmatic presuppositions, accepted without question and without rational justification. Rather, he finds justification in the discovery that such assumptions have to be made if the world of human experience is to be intelligible, since strictly materialistic assumptions fail completely to explain the value dimensions which are an undisputable part of our life experience. Such assumptions are the methodological parallels, he suggests, of such principles as causality and the uniformity of nature which are taken for granted by scientists and by naturalist philosophers. But the metaphysical content of his position turns out, surprisingly, to resemble naturalistic humanism more than monistic Idealism. He says explicitly that the idealist view he is advocating is "not committed to the doctrine that the world is made of mind."[4] And although he does occasionally speak of the ultimate oneness of everything and the formlessness of the ultimate being, he appears most interested in understanding and finding meaning in the multiplicity of the here and now, and he often seems to do it by means of a divine being which has the earmarks of a personal God. Perhaps in the long run Radhakrishnan envisions an ultimate realm of *mokṣa* wherein all multiplicity, all separateness, and all change are transcended, but the idealist view of life is concerned with the realm of *samsara* in which we strive to understand, to express our moral and aesthetic intuitions, and to find our lives worthwhile.

In the course of his discussion of the idealist view of life, i.e. of the human place in the world of time and change, he examines several current philosophical positions which he judges inadequate. The most conspicuous examples are evolutionary naturalism and humanism. These were among the most creative and widely advocated philosophical alternatives to Absolute Idealism during the period of his life when he produced his two "view of life"[5] books - the period before the corrosive influence of logical positivism poisoned the intellectual atmosphere of the West, and left a scorch and barren philosophical landscape virtually devoid of any constructive metaphysical work, a condition of philosophical devastation from which a third of a century would be required to recover. Indeed, to a considerable extent it is by contrasting his own views with naturalism and other "non-spiritual" philosophical positions that Radhakrishnan gives the clearest expression to his own philosophy. But the contrast, as I see it, it greatly overdrawn.

When a new philosophical position is being worked out, or when a position is undergoing creative rethinking and refining, its advocates tend to elaborate it by generating a variety of versions. In the heat of the argumentation among the partisan advocates, as well as debate with advocates of contrary positions, differences loom large, but when the works are viewed from the perspective of a few years or decades, it becomes clear that similarities are far more striking than differences. Indeed, sometimes the differences appear small, even trivial, to outsiders. But the differences often arise from attempts to answer perceived weak points in the position, or to respond to objections by advocates of slightly different versions of the position, or to take into account matters which some partisans believe that others have failed to notice. This was certainly true of the hustle of work which generated various versions of naturalism and humanism during the early decades of the twentieth century. What is even more striking to those of us who view that philosophical scene from the vantage of the 1980's is how similar certain "religious" or "theistic" positions are to the very naturalism they criticized as inadequate. Radhakrishnan's view of life is a conspicuous example. Radhakrishnan wrote fairly extensively about naturalism and was careful to distinguish his position from both naturalism and humanism. And yet his view of life shares a very great deal with both of those philosophies. Clearly, in his mind, the naturalists and the humanists were correct in the way they explained a large proportion of human experience. But as he saw it, they were wrong about certain points, and these points are the ones which, in his view, are of the greatest importance.

The central point about which nearly all of the naturalists and humanists agree is that the evolutionary model derived by analogy from biology is the key to understanding reality. It was, indeed, the discovery of evolution as a principle in the organic world, and then the extension of that principle to reality as a whole, which provided the stimulus for the growth of naturalistic theories. Earlier naturalisms had attempted to explain the world in mechanical terms, that is to say, in terms of mechanical rearrangements of matter. Even at their best, they provided a thin and strained account of the workings of a static universe on the analogy of a machine. Many of their critics maintained that they could be made even remotely plausible only if they were supplemented with a cosmic mechanic, a God, who built the machine and kept it oiled and running, a concession most were not willing to make. But mechanistic materialism seemed pitifully inadequate to account for the most complex and interesting aspects of reality, the organic and the mental, and this was so even if claims about spiritual dimensions were left out of account. One way in which critics made this point was to argue that even if mechanistic materialism explains adequately the how of the cosmos, it leaves completely unanswered the why questions. And even the most generous interpretation of mechanistic materialism recognizes that it is a static theory. Even if we admit that it gives a plausible account of reality seen as a stable and unchanging system, a "machine," it offers no explanation at all of how the system can grow and change.

It was on this point that evolutionary theory represented a major advance. Understood in evolutionary terms, the universe is more like an organism than a machine. It is a dynamic system one of whose most interesting characteristics is that it moves toward ever increasingly complex levels of order. This aspect of the theory made it possible to explain change and novelty by the plausible suggestion that the material world turns out to have the surprising feature of manifesting new and unprecedented qualities when a new level of complexity arises. Thus the objectionable reductivism of mechanistic materialism, which amounted to saying that life is nothing but matter more complexly arranged and that mind is nothing but a much more complicated material configuration, is avoided by the new naturalism. Its advocates worked it out in various ways, but it amounted to the recognition of genuinely new, novel emergent qualities not characteristic of matter itself or of less complex arrangements of matter. A living organism is no longer seen as merely a more elaborate mixture of material particles. According to naturalism, a living organism is a more elaborate mixture of material particles which, because of the greater complexity, turns out to have a new characteristic never before known in the world, something quite novel which could not have been predicted, namely, life. And mind is not simply matter mingled in more variegated patterns. Rather it is that, plus mentality, consciousness - an emergent quality without precedent in the world.

The non-reductive nature of the new naturalism gave it a much more plausibility, and also provided a better foundation for another central claim most naturalisms, namely that a complete explanation of reality is possible exclusively in natural terms. Nature can be seen as a self-sufficient system with the power which drives it as well as the principle which guides and orders it built right into the system itself. No longer was it necessary to introduce a *deus ex machina* in the form of a supernatural designer and operator. The elegance of a theory which avoided explaining some not-fully-understood things by postulating something else even less well understood was truly appealing.

While Radhakrishnan found the evolutionary metaphor attractive and integrated it into his philosophy of the physical world, he found the claim that all of reality can be explained in purely natural terms quite unacceptable. This was perhaps his most serious objection to naturalism. For he was convinced that a purely naturalistic explanation read all purpose out of the world and left it a lonely, valueless place. If the world process is to be seen as moving in some direction and having some purpose; and if human existence is to be understood, not as a temporary and accidental flourishing of a curious phenomenon but rather as the progression and the culmination of a plan for the realization of goodness and value in creation, then a supernatural creator who knows and cares about the process must be recognized.

But the dichotomy which Radhakrishnan sensed between his position and that of evolutionary naturalism seems not to be as substantial as it appeared to him. As it turned out, some of the leading advocates of the new naturalism themselves began to discover, the more they worked out the detailed implications of their theories, that explanation in purely natural terms did not quite suffice, and that after all they needed some further explanatory concepts. Bergson spoke of the *elan vital* and Samuel Alexander introduced the notion of a *nesis*.[6] They insisted that these were not extra-natural or supernatural forces, but many of their critics believed that the introduction of such qualities amounted to admitting that explanation in purely natural terms was not possible. Alexander went a step further, bringing in the notion of deity. But deity in his system is not the source of the existence or the order of nature; rather deity is the outcome, that toward which the cosmic process is moving. It is not that deity has produced nature according to

Alexander. Rather nature is in the process of creating deity and deity will be that as yet unknown quality which will characterize the world when it arrives at that highest and most complex arrangement to which it is moving.

But the introduction of forces or principles which seemed to smack of the supernatural, and the bringing in of deity, even in an unconventional way, were not the only instances of what looked like cracks in the strict naturalism of the naturalists. On another major teaching the naturalist divided sharply, with the French philosopher, Henri Bergson, taking what turned out to be the minority position. This has to do with epistemology and the source of our knowledge. Most naturalists were strict empiricists, maintaining that scientific method is the only way of attaining knowledge and that all scientific knowledge rests on sense impressions. Bergson, truly the naturalist voice crying in the wilderness, taught an enlarged epistemology which insisted that scientific knowledge, useful as it is in providing utilitarian insight into the mechanical workings of nature, utterly fails to make us acquainted with the inner reality of the world or of man. He worked out a doctrine of intuition, one which sounds remarkably similar to Radhakrishnan's understanding of intuition and religious experience. Bergson's version involved the notion that the human mind is capable of plunging, as it were, into the very temporal evolutionary flow of reality and knowing it in a direct and unmediated way as it really is in itself.[7] He did not see intuition in this sense as inconsistent with naturalism or as involving anything spiritual even though it was, of course, an extra-sensory way of knowing; a way of achieving a simultaneity and co-extensiveness with the process of the world which revealed dimensions of nature that since knowledge utterly missed.

It was emergent naturalism of the type advocated by Bergson and Alexander that Radhakrishnan studied but found wanting. However adequately naturalism accounts for the process of nature, however apt the evolutionary metaphor may be as a way of picturing the ongoing life of the natural world, Radhakrishnan sees fundamental omissions in these theories which render them ineligible. It is at the point of dissimilarity between naturalism and the idealist view that Radhakrishnan's most characteristic beliefs stand out in boldest relief. As a portrayal of the process of the mundane world seen in its strictly local setting of historical time and space, the naturalist account was a plausible description. Radhakrishnan was not concerned to modify or amend their narrative of the spacio-temporal unfolding of the natural world. But the naturalist tale, as he saw it, is only a chronicle about the how of the machinery of the physical world. It is not really a comprehensive philosophical account of the why of the entire scheme of things. It leaves out utterly any attempted accountings for ultimate origins, but more importantly it omits altogether any elucidation of the why concerns of human experience, and indeed virtually neglects to recognize the moral and spiritual aspects of conscious life. It gives a pretty good descriptive account of how things work, but it does not recognize or account for the fact that human experience involves a keen sense of how things ought to work, a strong urge toward ways of thinking and behaving which evaluate, which distinguish the factual from the ideal, and which lure toward the realization of more valuable states of affairs.

Radhakrishnan refers to science - and to naturalism as a philosophical elaboration of science - as an account of *saṁsāra*. It attempts what earlier materialist theories could not do, to account both for the continuity of nature and the discontinuity which marks the major evolutionary transitions from dead matter to life, and from the biological to the psychological. It also finds discontinuities at more fundamental levels in the form discovered by quantum physics. The philosopher expresses these truths in terms of *karma* and freedom. *Karma* is the recognition of continuity and the determination of the present by the past. Freedom is that special feature which characterizes moral spirits. It is an emergent quality which enables human persons to redirect the course of their lives - indeed, the course of the world. Freedom is not a denial of continuity. Just as living things, despite the astonishing new features they have which differentiate them from the inorganic, depend at every moment upon the proper functioning of the material processes which characterize their bodies, so also free spiritual human beings depend upon and are continuous with the organic processes which characterize them. And just as material processes are subject to the web of causation, so also are the organic ones, and indeed also the psychological ones. And yet, there really is freedom. Radhakrishnan explains it by an analogy with a card game. *Karma*, the principle of causal continuity, is the name for the fact that we are dealt a certain hand of cards. Freedom does not negate the effects of material law or the effects of spiritual continuity with previous deeds. The range of our freedom is limited. But the same hand of cards can be played in many ways. Freedom is that amazing capacity which rational spirits have to choose how they will play their cards and thus to create meaning and significance in their lives. The fact that they have been endowed with such a capacity is evidence that the universe supports their moral strivings and makes provision for the satisfaction of their need for beauty, goodness, and happiness.

At this point Radhakrishnan sounds very much like the humanism he criticizes. He certainly acknowledges that humanism is a step above naturalism. Humanism, he tells us, is religion secularized. Humanism recognizes that man is a value-conscious being, striving to realize moral ideals. But humanism refuses to recognize that the limitation of the realm of value to the domain of human dreams and imagination shrinks and dwarfs not only what man is, but what he ever could hope to be. It is ideals higher than any we have yet conceived which call out to us and lure us, not merely from within our own psyche but from a realm of spirit infinitely higher than the merely human. The lure is not merely to become better humans; it is a summons to embody the divine. Humanism, which believes that there is nothing higher than man, can hardly inspire in man the passion which has enabled a few great saints to rise to superhuman levels and to become the prophets, the enlighteners, and the saviours of mankind. Humanism calls man to dream great human dreams and to strive for great social reform. But Idealism challenges man to open his eyes to the spark of the divine in him which offers hope not merely of a better society but of, *mokṣa*, salvation.

One cannot help feeling that it is the theist in Radhakrishnan which speaks when he interprets Idealism thus. And yet an Idealism which is closer to Advaita Vedānta lies beneath the surface in his thought. It is that Advaita Idealism which, surprising as it may sound, I want to suggest is really quite close to humanism. Radhakrishnan the theist becomes, or verges on becoming, a *Dvaita* thinker, for theism is almost unavoidably dualistic. Absolute Idealists, whether Indian, German, or British, often tend to sound dualistic when they deal with the processes of the natural world, but they recognize that in the final analysis reality is one. It was Tagore who said that, in the end we will probably have to recognize that ultimate reality is the Absolute, formless One and that Ātman, the spirit of man, is identical with Brahman, that ultimate, impersonal, formless One. But he went on to argue that if love is to characterize our relationship to reality, we must imagine reality as a personal God who has a form which is man-like and from whom Ātman is separated. For love is the longing one feels for union with that from which it is separated, and the experience at least sometimes of touching and knowing the Beloved. Love disappears when the distinction between the self and the lover is lost in the merging of the no longer conscious or personal self with the formless and impersonal One.

Radhakrishnan, like Tagore, seems aware that Idealism in its full philosophical elaboration requires a concept of the Absolute which is formless, impersonal, and inseparable from the rest of reality. This conception of reality, I want to argue, is remarkably compatible with humanism. For humanism recognizes that reality soars to consciousness in man alone; that the source of meaning and goodness in the world is not a divine being separate from the world but is those processes in the world which create and sustain human consciousness and value. The humanist sees reality as one and mankind as an inseparable part of it. And yet, unable to shift responsibility for the well-being of the mundane world to a supernatural being, the naturalist recognizes the call and the challenge to embody those ideals of goodness and beauty which nature inspires and supports.

What predominates in Radhakrishnan's interpretation of Idealism is his concern for a practical philosophy in the sense of a view of life, philosophy which can inspire the devotion of the common person as the image in the temple inspires the *bhakti* of the devotee. And that is what makes him think that Idealism as he conceives it is something so different from and superior to humanism. Radhakrishnan is convinced that naturalistic humanism which omits the supernatural dimension of reality lacks not only an explanation of the source of the world and especially the value aspects of the world, but also lacks the power to inspire religious heroism or sainthood in humans. On this point he may well be right. Apart from Socrates, we do not find many martyrs to reason and the values which uniquely make us human. The fiery zeal of the world-shaking martyrs is usually the fruit of religious, indeed, most often of sectarian, enthusiasm - behaviour which Radhakrishnan deplores. If humanism, grounded in a metaphysics of evolutionary naturalism instead of theism, is slower to inspire humans to become martyrs and saints, perhaps it is also slower to enflame them to become fanatics. The humanist certainly does not use god-language, and does not call the totality of reality by the name of the Absolute. And yet the humanist vision of reality is not of a world cold and uncaring where, as the Existentialists suggest, human life is a fortuitous and tragic calamity. Neither is it necessary that humanism lack the experiential dimension which Radhakrishnan felt was an indispensible supplement of empirical scientific rationalism. Bergson's epistemology is explicitly and thoroughly intuitional. And the type of religious oneness with reality which Emerson expressed when his naturalism bordered on pantheism is not alien to or inconsistent with naturalistic humanism. Many humanists, particularly persons like John Dewey, are convinced that the universe, which has created by its natural processes, all of the capacities and the ideals of mankind, also is clearly on the side of human values. Dewey and other naturalists also believe that the highest ideals toward which humans do and ought to aspire may appropriately be called divine in at least a metaphorical sense. Humanism relinquished the concept of a divine person, a god separate from the world who makes and sustains reality. But then, so does Advaita Vedānta in its fully worked out expression. Brahman is not separate from the world, and does not have the form of a conscious god-being. Man's oneness with Brahman is hidden while samsara is pervaded with māyā. We glimpse it only in those mystical experiences in which our consciousness dissolves into the One. And the humanist's description of those experiences are not strikingly different from the description of the Advaita mystic.

References

1. Sarvepalli Radhakrishnan : *The Reign of Religion in Contemporary Philosophy*, London : MacMillan and Co., 1920.
2. Sarvepalli Radhakrishnan : *An Idealist View of Life*, London : George Allen & Unwin Ltd., 1932.
3. *Ibid.*
4. *An Idealist View of Life, op. cit.*, p. 10.
5. *An Idealist View of Life, op cit.*, and *A Hindu View of Life*, London : George Allen & Unwin Ltd., 1927.
6. Henri Bergson : *Creative Evolution*, New York : Henry Holt and Company, 1911. Samuel Alexander : *Space, Time, and Deity*, New York : MacMillan, 1920.
7. Henri Bergson : *An Introduction to Metaphysics*, New York & London : G.P. Putnam's Sons, 1912. *The Two Sources of Morality and Religion*, London : MacMillan and Company, 1935.

35
Perspectives on Social Philosophy : Radhakrishnan's View

T.S. DEVADOSS
University of Madras

That philosophy counts in human affairs is acknowledged by one and all. If philosophical ideas play a role in determining social practise, this indicates that some ideas have relevance to conduct. I understand by philosophical ideas or views as distinct from purely scientific ideas or views, interpretations of existence from the standpoint of value. Values may be rooted in interests, but whenever conflicts of value arise, they involve or are related to interests - and, to the extent that the content of interests is social, to social interests.

The most effective development is in the presentation of India's fundamental thought in the idiom of our age and its development in new directions. Today we find that humanity's search for Truth and fulfilment has taken man in two directions - the outer and the inner. The investigation of the objective world has resulted in the scientific heritage, and the investigation of the inner or subjective world has resulted in the religious heritage. The present era is marked by deliberate attempts to formulate social values and ideals and the political ends and means which they cherish.

The present age which is marked by the process of secularization and democratization of social life, shows that social philosophy has become less remote; it has entered the area of social struggle on which ideology is born. Social philosophy has now to rediscover man as a symbolising, evaluative, dialectic and integrated person whose nature, conduct and aspirations can no longer be artificially fragmented and segregated by separate scientific and social studies. The studies in future have to be all-comprehensive and all-encompassing. Similarly social philosophy has to discover society which defines, shapes man's nature, understandings and habits and also projects his desires, values and aspirations. Man's greatness is not in what he is but in what he can be.

The present paper is designed to contribute some thoughts concerning the changing needs of the individual as well as of the society from the perspective of Radhakrishnan's social philosophy.

The study of Radhakrishnan's philosophical system and of comparative philosophy in general, confirms the importance of understanding the culture within which a philosophy or philosophies develop and function. Radhakrishnan's system, including his theories of knowledge and reality as well as his theories of religion, exemplifies the influence of linguistic, geographical, economic, political, social and religious factors upon a philosophical system.

By attempting to revitalize the idealist view of life, Radhakrishnan tried to articulate the 'perennial and universal philosophy' and showed that it has its finest expression in traditional Indian thought. While he began his philosophic career defending Vedānta against the charge that it 'had no room for ethics,' he came more and more to treat Vedānta as the means for establishing a universal philosophy. But however one interprets his use of Vedānta, it would be difficult to deny that Radhakrishnan has consistently and explicitly worked toward a philosophy which most adequately synthesized Indian and Western philosophy. Further, there is textual evidence to show that this philosophical synthesis rests entirely on what Radhakrishnan calls the idealist view of life. In reply to D.M. Datta's question as to whether a synthesis of Indian and Western philosophy could fruitfully be based on a position other than idealism. Radhakrishnan affirms idealism as the most effective synthesizer of East and West :

> I do believe that the great idealist tradition has in it the possibility of bringing East and West together in a closer union on the plane of mind and spirit . . . . It is my conviction that, if the achievements of science and criticism are to be harnessed for right ends, we must develop certain universal aims, and the idealist tradition of the world provides us with these goals for human endeavour and action.[1]

It is quite significant that in this reply, and in virtually all of Radhakrishnan's references to a synthesis of East and West, idealism is synonymous with a universal spirituality or what the Vedāntist calls darsana, a spiritual insight. Radhakrishnan's goal is not only a particular philosophical system, but a unifying and universal vision as well. He notes that we may not be ready for a world philosophy, but it is at least time for a world outlook. The outlook which Radhakrishnan has fostered is consistent with Vedānta. In *An idealist View of Life*, he calls this outlook 'spiritual wisdcm.'

An idealist view of life is an absolute view of spirit. It is the affirmation of the primacy of the spiritual values. The primacy of spiritual values, the lack and necessity of the spiritual note in modern civilization, the logical inevitability of a spiritual absolutism in philosophy, the undeniable truth of our inner life or spirit - this is the ever recurring theme of practically all his books and lectures. He believed that the philosophies of the East in general, and of India in particular, have from the beginning, upheld the spiritual tradition.

Radhakrishnan's central teaching is that the spiritual should be given primacy, and reason and humanism, or science and man, should be explained in the light of the spiritual. The true Absolute is the spirit; our attempt to turn reason into an absolute has ended in some of the unhuman and inhuman results of science; and in similar view of man as an absolute has led to conflicting political philosophies and conflagrations. A true understanding of man requires viewing him from the standpoint of the spiritual.

'A spiritual view,' says Radhakrishnan, 'is sustained not by insight, but also by a rational philosophy.'[2] The uniqueness of Hindu thought, he holds, is the recognition and explication of the inwardness of man, of its freedom, sacredness, nobility and importance.

Radhakrishnan points out that the fragmentariness of man is overcome only in the whole. So he "strives after values, frames, ideals and struggles to build up a world of unity and harmony."[3] We began our life in a given or assured framework of values and we endeavour to realise that value which is the source of all other values, and this is assuredly a spiritual value that we strive after. Radhakrishnan contends : "The primal craving for the eternal and the abiding remains inextinguishable."[4]

The spirit in man always shines in him, even in the depths of his degradation, as the subject that transcends the empirical self and enlightens both. In realising his unity with the universal self or his own spiritual existence, man becomes one with the universe. The internal conflict among the different aspects of his life, passions, desires, feelings and thoughts disappears; and so also the conflicts between the self and the environment, his self and other selves. Only at this stage the human self is completely organised and integrated, and becomes a perfect self in the truest sense.

In the idealism expounded by Radhakrishnan, we have just that vital ideal for which the world is waiting - one which instead of dividing continents and sects within them, is capable of uniting them 'in a single allegiance, not to any material crown, or empire, but to the values which are the crown of life and, the empire of the spirit.' His idealism bears some marks of Platonic and Hegelian influence, but the perception of what appertains to spiritual consciousness becomes with Radhakrishnan a much more vital and subtle process, revealing as it does, the intuitive quality of an inner life.

Radhakrishnan has tried successfully to disentangle the strands of pure metaphysics from the complex web of Indian philosophical writings. Pure metaphysical ideas in Indian thought have yet to be thrown together into a perspective but the essential initiative has been taken by him. His contribution to Indian idealistic absolutism lies in making it clear that the Absolute can be reached positively, and not merely negatively. By trying to remove the elements of negativism from the general Advaita tradition and by pointing out a positive way, he has encouraged the development of a dynamic outlook which forms the basis of his social philosophy.

It is against this backdrop that an attempt will be made to analyse Radhakrishnan's social philosophy. His thought is philosophical and his vision is that of a great universal humanist. The presentation of his social philosophy has passed through three phases. The first phase is represented by his Upton lectures delivered at Oxford in 1926, and published as 'The Hindu View of Life.' They have been extremely popular both in India and in the West. The popular vein in which they are composed may explain the naivete of their assumptions. The second phase is more mature and published as 'Eastern Religions and Western Thought,' where a philosophical justification of basic social ideas in Hinduism is attempted. The third phase began with his lectures in 1942 delivered at Calcutta and Banaras, and published under the title, Religion and Society.

There are five aspects in Radhakrishnan's social philosophy. In the first place, he finds in it the spiritual equality of all men. But this has to be taken with a grain of salt, for prima facie only the Brahmin is born in getting where he can proceed with his spiritual development. Second, it is claimed that the four-fold scheme makes for individuality. In the positive sense, individuality is attained not through an escape from limitation but through the willing acceptance of obligations.[5] But if caste is determined by birth and birth determines functions, then it should be clear that there is no room here for a willing acceptance of obligations except in the sense that the average Hindu is a patient sufferer and, until lately, did not bother to break his head against the stone wall of caste. Third, all work is socially useful and from an economic standpoint equally important. This can hardly be adduced as an argument for the democratic nature of caste, since it is equally, and perhaps even more pertinent to an aristocratic organisation of society. Fourth, 'social justice is not a scheme of rights but of opportunities.' Every historic democracy in the West has been more insistent on rights that on duties, and this fact is cited as a weakness of democracy by its critics.

Radhakrishnan accepted democratic form of government, since the essence of democracy is consideration for others. He adopted the democratic method, because democracy is an expression of this life in man and his rights and duties to perfect himself, to govern himself and to build a society in which self-perfection is possible. No individual can be good unless the social structure to which he belongs is good.

Radhakrishnan realised that the freedom of spirit. Liberty from physical and social constraints, are essential. Liberty, has been interpreted in two ways. There is the liberty which saves from social compulsion, to liberate us from wants which can be satisfied only through right economic and social relationships.

If democracy is sound, we will work for social structure which assures work and security to all adults, proper education for the young for the development of their special capacity, a widespread distribution of the necessities and amenities of life, full safeguard against the distress of unemployment and freedom of self-development. Radhakrishnan holds that the social life is a movement in our destiny but not the terminus. The state must become the instrument of true civilization, and educate its member's to an entirely new conception of social responsibility. If we believe in religious discipline for achieving this end we need not be looked upon as soft and sentimental.

Radhakrishnan's views on social dynamics is worth noting here. Political wisdom cannot be in advance of social maturity. Social progress cannot be achieved by external means. It is determined by man's intimate transcendent experience. We are the guardians of the values of a society, the values which are the real life and character of a society. Radhakrishnan contends that if society is to be saved, resistance to the present order is necessary, but it should be resistance which will put down lies and insincerity. Death is not worse than a dishonourable life.

In the modern society, every one of us is responsible, for not bringing in radical change in the social conditions. Only education and employment opportunities can change the sad plight of the youth of the nation.

On the social side, we are attempting to spread education, scientific and technical. If we are to adjust ourselves to the rhythm of the new world, our people should adopt a rational and scientific outlook in matter of health, sanitation, etc. In schools and colleges, as well as in self-governing institutions, we have to develop a sense of decency in public affairs. Unfortunately at the present moment, Radhakrishnan contends, we have factional strife, personal rivalries, pressure groups and scrambles for power, which impede the development of a national ethos. Radhakrishnan advised us that we should subordinate our personal interests and group loyalties to the strengthening of the moral fibre of the nation.

Man, when truly human, is not merely the product of history, but is the moulder of history. What is called the contingency or unforeseeability of history is due to the free will of the human being. He is not a victim of necessity - naturalistic, historical or dialectical. He uses this necessity as a means for achieving freedom. Our hope for the future lies in the wise direction which the leaders of the world will make in the present context.

Radhakrishnan and Nehru have often displayed a marked identity of approach. Tolerance, liberalism and humanism form the basic ingredients of their political thinking. He observed : "when we accept democracy as a working principle, we mean that there are inalienable rights belonging to human personality as such, which must be respected in our dealings with all persons, whatever the sex or calling may be. Individuality is sacred and each individual should be allowed to develop his nature . . . The chief purpose of social organisation is to foster the spiritual freedom, human creativeness. All attempts at establishing a social democracy, a more equal distribution of wealth and opportunity, are a genuine manifestation of the religious spirit."

Radhakrishnan contends that 'if individuality is lost, all is lost,' but adds that 'both aspects, the individual and the social are essential.'[6]

Radhakrishnan lays the utmost emphasis on individual freedom and initiative. He was deeply influenced by the Gandhian stress on the purity of means and the message of non-violence. As a religious humanist, Radhakrishnan urges the necessity of a new social order with basic economic justice. All attempts at establishing a social democracy, a mere equal distribution of wealth and opportunity are a genuine manifestation of the religious spirit.

Radhakrishnan holds the view that human life is ever changing. It is not static but dynamic. As life changes, changes occur in society too. Society, in other words is a dynamic process. Every change in man's relation to society means necessarily some changes in his relation to his fellow beings. Society is a changing medium of creation and expression of his deep seated desires, values and aspirations. It outlines, shapes and refines man's social nature, conscience and morals, as he also frequently and insistently projects his own image, values and experiences from the depth of his consciousness when he is unique by himself. In other words, man is thus deeply embedded and moulded in the matrix of society and the society in turn has enabled him to reveal his true nature. Man is an integral whole as the career of values of complex dimensions. Man's values, his group structure constitute a single arch supporting the ascending, aspiring, activating moral spire of nobility, goodness, justice and love that gently touches sublime heights of infinite and the perfect. What is to be achieved is that the individual as an integrated person may have to realize to the fullest extent his own innate possibilities as a human being in and through society.

Radhakrishnan believed in complete regeneration of social structure as of the individual. Society was more important to him than the state and it was the former's reformation he sought. Society must restrain and control the state, and the individual should keeps the society strong and reasonable.

The main point to be noted is that the main contribution of Radhakrishnan is not so much in the realm of effecting actual social change as in awakening social consciousness about the necessity of change.

The ideal society for which we must work, says Radhakrishnan, should be one where there will be no inequalities among men. One must effect peacefully a social transformation which makes justice, individual and national, its objective. Radhakrishnan was convinced that mere constitutional structures will not suffice for the concrete realization of rights and hence he postulated the ideal of a dharmic society based on the doctrine of 'sarvadharma-samanatva,' as taught to us by Svami Vivekananda. In other words, it means the establishment of the kingdom of love, justice and righteousness.

We are living in an age of tensions between group and group, class and class, nation and nation. The world today is burning with unrest that seeks to right social and political wrongs, when violence erupts there is destruction and loss of life but no assurance of the outcome. The armaments race is wasteful and potentially catastrophic. Hence a group of the methods of struggle is needed. In this sense, Radhakrishnan's world view of 'Universal Man' and 'Universal Religion' is considered relevant.

Radhakrishnan was an ardent admirer and follower of Gandhi, particularly his technique of non-violence. Radhakrishnan objects to the use of violence because : 'when it appears to do good, the good is only temporary; the evil it does is permanent.' This is the lesson which mankind has to learn from history. According to his analysis, the prime cause of modern wars is the inhuman race for exploitation of the so-called weaker races on the earth. He thinks that the motive of exploitation accounts not only for the outbreak of war between two states, but also generally for chaotic situation that prevails at the national and international levels.

An analysis of Radhakrishnan's position will show that at a still deeper level there is another factor which serves to explain the inhuman race for exploitation, and that factor is selfishness. Exploitation is only the outer manifestation of the inward selfishness of the individual. When the selfishness of the individual gets organised, systematically pursued, and is given institutional form by a group of individuals of kindred interests, it culminates in class antagonism and class exploitation with all the attendant consequences.

Philosophers and peace lovers are earnestly in search for a moral equivalent of war which would embody the technique of war minus its violence as the surest way to establish peace. Radhakrishnan fully endorsed the technique of Gandhi, viz., non-violent resistance to get our grievances redressed.

To Radhakrishnan, what the individual does being moved by the idea of common good is of utmost importance, for the successful realization of the ideal of implementation of the scheme is dependent upon the individual. Like Gandhi, Radhakrishnan gave supreme importance to man - the individual. Man is never to be treated as a means to any other end.

Radhakrishnan held the view that the ideal of world government is bound to recede, so long as people believe in the view that their salvation and welfare would depend on their sovereign independence. What, then, is the remedy? A change of attitude on the part of the people is necessary, but that is not sufficient. What is required in addition to a change of attitude is sincerity to work it out. That is what may be called in the existential language commitment on the part of the individual. But whose commitment is that? Though it cannot be derived that it is the commitment of fallible men, it is the commitment of those individuals who want to realize an ideal in which disinterested service must find an important place. If so, this phase of morality is the precondition of any well-ordered social and political framework. It is not the case that men to start with are in a moral vacuum and that through the social order they come to have a moral stature. It is the capacity to conceive of, and contribute to, the common good that entitles the individuals for membership in a society and this capacity which is at the basis of social and political order is undoubtedly moral as well as rational.

Whether the formation of world government is the effective solution to international tension is another issue. Since a very important source of trouble arises from centralisation of authority in one place, it is to be seriously doubted whether at all it is conducive to the presentation of freedom and personal worth of the individual as well as the promotion of world peace. What is required today is not a unitary authority but a plurality of authorities which would function on the basis of non-violence in all matters in harmony with one another. The ideal to be pursued is a federation of friendly inter-dependent states whose entire set-up will be based on the principle of decentralization with non-violence as the principle of action. The way to peace lies through peace.

The struggle for the preservation and strengthening of peace is a key prerequisite of human rights because it is only in conditions of peace and international cooperation that the basic right of all people can be guaranteed.

Radhakrishnan, denouncing the use of violence, says : "In human relations the choice is not between good and bad, but between what is bad and what is worse. The unregulated use of force by the states is infinitely worse than the use of force by the world commonwealth as the sanction of law . . . . Non-violence may be unattainable if we wish to obtain it at one rush; but we may reach it if we are prepared to work towards it by stages."[7]

In the last analysis, Radhakrishnan like Gandhi believed in the efficacy of the principle of non-violence as a means to establish peace on earth and goodwill among mankind. He observed : "Peace on earth is our act of faith, and a :t of free will against determinism." He said : 'I have no doubt in my mind that we are moving forward, that all the great achievements of science and technology are there for the purpose of producing a single world, a kind of paradise on earth. All the resources are there, the intellectual achievements are there, the will is there, but not that dedication that capacity to raise above narrow group loyalties . . . and transforming those loyalties into loyalty to one single world community. He maintained : 'Ethical sublimity is the mark of the magnanimous man; ethical depravity is the mark of the low man. All other distinctions are irrelevant, *na kulam kulami-tyahu hacaram kulamucyate.*'

Philosophers, with a few exceptions, have throughout the history of civilization thought and worked for peace. This has been true largely because of the philosopher's confidence in reason and his belief in the possibility of man's control of his destiny through the exercise of his freedom.

Wars, as everybody knows are not natural cataclysms, but are made in the minds and hearts of men, or as UNESCO so eloquently expressed it in the justly celebrated phrase of its Preamble, the joint conception of a British statesman and an American poet, Clement Atlee and Archibald. Mac Leish : "Since wars begin in the minds of men, it is in the minds of men that the defences of peace have to be constructed." UNESCO has required philosophers formally to "engage upon a world philosophy, unified and unifying background of thought for the modern world." Several important conferences have been held in various parts of the world for the purpose of discovering whether or not there are insuperable differences of thought and world outlook that would make world co-operation impossible, in principle usually with reassuring and encouraging result, at least as far as philosophers are concerned. Philosophers are by nature and training usually interested in the universal rather than in the particularistic. Orchestrated harmony, not homogeneous sameness, is the ideal of philosophy. Philosophers, consequently, tend to stress what unites mankind, rather than what divides it. They are also pledged to attempt promote clarity of concept and of statement.

We have now come to the end of our consideration of Radhakrishnan as the spokesman for philosophy's concern for peace and harmony among the nations and the people of the world. Radhakrishnan spoke for all mankind in reminding us where man's true dignity resides, and what constitutes the true grandeur of peoples and nations. Let us work for the renewal of the heart, the transformation of values, the surrender of the spirit to the claims of the eternal. Dr. Sarvepalli Radhakrishnan the greatest acarya of the present century has left his footprints in the sands of time. May his life and teachings be a beacon of hope and courage to all of us.

References

1. Paul Arthur Schilpp (ed.), 'Reply to Critics.' *The Philosophy of S. Radhakrishnan,* Library of Living Philosophers, New York : Tudor, 1952, p. 820.
2. S. Radhakrishnan, *Eastern Religions and Western Thought,* Oxford : Oxford University Press, 1940, p. 76.

3. S. Radhakrishnan, *An Idealist View of Life*, London : George Allen & Unwin, 1952.
4. *Ibid.*, p. 345.
5. Paul Arthur Schilpp, op. cit., p. 775.
6. S. Radhakrishnan, *Religion and Society*.
7. S. Radhakrishnan, *Religion and Society*, London : George Allen & Unwin, 1969, p. 218.

36
Radhakrishnan's Philosophy of World-Involvement

KAISA PUHAKKA
Georgia State College

Bridging the gap between thought and action is a perennial concern for philosophers both Indian and Western. It is especially a concern for ethics. Yet decades of intensive work by ethicists has not changed the fact that our understanding of the world, no matter how pristine and clear by philosophic standards, often has distressingly little impact on our lives.

Sarvepalli Radhakrishnan stands out among modern Vedāntic thinkers as one for whom worldly action is of central concern. The purpose of this article is to compare and contrast the way the problem of action comes about in the Western and Indian contexts and to discuss Radhakrishnan's proposed solution to the problem.

The problem of ethical theory vs. ethical action is frequently expressed as the dichotomy between fact and value, 'is' and 'ought.' One does not get from fact to value or form 'is' to 'ought' and vice versa. The fact-value dichotomy thus sets up the problem to be unsolvable and doomed to be a pseudo-problem. I believe that a more productive way of setting up the problem is to view 'value' not as an ontological category juxtaposed to that of 'fact' but as a dynamic energy which, when it imbues thought and understanding, leads to action.

All action takes place in an interactional context. It is only when an action has an impact on someone or something that its ethicality becomes an issue. The interaction minimally involves an action by one of the participants and the receiving of its impact by the other. The interaction can thus be viewed as a communication between two terminals, one sending the message or doing the action, the other receiving the message or the impact of the action.

Three elements are necessary, I believe, for any successful communication. These are : *understanding, affinity,* and the act of *communication* itself. The last of these is self-explanatory : for the message to get across, the act of communication must occur. The other two enhance the likelihood of this happening. Understanding refers to the viewpoint, frame of reference, or conception of reality shared by the two terminals. The necessity of a shared frame of reference for a rational discourse is something that no philosopher or scientist today would doubt. It suffices for our purposes to merely call attention to the fact that the absence of a shared framework or the lack of agreement about reality is one of the most common reasons for a breakdown of communication among people. Thus a phenomenologist usually finds it impossible to talk to his or her analytic colleague and vice versa, and we all know the futility of trying to discourse on politics with someone who does not share our political views. Sharing viewpoints, or at least being willing to entertain the other's viewpoint, is necessary for successful communication. Once there is a shared framework of understanding, communication can occur regardless of who or what the other terminal is. For any contemporary model of communication the shared framework of understanding is a given, and indeed the models are largely concerned with spelling out the specifics of this framework.

But the presence of a shared framework does not yet mean that communication will actually occur. Affinity is the second necessary element in communication. Affinity refers to liking, feeling of closeness, willingness to share the same space with, the other terminal. Witness the rapt attention with which a man or a woman talks and listens to his or her beloved; at no other time in one's life is there so much eagerness to understand, to share with and open up to the viewpoint of another person. At the other extreme, people pass each other by in the crowded streets of New York, indifferent if not oblivious to each other as potential communication terminals. Between these extremes, there is our natural gregariousness which makes us start up conversations with strangers on trains and airplanes just for the fun of it. Affinity thus facilitates communication. Its absence, indifference, is not conducive to communication. Computer models of communication usually do not incorporate affinity among their elements. But then such models are meant to only describe how communication occurs, not to predict that it in fact does occur. However, I suspect that the AI workers and hackers who spend long hours devising or deciphering these models are fascinated by the likeness between their own minds and the models and feel a certain affinity with the latter. Because of this affinity, they sometimes prefer computers to their fellow humans as terminals of communication. The point of these remarks is that any communication, even that between humans and computers, is an action in the world, and as such it occurs because there is affinity between the terminals. The affinity need not be felt reciprocally - and many would maintain that it is not when the other terminal is a computer - but affinity, whether one-sided or reciprocal, provides impetus for communication.

Let us explore the above point further. In everyday commerce affinity refers to liking the other. But at a more fundamental level, it refers to the acknowledgement that the other is of equal ontological status with oneself. This is in keeping with the dictionary meaning of 'affinity' as 'similarity' or 'like nature.' For me to be willing to communicate with someone or something, I must take it to be in some ways like myself, and minimally this means that it is as real to me (though not necessarily as alive) as myself. An example may help clarify the point. Suppose on a lonely walk in the dark woods you encounter an eternal form suspended some three feet above the ground. It smiles at you and you hear it speaking to you. Assuming you don't flee from the spot, you may either take a swing at the form or you may listen to it. In either case, you are, at the moment, taking it to be as real as yourself albeit less solid and perhaps in other ways also different from yourself. Or you can look behind the bushes for the contraption that might be responsible for the apparition and hence the real terminal of this communication. Should the apparition turn out to be a hologram, you might still watch it, even with fascination. But a certain detachment would now characterize your way of relating to it. You would be, so to speak, looking through it and listening behind it in a way that is phenomenologically quite different from the moment before. Because what is in front of you now is only a representation, not the real thing. Lacking reality, it lacks the power to evoke a reaction.

One is reminded here of Śaṁkara's classic example of the person who was instantly freed of his fear of a snake upon realizing that what he had stumbled upon was only a rope. This example was meant to illustrate the power that illusions have on us - as well as the power of insight into the true nature of things of free us from captivity to illusions. But Śaṁkara's point applies to anything that is taken to be real, anything to which one is ontologically committed. The man who now sees a rope in front of him is guided in his action upon or reaction to the rope by the reality to which he is now committed : he may, for example, pick the rope up and tie it in a knot. But he would not do these things if he were uncertain as to the ontological status of the rope.

The point of all this is that action (i.e. interaction) and ontological commitment are inextricably bound up together. The connection between them is more intimate than that of cause and effect, and it is also more substantial than a logical or analytic connection. Action both presupposes and generates ontological commitments. I have also argued above that ontological commitments are akin to feeling rather than thought, and I have characterized this feeling as affinity. The empirical possibility that thought influences feeling is, of course, not denied. However, thought alone is not sufficient to generate action and engagement with the world. And thought alone is not sufficient to generate ontological commitments. The domain of thought ends where ontological commitment begins. No one has argued this point more persuasively than W.W. O. Quine.[1]

Let us now turn to ethical theory (i.e. values and ethical directives) and the world, and the gap between them. The gap can be viewed as a problem in communication, in getting the message (ethical theory) to have its intended impact (action) on the world. The problem of Western ethical theories has to do with the understanding component of our model. This is because Western ethical theories are applied to a value-neutral world view depicted by science.[2] Such a world view does not ontologically compel the acceptance of any particular ethical theory, and hence a gap remains between ethics as a *consideration* and ethics as *action*. I believe that one can safely make the following generalization about "the Western world view" - the overall framework in which both Western scientific and ethical thinking are embedded. It is that the world with its physical, psychological, and social manifestations is taken to be real in an unqualified sense. Philosophers and scientists may differ in their interpretations as to the nature of reality (e.g. whether it is ultimately physical or mental). But the reality of the world is not itself in question, and the notion that some things are more real than others is alien to Western thought. The world is thus acknowledged to be as real as oneself and can be embraced with affinity. The willingness to engage the world is indeed the hallmark of Western civilization. But how to conduct oneself in the world has remained problematic. The world as depicted by science just sits there silently, it does not seem to be going anywhere in particular nor does it tell us where we should be going or if we should be going anywhere at all.

The problem of the Indian theories of ethics has to do with the affinity component of our model. The relationship between the spiritual aspirant and the mundane world tends to be problematic, not so much in terms of the understanding conferred by the supramundane vision as in terms of the attitude or feeling inspired by this vision toward the world. This attitude or feeling has been elucidated in terms of the concept of 'renunciation' which is carefully distinguished from that of 'resignation.'[3] The distinction between these two is no doubt a crucial one as it marks the difference between the spiritual aspirant who may ultimately triumph over the world and one who is likely to succumb to the world. However, even the attitude of renunciation falls short of the kind of affinity toward, or feeling of liking and being close to, the world which inspires willingness to engage in exchange and communication with its various social and natural phenomena.

Let me expand a bit on my claim that Indian ethics has suffered from a lack of affinity for the world in its spiritual foundations. While renouncing the ways of the world, the spiritual aspirant is expected to show compassion toward his fellow beings. This compassion is, of course, a form of affinity. But it is directed toward the *beings as such*, not toward *socio-economic or cultural groups*. Humans and other beings are real by virtue of being *Ātman*. But the ways in which human beings organize their relationships with one another as socio-economic and cultural groups have tended to be viewed as part of the world which is to be renounced. The rationale for the renunciation is the consideration that, as *māyā*, the world is, if not wholly unreal, at least of lesser degree of reality than oneself as *atman*. Among the four paths (*bhakti, karma, jñāna, raja*), one (*karma*) does recognize action and good works in the world as a legitimate path of spiritual growth. But this path, too, is guided by the background vision of lesser value if not altogether illusory nature of the world and its ways. Thus the good works of the karma yogin, too, tend to be inspired by compassion toward the individual rather than affinity with the community which, because of its malfunctioning, may inflict suffering on the individual. The passive, duty-bound traditionalism of the Indian attitude toward society is something that was decried by the activists of the Hindu Renaissance, Radhakrishnan in particular. This passivity arises out of a background vision of transcendence that considers the world to be either unreal or not wholly real; in either case, not of value in and of itself.

On the other hand, Indian ethics have been praised for being grounded in a vision of reality[4] and as having in this regard an advantage over Western ethics which lack such a grounding. A world view which recognizes some things as more real than others does indeed provide powerful directives for action : to move away from the less real and toward the more real, to minimize the less real and maximize the more real, and so on. It imbues the world with an ethical dynamism that is lacking in the Western world view. The latter does not discriminate between the more real and the less real and thus does not ontologically compel one to move in any particular direction.

How to extend affinity and hence unqualified reality to the human community and the world at large while preserving the ethical dynamism that is transcendentally grounded? This, as I see it, is the Indian problem of ethics.

Radhakrishnan's idealism and in particular his concept of intuition offer a solution to the Indian problem by restoring the affinity component and thereby the willingness to engage in exchange with the world. This solution is not without difficulties, as we shall see shortly. Nevertheless, Radhakrishnan's life and work bear testimony to the fact that he came farther than most others in bridging the gap between thought and action. How it is that he accomplished this and that this is a genuine philosophy of world-involvement will be examined next.

Modern scientific thinking tells us that all knowledge is tentative and probabilistic and that nothing counts as knowledge unless it is operational or communicable. Against this, Radhakrishnan proposes "certainty and noncommuicability" as the "true test of knowledge."[5] These are the hallmarks of intuitive knowledge. There is a convergence of the epistemological and the ontological in *aparokṣa*, immediate, non-sensuous, intuitive knowledge. Says Radhakrishnan : "This intuitive knowledge arises from an intimate fusion of mind with reality. It is knowledge by being, not by senses or symbols."[6] As an example of knowledge by being Radhakrishnan mentions the inseparability of self-knowledge from self-existence. In Descartes' "cogito, ergo sum" there is really no "ergo," he maintains, for one's own existence is known directly, simply by existing.

Radhakrishnan's thesis regarding the unity of being and knowing is a radical version of my thesis regarding affinity between the knower and the known and, in general, between any terminals of communication or interaction. It could be put forth as a dictum : "to be something is to know it" or, equivalently, "to know something is to be it." Obviously, a weaker version of this dictum would be : "The more like something one can be, the more fully one can know it" and vice versa. There is thus affinity, or degrees of affinity, between mind the knower and the object of knowledge. The basis of affinity, I have argued, is ontological commitment. Further, ontological commitment is the first act of engagement with the world. One's own existence is ontologically given; as far as I know, it is the only thing in this world that does not require an act of ontological commitment. It, so to speak, stares one in the face before one has a chance to act in any way. And it is the source of all other ontological commitments.

But can anything else, besides one's own existence, be known directly, simply by being? Radhakrishnan does not offer other examples but does declare that "The deepest things of life are known only through intuitive apprehension."[7] It might be tempting at this point to demand a list of such "deepest things of life" or at least some guidelines as to how one goes about knowing things intuitively. Radhakrishnan himself may have felt the pressure of such a demand when he indulged in the following bit of reasoning: ".... If intuitive knowledge does not supply us with universal major premises, which we can neither question nor establish, our life will come to an end."[8] Our life as a species has not come to an end, and the implication is that therefore intuitive knowledge has supplied us with the universal major premises. Such logicisms and associated speculations regarding the interrelationships between the Absolute, God, and the world may have given cause to the rather forbidding characterization of Radhakrishnan as "a rationalist, a humanist, and a spiritual absolutistic monist" by P.T. Raju.[9] But however unsatisfactory in the end, such speculations certainly highlight Radhakrishnan's deeply felt need for bridging the gap between the transcendent reality and the mundane world and for generating a vision for ethical action, grounded in the transcendent but impacting on the mundane.

Radhakrishnan was profoundly influenced by Western ways of thinking and was committed to synthesizing the best of the Western tradition with his Indian heritage. His desire to bridge the gap between the transcendent and the mundane was pursued against the background mission of reconciliation of the Indian and Western traditions. The latter mission might be characterized as "ideological" as it is concerned with the rightness or correctness of thinking in given traditions. The quest for bridging the gap between the mundane and the transcendent might be described as "ontological" in that it is concerned with reality itself irrespective of tradition (even though, of course, the latter quest is usually pursued within some tradition or other).

Radhakrishnan's effort to solve the Indian problem of ethics was somewhat hampered by his ideological concern for reconciling the Vedāntic and the Western views. He admired the world-embracing activism of the Western tradition, but he shunned the "depersonalizing effect on the individual" of modern technology and mass societies."[10] He held to the deeper, all-embracing spirituality of his own tradition, but he decried the latter's complacent, passive attitude toward worldly affairs. The Western scientific and technological world view strips the mundane world of spirituality and, as Radhakrishnan saw it, threatens to strip people of their humanity. The rescue from this bleak prospect is provided in Radhakrishnan's Vedāntic tradition by Śaṁkara's *māyāvāda*, the doctrine of the illusory nature of the world. Yet the effect of this doctrine (not intended by Śaṁkara) has been to furnish the rationale for the kind of indifference toward the world that Radhakrishnan sees as burdening the Indian tradition. Thus *māyāvāda* was not an acceptable solution. Radhakrishnan's reinterpretation of

Śaṁkara's concept of *māyā* has been considered the latter's greatest contribution to Advaita Vedānta.[11] He tried to temper Śaṁkara's "ascetic" approach[12] to the world by declaring the world to be real, not illusory, and by emphasizing the active, creative principle of Īśvara. According to Radhakrishnan, the world as *māyā* is the self-expression of Īśvara.[13] Nevertheless, he affirmed Śaṁkara's distinction between the higher and the lower reality and, as an Advaitin, had to accept the notion of the disvaluation or sublation[14] of the lower reality by the higher, of Īśvara as *Saguṇa Brahman* by Ultimate Reality as *Nirguṇa Brahman*. Much as Radhakrishnan would have liked to embrace the world wholeheartedly, the ontological potency of *Īśvara* is unavoidably diminished by an Advaitic interpretation. Thus, in the end, he failed to provide a full philosophical justification for considering the world to be real.

But the world as depicted by Western science and shaped by technology, though unqualifiedly real, remains inhospitable to a way of living and being that is infused by spirituality. So, short of arriving at a coherent, rationally articulated view of how to fully embrace the world and yet not have the world tarnish one's spiritual essence, Radhakrishnan falls back on the notion of two separate orders of reality, one mundane and the other transcendent. Thus he says, "There is in us a level of being, an order of reality, a spark of spirit. We do not belong entirely to the world of objects to which modern scientific techniques are seeking to assimilate us."[15] But the reference to "the world of objects" to which "we do not entirely belong" implies a degree of alienation that is inimical to, or at least tends to undermine, the inclination to embrace the world and engage in interaction and exchange with it.

Radhakrishnan rightly saw the mechanistic-materialistic world view of science and technology as hostile to his ethical vision, but his attempt to temper this world view with

Vedāntic spirituality was not entirely successful. Adding on a spiritual dimension, understood as "another level of reality," will not restore as spiritually bankrupt world view. The world view itself needs to change. In this case, putting together the desirable elements of two incompatible world views does not work. Rather than juxtaposing the "spirit in us" and the "world of objects," Radhakrishnan might have considered the world of objects, technology and science, even pollution and crime, as the creative products of the human spirit. Such a view would not reduce humans into objects, helpless victims of a world gone awry.

Rather, in placing the human spirit at the source of it all, such a view would foster in us a joyful sense of confidence and responsibility for our actions and creations. In its infusion of the mundane world with spirit, this way of looking at things is alien to the West. And in its affirmation of the world as being real without qualification, it is alien to the Vedāntic tradition. But it is not alien to Hindu thought at large. Thus Radhakrishnan might have found the notion of *Līlā*, the dance of Shiva, the act of pure creation, prominent in some Tantric traditions of Hinduism as offering the kind of world-embracing philosophical basis that he could not quite find in his own Vedāntic tradition for his positive, dynamic view of the world.

In conclusion, the vision that emerges from Radhakrishnan's writings and inspires us all is that the Absolute, God, and the universe are all very near to us, very much like us; indeed, that we *are* all of these. I believe that this vision, available in Hindu thought but problematic in the Advaita Vedānta tradition, prompted the following exhortation from Radhakrishnan : "Man must become an active, purposeful force. He must cease to believe in an automatic law of progress which will realize itself irrespective of human ideals and control."[16] I might add that, as an active, purposeful force, one becomes a participant in the Dance of

Shiva - the dance that reveals the Divine in the most convoluted of human affairs.

References

1. Quine, W.V., "On What There Is," *From a Logical Point of View*, New York : Harper Torchbooks, 1963.
2. Values obviously enter into the presuppositions of the scientific worldview, but such a world view depicts the world as being value-neutral.
3. Potter, Kar H. *Presuppositions of India's Philosophies*, Englewood Cliffs, N.J. : Prentice-Hall, 1963, pp. 15-19.
4. Puligandla, r., *Fundamentals of Indian Philosophy*, New York : Abingdon, 1975, pp. 19-20.
5. Radhakrishnan, S. *An Idealist View of Life*, p. 145.
6. *Ibid.*, p. 138.
7. *Ibid.*, p. 142.
8. *Ibid.*, p. 156.
9. Raju, P.T. *The Philosophical Traditions of India*, London : George Allen & Unwin Ltd., 1971, p. 231.
10. Radhakrishnan, S. "The Difficulties of Belief". In P. Nagaraja Rao, K. Gopalaswami, & S. Radhakrishnan, eds. *Radhakrishnan Reader : An Anthology*, Bombay : Bharatiya Vidya Bhavan, 1969, p. 91.
11. Raju, P.T. *op. cit.*, p. 234.
12. Singh, Ram Pratap, "Radhakrishnan's Substantial Reconstruction of Śaṁkara's Vedānta. Excerpts reprinted in Nagaraja Rao *et al.*, eds., *op. cit.*, p. 621.
13. Radhakrishnan, S. *Indian Philosophy*, Vol. II, London : George Allen & Unwin Ltd., 1929, pp. 573-4.
14. Deutsch, E. *Advaita Vedānta : A Philosophical Reconstruction*, Honolulu : East-West Press, 1969, p. 15.
15. Radhakrishnan, S. "The Difficulties of Belief," *op. cit.*, p. 92.
16. Radhakrishnan, S. "My Search for Truth," *op. cit.*, p. 10.

37

Radhakrishnan's Philosophy of Art

FRED GILLETTE STURM
University of New Mexico

Although Radhakrishnan never addressed himself to the problems of Philosophy of Art and Aesthetics systematically, devoting an entire book or even an article to the field, he did have a genuine interest in artistic phenomena and in the philosophical issues which are raised by the world of the arts. In the course of writing about other matters he occasionally made reference to questions related to the arts and aesthetics. The closest he comes to anything approaching a systematic treatment of certain aspects of the arts and aesthetic experience is part of a chapter entitled "The Spirit in Man" in *An Idealist View of Life*, and a section entitled "Art and Morality" of his essay written for *Contemporary Indian Philosophy*. Despite the scattered nature of his analyses of the artistic dimension of human experience he does provide us with some insight into his understanding of a number of issues in the philosophy of Art, including (1) the nature of artistic "genius," (2) the nature of the creative act, (3) the nature of aesthetic appreciation and the appreciative act, (4) the nature of artistic communication, (5) the structure and function of the work of art, (6) standards for artistic judgment and criticism, (7) the nature of aesthetic value, and (8) the relations between the world of art and the worlds of morality, science and religion.

Because we do not have access to any systematic analysis of the world of the arts in Radhakrishnan's writings, I believe it will be useful at the outset to proide a simple conceptual scheme for viewing the component elements of that world as well as its relational structure. Within any art medium we can identify three fundamental elements which can be viewed independently. There is the work of art itself : musical compositions and performances, plays, painting, sculptures, poems, novels, buildings, etc. There is the artist who, working with the materials and instruments peculiar to the medium, creates the work of art : the composer and performer, the playwright and actor, the painter, the sculptor, the poet, the novelist, the architect, etc. Thirdly, there is the person who interacts with the work of art : the appreciator, the critic, the evaluator. These three - art work, creative artist, appreciator - constitute what we may call the *Ur-Welt* of Art, that without which no work of art as we know it could exist. Taken by themselves, however, they are merely abstractions or ideal entities, since to be existentially meaningful they must be defined in terms of each other. A creative artist does not exist as creative artist apart from the work of art created or in process of being created. An art critic or appreciator does not exist as critic or appreciator apart from the work of art being evaluated or appreciated. Even a work of art can not exist as a work of art apart from reference to the artistic creator whose vision and work within a medium caused it to come into being, or the appreciator who proclaims the piece to be a work of art through selection, interaction, and judgment. It is through their inter-relating with each other that the elements of the *Ur-Welt* of Art become existentially real. The matrix of three basic relations which link the elements together, thereby giving them existential significance, constitutes the Ver-Welt of Art, that world which appears to us experientially. Linking artist and art work is the creative act, the relationship of artistic creativity. Linking appreciator/critic and art work is the appreciative act, the relationship of aesthetic evaluation. Linking creative artist and aesthetic appreciator/critic is the communicative act, the relationship of meaning or significance.

If we were to picture the triad of basic and essential elements which constitutes the Ur-Welt of Art in the form of an equilateral triangle, the apex representing the work of art, the right base point representing creative artist, the left base point representing aesthetic appreciator/critic, and were we to superimpose a second reversed equilateral triangle to form a Star-of-David symbol, such that the second triangle stands for the Ver-Welt of Art, the right base point representing the relationship of creativity, left base point representing the relationship of appreciative evaluation, and the "apex" (now reversed) representing the relationship of significant communication, we would have a graphic representation of the fundamental structure of the world of art in both its elemental and relational dimensions. Each of the angles would represent a point at which the world of art is related to other world of human existence and experience, something which is of great concern for Radhakrishnan who emphasized the importance of always keeping in view the whole human person as over against compartmentalization. The creative artist, then, although an essential element in the world of art, is related, through creative ability, to the creative scientist, an essential element in the world of science, just as the relationship of appreciative evaluation in the world of art bears strong resemblance to axiological judgment in the world of ethics and morality. In Radhakrishnan's words, "the hero who carves out an adventurous path is akin to the discoverer who brings order into the scattered elements of a science or the artist who composes a piece of music or designs a building."[1]

Robert Browning, in his contribution concerning "Reason and Types of Intuition" to the 1952 Library of Living Philosophers volume dedicated to the thought of Radhakrishnan, distinguished between two uses of aesthetic terms in Radhakrishnan's writings : "At times, some of these . . . seem to be employed in contexts of psychological description; in other places, they seem to be incorporated in metaphysical propositions."[2] It is not clear to me how, exactly, Browning is using the terms "psychological" and "metaphysical." Indeed he apparently was not completely clear in his own mind just how to render the distinctions accurately with reference to Radhakrishnan's linguistic usage. Browning, in fact, declares that "Radhakrishnan's metaphysics of aesthetics is obscure."[3] I agree with Browning when he insists that "one cannot avoid it, however, if one tries to relate his view of the role of art to morality and religion."[4] Although it does not seem to me that the metaphysical grounding of Radhakrishnan's aesthetics is obscure. What Browning took to be a difference in linguistic usage of a given aesthetic term such as "creation" or "inspiration," now utilized in psychological description, now in metaphysical proposition, is, in fact, the distinction my conceptual scheme makes between the *Ur-Welt* and the *Vor-Welt* of art, and the different approaches Radhakrishnan considers to be appropriate for understanding each. The rational matrix that constitutes the *Vor-Welt* is open to ordinary sensory observation and can be described accordingly through empirical statements and logical inference. When discussing the relationships of the *Vor-Welt* of art, Radhakrishnan's use of the word "creativity" is empirical or, to use Browning's term, psychologically descriptive. However, a full comprehension of the relationships of the *Vor-Welt* of art requires, in Radhakrishnan's philosophy of art, a grasping of the elements of the *Ur-Welt*. This, presumably, is why Radhakrishnan, when describing an aesthetic relationship, such as the act of creativity which links creative artist and work of art, usually proceeds to a consideration of the elements related, in the case of creativity either the creative artist or the work which is the result of the acting of creativity. To comprehend the nature of creative genius, or the essence of the work of art, is not a task appropriate to empirical observation and description. It rather requires an act of intuition which, epistemologically, is significantly different in nature from the empirical and logical. The relations of the *Vor-Welt* are open to external observation, at least superficially, i.e. apart from a concern for the elements related. Yet, just as the elements can be defined existentially only in terms of their relationships to each other, so the relations can be understood fully only with reference to the elements being related. The relational matrix that I am designating *Vor-Welt* of art is the world of art as it appears to us. The triad of elements that constitute what I am designating *Ur-Welt* of art grounds the artistic world appearance and, in turn, is grounded, according to Radhakrishnan, in the universal spirit which is the ground of all being, and of all appearing. In his book *An Idealist View of Life* Radhakrishnan writes : "The endless variety of the sensible world becomes the symbol of an invisible ideal world which is behind and within it sustaining both it and the mind which perceives it."[5] Later, when analyzing the human self, he writes : "The true subject or the self is not an object which we can find in knowledge for it is the very condition of knowledge. It is different from all objects, the body, the senses, the empirical self itself. We cannot make the subject the property of any substance or the effect of any cause, for it is the basis of all such relations. It is not the empirical self but the reality without which there could be no such thing as an empirical self."[6]

Comprehension of this true subject or self comes only through intuition, an internal rather than external epistemological act, which is self-reflective, the grounding spirit coming to self-consciousness, as it were. When referring to the creative artist, apart from the empirical or existential activity of artistic creativity, or when referring to the appreciator, apart from the empirical or existential act of appreciation, or even when referring to the work of art itself through which something of both creator and appreciator is embodied and hence revealed, one points to the true subject or self which is the ground of empirical appearance, and is itself grounded in universal spirit, the ground of all being. Any adequate description of the elements of the *Ur-Welt* of art, therefore, must be intuitional rather than observational and empirical. "Strictly speaking," Radhakrishnan observes,

> "logical knowledge is non-knowledge, *avidya*, valid only till intuition arises. The latter is reached when we break down the shell of our private, egoistic existence, and get back to the primeval spirit in us from which our intellect and our senses are derived . . . the fact of the spiritual character of both subject and object is lost in our conventional life where we mistake our true self for the superficial one."[7]

When discussing "creativity" as rooted in the primeval spirit which expresses itself through the creative artist, Radhakrishnan's use of the world is intuitional rather than empirical, or, to use Browning's terminology, metaphysical rather than psychological.

Let us briefly examine Radhakrishnan's views concerning the three relationships of the *Vor-Welt* of art, and then his analysis of the three elements of the *Ur-Welt* of art.

1. The Creative Act

Speaking of poetry, Radhakrishnan remarks that "While poetry is in the soul, the poem is a pale reflection of the original, an attempt to register in words an impression which has become an image in memory. This is incommensurable, eluding expression in words."[8] The great poet has mastered language, just as the great artist in general can be said to have mastered the materials of his or her own artistic medium, and is capable of representing human experience "through words winged with magic,"[9] thereby evoking that experience in the imagination of reader or listener. "All art is the expression of experience in some medium," according to Radhakrishnan.[10] The difference between poet and non-poet is that the former's experience is richer, and "his verbal control greater"[11] - a statement which, of course, can be applied to the other arts as well. Technique is very important, then. "There is no more mystery in poetry than there is in engineering. If we observe a few tricks of the trade, we will get poetry. It is reduced to technical power."[12] The technical utilisation of the materials of an artist's medium constitutes the creative act whereby the creative artist is linked to the work of art. Yet more than technical skill and its proper application is required, and reference is made to the creative artist who either is, or is not, inspired by the spirit. "Technique without inspiration is barren,"[13] Radhakrishnan remarks, and results in "manufactured poetry," art works which "touch the mind but do not enter the soul,"[14] a criticism which he makes of most modern literature and art.

2. The Appreciative Act

"Aesthetic appreciation," Radhakrishnan writes, "demands the exercise of the whole mind and not merely of the logical appreciation."[15] The artist's initial experience, which is translated into sensuous form through technical manipulation of the material of a given medium, is described by Radhakrishnan as the mind grasping "the object in its wholeness," clasping "it to its bosom," suffusing it "with its own spirit," and become "one with it" in "a deliberate suspension of individually," "a complete absorption in the object . . . so as to breathe its life and enjoy its form."[16] So, too, the appreciator's experience is one of identification with the art object, taken as an objectification of the artist's experience. "We must share the world which the artist presents to us," Radhakrishnan writes. "The reader of poetry is one of a similar heart and temperament . . . . Appreciation requires sympathy and understanding though not belief and agreement."[17] The difference between the creative act and the appreciative act seems to lie in the degree of involvement. Creativity is the effort to translate experience into sensuous form, and requires passionate involvement; appreciation, on the other hand, requires distancing. "We must for the moment," writes Radhakrishnan, "become disinterested and severely contemplative."[18]

3. The Communicative Act

This aspect of aesthetic experience is dependent upon the artist's ability to - as Radhakrishnan puts it - "translate states of soul into words and images," and upon the appreciator's ability to read or interpret such artistic translation of the artist's experience in a meaningful way. There is an appreciator's part, a task of re-translation, as it were : "The meaning of the poet" - Radhakrishnan writes - "must become meaning to me, the image he suggests must be found in my mind, and his ideas must be thought by me . . . . We cannot understand great poetry unless we bring it to some fragment of a life experience."[19]

4. The Creative Artist

Radhakrishnan follows Plato in distinguishing "the man of genius, the madman inspired by the muses, from the industrious apprentice to the art of Letters . . . ."[20] The artistic genius is a person who is in touch with the universal spirit that grounds all human existence and experiencing;

capable, then, of being inspired and using technical skills to respond to, and communicate, that inspiration. "Great art is possible," writes Radhakrishnan,

> "only in those rare moments when the artist is transplanted out of himself and does better than his best in obedience to the dictates of a *daimon* . . . . In those highest moments, the masters of human expression feel within themselves a spark of the divine fire and seem to think and feel as if God were in them and they were revealing fragments of the secret plan of the universe."[21]

Although requiring technical skill, the true essence of the creative artist lies in openness to the "spirit in man," an ability to touch, and be touched by, the universal spirit which is the ground of all being.

5. The Appreciator

There is a sense in which the appreciator is also a creator, or perhaps it would be more accurate to say are - creators. "Those who appreciate beauty," Radhakrishnan remarks, "are artists in a degree."[22] As the creative artist is one who is open to the prompting of the universal spirit, so the aesthetic appreciator is one who is open to the prompting of the creative artist's spirit as communicated through the work of art. "The poet's words are claimed by us as our native speech . . . . We understand an object only when there is something in us akin to it. When any picture, poem or life produces in us a wonderful effect, we may be sure that there is an interior responding wonder that meets it."[23]

6. The Work of Art

It follows from what has been said about creative artist and aesthetic appreciator that the work of art is the objectification in sensuous and material form of the experience the artist has had which revealed to him/her the spiritual depths of reality, and the means of communicating that revelatory experience to the appreciator. Through the work of art the creative artist provides the aesthetic appreciator with "the power to know, love and appreciate the world in a new way," and the appreciator is led to share the artist's vision of life to the best of his/her capacity, thereby becoming illumined, transformed, and spiritually emancipated.[24] "The function of art," according to Radhakrishnan, "is to stir the spirit in us."[25] Using Rudolf Otto's terminology he writes that "poetry plunges us into the *mysterium tremendum* of life and suggests the truths that cannot be stated. An atmosphere of the *numinous* envelopes all poetry."[26] At first sight it is puzzling that with such high regard for art and its function Radhakrishnan did not choose to devote more time in his thinking and writing to an analysis of the artistic and aesthetic questions. Poetry and the other arts would seem to be the most important of all human endeavours if they indeed "stir the spirit in us." He states unequivocally that this is not the case, however. In a section of *An Idealist View of Life* he writes : "Each of the values of truth, beauty, and goodness has its own specific characters. We cannot arrange them in a hierarchy or subsume them one under the other."[27] Each is of equal value, no one can be left out of the full life of the human spirit, and the three need to be integrated into that life. "The nature of man is not built of parts which are independent of one another. Our instinct for truth, our moral sense and artistic craving are all organically bound up."[28] He speaks of the artist who "may be intellectually feeble and morally depraved,"[29] insisting that "an art independent of morality . . . which does not draw towards the divine in things is not true art."[30] Therefore, despite the unique function of art in stirring the spirit in us through a revelation to us of the truth of the spiritual, art does not occupy a privileged status. "The cognitive, the aesthetic and the ethical sides of our life are only sides, however vital and significant. The religious includes them all."[31] While this explains his great preoccupation with religion throughout his long life, it still leaves open the question of why he devoted much more of his writing to morality and ethics than to arts and aesthetics.

References

1. "The Spirit in Man," in *An Idealist View of Life* (London : George Allen and Unwin, 1937), p. 196.
2. Paul A. Schilpp (ed.), *The Philosophy of Sarvepalli Radhakrishnan* (New York : Tudor Publishing Company, 1952), p. 207.
3. *Ibid.*
4. *Ibid.*
5. *An Idealist View of Life*, p. 184.
6. *Ibid.*, p. 271.
7. *Ibid.*, p. 146.
8. "The Spirit in Man" (*op cit.*), p. 187.
9. *Ibid.*, p. 188
10. *Ibid.*, p. 182.
11. *Ibid.*, p. 188.
12. *Ibid.*, p. 185.
13. *Ibid.*, p. 188.
14. *Contemporary Indian Philosophy* (London : George Allen & Unwin Ltd., 1936), p. 489.
15. "*The Spirit in Man,*" p. 196.
16. "*The Spirit in Man,*" p. 184.
17. *Ibid.*, p. 196.
18. *Ibid.*
19. *Ibid.*, pp. 2-8.
20. *Ibid.*, p. 187.

21. *Contemporary Indian Philosophy*, p. 489.
22. "The Spirit in Man", pp. 2-8.
23. *Ibid.*
24. *Ibid.*, pp. 208f
25. *Ibid.*, p. 190.
26. *Ibid.*, pp. 19f.
27. *An Idealist View of Life*, p. 199.
28. *Ibid.*, p. 200.
29. *Ibid.*, p. 201.
30. *Ibid.*
31. *Ibid.*, p. 200.

38
Radhakrishnan, Religion and World Peace*

JERALD RICHARDS
Northern Kentucky University

My primary focus in this paper will be upon those aspects of the thought of Radhakrishnan that are related to the possible solution of the problem of war in the modern world. In particular, I have in mind Radhakrishnan's views on the place of religion in achieving world peace, his ideas on world unity, and his views about the necessity of replacing violence and warfare with nonviolent methods of conflict resolution.

Introductory Considerations

By the term "war" I have in mind those types of violent conflict between armed groups of individuals organized for the purpose of either maintaining or gaining political power in a particular nation or geographical region. These organized armed conflicts are either international or intranational in nature. The problem of war in the modern world would include, besides conventional international and civil wars, the threat of nuclear war (including the threat of unclear holocaust), with the attendant vertical and horizontal proliferation of nuclear weapons, and the huge expenditure of public monies and human talent in preparation for warfare.[1]

The problem of war is by no means the only crisis of global proportions that we face in the latter part of this twentieth century. The list of global crises would include the rapid increase in world population, malnutrition, starvation, the exhaustion of our nonrenewable resources, the creation of vast numbers of marginal human beings, economic instability, the suppression of minorities, forms of violence other than warfare, illiteracy, and environmental pollution. But the huge expenditure of money and talent in preparation for warfare[2] and the threat of nuclear war make the problem of war our most pressing problem. In a world of limited resources, until the problem of war can be brought under control, there are not enough resources available (both material and human) to solve our other pressing problems. In addition, the threat of nuclear war tends to chill, or even freeze, human resolve, dash human hopes, generate indifference toward our various problems, and create a general, at times pervasive, malaise of despair, hopelessness, and meaninglessness. A "nuclear winter" and an "ultraviolet spring" could mean the end of life (or life as we know it) on this planet. The thought of the possibility of a "nuclear winter" and an "ultraviolet spring" can lead to psychic numbing, exhaustion, and despair.

The Thought of Radhakrishnan

Radhakrishnan addresses the problem of the sense of meaninglessness and its attendant *ennui* and despair. For him, meaning or purpose is found in the recognition of the religious or spiritual dimension of human existence and, ultimately, in the experience of one's union or identification with Ultimate Being or the Absolute. Out of this experience flows the kinds of attitudes and actions that would contribute to world community and world peace, and the eventual solution of our global problems. After expounding the specifics of Radhakrishnan's approach to the place of religion in the quest for world peace, I shall consider criticisms of aspects of this approach, as well as offer some comments and suggestions.

The Unity of Religions

Radhakrishnan believes in the transcendent unity of religions. The ultimate goal of religious belief and practise is a mystical experience of the Absolute, and a resultant sense (or grasp or understanding) of the oneness of all beings and things. In this mystical experience of the Absolute, one intuits the highest truth, gains "the pure apprehension of the Absolute."[3] Religions differ among themselves due to the accidents of different histories and geographies. Different creedal statements about Ultimate Reality are just culture - and time-bound "historical formulations of the formless truth."[4]

One who has gained "the pure apprehension of the Absolute," and subsequently understands that different religions are just different attempts to grasp the nature, and to achieve an experience of, the Absolute, is tolerant toward other and all religions and beliefs. Says Radhakrishnan :

> He who has seen the real is lifted above all
> narrowness, relativities, and contingencies.[5]

And again,

> The sense of the present reality of God and the joy
> of His indwelling make the mystic indifferent to all
> questions of history. Toleration is the homage
> which the finite mind pays to the inexhaustibility
> of the infinite.[6]

This toleration, for Radhakrishnan, is not the outcome of political expediency, skepticism, or indifference. It is not a matter of being tolerant in order to guarantee one's continued existence. Nor is it based upon a general epistemological thesis that truth about reality is not attainable. Nor, further, is it grounded in shallowness of conviction regarding one's religious beliefs. It is not negative, a mere putting up with other beliefs. It is positive, involving an attitude of genuine sympathy and respect toward other beliefs and forms of worship, as well as the willingness to incorporate into one's own view those aspects of other religions one finds important and valuable.[7] This positive attitude of toleration leads to genuine dialogue among adherence of different religions, generates mutual understanding, encourages positive fellowship, leads over time to the transformation of irrational beliefs and repugnant practises, and ultimately results in the creation of world unity and world peace.

For Radhakrishnan, the greatest obstacle to genuine religious dialogue and the eventual recognition of the essential unity of religions is belief in the finality of one's own religion. This belief leads to exclusiveness and intolerance. Says Radhakrishnan, "Finality of conviction easily degenerates into the spirit of fanaticism, autocratic, over-positive, and bloodthirsty."[8]

World Unity and World Peace

The essential unity of religions, for Radhakrishnan, is grounded in the essential unity of Reality which, in turn, entails the essential unity of the human race. Given these views, it should be no surprise that Radhakrishnan is concerned about world unity and world peace. Essential to the emergence of world unity are the same kinds of positive tolerance, mutual respect and regard, and genuine dialogue in the social and political arenas as are necessary for unity in the religious arena. In fact, for Radhakrishnan, there is a direct connection between religion and politics. He writes, "religion includes faith in human brotherhood, and politics is the most effectual means of rendering it into visible form.

Politics is but applied religion."[9] Essential for human brotherhood, for Radhakrishnan, are the recognition of the value of the individual, freedom to develop individual capacities, equal treatment before the law, political liberty, social justice, economic equality, and racial tolerance. Such values can be developed only in democratic societies.[10] The good of individuals is not the good of atomistic individuals but of individuals in community. A concern for the common good should be of major significance, not only within nations but also among nations.

Concern for the common good among nations that will result in genuine world community requires creative thinking and the realization of new possibilities. Of necessary and fundamental importance for achieving world community is some form of federalism as an alternative to international anarchy and as the foundation for devising alternatives to militarism and the methods of warfare. Writes Radhakrishnan, "A world federal government with powers limited to those necessary for establishing and maintaining law and order among the nations of the world is a practical way of achieving just and lasting peace."[11]

Of course, the existence of some type of international authority would not necessarily entail the total absence of warfare. At least in the early decades of some type of world federalism, coercive violence may be necessary, as a last resort, against rebellious groups, both within and among nations. But the bias of a world federation would be in favour of the development and use of non-violent alternatives in conflict resolution. For Radhakrishnan, the origination of and inspiration for this non-violent bias is found in religion or the religious dimension of human existence.

Thinking realistically, effective world federalism will not develop unless we can achieve world understanding or world community. But world community cannot be achieved without significant changes in the current moral, social, and political conditions of the world.[12] On this issue, Radhakrishnan's thought seems to be caught in a kind of "catch-22" bind. Of fundamental importance for achieving a just and lasting peace is some kind of world federalism. But world federalism will not develop unless we can achieve world understanding or world community. To which, if either, of these alternatives does Radhakrishnan give primacy? Given my reading of Radhakrishnan, it seems he would give primacy to the latter, to the achievement of world understanding and world community. And, for Radhakrishnan, to repeat what I said above, primacy among the ingredients for achieving world understanding is given to religion, or the religious outlook and spirit. Crucial to the functioning of the religious outlook are (1) the ability of the religiously enlightened person to relate to diverse cultural conditions in a spirit of positive and sympathetic toleration, and (2) the cultivation and expression, in the lives of the religiously enlightened, of a number of peace - and comunity-creating virtues. Chief among these virtues, for Radhakrishnan, are the following : ". . . quiet confidence, inner calm, gentleness of the spirit, love of neighbour, mercy to all creation, destruction of tyrannous desires [including atomistic individualism and selfishness], and the aspiration for spiritual freedom."[13]

Radhakrishnan's approach to religious transformation (and, thus, to socio-political-economic transformation) is elitist rather than grassroots. The model for transformation is the exceptional person or exemplar, including such ancients as Buddha, Jesus, Hosea, Isaiah, Śaṁkara, and Rāmānuja, and such moderns as Ramakrishna, Tagore, Gandhi, and Nehru.[14] Without the lives, actions, and examples of these exceptional persons, it is highly unlikely that religious and other types of transformation would occur. Radhakrishnan's view of the religious practises of the masses is not very complimentary. On this point, he writes :

A welter of superstitions and taboos, primitive myths and unhistorical traditions, unscientific dogmatisms and national idolatries, constitute the practising religion of the vast majority of mankind today.[15]

For Radhakrishnan, world community and world federalism have become absolute necessities for human well-being in the modern world given (1) the global dimensions of economic, political, environmental, and technological developments and policies, and (2) the nature of modern warfare including, among other things, the mass murder of millions of noncombatants and the potential annihilation of the human race by the firing of nuclear weapons.[16] For Radhakrishnan, to return to a point made above, a major contribution of the religious orientation, in generating the placing of strict limitations upon the use of organized violence and in the eventual replacement of violence by other means of conflict resolution, is the bias toward non-violence. Non-violence is the ideal of many, if not all, historic religious faiths, including Hinduism, Buddhism, and Christianity.[17] However, the historical record of religions has been checkered. All too often, violence and warfare have been advocated, supported, or at least acquiesced in.

Nevertheless, for Radhakrishnan, we can and must work toward the gradual realization of the ideal, the displacement of faith in violent force by non-violent method of conflict resolution (threat systems, deterrence, arbitration, mediation, negotiation, mutual adaption) leading to alliances, cooperation, and integration.[18] The gradual road to such replacement requires, among other things, the achievement of social, political, and economic justice (both nationally and internationally), rethinking the idea of national sovereignty, and especially a re-education in values. These transformed values will be universal human values grounded in love, compassion, a sense of justice, and fellow-feeling.[19] The modern exemplar of non-violence is Gandhi.[20] Those who would be contemporary exemplars should model themselves after Gandhi.

Comments, Observations, and Suggestions

There seems to be no question that religions have functioned historically and function today as organizing wholes that provide meaning and purpose to millions of human beings. A particular religion provides its adherents with a sense or understanding of the nature of Ultimate Being, human nature, the possible relations between human beings and Ultimate being, how human beings should live, and human destiny. The various dimensions of religion (doctrinal, ritual, mythical, social, ethical, and experiential) touch on all aspects of human life.[21] Against the possible tendency to deny or to disregard the pervasive influence of religion in the world today, J.W. Bowker would remind us :

> Contrary to what Karl Marx predicted (and contrary to what some Western commentators seem to suppose), religion is not withering away. It remains the context, or at least part of the context, in which the majority of people alive on this planet today live their lives or from which they derive important inspiration and judgment for their lives.[22]

However, there are facts about religions that seem to militate against their value as major contributors toward world peace. These facts are their incredible diversity (both internally and externally), the relatively high incidence of religious conflicts (including violent conflicts), and the involvement of religions in larger socio-political conflicts (including violent conflicts and warfare).

The Problem of Religious Diversity

It is possible, perhaps probable, that the diversity among world religions is much more profound than Radhakrishnan believed. There is a great diversity of religious belief and practise among religions in the contemporary world, including different views of the Divine, different views about human nature and destiny, and different social, ethical, political, and economic orientations and behaviours. Some of these differences seem to be of a fundamental, radical nature. Even if we focus our attention upon a study of the experiential dimension of religion, more particularly, upon the mystical experiential dimension of religion, in an attempt to isolate a presumed essential or transcendental unity, we discover that the results of more recent comparative research are inconclusive. The plea of many researchers in this area is for the recognition of fundamental differences. Representative of this standpoint is Steven Katz. In sum, Katz argues that a pluralistic account of mystical experiences among world religions does justice to all the currently available evidence without being reductionist (i.e., forcing the evidence into comparable categories) and without making *a priori* assumptions about the nature of ultimate reality.[23]

It would seem that much more research, study, and analysis are needed if Radhakrishnan's claim about the essential, transcendental unity of religions is to be established. Specific epistemological issues that need to be addressed, among others, are (1) the status and verifiability of claims to intuitive knowledge, and (2) the claim that the content of mystical experience is ineffable.[24]

The Violent Side of Religion

The violent side of religions is directly related to their diversities of belief and practise, and to the importance of religion in the lives of their adherents. Since a religion provides its adherents with a world view that organizes all aspects of life into a meaningful whole, giving sense and direction to life, its adherents are passionately committed to it and are deeply disturbed when it is threatened, either by other world views or by larger socio-political factors. These disturbances often erupt into violent conflicts. Violence, including its Ultimate expression in warfare, has been a part of all religious traditions. Although all (or most) religions contain a culture of peaceableness, they also contain a "culture of violence and war." About this negative side of religion, Elise Boulding writes:

> Every religion ... has a vision of holy war, of divinely legitimated violence .... Either God enjoins battle on his people to destroy evildoers, as has happened frequently enough in Judaism, Christianity, and Islam, or violence itself is elevated to the realm of the sacred, as a part of the created order, as in some Hindu and Buddhist teachings. This set of violence-justifying teachings has made it possible for every religion to support the state that honours it in time of war.[25]

The negative side of religion either erupts in violence against dissenters and adherents of other religions, or supports and justifies violence by the host nation. This "shadow-side" of religion existed not just in past centuries. The twentieth century is no stranger to demonic and destructive forms or expressions of religion. On this point, Langdon Gilkey writes,

> ... in our century intolerable forms of religion and the religious have appeared: in a virulently nationalistic Shinto, in Nazism, in aspects of Stalinism and Maoism, in Khomenei - and in each of these situations an absolute religion sanctions an oppressive class, race, or national power.[26]

Nor is the end in sight of such involvement of religion in violence. Ninian Smart writes,

> Not only are advances in unity accompanied by hardline backlash phenomena, but the difficult relations between Christianity, Islam, Judaism, and Marxism and the friction between radical Hindu and Islamic values could be major factors in warfare over the next thirty years.[27]

Even if we assume, with Radhakrishnan, the importance of religion in promoting world community and world peace, a great amount of work remains to be done in fostering goodwill and dialogue among religions, and between adherents of religions and adherents of other world views, before the positive dimensions of religions exert significant influence.

The Problem of Toleration

As noted above, Radhakrishnan advances a view of positive as opposed to negative toleration toward religions (as well as ideologies and world views) different from one's own. The two aspects of this positive toleration are (1) an attitude of sympathy and respect toward other beliefs and forms of worship, and (2) an appreciation of the values of other religions and the willingness to assimilate into one's own religion what is true, valuable, and best in them. This positive tolerance is grounded in the mystical experience of the Absolute, a belief in the essential unity of religions, and the rejection of the claims to finality, exclusiveness, and/or absoluteness.

It has been claimed that, in the final analysis, Radhakrishnan's positive tolerance is limited to a tolerance of his own position, while his tolerance of other positions (including Hindu views different from his own) is merely a negative "putting up with" them as inferior, inadequate, partial, and/or subordinate.[28] In support of this claim, the following lines of argument are advanced : (1) Radhakrishnan judges what is true, valuable, and best in other religions in terms of his nondualistic Advaita Vedāntic interpretation of the experience of the Absolute; (2) he is not critical of his interpretation or formulation of the nature and experience of the Absolute, as he is of all other interpretations; (3) thus, he assumes the absoluteness of his understanding and the finality of his interpretation of the Absolute; (4) on the basis of this assumption, he ranks religious beliefs and concepts as higher or lower, and of more or less intrinsic significance; and (5) his position leaves little, if any, room for dialogue and has frustrated persons who have confronted him and his admirers with a claimed conflict of positions.[29]

In an attempt to rescue Radhakrishnan from this understanding of the limitations of his concept of tolerance, it has been argued that his distinction between a personal God and the Absolute (a major conflicting view among world religions) is a logical rather than an ontological distinction. On this interpretation of Radhakrishnan, the personal God is the relational aspect of Divine Being and the Absolute is the non-relational aspect of Divine Being. Thus, the personal God is not a lower, illusory representation.[30] But this interpretation of Radhakrishnan's understanding of a personal God is problematic. Even when rejecting the view that the personal God (*Īśvara*) is on a lower level than the impersonal Brahman, Radhakrishnan says :

> *Īśvara* is not the Ultimate ideal. A Personal God even when theologically sublimated is only a realisation of that which is beyond both being and its opposite non-being. We must leave behind the categories of religious thought and have a direct ascent. In the concept of *Īśvara*, we objectify what is essentially non-objective. We try to naturalize what is beyond nature.[31]

Unless Radhakrishnan would say that same thing about the interpretation of Brahman as impersonal Absolute, then he is either placing the idea of a personal God on a lower level or contradicting himself, in one place claiming parity and in another place disparity of the two concepts of the divine.

Given (1) the problematic nature of Radhakrishnan's thinking about the essential or transcendental unity of religions, and (2) the limitations of his concept of tolerance, it seems that a more fruitful approach to the problem of conflicting truth-claims and practises among world religions would include both the acknowledgment of pluralism (fundamental differences in belief and practise) and the attempt to generate genuine dialogue on the basis of mutual regard and respect. Mutual respect would include both constructive criticism of and learning from one another, and moral compassion.[32] One of the goals of dialogue would be greater unity among world religions, but a unity, given the limitations of the human mind and the possible inability of establishing much if any common intellectual ground among rival viewpoints, that recognizes diversity and accepts plurality in matters of belief and practise.[33]

Given the pressing concern for world community and world peace, and given the facts that major religions are transnational (and thus in a position to influence persons and events in the direction of world community and world peace) and major forces (and sources of meaning and significance) in the lives of millions of human beings, the focus in dialogue might best be centered on the ethical dimension of religions (and other world views) with the goal of identifying and emphasizing those shared or overlapping beliefs in universal human values that have direct bearing on the constructive solution of our global crises, especially violent conflict between religions, warfare, and the threat of nuclear destruction.[34] Once these major global crises are under some semblance of control, then proponents of different world views can go on to dialog about the more particularistic aspects of their respective moral dimensions as well as about their doctrinal, mythical, and experiential dimensions.

Finality of Conviction and Intolerance

A corollary of Radhakrishnan's doctrine of positive tolerance is his view that the greatest obstacle to genuine religious dialogue is belief in the finality of one's own religion that leads to exclusiveness, intolerance, and even violent conflict. It is not clear to me that finality of conviction alone is the cause, or even the major element in, intolerance. Radhakrishnan himself, writing about Hinduism and Buddhism, says that the Hindu or Buddhist (or at least the "cultivated" Hindu or Buddhist) may have certainty (an unquestioning belief) in the truth of his religion, but still express an attitude of sympathy and respect toward other religions. Radhakrishnan writes, "It is not historically true that in the knowledge of truth there is of necessity great intolerance."[35] For Radhakrishnan, we can reach stable truth, achieve certainty and depth of conviction, and claim finality or absoluteness for our ultimate viewpoint without any accompanying intolerance.[36] Unless Radhakrishnan is contradicting himself, he is implying that other factors in combination with belief in the finality of one's religious world view leads to intolerance. These other factors would include specific elements of one's world view, individual psychological factors, and larger social, political, and economic factors. Relevant elements of one's world view would include specific views about the nature of God and God's will for mankind. Individual psychological factors would include a sense of insecurity, a desire for power, and the "need" to have the truth. Larger cultural factors would include threats to continuing cultural existence, political ideologies, ethnic differences, and the pernicious influences of mass media in the hands of unprincipled and power-hungry leaders. Given a combination of some of these factors (and the effective combination would vary from individual to individual and from culture to culture), a belief in the finality of one's religion (and the sense of meaning associated with this religion) can be and often is exploited in ways that generate intolerance and the eruption of violent conflict. In these conflicts, belief in the finality of one's political or economic ideology may override belief in the finality of one's religion, leading to the subordination or ignoring of the religious beliefs.

Some clearer sense of the nature of world view epistemology might help us to understand how an adherent of a particular religious world view can have finality of conviction about his religious beliefs, while at the same time engage in genuine dialogue with adherents of other religions in openness to new insights and truth. World views seem to be epistemologically "soft" (to borrow a term from Ninian Smart)[37] in that alternative world views are possible and cannot be ruled out *a priori* as implausible, and in that proof for a particular world view does not yield logical certainty. That world views are epistemologically "soft" does not, for Smart, entail relativism. Various tests - ". . . consonance with science, richness of relevant experience, capacity to bear fruits," and consistency - can be applied to them.[38] So that the best linguistic handle to apply to them is "soft non-relativism."[39] Assuming this analysis of world view epistemology is correct, proponents of a particular worldview cannot claim logical certainty or absolute finality for their beliefs. But quite legitimately they can claim finality of conviction and/or psychological certitude for them. At the same time, they can be open to the search for new truths and new perspectives on the truths they hold in genuine, compassionate dialog with others.[40]

Whether the acceptance of such a world view epistemology is necessary for genuine tolerance and dialogue may be debatable, but Smart and others seem to imply they can be generated only by its acceptance. But to accept such an epistemology, not only by the leaders but also by the ordinary adherents of a particular religion requires a high degree of maturity and self-confidence, and a deep sense of meaning and purpose in one's own existential viewpoint. This may be too much to expect of most people. To accept the limitations of knowledge opens up the possibility of meaninglessness, and can create anxiety. This anxiety, in turn, can lead to claims of final truth as well as to intolerance. Using the philosopher as an example, Reinhold Niebuhr illustrates the dynamics of this possible problem. He writes,

> The philosopher is anxious to arrive at the truth; but he is also anxious to prove that his particular truth is the truth. He is never as completely in possession of the truth as he imagines. That may be the error of being ignorant of one's ignorance. But it is never simply that. The pretensions of final truth are always partly an effort to obscure a darkly felt consciousness of the limits of human knowledge lest he fall into the abyss of meaninglessness. Thus fanaticism is always a partly conscious, partly unconscious attempt to hide the fact of ignorance....[41]

In spite of the difficulty, for leaders and followers alike, in achieving and maintaining a proper balance between finality of conviction and openness to genuine dialogue, such a balance would seem to be necessary for the generation of international understanding and world peace, regardless of the particular world view epistemology one adheres to.

Attitude Changes and Non-violence

In conclusion, two things Radhakrishnan considers important contributions of religion toward world peace, the necessity of changed attitudes and the bias toward non-violence, are worth special notice.

Although attitudes and environmental conditions often interact with one another in a dialectical fashion (e.g., favourable changes in environmental conditions may lead to the softening of belligerent attitudes toward others, or positive changes in attitudes toward others may lead to positive changes in their attitudes toward us as well as in attempts to bring about more favourable environmental conditions), it seems that attitude changes are foundational and necessary for any substantial moves toward world peace. Primary attention must be given to a re-education of values. Radhakrishnan's emphasis on the nurturing of a spirit of positive and sympathetic toleration, a number of peace - and community - creating virtues (love, compassion, a sense of justice, and fellow-feeling), and rethinking the idea of national sovereignty (replacing or combining patriotism with humatroitism)[42] should be the core of this re-education in values, which would lead to the reformation of the operations and policies of national governments, and the eventual reforming of the nation system.[43]

One attitude change that is a necessity is the change from the readiness to the reluctance to use violence to settle disputes and conflicts. It may be that the religious bias in favour of non-violence is the major contribution religion can make toward the abolition of war and the establishment of world peace. Although the tendency in conflict situations, by both individuals and nations, is to use violence early on in a conflict, the chances of peace would be much greater if there existed a general attitude that conflicts should be settled by non-violent means, and that limited and restrained violence should be used, if at all, only as a last resort. This attitude shift could be promoted by a dissemination of the philosophy and techniques of non-violence,[44] as well as by increased exposure to the lives and thoughts of persons like Gandhi and Martin Luther King, Jr.[45]

References

* Since published in *Darshana International*, India. Reprinted with the kind permission of the Author and Editor.

1. On the definition and facets of war, see Ronald J. Glossop, *Confronting War : An Examination of Humanity's Most Pressing Problem*, Second Edition (Jefferson, North Carolina : McFarland and Company, Inc., Publishers, 1987).
2. See Glossop, *ibid.*, pp. 3-4. For the most current comprehensive data on comparative global military and social expenditures, see Ruth Leger Sivard, *World Military and Social Expenditures 1987-88*, 12th Edition (Washington, D.C. : World Priorities, 1987).
3. S. Radhakrishnan, *Eastern Religions and Western Thought*, Second Edition (London : Oxford University Press, 1940), p. 317. Hereafter cited as *ERWT*.
4. *Ibid.*, p. 327.
5. *Ibid.*, p. 317.
6. *Ibid.*
7. *Ibid.*, p. 314.
8. *Ibid.*, p. 324. On Radhakrishnan's thinking about toleration, see also his "Religion and World Unity, "*The Hibbert Journal*, vol. 49/50 (April, 1951), p. 222.
9. Address to UNESCO Conference, May 30, 1950, quoted in Humayun Kabir, "Radhakrishnan's Political Philosophy," in Paul Arthur Schilpp, editor, *The Philosophy of Sarvepalli Radhakrishnan* (New York : Tudor Publishing Company, 1952), p. 706.
10. See *Ibid.*, pp. 706-707.
11. S. Radhakrishnan, *Religion in a Changing World* (London : George Allen and Unwin Ltd., 1967), p. 157.
12. See *Ibid.*, pp. 156-158.
13. *Eastern Religion and Western Thought*, p. 323; see also pp. 320-323.

14. See *Religion in a Changing World,* pp. 158-160. Hereafter cited as *RCW*. See also Robert A. McDermott, ed., *Radhakrishnan : Selected Writings on Philosophy, Religion, and Culture* (New York : E.P. Dutton and Company, Inc., 1970), pp. 23-25.
15. *ERWT,* p. 290.
16. See *RCW,* pp. 155-156.
17. For a discussion of non-violence in Hinduism and Christianity, see S. Radhakrishnan, *Religion and Society,* Second Edition (London : George Allen & Unwin Ltd., 1948), pp. 201-211. Hereafter cited as *RS.*
18. See the conflict continuum that includes these methods in Elise Boulding, "Two Cultures of Religion as Obstacles to Peace," *Zygon,* Vol. 21, No. 4 (December, 1986), pp. 502-503.
19. See *RS,* pp. 222-229.
20. See *ibid.,* p. 229-238.
21. For a discussion of these dimensions of religion, see Ninian Smart, *The Religious Experience of Mankind,* Third Edition (New York : Charles Scribner's Sons, 1984), pp. 6-12. See also Smart's *Worldviews* (New York : Scribner's, 1983).
22. J.W. Bowker, "The Burning Fuse : The Unacceptable Face of Religion," *Zygon,* Vol. 21, No. 4 (December, 1986), p. 417.
23. See Steven T. Katz, "Language, Epistemology, and Mysticism," in Steven T. Katz., ed., *Mysticism and Philosophical Analysis* (New York : Oxford University Press, w1978), pp. 22-74. See also the other articles in this same volume which, on the whole, tend to argue for a pluralistic account of mystical experience.
24. On the special problems of the epistemology of intuition in Radhakrishnan, see *Robert* W. Browning, "Reason and Intuition in Radhakrishnan's Philosophy," in Schilpp, *op. cit.* pp. 173-277.
25. Boulding, *op. cit.,* 502.
26. Gilkey, *op. cit.,* p. 44.
27. Ninian Smart, *Religion and the Western Mind* (Albany : State University of New York Pres, 1987), p. 119.

28. See Robert N. Minor, "Sarvepalli Radhakrishnan on the Nature of 'Hindu' Tolerance," *The Journal of the American Academy of Religion*, Vol. L, No. 2 (1982), p. 287.

29. See *ibid.*, pp. 275-290.

30. See Ninian Smart, "Sarvepalli Radhakrishnan," *The Encyclopaedia of Philosophy* (New York : MacMillan Publishing Company, 1967), Vol. 7, pp. 62-63.

31. S. Radhakrishnan, *The Brahma Sūtra: The Philosophy of Spiritual Life* (London : George Allen and Unwin Ltd., 1960), pp. 175-176. Quoted in Minor, *op. cit.*, p. 282. On this issue, see Minor, pp. 280-284.

32. See Harold Coward, *Pluralism : Challenge to World Religions* (Maryknoll, New York : Orbis Books, 1985), p. 107. On interfaith dialogue, see also, among others, John. V. Taylor, "The Theological Basis of Interfaith Dialog," in John Hick and Brian Hebblethwaite, eds., *Christianity and Other Religions* (Philadelphia : Fortress Press, 1980), pp. 212-233.

33. See Coward, *ibid.*, pp. 96, 101-102.

34. See Smart, *Religion and the Western Mind*, pp. 120-131, who argues for this kind of approach.

35. *ERWT*, p. 314.

36. See *ibid.*

37. See Smart, *Religion and the Western Mind*, p. 124.

38. See *ibid.*, p. 125. Given the "shadow side" of religions, the application of tests and of criticism is a necessity.

39. See *ibid.*

40. See Langdon Gilkey, "Plurality and Its Theological Implications," in John Hick and Paul F. Knitter, eds., *The Myth of Christian Uniqueness : Toward a Pluralistic Theology of Religions* (Maryknoll, New York : Orbis Books, 1987), pp. 44-47, where Gilkey develops a view similar to the view of Smart, but calls it "relative absoluteness."

41. Reinhold Niebuhr, *The Nature and Destiny of Man, Vol. I, Human Nature* (New York : Charles Scribner's Sons, 1964 (1941)), pp. 184-185.

42. On the term, humatriotism, see Theodore Lentz., "Introduction," in Theodore Lentz, ed., *Humatriotism* (St. Louis : The Future Press, 1976), p. 28. See the discussion of this concept in Glossop. *op. cit.*, 223-227.
43. On these reformations, see Glossop., *ibid.*, pp. 218-302.
44. Se among others, the many works of Gene Sharp, including *The Politics of Non-violent Action* (Boston: Porter Sargent, Publishes, 1973), *Social Power and Political Freedom* (Boston: Porter Sargent Publishers, 1980), *Making Europe Unconquerable : The Potential of Civilian-Based Deterrence and Defense* (Cambridge, Mass. : Ballinger Publishing Company, 1985), and *National Security Through Civilian-based Defense* (Omaha, Nebraska : Association for Transarmament Studies, 1985 (1970)).
45. See Louis Fischer, *The Life of Mahatma Gandhi* (New York : Harper and Brothers, 1950), Joan V. Bondurant, *Conquest of Violence : The Gandhian Philosophy of Conflict* (Princeton, New Jersey : Princeton University Press, 1958), Krishnala Shridharani, *War Without Violence : A Study of Gandhi's Method and Its Accomplishments* (New York : Harcourt Brace, 1939), Martin Luther King, Jr., *Stride Toward Freedom* (New York : Harper and Row, 1958), John J. Ansbro, *Martin Luther Kind, Jr. : The Making of a Mind* (New York : Orbis Books, 1982), and James Melvin Washington, eds., *A Testament of Hope : The Essential Writings of Martin Luther King, Jr.* (San Francisco : Harper and Row, 1966). On the need for this attitude shift from violence to non-violence, see Glossop, *op. cit.*, pp. 221-222.